John Kerr

The History of Curling

John Kerr

The History of Curling

ISBN/EAN: 9783337330422

Printed in Europe, USA, Canada, Australia, Japan

Cover: Foto ©ninafisch / pixelio.de

More available books at **www.hansebooks.com**

ISTORY OF CURLING

Scotland's Ain Game

AND FIFTY YEARS OF
THE ROYAL CALEDONIAN CURLING CLUB

By JOHN KERR, M.A., F.S.A. Scot.

MINISTER OF THE PARISH OF DIRLETON

ENER OF THE LITERARY COMMITTEE OF THE ROYAL CALEDONIAN CURLING CLUB

PUBLISHED UNDER AUTHORITY OF THE CLUB BY

DAVID DOUGLAS, EDINBURGH

MDCCCXC

[*All rights reserved.*]

RESPECTFULLY DEDICATED,

BY PERMISSION,

TO

HER MOST GRACIOUS MAJESTY

THE QUEEN

BY

HER MAJESTY'S LOYAL SUBJECTS

THE MEMBERS OF

THE ROYAL CALEDONIAN CURLING CLUB.

PREFACE.

IN view of the Fiftieth Annual Meeting of the Royal Caledonian Curling Club in 1888, a Special Committee was appointed at the Meeting of the previous year to consider what should be done in the way of celebrating the Club's Jubilee. Among the suggestions sent up in the Report of this Committee, and adopted by the Club, was one to this effect :—"That a Literary Committee be appointed, with powers, for the purpose of preparing a sketch of the Royal Club's history during the last fifty years." Of this Literary Committee, the Rev. John Kerr was appointed Convener, and the preparation of the volume was thereafter entrusted to him to be carried through under the Committee's supervision.

Some words are necessary to explain how a work thus primarily intended to be a sketch of the history of the Royal Caledonian Curling Club should gradually have developed into a "History of Curling." The story of the Royal Club was obviously but the concluding chapter of a long history which had yet to be written. It was thus very early seen that, to do justice to the subject, it would require to be treated more fully than was at first contemplated. At the Jubilee Dinner in 1888, Lord Balfour of

Burleigh said "that one of the wants which might reasonably be filled in the Jubilee year of the Club was a really good painstaking history of the game, which would hand down to posterity all that was known of it at the present time." That want, it is hoped, has now been supplied; at all events, every effort has been made to do so.

To all who have assisted in the work hearty thanks are due—to the Secretaries of local Clubs for their answers to the queries sent out by the Committee; to Professor Forster Heddle for his valuable contribution; to T. Thorburn, Beith, for the great amount of trouble he has taken to give us information of a practical kind on stone-manufacture; to Messrs Kay & Keanie for similar information; and last, but certainly not least, to Mr William Douglas, the son of the esteemed publisher, who has in every possible manner done his best to make the volume worthy of the subject.

All curlers will join in an expression of regret that while the work was being written three noble veterans have been removed from the ranks—Mr Charles Cowan, Admiral Maitland-Dougall, and Sir John Ogilvy.

The volume having greatly exceeded the limits originally designed, it has been found necessary to omit a Glossary of Curling Words and Phrases, also a large collection of Songs and Humorous Stories marked as worthy of preservation. The ground having been so far cleared by this "History," justice may yet be done to the other subjects referred to, in a second volume, which will be forthcoming whenever an earnest demand is made for its production. The trouble and anxiety connected with the preparation and publication of a work such as this commemorative volume is have been great; but these, it is believed, will soon be forgotten if by its means a fresh enthusiasm be inspired in a game which develops all that is manly and good in social life, and unites in one brotherhood all ranks and conditions of men.

EDINBURGH, *15th April 1890.*

CONTENTS.

PART I.—ANCIENT CURLING.

CHAP.		PAGE
I.	THE ORIGIN OF THE GAME,	3
II.	A STUDY OF STONES,	27
III.	HISTORICAL AND POETICAL REFERENCES,	69
IV.	ANCIENT CURLING SOCIETIES,	113

PART II.—MODERN CURLING.

I.	THE TRANSITION PERIOD—1800-1838,	171
II.	THE VICTORIAN ERA—ROYAL CALEDONIAN CURLING CLUB,	229
III.	CURLING FURTH OF SCOTLAND,	307
IV.	"THE MYSTERIES,"	351

PART III.—MISCELLANEA.

I.	CURLING EQUIPMENTS,	367
II.	THE SCIENCE OF CURLING,	379
III.	THE ART OF CURLING,	387
IV.	BIBLIOTHECA CURLIANA,	419

APPENDICES.

A.—	CONSTITUTION OF THE ROYAL CALEDONIAN CURLING CLUB,	425
B.—	PROVINCES (AS IN 1889),	432
	INDEX,	435

LIST OF ILLUSTRATIONS.

The Illustrations are engraved by Messrs Walker and Boutall, Alexander Brown, John Adam, Lemercier et Cie., Angerer and Goschl, and others.

	ARTIST	
THE MARQUIS OF BREADALBANE	Geo. Reid, R.S.A.	Frontispiece
		PAGE
Heading—'CURLING IN THE PAST,' and *Initial Letter*	W. S. Cumming	3
'ICE-STICK'		14
Tailpiece—'THE LUNCHEON BASKET'	W. S. Cumming	25
Heading—'THREE PERIODS OF CURLING,' and *Initial Letter*	W. S. Cumming	27
ANCIENT CURLING STONES—		
Stirling		30
Newton Loch		32
Lochleven		34
Roslin		35
Rev. W. Guthrie's		36
Ardoch, Rev. W. Hally's		40
Blairgowrie and Delvine Clubs		41
Coupar-Angus		42
Lochlane		42
Birkhill		43
Muthill		46
Strathallan		47
'Jubilee Stone'		48
From Fisher's *Winter Season*		60
From Broun's *Memorabilia Curliana*		61
East Kilbride		62
Penicuick House		63
Tam Samson's		63
Old Canonmills Club		64
From Cairnie's *Essay*		65
Fala Estate		67
DIAGRAM, shewing Angles of Play		57
Heading—'AMONG THE TOMES,' and *Initial Letter*	W. S. Cumming	69
Tailpiece—'HARD TIMES'	Samuel Reid	111
Heading—'LINLITHGOW,' and *Initial Letter*	W. S. Cumming	113

LIST OF ILLUSTRATIONS.

	ARTIST	PAGE
SIR GEORGE HARVEY'S CURLERS	From a woodcut lent by Messrs A. & C. Black	To face page 114
CRAMPITS—		
Hamilton		130
Harvey's Picture		158
Currie		158, 159
Cairnie's Essay (Foot-Iron)		159
Fala, Linlithgow, Doune, Strathallan Meath Moss, Markinch		160
ROSLIN TEE-MARKER		155
ANCIENT CURLERS	The late Jas. Drummond, R.S.A.	156, 157
HACK IN THE ICE		161
Tailpiece—'A COLLIE'	W. S. Cumming	167
Vignette—'MAKING THE BROUGHS'	C. A. Doyle	168
Heading—'LOCHMABEN,' and Initial Letter	Samuel Reid	171
DR CAIRNIE	From a picture	178
ROBERT PALMER	From a photograph	200
G. A. WALKER ARNOTT, LL.D.	From a photograph	214
SIR JOHN OGILVY, BART.	From a photograph	224
Tailpiece—'HELP IN TIME OF NEED'	John Smart, R.S.A.	227
Heading—'MEDALS OF THE R.C.C.C.,' and Initial Letter	T. Bramah	229
CAPTAIN J. OGILVY DALGLEISH	From a photograph	240
DUKE OF ATHOLE'S RINK	From a photograph	253
BAILIE CASSELS	From a photograph	255
REV. C. GIFFEN	From a photograph	257
KEY TO MR LEES' PICTURE OF THE GRAND MATCH AT LINLITHGOW IN 1848		270
GRAND MATCH TROPHY		277
DR SIDEY	From a photograph	284
CHARLES COWAN	From a photograph	291
A. DAVIDSON SMITH	From a photograph	304
LORD BALFOUR OF BURLEIGH	From a photograph by H. S. Mendelssohn, London	To face page 305
Heading—'CANADIAN SCENE,' and Initial Letter	Samuel Reid	307
MARQUIS OF DUFFERIN AND AVA	From a photograph	319
MARQUIS OF LORNE	From a photograph	323
CANADIAN IRON-PLAYERS	From a photograph	330
CANADIAN STONE-PLAYERS	From Ontario Branch 'Annual'	337
HON. ALEX. MITCHELL	From a photograph	343

LIST OF ILLUSTRATIONS.

	ARTIST	PAGE
Heading—'THE MYSTERIES,' and *Initial Letter*	Samuel Reid	351
J. W. WILLIAMSON (and *Cerberus*)	From a photograph	357
Heading—'AILSA CRAIG,' and *Initial Letter*	Samuel Reid, from a photograph	367
THE STONEMAKER'S GRINDING MACHINE		371
,, POLISHING MACHINE		371
SHIPPING STONES FROM AILSA CRAIG	Samuel Reid, from a photograph	373
MARKING THE RINK		376
Tailpiece—'CURLERS' IMPLEMENTS'	W. S. Cumming	378
Heading—'THE CHAIR OF CURLING,' and *Initial Letter*	Samuel Reid	379
COLOURED EXAMPLES OF STONE USED FOR CURLING	To face page	382
Do. do. do.	To face page	384
Tailpiece—'STONE-HOUSE'	C. A. Doyle	386
Heading—'ART OF CURLING,' and *Initial Letter*	Samuel Reid	387
CURLERS AT PLAY	C. A. Doyle	389
DIAGRAM OF THE RINK		392
THE SOLE OF THE STONE	From Cairnie's 'Essay'	399
POSITION OF CURLERS—		
'Fitting the Tee'		400
'Shew me the Winner'		401
'A Canny Swing'	These have been drawn by W. G. Stevenson, A.R.S.A., from instantaneous photographs	403
'A Hair o' Pith'		403
'A Thunnerin' Cast'		404
'Sharp-Edged Soling'		405
'Weel Laid Doun'		405
'A' the Curl'		406
DIAGRAMS OF THE POINT GAME		414, 415
,, ,, CANADIAN PORT SHOT		417
Heading—'BIBLIOTHECA,' and *Initial Letter*	Samuel Reid	419
Tailpiece—'THE SPIRIT OF CURLING'	C. A. Doyle	433
PORTRAIT OF REV. J. KERR	From a photograph	434
Tailpiece—'FINIS'	C. A. Doyle	440

Auld Daddy Scotland sat ae day,
Bare leggit on a snawy brae,
His brawny arms wi' cauld were blae,
　　The wind was snelly blawing :
As icicles froze at his snout,
He rowed his plaid his head about,
Syne raired to heaven a roupit shout,
　　Auld Albyn's Jove miscaʼing :
Chorus—"Oh! for a cheery, heartsome game,
　　　　To send through a' the soul a flame,
　　　　Pitt birr and smeddum in the frame,
　　　　　　And set the blude a-din'ling.

" Oh, dool and wae! this wretched clime ;
What care I for our hills sublime,
If covered aye wi' frosty rime ?
　　I'm right mischantlie dealt wi'."
Quo' Jove, and gied his kilt a heeze,
" Fule carle ! what gars you grunt and wheeze ?
Get up ! I'll get an exercise
　　To het your freezing melt wi'.
　　　I'll get a cheery, heartsome game, &c.

" Gae, get twa whinstanes, round and hard,
Syne on their taps twa thorn-roots gird,
Then soop the ice for mony a yard,
　　And mak' baith tee and colly ;
If in the hack your fit ye hide,
And draw or inwick, guard or ride,
Syne wi' your besom after 't stride,
　　We'll hear nae mair o' cauld aye.
　　　That, Sawney, 's what I ca' a game," &c.

" Great thanks !" auld Daddy Scotland cries,
" Sly, pawky chield, for thy advice,
We'll birsle now our shins on ice,
　　Instead o' owre the ingle :
Let ilka true-born Scottish son,
When craureuch cleeds the snawy grun',
'Mang curling cores seek harmless fun,
　　And gar his heart's blude tingle."
　　　Oh ! curling, cauld-defying game, &c

OLD SONG.

PART I.

ANCIENT CURLING.

"We are sons o' the true hearts that bled wi' the Wallace
 And conquered at brave Bannockburn wi' the Bruce;
Thae wild days are gane, but their memories call us,
 So we'll stand by langsyne and the guid ancient use.

"And we'll hie to the spiel, as our faithers afore us,
 Ye sons o' the men whom foe never could tame:
And at nicht round the ingle we'll raise the blithe chorus
 To the land we lo'e weel and our auld Scottish game."
         Principal Shairp.

"Hail! Scotland, wi' thy ancient play
 When winter cleeds the plain!
Thy buirdly race shall ne'er decay
 While Curling doth remain."
     Irvine Miscellany.

"Sic Scoti: alii non æque felices."
    Motto, Duddingston C. C.

CHAPTER I.

THE ORIGIN OF THE GAME.

N enquiry into the origin and antiquity of the game of curling is not only an appropriate introduction to a work that is written with the aim of being a handbook to the game, but is also a chapter of interest and importance in the history of our nation. Without trenching on what we may hereafter have to say "in praise of curling," we may here affirm that no other game so well illustrates the national character, or tends so much to its healthy development; and, if this be so, then the history of the game has an intimate connection with the history of our people. In the pages of the historian, such influences are too often ignored, and attention directed to those great and striking events that are supposed to be the only constituent elements of a nation's history. It ought not to be so; and, therefore, in gathering together such information as is available on the past and present of this most truly national of all our amusements, we hope to have the approval of the historian as well as of "the brethren of the broom." At the outset of our enquiry, we find that there are no facts by which

we can determine precisely the antiquity of the game or the manner in which it was at first played. This is not perhaps to be wondered at, for, as a writer on our other great national game—golf—remarks,* "If the origin of the most valuable institutions of civilised life, the laws and usages of the most enlightened nations, are lost in the mist of antiquity, eluding the researches of the philosopher and historian, it was not to be expected that any distinct record would be found setting forth the invention and progress of a mere popular recreation." Our author is evidently tainted with the vice to which we have referred. He does not esteem the games of a country—as Fletcher the patriot esteemed the songs—of greater importance than its laws. He depreciates the national importance of both golf and curling by his phrase, "mere popular recreations," against which we protest; but, in the general nebulous haze that surrounds all the "origins," we need not be surprised to find "our ain game" floating in shapeless, unrecognisable form, unable to give any clear account of itself. In the case of the game of curling, it is as well, however, to bear in mind that while it is a game of great antiquity, and can be traced back for nearly 400 years, it was only about the middle of last century that it began to take on the dignity of a truly national game. Unlike its neighbour—golf, which, barring the *gutta*, has been played in much the same method from the beginning, and unlike lawn tennis, which is simply the revival of a game played centuries ago in a form that required as much skill as the present—curling has so completely developed out of its ancient mode, that it is only by the help of an evolutionary theory, which requires great faith on our part, that we can trace connection between the modern and the ancient game. Since the game, through the rounding of the stone fully a century ago, made such a break away from the style of previous centuries, its progress has been remarkable. It has taken a firm hold on the national character, and has drawn around it a literature of its own well worthy of attention. If we find, as is the

---

* *Historical Notice for the Thistle Golf Club*, Edinburgh, 1824.

case, that prior to the middle of last century we have scant records of the game, we need not therefore suppose that much of value has gone amissing. When Edward I., taking advantage of his position as arbiter between Bruce and Baliol in their contention for the throne of Scotland, carried off to England such records as he could lay hold of, and destroyed them that he might thus destroy our nationality, he doubtless put out of the way much that might have dispersed the mist from our early Scottish history; but we as curlers need not suppose that any curling records perished at his hands, or that anything particularly precious has been lost since his time. With no authentic facts, as we have said, to determine accurately the history of curling, our enquiry into its origin and antiquity resolves itself very much into a question of *Etymology*.

"Many ancient customs," says Dr Jamieson,* "otherwise unknown or involved in obscurity, come to be explained or illustrated from the use of those words which necessarily refer to them." This is true, but the opening sentence of the Preface to Jamieson's great work suggests another view of the study of words. "Some,' he says, "affect to despise all etymological researches, because of their uncertainty." Etymology seems to be like curling—a slippery game: it is not safe to depend on it very much for historical information, or for proofs of antiquity. Herodotus tells a story of ancient Egypt, which may be read as a warning by etymological historians. The Egyptians used to boast that their language was the most ancient. Psammitichus, their King, made a practical test which destroyed their boast. He placed two infants apart from human society, their attendants being forbidden to speak in their hearing. One day, when about two years old, they ran to their keeper, crying "Bekkos," "Bekkos." This being Phrygian for bread, the palm of antiquity was given by Psammitichus to the Phrygians. But the test was not satisfactory. Deprived, in the circumstances, of natural nurses, the infants were suckled by goats, and their first cry, it was said by some Philistines, was just

* Preface to *Etymological Dictionary of the Scottish Language*, Edin., 1808.

an imitation of the bleat of the goat. The Germans however recognise in it their word *bakken* = bake: the Scotch would have it that the bairns demanded *baiks;* while certain etymologists claim the word as the Sanscrit root *pac,* whence the English "cook;" and a sly Englishman finishes off by suggesting that it may have been a feeble attempt to call for "breakfast."* So we are told Etymology or Philology has acted the Psammitichus for this curling nation. We have boasted of curling as "Scotland's ain game," as of unknown antiquity, and certainly indigenous; but away beyond the gabble of historians we have been taken by Etymology to find that we are mistaken. The infancy of curling breaks out, we are told, in a language which proves that the game is not ours in origin, but that it belongs to another country. Like Psammitichus with the Egyptians, the test has been applied, as far as we can see, by one of ourselves, and after its application the origin of curling is still left in Egyptian darkness. No other nation has attempted to filch from us our reputation, or lay claim to the origination of curling. Perhaps no other would care to do so; but, if the Egyptians submitted to the verdict of their King in favour of the Phrygians, the Scots have certainly not agreed to the statement that the earliest words in use at curling prove it to have been imported into our country by the Flemings. For this is what it amounts to. The statement, as far as we can judge, was first made by the Rev. John Ramsay (1777-1871), who has given the earliest account we possess of the history of curling.† Ramsay, no doubt, found a difference of opinion on the subject among curlers before he wrote, but the opinion as to the Continental origin of the game was first distinctly formulated in his work.

"We have *all the evidence,*" he says (pp. 18-19) "*which etymology can give in favour of its Continental origin.* The terms, being *all Dutch or German,* point to the Low Countries as the place in which it most probably originated, or, at least, from whence it was conveyed to us. For if it

---
* In the circumstances the Spanish, as far as we know, have not put *tobacco* into the mouths of the young people, nor have the Greeks suggested such an early worship of *Bacchus.*
† *An Account of the Game of Curling.* By a member of the Duddingston Curling Society. Edinburgh, 1811.

was not introduced from the Continent, but was first invented in this country, it must have been at a time when the German and Low Dutch were the prevailing languages. Now, though the Saxon was once pretty general in this country, and there are still many Dutch words in our language, yet those German dialects were never so general as to make it credible, that our countrymen, in any particular invention, would employ them alone as the appropriate terms. In the history of inventions, such a phenomenon is not to be found. Had there been only one or two foreign terms, these would not have militated much against the domestic origin of the game, but *the whole of the terms being Continental, compel us to ascribe to it a Continental origin.*"

The italics in this passage are ours, and they shew on what basis the Continental origin of our great national game is supposed to rest. Without further enquiry this statement is simply repeated, time after time, by writers on the subject,* and accepted by them as gospel—they follow the first historian like a flock of sheep; and even those whose *amor Scotiae* will not hear of such a *low* view of the origin of the game, do not attempt to meet him on his own ground, or to overthrow his argument from etymology.

Let us therefore look at the etymological argument by itself, apart from any historical facts that may be brought forward in its support. On the face of it, the assertion that the whole vocabulary of the curler is a foreign one, is absurd, and overshoots the mark. The curler's language,

---

* "Curling is a comparatively modern amusement in Scotland, and does not appear to have been introduced till the beginning of the sixteenth century, when it was probably brought over by the emigrant Flemings."—*Encyc. Metrop.* (Brewster) vol. xvii. p. 469.

"Powerful etymological evidence supports its foreign origin. The terms, being all Dutch or German, point to the Low Countries as the place whence we, at least, derived our knowledge of it. . . . . It is supposed that the Flemings were the people who, in the fifteenth or about the beginning of the sixteenth century, introduced Curling into this country."—*A Descriptive and Historical Sketch of Curling,*" &c. Kilmarnock, 1828.

Sir R. Broun gives both sides without his own opinion, but suggests that some Scottish traveller may have introduced the game on his return from the Continent.—*Memorabilia Curliana Mabenensia.* Dumfries, 1830.

Dr Cairnie remarks, "After all we have seen or heard, we may say that its introduction or commencement is involved in mystery."—*Essay on Curling.* Glasgow, 1833.

Mr J. Brown, in his *History of the Sanquhar Curling Society* (Dumfries, 1874), is inclined "to regard Scotland as the birthplace of Curling."

Dr James Taylor, after strongly combating the Continental theory, concludes, "There is good reason to believe that Curling originated in Scotland, probably in the south-western district of the country, which has always been its stronghold."—*Curling—the Ancient Scottish Game.* Edinburgh, 1884.

as he plays the old game, is certainly peculiar. It would defy the wisest philologist to explain its formation. Even a native, if he were unacquainted with the game, might, from the shores of the loch that resounds with the shout of the bonspeil, suppose that the players were foreigners, so peculiar is their language. The curling *lingo* is, however, essentially native. It drags into its service words and phrases that look very queer in their new employment, and "piles on the agony" for philologists by the strange use it makes of these servant-words; but, for all that, the native Doric is, and has always been, the staple speech of the curler; and, while its use since the union of the kingdoms has been gradually dying out, it has been preserved by curlers more truly than by any others. Nay, more—as if the game could not be properly played without it—the native dialect has accompanied it to those other countries into which it has so happily been transferred in later times. To assert that the whole vocabulary of our national game is Continental is just as much as to assert that our whole national vocabulary is the same: it proves too much.

There are, however, some "foreign terms" that may seem to "militate," as Ramsay puts it, "against the domestic origin of the game." Let us select a few specimens of curling words that were in use at the time Ramsay formed his conclusion (and most of which still do duty) *e.g., Boardhead, bonspiel, brough, bunker, channelstane, chuckle, cock or cockee, cowe, cowl, colly or coal-score, crampit, curl, director, draw, hack or hatch, hog, kuting, quoiting or coiting, rack, rink, skip, stug, tee or toesee, trickers, wick, witter or wittyr*. It cannot be denied that there is a far-away sound about some of these. Some are no doubt of Dutch or German origin, as stated by Ramsay, but that they all connect the game with the Low Countries, and compel us to own its Continental origin, is an entire mistake, and may be met with a distinct denial. The great dictionary of Dr Jamieson had only been published a year or two before the "member of the Duddingston Club" drew up his "account," and he must have rested his case against the native origin of curling very much on Jamieson.

Now, while the Dictionary is a perfect storehouse for the student of Scottish literature, its references being very full and very reliable, Jamieson's etymologies are quite unreliable, and in many cases misleading. Some of Ramsay's derivations are, however, more far-fetched and absurd than anything found in the lexicologist's work, as for example—

Curl, from the German *Kurzweil*: an amusement: a game: and *Curling* from *Kurzweillen*, to play for amusement.
Rink, from ancient Saxon *hrink*, *hrincg*, a strong man.

Jamieson, to his credit be it said, does not commit himself to such a couple of evident errors. There is one word among the number on which more stress has been laid than on any of the others, because it is said to imply a distinct connection between a game played in the Low Country and our game of curling. It is the word *kuting*, *quoiting* or *coiting*. Kilian, it would appear, in his *Etymologicon Teutonicae Linguae* (1632), renders the German words *Kluyten*, *Kalluyten*, "*Ludere massis sive globis glaciatis: certare discis in aequore glaciato.*"—to play with lumps or balls frozen: to contend with quoits on an icy plain. *Kuting* or *coiting*, as will appear (Chap. II.), was for a long time the name given to curling, and its primitive style was more allied to quoit-playing than its style is in modern times. The implements of the game were originally called coits; and so Jamieson throws out the suggestion *(Dict.—sub voce,* to coit)—"Can it be supposed that this west country name has been softened from Teut. *Kluyten, certare discis in aequore glaciato?*" Ramsay jumps at this suggestion, and regards it as further proof that all the evidence of etymology is in favour of the foreign origin of the game. Now, it may be evidence—it is evidence—that Dutchmen had two kinds of ice-games: one apparently a kind of "shinty" played on the ice with snowballs, the other a kind of pitch-penny played with small quoits; but it is not etymological evidence; for *kuting* or *coiting* and *kluyten* or *kalluyten* can only be made one term by a very great stretch of imagination. Had our word *cloyte* or *clyte*, to squat down, been attached to the game at first, or had Kilian given us under Dutch *cote* a reference to something like our early curling, we might at once have granted some connection between the ice-game of the Dutch and our own on etymological grounds; but on these grounds alone—and this is what we are now considering—the evidence is insufficient to prove that our curling was the game spoken of by Kilian, and that it was introduced from the Low Countries. Indeed Jamieson shrinks from his own suggestion when under the word *Curling* he acknowledges that Kilian's *kluyten*, though applied to a similar amusement, is a *different name*. Thus far our enquiry into etymology does not support the statement which ascribes the origin of curling to the Low Countries. The most thorough investigation of this statement since it was first hazarded by Ramsay is to be found in the *Annals of the Parish of Lesmahagow*, 1864. The able author of this work (J. B. Greenshields) thus concludes—

"After careful examination of these words . . . the conclusion appears certain that many of them do proceed from foreign roots; but the same remark is applicable to almost every word in the English language. Of the original language of our own country, it is sufficient to state that it was Celtic; but the venerable Bede, the Saxon historian, informs us that in his day four languages prevailed in Britain, viz., the Irish, the British or *Cymraig*, the Pictish or Scandinavian, and the Anglo-Saxon. 'Twice was the languishing Anglo-Saxon energy stirred up by the admixture of northern blood; and the "salt blood" which makes British youth turn almost instinctively to the ocean, and which forms so notable an ingredient in Britain's dauntless seamanship, is probably due in no small degree to the daring spirit infused by Scandinavian sea rovers (*Northmen in Cumberland and Westmoreland* p. 3). With the blood of Denmark came a mixture of the Danish language, and with the Norman conquest Norman French was partially introduced. That foreigners in considerable numbers subsequently settled in our country is an undoubted historical fact; but, as the most skilful philologists pronounce the German, Danish, Swedish, and ancient Saxon, to be all of Gothic origin, and that the English language is mainly compounded of these, it does seem unwarrantable, from etymology alone, and in the absence of all historical proof, to decide upon the foreign origin of the game, seeing that our ancestors could not avoid using words of foreign derivation. 'The whole fabric and scheme of the English language,' says that great authority, Dr Johnson, 'is Gothic or Teutonic.'"

In our desire to deal fairly with this question, and to place before curlers the whole case, we have not simply formed our own opinion on an unbiassed investigation of the subject, but have secured the verdict of some of our ablest philologists on the words above given (with many others), and the assertion of Ramsay as to what is implied in them regarding the origin of curling. Professor Masson, whose opinion is of the greatest value, thus writes:—

"I see no proof in them collectively that the game came from the Continent. Most of the terms are of Teutonic origin in a general way; some are of French original; some might even be claimed as of Celtic original; and a few seem recent inventions by the natural *nous* of players of the game within the last century or so, to define recurring circumstances and incidents of the game previously unnamed.

"I do not think much can be made for your question on either side by chasing up etymologies. The matter seems mainly a *historical* one.

"Wherever there was ice, there must have been, since man existed, games on the ice; and the question is whether the particular game of Curling can be proved to have been in use anywhere out of Scotland, without clear derivation from Scotland. If it ever existed anywhere else, it ought to be found in that place now; for, the ice still remaining, the extinction of the game, if once in use, may be voted impossible. Curlers, therefore, ought to drive at this question—'Is there any Curling now, or anything like Curling, anywhere in the world out of Scotland, except by obvious and provable derivation from Scotland?'

"The terms of the game, on the supposition of its Scottish origin, are easily accounted for. The original inventors of the game, or of the germ of the present game, would use the words of their composite Scoto-English vocabulary—mostly Teutonic, but some French and some Celtic—for the purposes and situations of the game, just as they would for any other business; and, as the game grew, other words would be added for new developments of it or new intricacies—some of these with no antique reference in them at all, but mere modern phrases of course."

Professor Mackinnon states his opinion thus:—

"The great majority of the words are not only Teutonic, but seem to me to be native. *Hack*, e.g., is an old English verb, and a noun used in the same sense is but what may be looked for. On the other hand *bonspiel* is foreign, and made up of *bon* (Fr.) and a form of the Teutonic *spielen*. I may say that in the West Highlands we have borrowed *spel* from the Norsemen in the sense of 'a game.' *Rink*, evidently the same as *ring*, looks a loan from the Continent, though the Scotch often pronounce their medials pretty strongly, perhaps under Continental and Highland influences. On the general question: if the words were proved foreign, the presumption would be a strong one, that the game was imported—so strong indeed that it would "hold the field" until a native origin was proved by other evidence. But my knowledge does not enable me (it is to Celtic philology that I give chief attention) to say with any degree of confidence that the words you quote or many of them are borrowed into Scotch."

Professor Blackie adds:—

"I am no adept in the Scandinavian and other dialects of the Teutonic that skirt the Baltic. The presumption, however, seems quite plain that the vocabulary of a game that belongs to frozen water, should claim a descent from the nations whose skates were frequently their shoes for four months in the year, but whether in addition to this presumable kinship there may not have been a direct historical introduction of technical terms from Flanders, is a historical question which would require a detailed historical knowledge to decide."

A survey of the evidence thus far produced, seems to warrant our laying down the double conclusion :—

(1) That the proportion of words of Teutonic origin in the Curling vocabulary has been over-estimated ; and

(2) That, even if a great many are Teutonic, it does not follow that the game of Curling must have had its origin in the Low Countries.

The argument from etymology must, therefore, if left to stand alone, fall to the ground.

To complete our enquiry we must, however, go further afield ; and, though we may have to trespass a little on our third chapter, it is necessary to investigate here in how far the etymological position, though weak in itself, may be supported by historical facts. "Curlers," says Professor Masson, "ought to *drive at** this question, ' Is there any curling now, or anything like curling, anywhere in the world out of Scotland, except by obvious and provable derivation from Scotland ?'" A good straight shot " up the howe," for it is a case of " chap and lie," is here sufficient. We may confidently say there is not; and, if any one has any objection to this direct negative, let him " now speak out or be for ever silent."

To the game on ice described in *Kilian's Teutonic Dictionary* we have already referred in discussing the point of etymology pure and simple. As to its resemblance to curling we may now quote Dr Cairnie—

"The explanation referred to by the writers on this sport, as to the interpretation of the words *kluyten, kalluyten*, in *Kilian's Dictionary*, throws no light on the game we now call Curling. Kilian's definition of it is thus given : '*Ludere massis sive globis glaciatis in æquore glaciato.*' This sport certainly must have been different from our Curling ; and now-a-days, from our want of frost, we should find it difficult to procure icy missiles to play with. We find the word *Klyten* in the Dutch

* This is a good curling expression, used no doubt unwittingly by the learned Professor, but all the more truly illustrating his statement.

language signifies a *clod;* and, had there been want of better *material,* it might be argued that iced clay clods had been originally in use for Curling." "We may notice," he adds in a note, "the remark of a noted stone-maker on the subject. He says that 'it must have been bairns' play, for that neither the ice nor clod-iced blocks would have stood the nidge of an Ayrshire hammer.'"*

The Icelanders had a game called "Knattleikr." It was played upon the ice by means of what are called bowls.† Such a parentage of curling is quite as feasible as the Continental one on etymological grounds; but it does not seem to exist now, and its relationship to curling must have been very distant. In the *Royal Caledonian Curling Club Annual*‡ *for* 1848, there is an interesting communication from Professor Ferguson, King's College, Aberdeen; and, as it is necessary to throw all the light on the subject possible, we transcribe it for our readers. It was addressed to the Professor by Thomas Purdie, and certainly describes the nearest approach to anything like curling that has come under our notice. It is as follows :—

"When I was in Munich, as I promised, I made a point of seeing the Curling Ponds and Curling Apparatus in use in that part of the world, and subjoin a description of the game as there practised, so far as my imperfect knowledge of German enabled me to understand it. In regard to such a subject the dictionary was of course useless, the technical terms in use having no place there among their more classic friends, and many of them having no equivalent even in the Curling language of our own country. I believe, however, you may depend on my information being pretty correct, as I was not content with a mere verbal description, but played a game on a barn floor with the man who takes charge of the Pond and Curling Stones, and vindicated the honour of Scotland by beating him with his own weapons and on his own ground. The game is a very ancient one, and is played generally throughout Bavaria, but more especially in the neighbourhood of Munich, the capital. It is common for gentlemen to have within their grounds artificial ponds for the practice of the game. These consist generally of one rink, fifty or sixty yards long, which is the common length between the Tees. The Tees, called *Taube,* are moveable, and the nearest stone counts wherever the Tee may be moved to. They are formed of square pieces of wood four inches long by two thick. The "stones" are made of wood, and are in German called "ice sticks,"

---

* *Essay on Curling and Artificial Pond Making.* Glasgow, 1833.
† "To their diversions likewise belongs that called *knattleikur,* or playing with bowls on the ice."—Von Troil's *Letters on Iceland* (1780), p. 92.
"*Knattleikr,* a kind of cricket or trap-ball, a favourite game with the old Scandinavians. . . . The ice in winter was a favourite play-ground."— Cleasby and Vigfusson's *Icelandic-English Dictionary.* Oxford, 1874.
‡ To be afterwards referred to simply as the *Annual.*

for an equally good reason that in Scotland we call them stones. You recollect some attempts being made to supply the place of stones with wooden fabrications: these naturally got the name of wooden stones, and, when some daring spirit attempts to introduce stones into Germany, I doubt not they will be called "stone sticks." Their sticks weigh from 12 to 25 lbs. English; run on a sole of from 10 to 13 inches, encircled close to the sole by a heavy rim of iron, to give weight and solidity. The handle is perpendicular, about 9 inches long and slightly curved at the top. The following drawing will give you some idea of the shape.

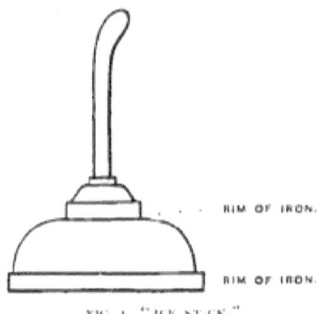

FIG. 1. "ICE STICK."

"There are from two to four players a side: the sides are chosen by ballot. Numbered balls are put into a box, and each man takes his side according to the number of his ball. The places of the players are fixed by playing one end, and each man ranks according to the distance his stick measures from the Tee. The first player is called Maier, the second Engmaier, the third Helfer, and the fourth, when there is one, also Helfer. The Maier directs the game, and his is reckoned the most important stick. The sides do not play alternately, as with us; but, when one side has the shot, the other must play till they take it out. Each side has a right to play the Maier stick twice. When all the sticks are played, including second playing of the Maier's —the party gaining the end counts six. If any party take the end without playing their Maier the second time—it counts nine. For example :—Suppose A and B to be on one side—C and D on the other. A plays, then C. If C has the shot B plays—If B takes the shot D plays—If D takes the shot, A plays his Maier, and supposing him also to take the shot—C follows with his Maier—and on taking the shot counts six, and it requires another end, probably two to finish the game. Again, suppose A plays, then C—If A has the shot then D plays—If D take the shot, A plays his Maier—if he fail to take the shot, C and D count nine and the game is ended—the right of C to play his Maier not having been exercised. Again, suppose A and C play—A has the shot—D plays, and afterwards C plays his Maier, both failing to take the shot, A and B count nine. The stakes are paid at the end of each game, and there is always some stake played for. The rinks played on are at least ten yards longer than with us, and it must require considerable force to propel the sticks. They are swung backwards and forwards in the hand before being thrown off.

"You will see, however, from the above, that it has little in common with our roaring game—no wicking, guarding, or running a port ; and, famed as Bavaria is for its brooms and broom girls, there is even no sweeping, so that their game is but child's play compared to our noble science. In fact we may consider the Bavarians to be in a state of heathenish ignorance on the subject of Curling—most degenerate sons of worthy sires, if the game has descended to them, as to us, from our common Gothic ancestors ; and I conceive this to be a fair field for the

missionary exertions of the Royal Grand Caledonian Curling Club,—
the manifold corruptions which have crept into their game rendering
reformation of the utmost consequence, and the superiority of orthodox
Curling so manifest as only to require exhibition to ensure conviction.
Armed with a few copies of the 'Annual' translated into German,
a few stones to show the pattern, I could undertake, in one winter, to
convert the whole nation to the true faith."

These three—the Teutonic *Kluyten* or *Kalluyten* of Kilian, the Icelandic *Knattleikr* of Von Troil, and the Bavarian game so minutely described by Mr Purdie, are all the instances we have yet heard of a kind of ice-game which might be considered as in any way related to curling, and they are clearly not derived from Scotland. But is it not as clear that our game of curling is not derived from any of them? Is the resemblance so strong that the argument from etymology, unable, as we have seen, to stand alone, draws from it sufficient support? No one, we presume, will venture to say so. "Wherever there was ice," says Professor Masson, "there must have been, since man existed, games on the ice;" and it is not improbable that the Scots *Curling*, the Dutch *Kluyten*, the Bavarian "*Ice-Sticks*," and the Icelandic *Knattleikr*, are all descendants from a common ancestor whose "period" is as ancient as the human race. Given a cold climate, where a man must exercise himself to keep his blood warm, an inherent tendency from Old Adam to "throw stones," and a struggling aversion to that mischief which Satan provides for the unemployed, with a sheet of ice to disport upon—we have all the "makings" of our national game, without requiring to search far away for its origin.[*]

---

[*] Since we have noticed most of the accounts of the origin of Curling, we should not omit that of the author of *Sixty-six Years of Curling: being Records of North Woodside Curling Club, 1820-1886.*" Captain Crawford quietly passes by the Native *versus* Continental discussion, and shews how the question of origin has endless ramifications, by pitting field-labourers against masons as the most likely originators of the game. He dismisses the *masonic* origin as rather fanciful; and, if his support of the other side is liable to the same objection, it is at least a capital piece of *evolutionary* logic. . . . "We believe," he says, "that the game originated among rural workers and the tillers of the land, in those moorland districts where undrained lochs and tarns were numerous centuries ago. Let us suppose a hard frost sets in: the rural labourer finds his plough frozen in the furrow; the earth is hard as iron; everything is bound in the cold embrace of the frost king. The rural workers meet together in their enforced idleness.

Those amusements we have mentioned are the ways in which other nations have protected themselves in times of cold, and this Curling is ours; but it is just as much proved that they got their games from us as that we got ours from them. We therefore conclude—

(3) That no game is proved to exist, or to have existed, in other countries, so much resembling Curling as to imply that the game was borrowed into our country.

In adding this to our former conclusions, we ought in justice to say that Ramsay, in supporting the Continental origin of the game, does not forget to deal with the objection; and he does so in these words:—

"Even though it do not exist on the Continent, and though no traces have been observed, by many of our countrymen who resided there, of its ever having existed, still this circumstance is far from being sufficient to prove that it is not of Continental origin. Within these two hundred years, the occupations, manners, and customs of the different countries of Europe have undergone the greatest revolutions. The vast improvements that have been made in agriculture and

The exhilarating winter air acts like a stimulant on their spirits, and the country-folk are full of fun. The loch and stream are frozen; they venture on the ice for the purpose of sliding; one mirthful fellow seizes a boulder, he putts it along the ice, and he and his fellows are astonished at the distance it is carried on the smooth surface of the frozen waters. He challenges his companions to a test of strength, and they begin to select suitable stones from the beds of the rivers, and from the dry-stone dykes, and play one against the other, by hurling the stones along in rude fashion. Ultimately, they fix a mark at which the stone is to be thrown; and in process of time the game becomes developed into an exhilarating pastime, where otherwise the country people would suffer from *ennui*. The rude stone selected, from its natural adaptation for playing, soon becomes moulded into more fitting forms. It is chipped to a shape, its under-surface is polished; a rude handle or grip is inserted; and the enjoyment afforded in the bright winter days by meeting together in this friendly rivalry brings out the whole rural population to enjoy the fun. The farmer and the ploughman keep themselves in good humour during the enforced idleness of the winter. The village workers find their labour impeded by the frost as well as the ploughmen. The smith is unemployed, because all farm and rural labour is suspended, and he joins in the fun and frolic of the game. The joiner and the artizan of the district catch the infection, and play sides against one another. The laird and the parish priest enter into the enjoyment, and encourage the innocent and exhilarating pastime, which has many salutary social influences, and keeps the hands of the people out of mischief. If the frost continues for long periods, as it often does on the upland districts of Scotland, one hamlet challenges another to a game of Curling, as was also their wont in olden days to challenge each other to games of shinty, football, and the like. Thus the game grew into district and national importance, and the implements of the sport, rude and primitive at first, have been developed into handsome and fitting accessories of the exhilarating recreation."

commerce, by giving employment to persons of all descriptions, have
had a fatal influence upon our sports and amusements, particularly such
as are practised in the open air. Hence many of the amusements of
former times are now forgotten, or fast going into disuse. . . . .
Curling, therefore, may have once flourished, where now, among an
industrious and laborious people, it is completely forgotten."

So it may, and there is proof here and there that in parts
of our own country it has died away after having been played
for a time; but it is not likely to have wholly disappeared
from any country where it was ever practised; and Professor
Masson's *dictum* may be set against Ramsay's explanation
as much more likely to be true, viz., that "the extinction
of the game, if once in use, may be voted impossible."[*]

Our task is not, however, done. "The matter," says
Professor Masson, "seems mainly *a historical one ;*" and
Professor Blackie—"Whether . . . there may not have
been a direct historical introduction of technical terms from
Flanders, is *a historical question* which would require a
detailed historical knowledge to decide." Is there, then,
any direct historical evidence bearing on the introduction
of curling from the Low Countries, and buttressing the
philological argument, which in itself is weak? The
upholders of the foreign origin of curling profess to have
such evidence, fitting in exactly with their argument from
philology, and, though destroying the idea of a national
origin of the game, giving it, nevertheless, great antiquity.
This evidence, as far as we can make out, is furnished
(though Ramsay gives no authority) in Buchanan's *History
of Scotland*,[†] where, describing the reign of James I. (1424-
1437), the historian says :—

"There was one admirable quality which the King possessed. In
the midst of his most anxious solicitude about the greatest affairs, he
thought nothing, however small, beneath his notice, from which any

---

[*] Since this chapter was in type, the publisher of this work has a communication from J. G. Robbers, Amsterdam, of date April 2, 1889, in which there is this statement:—"The game 'Curling' is quite unknown in our country. Mr H. C. Ragge, keeper of the library of the University in town, to whom I have applied for information on the subject, writes me to-day that he could not trace a similar game in the present or last century, and that he believes he may assume that curling or a game similar to it has never been in use in this country."

[†] Aikman's *Buchanan*, Vol. II. Book X. p. 41.

advantage could arise to the public. As during the constant state of warfare in which Scotland had been engaged, for nearly a hundred and fifty years from the death of Alexander, her cities had been wasted and burned, and her youth trained to arms, while the other arts had been neglected, he invited tradesmen of every description from Flanders, and encouraged them to settle by rewards and immunities, and filled the almost deserted cities with artisans; the nobility, according to the ancient custom, residing on their estates. Nor did he by this restore only the ancient appearance and trade of the towns, but he likewise induced a great crowd of vagabonds to betake themselves to industry, and superseded the necessity of bringing, at a great expense, from abroad, what could with little cost be produced at home."

Now, though Buchanan is more esteemed for his classical accomplishments than for historical accuracy, we have no reason to doubt the facts here narrated. It was quite a common thing for the English and the Scottish Kings in those early times to "beg, borrow, or steal" Flemish peasants and tradesmen, not always with such high motives as are here ascribed to James I. of Scotland by Buchanan, but to curb the influence and power of their nobles, which always increased as the industrious classes diminished. On the other hand, the Flemings themselves were often led to seek refuge in England, Wales, and Scotland.

"The year 1108," says an old Welsh historian,* "did overflowe and drowne a great part of the Lowe countrie of Flanders in such sort that the inhabitants were driven to seeke themselves other dwellings: who came to King Henrie and desired him to give some voide place to remain in: who, being very liberal of that which was not his own, gave them the lands of Ros in Dyvet or West Wales, where Pembroke, Tenby, and Haverfordwest are now built, and there they remaine till this daie, as may be well perceived by their speeche and conditions, farre differing from the rest of the countrie."

And Holinshed, evidently referring to the same or a similar inundation, writes:—

"About this season (A.D. 1107), a great part of Flanders being drowned by an inundation or breaking in of the sea, a great number of Flemings came to England beseeching the King to have some void part assigned to them wherein they might inhabit. At the first they were appointed to *the countrie lieing on the east part of the Tweed;* but within four years after they were removed into a corner by the sea-side in Wales, called Pembrokeshire, to the end that they might be a defence there against the unquiet Welsh." †

---

* Powell.
† The words in italics shew that Flemings were near us as far back as the twelfth century.

Giraldus Cambrensis favours us in addition with some insight into the character of these early emigrants:—

"The inhabitants of Haverfordwest," he says, "derived their origin from Flanders, and were sent by Henry I. to inhabit these districts: a people brave and robust, ever hostile to the Welsh: a people, I say, well versed in commerce and woollen manufactures: a people anxious to seek gain by sea and land, in defiance of fatigue or danger: a hardy race equally fitted for the plough and sword: a people brave and happy," &c.

Religious persecution seems also from time to time to have driven refugees from the Low Countries into ours; and Samuel Smiles in his *Huguenots* states that—

"Colonies of **Flemish fishermen** having settled during the reign of Henry II. at Brighton, **Newhaven**, and other places along the south coast, their lineage is still **traceable** there in local words, names, and places."

Curious documentary evidence can be adduced* to shew that, in the year **1601**, at the instance of George **Heriot**, and others who were then **Commissioners** of the Royal Burghs of Scotland, Flemish workmen were brought from Norwich to Edinburgh, to introduce the manufacture of "all sortis of claithis."

The influence of the Low Countries on our arts, industries, and literature, is as yet, we believe, an unwritten chapter of British history. To them we owe the printing press, and from them, we are told, Shakespeare got much of the information that enabled him to write his matchless plays. On many of our manufactures and arts they have impressed their versatility and skill; and agriculture, it is said, owes to them the method of drainage, to which its development is in great measure due.

The point, however, for us to determine now is whether we also owe to the Flemings our great national game. The answer to this question is the final conclusion of the series which we have tabulated as we proceeded with this enquiry. It is that—

* *Notes and Queries*. Sec. IV. vol. 8. p. 259. Chambers *Domestic Annals of Scotland*, I. 352.

(4) No evidence is forthcoming to prove that Curling was introduced into our country by Flemish emigrants.

The period of 150 years, to which Buchanan refers as following the death of Alexander III. (1286), though lit up by Bannockburn, was indeed a dark and troublous time, and we need not wonder that through that period no word is heard of any amusement on the ice in our "most distressful country." There was no "gamyn and gle," as the pathetic lines preserved by Wyntoun—the earliest we have in our mother tongue—so touchingly relate:—

> "Quhen Alysandyr, oure Kyng, wes dede,
> That Scotland led in luwe and le;*
> Away wes sons † of ale and brede,
> Of wyne and wax, of gamyn and gle :
> Oure gold wes changyd into lede,
> Chryst, borne in-to Virgynyte,
> Succoure Scotland, and remede,
> That stad ‡ [is in] perplexyte."

It is not unlikely that, when, under the able, though ill-fated, James I., the condition of matters was improved,—when the cities that had been wasted and burned were filled with artisans, and the youth turned from arms to cultivate the arts—that amusement, which had been forgotten, would be revived. Forms of amusement hitherto undeveloped would also receive attention, and the Scots, and their Flemish friends, might exercise themselves together on ice in the cold season; but certainly the link that connects the origin of our curling with Flemish immigration is wanting. It is only conjecture, and we do not see how the argument from etymology can receive from a mere conjecture such proof as to enable it to "hold the field." The member of the Duddingston Club who asserted the Continental origin of curling, to do him justice, does not base upon the immigration of these mechanics and manufacturers into our towns and villages, "in the reigns of Henry V. and VI. of England, and James I of Scotland," any decided proof of his theory. "There is," he says, "a very strong probability that

---
* Joy.   † Abundance.   ‡ Placed.

THE ORIGIN OF THE GAME. 21

the game of curling was introduced into this country by the Flemings in the fifteenth or about the beginning of the sixteenth century." This strong *probability*, as far as we can judge, must be reduced to a mere *possibility*, and nothing more; and, until some more direct evidence is forthcoming, we are not warranted in believing that the game had its origin furth of Scotland. Why, even in the time of Alexander III., there were Flemish settlers in our country; and we have seen that, centuries before the time at which it is suggested that curling was introduced here, there were Flemish colonies in England and Wales, some so near us as to be settled in the country lying on the east part of the Tweed. How is it that no trace of it exists in England and Wales, if it was carried by Low Country people along with them, and how is it that no earlier trace of it is found in our own country than the sixteenth century? Surely, if the game had been introduced by the Flemings in the time of James I., we should have expected to hear something of it in the time of James IV. (1488-1513), who himself personally took an interest in such games as he found among his people. But we hear nothing. Tytler* gives us an account of ancient games and amusements of the period, and, from the MS. accounts of the Lord High Treasurer, gives references to some of them, but no mention is made of the game of curling; and, as we shall see hereafter, it is not noticed by any writer till about the beginning of the seventeenth century. It will be found, as we proceed, that the earliest date as yet discovered on a curling-stone of the primitive type is 1511, and it may be said that this Stirling stone is a discovery that adds another link to the evidence in support of the introduction of curling from Flanders at this time. It is to be hoped that other stones will be forthcoming; but in the meantime every stone of the kind found in this country is only evidence that the game, even in its earliest form, is "our ain," since neither in Wales, England, the Low Countries, nor anywhere else, are such relics cast up; for it is absurd to suppose that, if

---

* Vol. III., *Lives of Scottish Worthies.*

the game were Flemish, and carried with Flemings wherever they settled, it would only be in Scotland that the primitive stones would be found. Let us have plain proof that the *discus* referred to by Kilian, as played by the Teutonic *in æquore glaciato*, is connected with the stone of antiquity, and we will begin to suppose that there is some support for the etymological position which has thus been discussed; but in present circumstances—though we must own to our having begun this enquiry with an inclination to favour the Continental origin of the game—it seems that the native origin of curling is more likely to stand the test of historical proof than the other. We have not denied the possibility, but we have certainly denied the proof, of the Flemish origin; and we hold that there is no more evidence to prove that we got our game from the Low Countries than there is to prove that they got their game of "ice-clods" from us. The argument crumbles away piece by piece as we examine it, and all that seems to be left, if the conclusions we have come to are correct, is, as we have said—not a proof, nor even a *probability*, but only a *possibility*. Such is our verdict; but we leave it to be reviewed by any further light that may be cast upon the subject.

"Wherever there was ice, there must have been, since man existed, games on the ice," and the likelihood is that, long before any Fleming ever landed on our shores, our ancestors had ice-games of a kind; for John Frost is a pre-historic monarch, older than any of the mythical Kings of Scotland whose doubtful doings are recorded by our early historians; and self-protection is a power as old as Adam, that, acting of itself without any Dutch example to imitate, would lead the ancients "on to the ice," where they would be more likely to engage in "throwing stones" than in throwing "frozen clods." It is more difficult for us to believe that no kind of ice-game ever existed in Scotland than it is to believe that such a thing was only thought of in the sixteenth century for the first time; and, if it be said that we cannot prove this native origin, we reply that the *onus probandi* has been thrown upon those who deny it, and we leave the origin of curling where we have to leave other origins, in the mist and haze of an unknowable antiquity.

Such an inquiry has not been uninteresting, for it has led us into corners of national history that we have not previously visited; but, after all, may we not add that Scotland's claim to the origination of the game of curling is not affected, even though it were proved that in the sixteenth century we began to "throw stones" on the ice like the Flemings, and to speak of this exercise in a Flemish tongue. "That's no' Curlin'" may well be said of each of these early forms of ice-games to which we have referred. Each is further removed from our game than the "anthropoid ape" is from the cultured man of the nineteenth century.

It is not, therefore, the origin of the game, but the origin of the germ of the game that is questioned; and, even if it were proved that the game of the sixteenth century was unoriginal, the originality of the game of curling, as we play it, and the credit of the development of the germ, can never be taken from us. We do not, as a nation, invent every good thing, but we know a good thing when we see it. We are said to "keep the sawbath, and everything else we can lay our hands on," and we are not ashamed of this trite definition of national character; but we add—"provided it is worth keeping." Be sure it is not for nought that we value and praise our national game, and jealously guard our interest in its origin and development. We know what it has done for us, and we know what its enjoyment will do for the generations that come after us; and so we are proud of its nationality. Like the ice-games of other countries, it may for centuries have been a mere germ floating about without form, and not worthy of notice by those who chronicled the beginnings of all that is now best in our national character; but it was in our country that the germ found its true development, and no other can take away the honour of its evolution from Scotland. "Soopin's everything," as we say upon the ice, and so here. Even though a Dutchman may have delivered it from a Flanders crampit, it is to our credit that we did not suffer it to die a *hog*, as other nations have done, but sent it "snoovin' up the howe," through the "port," into the "parish," so that it now lies a "pat-lid o' perfection" among games, suiting our national character to a *tee*.

"Sic Scoti : alii non æque felices."

Others have not carried it to such happy issues (though it is our fervent wish that the day may speedily come when the *non* of the old Duddingston motto will be changed into *nunc*); but in Scotland, by the attention we have given to it, and the glory we have thrown around it in thousands of bloodless bonspiels; by the sociality, the robustness, the "smeddum," and the enthusiasm it has imparted to our national life, we have made it as truly a national institution as the haggis, the parritch-pat, the pibroch, or the "auld kirk"; and it is as truly our national game as the thistle is our national emblem, or Saint Andrew our national saint.

After all, "brither curlers," is it not, when we come to think of it, something to be thankful for that the inventor of curling is unknown—that no Jove sent it forth from his powerful brain fully equipped, like Minerva, "stanes, an' besoms, an' a'" (though the poet, in our prefix, seems to have ascribed to *Albyn Jove* a feat of this description); but that the game has slowly evolved from stage to stage, through many imperfections, to its present perfect form; a tendency to infinite variation being ever checked by a process of natural selection, and the survival of the fittest type? Is it not a blessing that we have not to march once a year, "besoms up," to the shrine of our great originator, like Birnam wood coming to Dunsinane? What a mighty cairn would by this time have towered over his grave, if curlers had only known it! Blocks and boulders of the curling times of old—Sanquhar Blacks, Crawick Greys, Carsphairn Reds, Crawfordjohns, Crieffs, Burnocks, and Ailsas—all worsted in the wars, would have found a last resting-place there, till a veritable Tower of Babel threatened the skies.

> "Then drain deep the cog, till the brain is a-whirling,
> And pledge me, ye lovers o' Scotia's ain game,
> To the memory of him, the inventor o' Curling,
> Though the mists of oblivion envelop his name."

So saith one to whom it seemed good to honour the unknown by whirling through the switchback of the "cog," into the same regions of oblivion. We recommend no curler to go so far, or to be so foolish; for surely the intoxication of the living is a sorry commemoration of the dead: but, according to our curling motto, where we cannot be clear let us not be too keen, for controversy too often waxes in its keenness as it wanes in its clearness. At any rate, agreement over wine is better than war over words; and, since the game itself is ours, with all the benefits that flow from it, we may leave its real origin in the darkness where it lies, and "fill ae bumper," at least, to the memory of its author—not in solemn silence, for that always seems to us as gruesome as a cold shower-bath over a warm tumbler of toddy—but in the genial glow of gratitude that every true curler feels when he thinks of what "Scotland's ain game" has done for his country, his kindred, and himself.

"The baby-figure of the giant mass
  Of things to come."
                  Troilus and Cressida, Act I. Sc. iii.

"The channelstane,
The bracing engine of a Scottish arm."
                  Davidson.

"Loud throughout the vale the noise is heard
Of thumping rocks, and loud bravadoes' roar."
                  Davidson.

"Now mark the dread sound as our columns move on,
So solemn, so awful, so martial's the tone,
The clouds resound afar, whilst the waters groan :
        Stable rock
        Feels our shock
    As if stern Mars in transport spoke :
Such the thunder and crash of the curling-stone."
          Canonmills "*Curler's March,*" 1792.

CHAPTER II.

A STUDY OF STONES.

OUR enquiry into the origin and antiquity of curling brought us into contact with a controversy about words. Our next chapter is a case of "sermons in stones." Of crampits, brooms, and other minor implements used in the early game, there are few relics to be considered; but the different stages in the development of curling are distinctly traced by the monumental stones that have been brought under notice, especially since the formation of the Grand Club in 1838. Of these we have three types or varieties distinctly marked, in the examination of which we are able to trace the progress of the game. These types are—

(1.) The KUTING-STONE, KUTTY-STANE, or PILTYCOCK.
(2.) The ROUGH BLOCK (with handle).
(3.) The POLISHED and CIRCULAR STONE.

FIRST TYPE: THE KUTING-STONE.—Curling, when first practised, appears to have been a kind of quoiting on ice. The stones had no handles, but merely a kind of hollow or niche for the finger and thumb of the player, and they were evidently intended to be thrown, for at least part of the course, the rink being shorter than it is now. In handling these stones, it seems natural to infer that they were not delivered after being drawn straight back, but swept round from behind, and sent toward their destination by a curving sweep. As might be supposed, they were much smaller than stones of the *handle* type, running from 5 or 6 to 20 or 25 lbs. in weight. They would seem to have been picked up from the channels of the rivers (hence the term *channel-stanes*, though this may have been given to them because of the channel or *howe* made by them in their course on the ice). Mactaggart, in his amusing work,* says that " when curling first began it was played with flat-stones or *loofies*." † We have seen that *kuting* and *kluyten*, the Dutch name for a game on ice, are not the same word: but that curling, though now more allied to bowls or billiards, did at first more nearly resemble the ancient game of quoits cannot reasonably be denied. The Ettrick Shepherd, in his famous song, contrasts the two games thus :—

> " I've played at quoiting in my day,
> And maybe I may do't again ;
> But still unto myself I'd say
> This is no the channel-stane."

But it is certain that the word *coiting*, *kuting*, or *quoiting*, was for a long time the word in common use to describe the game, and in some districts it is still applied to it. Thus writes the curling-poet of Chryston, W. Watson—

> " The loch's aye the loch, whaur in cauld days o' yore,
> The lee-side was cheered by the *quoitin-stane's* roar,
> Whaur aft our auld daddies wad off wi' their plaidies,
> As they had been shown by their daddies afore."

And Grahame, of " Sabbath " fame, at an earlier date speaks of

> "The player as he stoops to lift his *coit*."

Andrew Crawfurd of Lochwinnoch, in a letter to Cairnie in 1833, writes thus about a certain ice-hero :—

"Old Will M'Adam was a famous curler ; he was once in a bonspeil between the Glen and the Muirland conjoined against the Brig-o'-Weir

---

* *The Scottish Galloridian Encyclopædia* (1824), p. 130.
† *Loofie*, a flat or plane stone resembling the palm of the hand. Gall.—Jamieson's *Dictionary*.

quoiters, with 14 a side. M'Adam was a very ugly man (like the devil) in countenance. But he was an ingenious man, up to the craft of mounting of all manner of weaving work : he was a grand *quoiter*, he never missed a shot ; he was dignified by the Brig-o'-Weir folk with the appellation of a warlock."—*Cairnie's Essay*, p. 93.

Sir Richard Broun, in his interesting *Memorabilia*, calls curlers "the merry handlers of the quoit;" and at p. 103 he gives a letter from Principal Baird to the Duddingston Club in 1822, in which the Principal presents the club with "five stones, as specimens of the original or earliest form of curling or coiting stones" which had been recovered, one from a loch at Stirling, and four from the loch of Linlithgow.

"The stones, as will be seen, are from three to four inches in thickness —of rather an oblong shape, and thinner towards the point extremity. At the opposite and thickest extremity, there is on the bottom (which has been artificially made quite smooth) a long thin hollow cut out for admitting the fore part of the player's fingers : and on the upper side of the stones there is a small hole for the point of the thumb. From this form," the Principal goes on to remark, "it appears that the stone has been *coited* or thrown by the hand to a short distance on the ice : if thrown with force, and rightly floored, it must have been capable of being propelled a very considerable length."

There are no dates on these stones, and Sir Richard propounds a query in regard to their antiquity which it was impossible at that time to answer. It was suggested by the following discovery that had then just been made of a very ancient stone of the Second type :—

"Last week, while the foundation of the old house of Loig, in Strathallan, was being dug out, a curling-stone of a very different shape and texture from those now generally in use in that district, was discovered. It is of an oblong form, and had been neatly finished with the hammer. The initials 'J. M.' and the date 1611 are still distinctly legible, having been deeply though uncouthly engraven. This discovery affords a curious and striking proof of the antiquity of the game of curling."—*Caledonian Mercury*, 20th Dec. 1830.

Sir Richard's query was thus put :—" If a curling-stone of an oblong form, ' neatly finished with the hammer,' gives the date 1611, what date will the pilty-cocks or kuting-stones give ?" For a long time it was supposed that the oldest stone was that noticed in the *Annual* of 1841, p. 11—

"This last summer a curling-stone has been found in an old curling-pond near Dunblane, bearing date 1551. It is 10 inches broad by 11 long and 5 thick, and seems to have been taken from the bed of the river, and not to have been dressed. There are two holes for the handle, as in the close-handled stones still preferred in the district."

This Dunblane stone, it will be noticed, though of very ancient date, is not of the primitive type, and it did not furnish an answer to the query of Sir Richard Broun. It is only recently that a kuting-stone, of date 100 years earlier than the Strathallan stone, has come to light, and the Dunblane stone, so long supposed to be the most ancient, has had to retire from the field. Not content with the custodiership of the relics of Sir William Wallace, Stirling, it would appear, now claims the honour of guarding the most ancient relic of early curling —

"In the Macfarlane Museum, Smith Institute, are two old curling or rather *kuting* stones, one of which bears a date shewing it to be the most ancient stone in Scotland which has yet been discovered. In shape this stone is nearly an oblong square, the sides being straight and the top and bottom slightly rounded. The length is 9 inches, width 7½ inches, depth 4½ inches, measurement round the middle 24 inches, vertically 26 inches, and its weight 26 lbs. The hollow for the thumb is 1½ inches wide at the mouth, while the place for the fingers, which is carefully carved, is 3½ inches long. On the upper side of the stone a small space has been polished to receive the inscription, in Roman capitals, A GIFT, while on the sole, which has been smoothed for the purpose, is the following :—

'S[T] J[S] B.   STIRLING.   1511.' *

"It can only be surmised that S[t] J[s] stands for 'St James,' a popular saint in Stirling, and B may be a contraction for 'Bridge' [or

FIGS. 2 AND 3. "STIRLING STONES."

---

* It is right to note that the figures on this stone are certainly not as old as they make out the stone to be. Dr Anderson is of opinion that they have been cut out as late as the present century. This does not, of course, disprove the antiquity of the stone, but tends to cast a doubt upon it.

'Brotherhood.'] It is known that there was a St James' Hospital at the Bridge-end of Stirling prior to the Reformation. The stone is made of blue whinstone, similar to that of Stirling Rock, and, having been a gift, it may be accepted as a fine specimen of the curling-stones of the period.

"The other stone in the Smith Institute is of the same material, but has the appearance of being older and more primitive, and may have been originally a water-worn boulder taken from the bed of some stream. Its shape is triangular, the sides and angles being rounded. It is 8¼ inches in length, and about the same in width, depth 4 inches, circumference 22 inches, and weight 15¾ lbs. The thumb-hole and finger-catch are roughly cut. A search through the records of the Museum has failed to elicit any information regarding the history of these stones."

The above account of the remarkable relics (Figs. 2 and 3) is given by Captain Macnair, in his interesting collection of curling-lore,* and is here reproduced by his permission. The present curator of the Museum, Mr Sword, tells us that the stones are much prized, and carefully preserved in a glass case, and that no further information regarding their history has yet been furnished. It will be observed that one of the stones referred to by Principal Baird was also found at Stirling, which evidently bears the palm of antiquity. Thus, when Buchanan (who was a Stirlingite, and is said to have written his *History of Scotland* at Stirling) was only a boy of five, we have it proved that our national game was in existence at his native place, though not worthy of notice afterwards by him or any other historian of the time. We had the pleasure of seeing the Stirling stones in the great Exhibition at Glasgow, 1888, where they were exhibited alongside the no less venerable relics of our old archery and golf clubs in that wonderful antiquarian temple—the Bishop's Palace; and it is needless to say that they were viewed with great interest by all curlers. At the same Exhibition, on the stand of T. Thorburn, Beith, where the beautiful symmetry and polish of the modern stones of this celebrated maker stood out in striking contrast to their venerable *forbears*, the Marquis of Breadalbane exhibited a pair of old stones†

---

* *The Channel Stane.* Fourth series, p. 66. The stones themselves have, however, been specially sketched by our artist for this work.

† These stones were also exhibited at the Jubilee Dinner of the R.C.C.C., Nov. 28, 1888.

(Figs. 4 and 5) which were taken about thirty years ago out of Newton Loch, a mile below Tyndrum, while it was being partially drained to make it safer as a curling-pond.

FIG. 4.
FROM NEWTON LOCH, TYNDRUM.

The Marquis, rightly regarding "the auld channel-stanes" as precious, insured them in transit for £25; and they were laid aside with proportionate care at Glasgow station, till it was almost too late for their entry at the Exhibition. A porter was sent off at steam-speed with what he was taught to regard as a valuable burden. He succeeded in reaching the place in time, and, with the sweat streaming down his face, he watched the opening of the heavily-insured box. Imagine his disgust when he saw what, in his eyes, were only two old useless "blocks" turned out. It was too much for the poor fellow, and, in wrath, he thereupon uttered words such as railway porters in our country are unfortunately too often heard to utter, with less excuse. The stones which

FIG. 5.
FROM NEWTON LOCH, TYNDRUM.

have so much to answer for are, no doubt, very old; but as they are without date, we are left to conjecture regarding them. Though they are about the weight of the early kuting-stones, yet, as the holes in them are evidently not for the insertion of fingers or thumb, but for handles, they probably belong to a later period than the Stirling stones. This is borne out by the fact that, along with them were other stones, with iron handles almost rusted away, which have since been lost sight of. This much is, however, proved by these interesting relics that curling was once enjoyed in certain districts from which it has quite disappeared. When the Breadalbane, Strathfillan, and Glenfalloch Club was instituted in 1858, the people, we are told, were astonished to see the *new game;* and an old lady, who died about six years ago, aged over 100 years, had never seen or heard of such a game. An interesting point in connection with this, as pointed out by Mr R. Macnaughton, Comrie, is that nearly as far back as the middle of last century the game must have been played in some parts of the Highlands, though there are some who think that it had not at that time got beyond the Lowlands.

At Linlithgow we seem to have evidence of an unbroken connection between the ancient and the modern game. From the same loch that now resounds with the "roar" of many a keen battle, and which Lees has immortalised by his famous painting of the Grand Match of 1848, several samples of the old finger or kuting-stone have been recovered. Some of these, as we have seen, were given by Principal Baird to the Duddingston Club in 1822, but of their present existence we have no intelligence. Mr W. H. Henderson informs us that about twenty-five years ago a kuting-stone was sent by him from Linlithgow to the Antiquarian Museum, Edinburgh. From the description furnished by him, this stone must have been a good specimen of the earliest type; but the Linlithgow relics seem to be unfortunate in their destiny, for, after diligent enquiry, we have been unable to find any trace of this stone. In the Museum there are, however, two specimens of the earliest type of stone. One of these is the smallest we have seen, and is much like an ordinary paving-stone. It was found embedded in the wall of an old house in the High Street, Edinburgh, which was being demolished some years ago, and brought by a workman to the Museum. Dr Anderson tells us that he was at first inclined to regard it simply as a disused cobbler's lapstone, but the marks for finger and thumb led him to suppose that it was a kuting-stone, and there is little doubt that he is right in his supposition. That such a stone should have been found in such a place is very remarkable, and may suggest to Edinburgh curlers a claim of antiquity for the game on the Nor' Loch that they have not as yet put forward.

Of the antiquity of curling in the Galloway district we

c

have several proofs in the form of *loofie-stones*, as they are called by Mactaggart. The late Rev. G. Murray of Balmaclellan had a good specimen among his collection of curling curiosities—"flat and wedge-shaped, with places for the fingers on one side and for the thumb on the other." The stone is now to be seen at his sister's house, Meadowbank, New-Galloway. A similar stone is the property of a merchant there—R. Mackay. Two of these ancient stones are also to be found in the Museum at Kirkcudbright, of which Mr M'Kie is curator. They were found in Loch Fergus.

The Doune Club have in their possession a good specimen of the Kuting-stone. It was found some years ago in digging up the foundation of an old house in Doune, which stood on a feu dating from 1664. It is a flattish, smooth whinstone nearly circular, a little rounded on the top with flat bottom. It is about $8\frac{1}{2}$ inches in diameter, and weighs $14\frac{1}{2}$ lbs. The upper edges are a little clipped to give it proper shape, otherwise it has its natural smooth surface. It has no handle, but has a hollow for the thumb, and a catch underneath for the fingers.

Lochleven, like Linlithgow, seems to have an unbroken record; and no doubt the game has had there a "local habitation" as long as in any other part of Scotland. Wyntoun, the author of our first national history—the *Oryggnall Chronykill of Scotland*, was Prior of St Serf's Inch, Lochleven, in the end of the fourteenth century; and it may yet appear that he heard the boom of the channel-stane in the silence of the monastery, but he makes no complaint about it, and most likely it was not such a roaring game at that time as to disturb the Prior at his

FIG. 6. FROM LOCHLEVEN.

"Chronykill." That it was played on Lochleven from time immemorial is, however, abundantly evident. Alongside

of the small High Street stone there is a larger-sized
specimen of the Kuting-stone (Fig. 6) lent to the
Antiquarian Museum by D. Marshall, F.S.A., to whom
it had been gifted by R. Wylie, shoemaker, Kinross.
It was got out of Lochleven about fifty years ago, and
for the most of that period did duty, like its neighbour,
as a cobbler's lapstone. This Kinross stone is of whin,
flat in appearance and triangular in shape.

"In its general contour," says Mr Burns Begg, "it may be said to
resemble a small but thick Belfast ham, with the shank-bone somewhat
shortened. It never has been graced with a handle of any kind, but
it has on its lower side or *sole* an oblong hollow hewn out for the
accommodation of the fingers of the player, while on the upper side
there is a corresponding hollow for the thumb. The stone shews no trace
of ever having been polished artificially, but has been worn smooth by
the action of the water in the channel out of which it was taken."

It is stated in a Montreal paper (*V. Annual 1885-6*.)
that the Club there has in its possession, among other
historical relics, an ancient Kuting-stone found at Roslin
in 1826, and dated 1613, which was presented to them
by the late Dr Sidey. If the drawing which accompanies
the statement is correct there must be some mistake, or
the Dr must have played a cruel joke upon his Transatlantic "brithers," or the *Annual* of 1843 must have
given a false drawing; for, while this latter is reproduced
here (Fig. 7), the Montreal
drawing is that of an ordinary
handled block of the second
type, in shape like the Jubilee
stone. A very good sample
of the Kuting-stone, dated
1611, is claimed by Tor-
phichen, where it was found
in 1840 built in a wall,

FIG. 7. FROM ROSLIN.

and a notice of which appeared in the *Annual* of 1843
by Mr Durham Weir. It is of grey whin, and the
notch for the finger is 4 inches in length by $1\frac{3}{4}$ inches
in depth. The curling-stone of the Covenanter Guthrie
(Fig. 8), still preserved in Craufurdland Castle, is also a

legitimate type of the early stone, though it must have been in use after 1644, when Guthrie was ordained Minister of Fenwick.

FIG. 8.
REV. W. GUTHRIE'S CURLING STONE, 1645.

The period in which this Kuting-stone, Kutty-stane, Piltycock or Loofie was in use may therefore be put down as extending from the beginning of the sixteenth to the middle of the seventeenth century (1500-1650); though in that time we have also proof of the second or handled type of stone. From their construction it is evident that early curlers *coited* or *skuyted* the stone along the ice; but as to the style of the primitive game little further can be inferred. If further light is to be thrown on ancient curling it is in this direction more than the etymological that we look for information; and certainly, until specimens of these curious stones are found in other countries, we are entitled to hold that the game is indigenous to Scotland. No doubt other and earlier ones will be found,* for the *loofie* oracle has not spoken its last word at Stirling, Linlithgow or Lochleven; but Curling antiquaries will do well on this point to remember Aiken Drum's Lang Ladle, for Curling Clubs are keen to make it clear that the most ancient relics are in their keeping, and some of them, after paying for the *Prætorium* of an old Kuting-stone, may meet with an *Edie Ochiltree* to take away their joy.†

SECOND TYPE: THE ROUGH BLOCK.—Of the description of stone that marks the second stage of ancient

---

* For an Account of the latest, see note p. 47 under Strathallan.
† It is not a little curious to find that Quoiting and Curling have resumed their early relationship among our Kinsmen "across the pond." In the admirable *Annual* of the Grand National Club of America there is published each year, alongside of the Rules of Curling and the bonspiels of States' curlers, an account of a great contest held each year for a *Quoit* medal with "Rules for Quoiting." In the days of the old Duddingston Society the members also got up quoiting matches to bring them together in the summer season.

curling, there are innumerable specimens "of all sorts and conditions." An ordinary human being when he gets *a handle* to his name is thereby lifted into greater importance, and certainly acquires more power if he makes a proper use of his title ; so, when the leverage of a handle was applied to the channel-stane it completely left behind the puny piltycock, and developed enormously in bulk and weight. In its development, however, it did not follow the curves of the beautiful. Another century and a half must elapse before the rough block is hewn into proper form, and the curler realises that scientific skill is higher than brute force. The corners have to be rubbed off, the angularities have to be rounded, the wild diversity has to be reduced, and it takes time to do it. Yet, withal, this bulging, unshapely, heterogeneous age of the curling-stone, when the curler—under the newly-gotten power of the handle—took the hinge from the gate-post, soldered it into the big boulder, bent incumbent under the weight, swung the block in air, and hurled it up the rink with giant strength, is an interesting one. "An affectation of minute accuracy," some wise writer says, "in cases where in the nature of things accuracy is impossible, is always a suspicious feature in a historian." In dividing our study of stones as we have done, we do not presume to draw a distinct line—saying here the handle type begins and there the no-handle type ends. The Dunblane stone and the Tyndrum stone, while veritable *loofies* in other respects, had evidently been played with handles in the period of our handle-less type of stone. Sometimes, as we shall see, the handle was an after-addition to an old stone that had been played without it ; and it is plain that handles were in use before the finger-and-thumb stone was discarded. We find also among stones of the later period many as diminutive as any of the Kutty-stanes, their weight being under 20 lbs., pigmies among the giants. This granted, we can, however, mark off a second period of 150 years, from about the middle of the seventeenth century on toward the end of the eighteenth, when the stone in common use was in some respects as unlike the early Kuting-stone, as it is to its polished and aristocratic descendant of modern times. In this period stones (and handles also) were of infinite variety and shape. Sir Richard Broun (p. 42), in describing those in use at Lochmaben, describes generally the stones of the period.

"They were of a wretched description enough. Most of them being sea-stones of all shapes, sizes, and weights. Some were three-cornered, like those equilateral cocked hats, which our divines wore in a century that is past—others like ducks—others flat as a frying pan. Their handles, which superseded holes for the fingers and thumb, were equally clumsy and inelegant: being malconstructed resemblances of that hook-necked biped, the goose."

Wretched as they may be, and useless for all practical purposes in modern curling—as much behind our modern Ailsa or Crawfordjohn as the flint-lock of Marston Moor and Culloden is behind the modern Martini-rifle; yet now-a-days, when the *Zeitgeist* of historical research is at work everywhere, Curling Clubs vie with each other in collecting from out-of-the-way corners these uncouth stones of other days. Time was when little respect was shewn to them—when they had to do duty as weights for weavers' looms and thack-ropes and cheese-presses, or lie neglected among the rubbish at the back of the curling pond; but now they are sought after, and, when found, readily elevated to places of honour. Many, alas! have met with the fate of "Whirlie," so pathetically described by J. J., a member of the Penicuick Club in the *Annual* of 1847.

"Whirlie" was of oblong triangular shape, and altogether a curling stone of nature's own making, being untouched with the workman's hammer, except the hole in which the handle was inserted. It was a jet black whin, and the sole, altogether a natural one, was very smooth, which, with the dense and fine quality of the stone, made it a keen runner even on dull soft ice. Tradition states that it was the favourite stone of Sir John Clerk, one of the Commissioners of the Union, but nothing is transmitted regarding its previous history. It was the first stone which the writer of this ever played with, when but a very young lad about fifty-five years ago ; and we have never forgot the diversion which our youthful play and this ancient stone afforded to both curlers and spectators. It being our first attempt at curling, we were appointed to lead, which we happened to do in such a manner that Whirlie was uniformly laid on or near the Tee ; to remove it from that position on which it had taken rest was no easy matter, because, should the stone which was destined to remove it strike any one of the angled corners, round went Whirlie, round and round, without ever shifting from its position, while the stone which struck it went at right angles across the rink. Stimulated with the success of our first attempt at curling, we were early next day on the field of action with Whirlie in our hand. But to our utter disappointment, poor fellow, a Curling Court was held upon him, and he was unanimously condemned to perpetual banishment, or rather to solitary confinement. This, however, we could not stand. We got him mounted in a more modern and fashionable uniform, by rounding his more acute angles, and in this capacity we introduced him as a stranger on his ancient domain. A bad character and bad habits, however, have a mark put upon them, and are not easily surmounted. The rogue, in spite of all our endeavours, was still seen in his new shape and in his habits likewise, for his roundabout way of going to work never forsook him, and again and again has he been banished from, and restored to the society of his fellows; until at last we had the galling mortification to hear his final doom decreed by the present Baronet, that this favourite stone of his illustrious ancestor should be played with no more. Since then the Ice, and all the curlers, except ourselves, who well knew him once, know him no more, and perhaps for ever. But many are the lingering emotions of fond affection with which we have sought after him; nor will we desist from the search until we in our turn shall be consigned to oblivion. But should we have the good fortune to find him, he shall have a 'museum' for his abode, and be henceforth preserved as an 'Ancient Curling curiosity.'"

"Whirlie" is a type of many in appearance and in habits, and we are afraid in destiny also; but "the lingering emotion of fond affection" that followed him to his unknown bourne now protects hundreds of his contemporaries from such an unwished-for ending to their curling career; and as the Royal Club, in its year of Jubilee, has decided to form a collection of historical relics such as these, curlers will by-and-bye have an opportunity of meeting face to face many of these brave old warriors, and many that now lie outcast and neglected will, it is hoped, be rescued from oblivion. It is not in the power of every club to secure such specimens, but those that have them ought to be proud of them. From returns furnished to us we give the names of some of the clubs that either possess or can account for old curling-stones of the second period, and statements regarding them, which will demonstrate forcibly what we have said as to the variety in weight and appearance of these rude engines of ancient curling warfare.

ABERDOUR.—Some stones, with fixed iron handles, are in the possession of the Club, which weigh 83 lbs. each.

ALLOA—PRINCE OF WALES.—Two very ancient stones

were found when cleaning Ardoch pond about ten years ago. They are in the hands of the President, Alexander Gall.

ALYTH.—The Secretary of this Club (J. Ferrier) says :—

"The curlers in olden times took the stones as they got them from the bed of the stream or the hillside, and all the workmanship bestowed on them was the fixing of a bent piece of iron into each as a handle. The forms of the stones generally suggested the names of them. There were 'Rockie,' 'The Goose,' 'The Deuk,' &c., &c. In these days curlers must have been powerful men, for the stones were very heavy and none of the keenest. Instead of a house, the curlers had only a small piece of ground fenced in with a rough paling in the form of a circle, and in the centre the stones were all tumbled together in a heap. This looks as if the Druidical circle had still been held in reverence among them."

ARDOCH.—Several stones were dug out of a pond on the estate of Mr Drummond Moray when it was drained some years ago. One (Fig. 9) is dated 1700, and is lettered M. W. H. In the interesting records of the Muthill Club, which go back to 1739, we find the first name entered "The Rev. Mr William Hally, Minister, Muthill," and this stone is supposed to have belonged to him, he being the first minister at Muthill after the abolition of Episcopacy in 1690.

FIG. 9. FROM ARDOCH.

This stone is unique in its way, having a three-legged handle inserted into it. It has now become the property of the Royal Club, having been gifted by J. M'Callum, Braco.

BLAIRGOWRIE and DELVINE Clubs both claim an interest in the set of ancient stones here presented, these having, we are informed, been formerly in the keeping of Blairgowrie, but presented or sold to the Delvine Club, in whose custody they have been for many years. Fig. 10, "The Soo," weighs 79 lbs., and measures $16\frac{1}{2} \times 11$ inches. Fig. 11 is "The Baron," weighing 88 lbs., and measuring $14\frac{1}{2} \times 14$ inches. Fig. 12 is called "The Egg," and weighs 115 lbs. It measures 17×12 inches. Fig. 13, "The Fluke," weighs 52 lbs. and measures $12\frac{1}{2} \times 11$ inches. Fig. 14,

"Robbie Dow," weighs 34 lbs. and measures 9 × 9 inches. This last and least was called after one of the Baron Bailies, a son of the parish minister of the time. They were all doubtless taken in a natural state from the famous Ericht Channel, and they seem to have done a good deal of work in

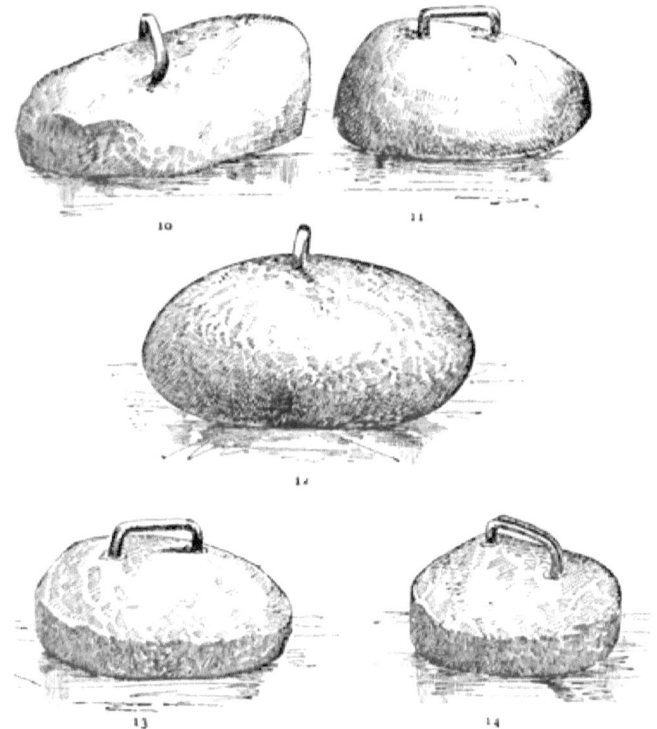

FIGS. 10, 11, 12, 13, 14. FROM THE BLAIRGOWRIE AND DELVINE CLUBS.

the hands of their strong masters. Their double handles are noticeable. A metrical account of these and others is found in Mr Bridie's Centenary Ode of the Blairgowrie Club:—

> "In early years the implements were coarse,
>   Rude, heavy boulders did the duty then,
> And each one had its title, as 'The Horse';
>   One was 'The Cockit-hat' and one 'The Hen';
> 'The Kirk,' 'The Saddle,' President' and 'Soo,'
> 'The Bannock,' 'Baron,' 'Fluke,' and 'Robbie Dow.'"

BRECHIN.—At Brechin Castle are old stones, found in making present pond thirty years ago. They are river boulders in natural shape, with a piece of iron inserted for handle.

CAMBUSNETHAN.—Specimens of rough stones with wooden handles and one sole, in use from 1789 to beginning of present century.

CHIRNSIDE.—Six pairs of very old stones are in possession of T. A. Calder, a member of this club. They were found in mud in the bottom of Bonkyll Curling Pond about forty years ago. They are hard unpolished whinstones with iron handles.

CLUNIE.—Several of various shapes and weights: blocks of unhewn stone, with smith-made iron handles. One is oval, measuring 46 inches in circumference, and weighing 95 lbs.; another, $90\frac{1}{2}$ lbs.

FIG. 15.
"BLACK MEG," FROM COUPAR-ANGUS.

COUPAR-ANGUS.—The following are the names and weights of a few of the more celebrated stones in the possession of the club:—"Suwaroff," 84 lbs.; "Cog," 80 lbs.; "Fluke," 72 lbs.; "Black Meg," 66 lbs.; "The Saut Backet," 116 lbs.

CRIEFF.—Several stones were found in 1881 at Lochlane, on Lord Abercrombie's estate of Ferntower, near Crieff, and all or several of which fell into the possession of Mr James Gray, builder, Bridge of Allan. One of these (Fig. 16) was given to Mr Henderson, Linlithgow, and presented by him to the Royal Caledonian Club. The stones were found under the lower steps of a spiral stair, the cavity having been built up with masonry.

FIG. 16.
FROM LOCHLANE, NEAR CRIEFF.

A similar stone (Fig. 17) is to be seen in the Antiquarian Museum, with the initial W incised in it. It was found in Birkhill Pond, Stirling, and belonged to the late Dr Mushet.

DALTON, ST BRIDGETS.—An oblong, oval stone is in possession of Robert Underwood, Hightae. It is supposed to have been formerly in use on the southernmost of the "mony lochs" of "Marjorie" (Lochmaben).

DELVINE.—(See above under Blairgowrie).

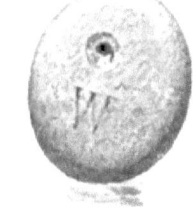

FIG. 17.
FROM BIRKHILL POND, STIRLING.

DOUNE.—A stone, with the inscription I. M^C, 1732, is possessed by the club. It weighs about 50 lbs. This stone was found some years ago when re-causewaying the close that leads to what is known as The Clans' Hall—a famous hostelry and favourite resort of curlers in the latter half of last century. It is $10\frac{1}{2}$ inches long, and $9\frac{1}{2}$ inches across at the broad end, and its contour is altogether quite unique, even among stones of the boulder type. Another stone of similar shape, but larger, used to be seen on the table at the annual feasts of the club, when the late James Macfarlane, Woodside Cottage, was president. It belonged to Archibald Greig, a noted and powerful curler of last century. This stone, we believe, is now the property of William Forrester, at Campsie.

DUNBLANE.—There are two ancient stones here, "The Provost," and "The Bailie," weighing about 60 lbs. each.

DUNFERMLINE.—A stone with $\substack{D\ M \\ 1696}$ carved on it. It weighs 66 lbs., and resembles the half of an egg cut long ways. It has an iron handle, run in with lead, is 38 inches in circumference lengthways, and 30 inches measuring over top and round sole.

DUNS.—An annual expedition used to be made in olden times to the Pease Burn, near Cockburnspath, to procure boulders, into which rough iron handles were fastened. This custom existed till the publication of the Rules of the Duddingston Society, when round stones came gradually into use. The pride of this club, in the way of old specimens, used to be "Rob Roy," a large whinstone block, 18 inches in diameter, and 54 inches in circumference, without chisel or hammer mark. "Rob" was purchased, in 1826, by David M'Watt, from a mason in Polwarth, for the sum of 10s. 6d.; but he has been missing since 1856. "The Gase" and "Bluebeard" have also gone astray; but "The Egg" is to the fore in the safe keeping of Charles Watson.

EDINBURGH.—That the game of curling was in ancient times practised in and around Edinburgh there is no doubt. We have already noticed the stone of the early type to be seen in the Antiquarian Museum, and later on we refer to stones that point back to the days of the old Canonmills Club. A specimen of the second type of stone—the rough boulder—is illustrated in the *Annual* of 1841-42; and the following notice by Mr Palmer of Currie would seem to suggest that curling was practised in other parts of the town besides the Nor' Loch and Canonmills:—

"In digging a drain to the east of Watson's Institution,* near Edinburgh, a layer of mud and refuse, to the depth of 3 feet, such as are usually deposited in the bottom of old ponds, was found. A regularly laid causeway, 8 or 10 yards in width and about 20 in length, shewed, from the slight embankments at the sides of the causeway, that it was evidently laid down as a bottom for a pond.

"In removing the mud, there were discovered about half-a-dozen roughly made curling stones, which were allowed to lie about the field for about a fortnight, during which time they were all broken to pieces (apparently for the sake of the old iron of the handles—*proh pudor*) save one, a fair sample of the rest, which luckily escaped the Gothic destruction, and yet remains to tell the tale.

"It is a semi-spheroidal block of coarse-grained whinstone, weighing 65 pounds. The sole is 11 inches in diameter, and hollowed out a little in the middle, so that it runs upon a ring about 2 inches wide. The stone is about 6 inches high, and has an iron handle of the common kind fixed in the usual place.

"There is no person in the neighbourhood (and there are some who have laboured in the fields about for more than half a century) who has any recollection of the place being anything else than an 'old pond'; and not one who ever heard, even by tradition, that curlers had erst practised their manly game upon it; and of course they were not a little surprised when the hand of modern improvement revealed the secrets of old Father Time.

"From this circumstance, and the depth of the deposit over the causeway, it is evident that the pond must have been made 'langsyne,' but the precise date must be matter of mere conjecture."

---

* Situated about half-way between Dean Bridge and Coltbridge.

What has become of this old stone, and was this submerged pond an earlier specimen of an artificial curling-pond than either Cairnie's or Sommerville's?

FOREST.—Two stones of early date are in possession of W. Richardson, St Mary's Cottage. One (whin) flat on both sides—the other of coarse granite, flat below but round above, thus ⌂ with hole in centre for handle.

GARGUNNOCK.—Here are some old stones "like a tailor's goose."

GLADSMUIR.—An old curling-stone is to be seen at the door of a house which was formerly the old coaching-inn, and its handle does duty in scraping the mud off the boots of the inmates and their visitors.

HADDINGTON.—Regarding a *find* of old stones here, Canon Wannop writes :—

> "Dr Howden (father of the present venerable practitioner of that name) told me soon after I came to Haddington, thirty-four years ago, that when he was a boy some alterations were being made on the Bowling-green (which is said to be the oldest in Scotland), when some old curling-stones, in the form of unpolished boulders with iron handles battened into them, were dug up. Nobody at the time knew what they were or for what they had been used. The Bowling-green was close to the River Tyne ; and the inference is that the game had formerly been played there, but had been given up for some time in the end of last century."

HAWICK.—There is here an old curling-stone called "The Whaup," the handle being like a whaup's bill. Another is called "The Town-Clerk."

JEDBURGH.—One old stone is called "The Girdle," another "The Grey Hen,"—the property of A. Smith, Paradise.

LOCHMABEN, according to Sir Richard Broun in 1830, had then several relics of the olden times—and of the introduction of the game,

> "Which are looked upon with a sort of filial veneration as being monuments of the fathers of those far-back times, whose names are associated with the art, and whose fame in the past still sheds, as it were, upon the present a reflected gleam. . . . The greater part, however, were borrowed in the end of last century by Herries of Halldyke, and could never find their way back from the banks of the Milk. Amongst these remaining, the most remarkable is the famous 'Hen,' which still exists in all the pristine elegance and simplicity of form, as discovered by old Thornywhat and the late Provost Henderson in a

cleugh upon the estate of the former, and conveyed down to the Burgh in a plaid. She was used, says our informant, in all our parish spiels, till, taking her to Dumfries, where stones of an improved make were earlier introduced than with us, we were ashamed of her; for, when once near the tee there was no removing of her. Wherever she settled, there she *clocked;* and the severest blow merely destroyed her equilibrium, turning up her bottom to the light."

The "Sutor" was the name of another Lochmaben stone. Then there were "Skelbyland," "The Craig," "Wallace," "Steelcap," "The Scoon," "Buonoparte," "Hughie," "Redcap," and "The Skipper," all noted and associated with the names and feats of other days. Doubtless the Lochmabenites whose prowess Sir Richard immortalised, and who are still ready to *souter* their opponents on the ice, will continue to hold these old heroes in reverence.

MUTHILL.—One stone in possession of this club is a square block named "The Bible" (Fig. 18); another, oval shaped, "The Goose" (Fig. 19); another, "The Hen." One since lost was said to be the weight of "a boll of meal."

FIG. 18.
"THE BIBLE," FROM MUTHILL.

FIG. 19.
"THE GOOSE," FROM MUTHILL.

MARKINCH.—Old stone (in possession of the patron, John Balfour of Balbirnie) which has for more than a century borne the name of "The Doctor," of the same shape as an old triangular smoothing iron, with a well-fastened old iron handle. The stone is about 60 lbs. weight.

NEWTYLE.—One old specimen is still preserved—a natural quartz boulder of unshapely build, with an iron handle inserted, and weighing about 70 lbs. Smaller boulders with three finger holes were once on the pond, entitled "The Goose" and "The Gander," but they have both flown away. Other old stones were known as "The Prince" and "The Kebbuck."

PITFOUR.—Within the last few years stones have been found in this district doing duty in keeping the thatch on the roofs of houses and hay-ricks, and supposed to be at least 150 years old. They are rough and round or oval in shape, weighing from 20 to 30 lbs., with a piece of rusty iron sunk into the top for a handle. They are evidently water-worn and picked up from the sea-shore, or the bed of the nearest river. Colonel Ferguson of Pitfour has two pairs of such stones.

STRATHALLAN MEATH MOSS.—Several old stones with iron handles, very rough, and with no trace of work on them. One very old (Fig. 20) called "The Grey Mare," used to be set on the table at curling dinners. The stone is just as it would be when taken from the channel of the river. It has a handle inserted in it, but from the holes that are also found pierced on its upper side it is supposed by its owners to have been played once upon a time without a handle. If this be so (but the size of

FIG. 20.
"THE GREY MARE," FROM STRATHALLAN.

the stone makes us doubtful) it is interesting as shewing the transformation from the first to the second type of stone.*

TWEEDSMUIR.—One ancient specimen, shaped somewhat like a Tam o' Shanter bonnet, is in possession of a member of this club. It was found in the bottom of a deep pool in the Tweed, near Crook Inn.

TYNRON.—The curling-stone which belonged to John M'Call, farmer, Glenmanna, Penpont, can be seen in Dr Grierson's Museum, Thornhill (parish of Morton), where

---

* Since this notice was in type we have received information from the secretary of this club (R. Maxtone) of the discovery of a stone of the earliest type by James Brydie, Hillhead, on the site of an old curling pond. The stone weighs 23 lbs., and is an admirable specimen of the "loofie channel-stane."

there is a famous collection of antiquities. It is a ponderous block weighing some 75 lbs. This John M'Call was a very powerful man. Many stories are told of great feats of strength performed by him. He "flourished" about 100 years ago.*

We have kept to the end of the list "the king o' a' the core,"—the "last but not the least:" the greatest in fact, of all that mighty race. In the circumstances in which he has made his appearance he claims a special title underneath his portrait, and we have therefore called him "The Jubilee Stone." This extraordinary stone that now beats the record formerly held by "The Saut Backet" of Coupar-Angus, was presented to the Royal Caledonian Club by John Wilson, Chapelhill, Cockburnspath, and exhibited on its arrival, at the Jubilee meeting of the club, held on the 25th July 1888; and its portly presence also graced the banquet on November 28th. It weighs 117 lbs., and belonged to John Hood, a keen curler of that district, who died

FIG. 21. "THE JUBILEE STONE."

---

* From the following Clubs we have also been favoured with notices regarding old stones either in their possession, or in the neighbourhood. They do not all refer us back to the time under consideration, but they supply information that certainly links the present with the past in an interesting way. The clubs are given in alphabetical order:—Achalader (Airth, Bruce Castle, and Dunmore), (Ancrum, Alewater and Mounteviot), Ballingry, Balmerino, Belfast, Breadalbane (2 clubs), Bridge of Allan, Cardross and Kepp, Castlecary Castle, Ceres, Croy, Cupar-Fife, Dirleton, Doune, Dumfries, Dunglas and Cockburnspath, Eaglesham, Earlston, Forrestfield, Fort-Augustus, Greenlaw, Hamilton, Hercules, Inverness, Kinnochtry, Kinross, Kirknewton, Lees and Lithtillum, Lilliesleaf, Lochwinnoch, Logiealmond, Manchester Bellevue, Megginch, Melville, Methven, Minnigaff, Montreal, Newport, Orwell, Penninghame, Pitlessie, Reston, Roslin, Scotscraig, Shettleston, Spean, Stoneycreek, Stow, Strathkinnes, Tinwald, Trinity Gask, Woodside (North), Upper Nithsdale.

at Townhead in January 1888. Mr Hood, it appears,
had often seen his father play the stone, and he himself
had played it occasionally before dressed stones were
introduced. It was sent by Mr Wilson to be preserved
in the archives of the Royal Club; and we are sure that
future generations of curlers will look upon it with interest
and astonishment, if not with dismay.

Such, then, are the memorial stones of the giant age of
curling. Varied is their destiny from the ignominious lot
of the poor outcast that acts as a foot-scraper in the parish
of the first historian of the game, to that of "the doctor,"
snugly ensconced in the patron's private parlour at Markinch, or, higher than all, of the great monarch who presides
at our banquets, and then sits in state at the secretary's
office to receive the admiring homage of his subjects, who
hail from every frosty clime to pay respect to His Majesty.
They are indeed a "core" of matchless weight and power.
In measuring against them our modern capabilities, we
ought, no doubt, to bear in mind that the rink in those
days was, in all likelihood, much shorter than it is now, and
each player used only one stone—the number of players on
each side being usually eight; but, even with such differences taken into account, we must own that these big blocks
alarm us with the conviction that the dissipation of energy
is going on more rapidly than natural philosophers seem to
think. Few of us would care to have our life depending
on the chance of sending the Jubilee stone "owre a' ice."
"Tak 'm by the handle" would be the cry that sealed our
doom; but the Titan of Cockburnspath thought nothing of
the burden as he enjoyed the play; and, if these weighty
stones could speak, they would doubtless relate how sweetly
they were swung by the arms of their owners, and how
gently they were carried to and from the loch—very often
in the cosy corner of the shepherd's plaid. We have no
reason to suppose that Cairnie's heroes, William Gourlay
and Aleck Cook were mythical—though we "sing small"
as William plays his 72-pounder, which takes off the guard
full, moves on, and in its progress raises half-a-dozen stones

in succession, and gains the shot that was declared to be impregnable. *We* cannot do that! nor can we rival Aleck the "ambidexter," who swung his long arm "so high, with the curling-stone behind him, that, when about to raise the double guards, a person standing on the tee opposite could see its entire bottom!" We listen and believe (?) all that Broun tells us about the irate Clapperton, who "seized the Lochmaben 'Hen' with an air of triumph, and whirled her repeatedly round his head, with as much ease, apparently, as if she had been nearer seven than *seventy* pounds;" and when he relates how the president, in reply to Laurie Young, the strongest player in Tinwald, who had challenged the Lochmaben party to a trial of arm, stepped out, took his stone and threw it with such strength across the breadth of the Mill Loch (nearly a mile), that it stotted off the brink upon the other side, and tumbled over upon the grass, adding thereafter—"Now, sir, go and throw it back again, and we'll then confess that you are too many for us."

"There were giants in those days." We had better just allow at once that the former days of curling "were better than these," in the physical force line. Herein just lies the difference between the ancient and the modern game. As we engage in it now, we do so that we may improve our physical as well as our mental and spiritual condition; but, with the beautiful implements now in our hands, we have something else to do than to make a display of force. In curling, as in other accomplishments—

> "It is well to have a giant's strength,
> But tyrannous to use it like a giant."

To "draw," and "wick," and "creep through the port," and "curl round the guard to the winner;" to "elbow in," and "elbow out," and, in a hundred other ways, to temper force with discretion and "canniness"—to reduce stone-throwing to one of the fine arts—this is the modern curler's ambition, and, in as far as he succeeds, he advances beyond the possibilities of ancient curling. It can easily be understood that, with these coarse three-neukit stones, the niceties

of the modern game were out of the question: they played—
they had to play, a striking game, and stone-breaking was
heroic at a time when stones cost nothing, but had simply
to be lifted off the nearest dyke or out of the nearest burn.
It is not surprising, therefore, to find that *thunder* is pre-
dominant in any descriptions we have of the middle age of
curling. One or two of these are found heading this chapter. Mr Muir's picture recalls a style of play that must
have been on the wane when he sung his spirited song to
the Duddingston Club—

" A stalwart chiel, to redd the ice,
  Drives roaring down like thunder;
Wi' awfu' crash the double guards
  At ance are burst asunder;
Rip-raping on frae random wicks,
  The winner gets a yether;
Then round the tee we flock wi' glee
  In cauld, cauld, frosty weather."

As a Yankee would say, " I guess they found some road
metal beside that tee."

When Davidson (1789) describes the great contest which
took place at Carlingwark, between Ben o' Tudor and Glenbuck (Gordon of Kenmure) in the olden time we " hear afar "
the noise of rattling shots and reckless shooters:—

"The stanes wi' muckle martial din,
  Rebounding frae ilk shore:
Now thick, thick, thick, each other chased
  An' up the rink did roar.

They closed fast on every side,
  A port could scarce be found
An' many a broken channel-stane
  Lay scattered up an' down.

Shew me the winner, cried Glenbuck,
  An' a' behind stan' off:
Then rattled up the roaring crag
  An ran the port wi' life."

Rough as the ancient game might be, it was, however, on
such a *granite* foundation that the sociality and brotherhood
of curling meetings were built up. The pillars of the
bonspeil, "rivalry and good fellowship," were then laid
strong and deep—never to be shaken.

> "Thus did Bentudor and Glenbuck
> Their curling contest end ;
> They met baith merry i' the morn,
> At night they parted friends."

And thus did other contests begin and end. Then, as now, the motto was, "meet friends and part friends:" and in their hard fighting our forefathers did not forget what we try to remember, that, on the icy plain, courtesy is due as much to those who vanquish us as to those who are vanquished by us.

"In those days," says Mr Wilson in sending the Jubilee stone, and referring to the time when such toys were used by his own and John Hood's ancestors, "the gude-wife of the farmer used herself to carry to the pond luncheon in the shape of a 'bicker of brose' made with the 'broo' of the beef and greens being prepared for dinner, and all the players sat around and partook of this substantial fare, washed down, we may safely assume, by a little of the national beverage. After play was over they adjourned to discuss the said beef and greens, and to 'fight their battles o'er again' over unlimited tumblers of toddy." We have not, with all our advancement, beaten that record of simple, homely, social enjoyment ; the curling of the future never will, for in such fellowship we "gie the grip" to a' keen curlers. The *manner* of play—be it of the *loofie* days or the big boulder age, or of some unimagined period which shall yet cast our own, with its boasted perfection, into the shade, matters not : we are brithers a', and the good fellowship that binds us together in every age is stronger than the developments that distinguish one age from another in the history of "our ain game."

THIRD TYPE: THE CIRCULAR STONE.—The acquisition of a "handle" by the typical mortal to whom reference has been made, with the consequent power and influence, does not at first bring polish and refinement : the *angles* or *corners* have still to be rubbed off ; and this is the next stage of development entrusted to the forces of

civilisation, culture, and society. The evolution of the
curling-stone proceeds on similar lines. The squaring of the
circle is proverbially impossible, and the problem, happily,
was not set before the curler. His task was to make circular
what was found square, oval, three-neukit, hexagonal, or indescribable, as the case might be; and it is evident, from
our illustrations, that he had every form and shape to work
upon. Who first accomplished this? For, was not the
inventor of the circular stone the true originator of curling?
Did he not draw the game away, as we have said, from its
former modes and conditions so completely as to leave no
connection, except what can be recognised by the faculty
that deals with the evidence of what is not seen? The
game of curling, in its origin, and in the incidents of its
progress, seems to be the work of some power other than
human: it comes as a gift from the unseen—keen curlers
call it a divine gift; and, no doubt, it is such if they use it
aright, for it is the use of them that makes all gifts divine
or the opposite. The inventor of the circular curling-stone,
like the inventor of curling, is, and must remain, a "great
unknown." In our historical survey of the subject we
content ourselves by saying that the development was
natural, and we wonder with those who wonder that it did
not come about sooner. We make a polite bow of thanks
in name of our countrymen to those writers (generally
countrymen themselves) who argue that the late appearance
of the circular stone is an argument for the recent origin of
the game, on the ground that our intelligence would not
have allowed it to remain so long so imperfect.*

---

* "Had the game been of very ancient origin, we should expect many
of these improvements to have been made long before the time when they
actually were made. As society advances in improvement, arts and
sciences advance at the same time. No human thing remains stationary.
If, then, we find curling-stones, at any period, in the rudest possible form,
having received no improvements, we have reason to conclude that the
origin of the game cannot be far distant from that period."—*Duddingston
Account*, etc., p. 17.

"That the game cannot boast of hoary antiquity is a conclusion which
may also be arrived at by a process of reasoning which dispenses with
written records, viz., from the rude shape and finish of curling-stones
and handles until within a very recent period. It is alleged that, in

But the argument won't do. Old channel-stanes, like facts, "winna ding, and downa be disputed," and we have now got evidence that they were in existence more than two centuries before the rounding of the stone brought in the new era of curling, and the intelligence of our countrymen was applied to the improvement of the stones. The proof of antiquity assails the pride of intelligence. The compliment is changed into a reflection, containing a rebuke. The bright *palladium* marked "1511," which, as we have seen, guards us against a foreign origin, within a glass case at Stirling, becomes a bitter pill which (*pace* the Curator of the Smith Institute) must be swallowed *nolens volens*; and we have simply to confess that the *lateness* of the circular stone is a great discredit to Scotland, and is unaccountable, except, perhaps, on the ground that our forefathers found so much enjoyment in the imperfect game as to keep them from thinking of improving upon it. Dr Samuel Johnson held that Scotland consisted of two things—stone and water; and, as these are the primal elements in the ancient game, he doubtless referred to this deficiency when he remarked that, with all our learning and advantages, we were devoid of elegance and embellishments till the Union!* It is interesting to notice that the visit of the grand old grumbler

---

some instances, within the memory of men still living, the stones had merely a niche for the finger and thumb to serve as a handle, and the they were really 'channel-stanes' taken from the river or brook. The improvements in handles and stones went on simultaneously at a good rate, until a near approach to mathematical precision was attained. Had curling been known in the Middle Ages these improvements would doubtless have been effected sooner, for our noble ecclesiastical piles and feudal strongholds bear ample testimony to the fact that stone-masons, who usually mould and fashion curling-stones, were no less accomplished tradesmen in mediæval times than they are now. It may be argued, however, that the blocks of which curling-stones are made are more difficult to mould than stones hewn for cathedrals and fortresses. While this is readily admitted, it is equally true that not one of the curling-stones, even of so recent a date as the last century, possesses the polish or finish usually met with in the ancient *querns*, or hand mill-stones, which for many centuries were in universal use for grinding corn, and which were often moulded out of solid whinstone."—J. B. Greenshields, *Annals of Lesmahagow* (1864), p. 205.

* He (Dr Johnson) owned the Scots had been "a very learned nation for one hundred years—from 1550 to 1650, but they afforded the only instance of a people among whom the arts of civil life did not advance in proportion with learning: that they had hardly any trade, any money, or

who did so much to take the conceit out of us, was made about the time that curling set out on its career of elegance and embellishment; and it would, perhaps, be more correct to ascribe the improvement in curling to Dr Johnson's Tour to the Hebrides in 1773, than to the Union. It is certain, indeed, that neither had anything to do with the matter; and, as far as we can judge, the time of the improvement is neither an argument for the recent origin of the game, nor a reflection on the want of intelligence in those who played away so long with loofie-stones, and sea, stream, or dyke boulders. Greater latent possibilities than the circular channel-stane have lain for ages undiscovered and undeveloped, and very often accident, or what is so-called, only brought them to light. Then everybody wondered that they had never been discovered or invented before—they were so simple. The greatest genius is he who can write something, or invent something, so true to nature that everybody admires its simplicity, and feels that it ought to have been done long ago, and that everybody might have done it.

Among the motley throng of boulders that gathered within the *brough* as the ancient game went on, there were to be found now and then stones worn quite circular, as we may find them yet by the action of stream or sea—nature's productions. The players could not fail to see a fitness about these that the others did not possess for dealing with certain situations occurring in the struggle to lie nearest to the tee, and out of this, doubtless, arose the idea of making *all* stones circular.

An outsider may have followed us till now without being led to inquire as to the manner of playing the game and the aim of the players, and we may take him so far into confidence at this stage as to furnish him with the earliest description of the game—that of Pennant, who made a tour in Scotland in 1772 :—*

---

any elegance before the Union: that it was strange that, with all the advantages possessed by other nations, they had not any of those conveniences and embellishments which are the fruit of industry, till they came in contact with a civilised people."—*Boswell.*

* *A Tour in Scotland and Voyage to the Hebrides*, 1772. 2nd edition. Part I. page 93.

"Of the sports of these parts," says Pennant, "that of *Curling* is a favorite; and one unknown in England: it is an amusement of the winter, and played on the ice, by sliding from one mark to another great stones of forty to seventy pounds weight, of hemispherical form, with an iron or wooden handle at top. The object of the player is to lay his stone as near to the mark as possible, to guard that of his partner, which had been well laid before, or to strike off that of his antagonist."

There is little to add to this concise description, except to say that in these times the *rink*, or distance from mark to mark (tee to tee), was generally not more than 36 yards; that the player steadied himself in delivering his stone, and kept his footing on the ice by means of *crampits* (*grippers, crisps*), in appearance like stirrup-irons, and fixed on his shoes like skates, having prongs underneath to grip the ice. In a contest there were then generally eight players on a side, each playing one stone. With this preface we may introduce a plain diagram (Fig. 22) to shew the difficulty of skilful play with the ancient stones, and the possibilities developed by the circular ones. It is not certain that in these times the players were particular in playing over one tee to the other, but, with their *crampits* on their shoes, they would move off and make a flank attack when the enemy's front lines were impregnable. This was, however, even in these times, bad form, and we may suppose the player's stone to be coming in the direction of the arrow.

One circle or brough is drawn, of 8 feet in diameter (the diameter in the early days ranged from 2 to 12 feet). In (1) we have an oval stone, T, on the tee, guarded by an angular stone, A. These are both the enemy's; and the player, with a three-neukit stone, is about to play, his object being to remove the oval stone of the enemy from its position on the tee. Touching the circle on the right of the triangular stone or guard is the square stone B on his own side. What is he to do? How will his three-neukit stone find the winner? The shot is no doubt a possible one; it may even be demonstrated as such by mathematical science, or taken in at a glance by a warlock like the renowned Tam Pate, who, with a three-neukit stone, never missed a shot in the famous match of the Duke of Hamilton against

M'Dowall of Garthland in 1784. We venture to say, however, that in an ordinary case the player would simply send up his stone and let it take its chance, not knowing what it

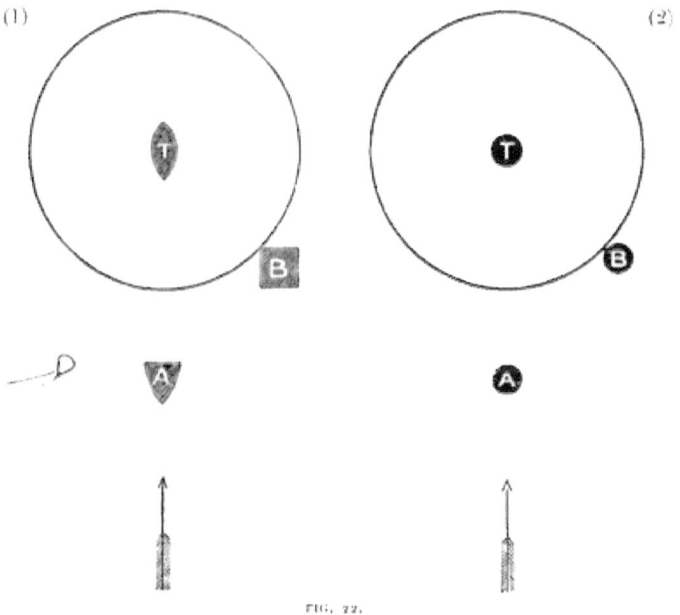

FIG. 22.

might do. In (2), with the same object in view, the stones in their corresponding positions being circular, and the stone which the player is about to play being also circular, it is at once evident that he can find the winner on the tee, and displace it in several ways. The proverbial three courses, at least, are open—to curl past the guard with the Fenwick twist (of which more under "The Art of Curling"), and change places quietly with the winner; to cannon or wick on the inner side of B, and at an angle do the same thing; or to wick B on the outer side, and force it to displace the winning-stone, and rest itself on the tee, which would be equally successful, since B is on the player's side. In the position of this game it will be noticed that only three have played out of the sixteen which were generally found in conflict—eight against eight, in ancient times; but as the number of stones within the circle increases in (1), the difficulty of *skilful play* will increase, and *force* and *chance* will more and more rule the destinies of the fighters; while in (2), though *force* will at times be needed to clear complications, and *chance* continue to give its spice of interest to the game, the player of *skill* will more and more be required for the *little* shot, and the last of all will most likely require to be the most skilful.

Now there may be a dubious precision in the situation of affairs thus sketched, for it is not likely that the variegated implements would ever fall into position exactly as above described; but it is enough if we have illustrated the nature of the change brought about in curling by the circular shape of the stones. It was a complete revolution in the game that was thus quietly effected, and by it the game was elevated into a position of national importance. It was thereby brought to a condition of perfection, such as to entitle it to be transferred as a winter game to every corner of the world, where the need of such amusement is felt. It was, without doubt, the most far-reaching event in the history of curling. We have given the Kuting-stone type, 1500–1650, and the boulder block, 1650–1800. And for practical purposes this holds as correct, but we shall find the great change working a good many years before the beginning of this century, when the boulder was in disgrace and doomed to extinction, or to the (perhaps) less enviable fate of being placed in an Antiquarian Museum as a relic of the olden time. The old block had lived a hard life, and it died *hard*, as if struggling to the last to avoid being left on the hog-line of history. It took from 50 to 80 years to die—an unconscionably long time to be moribund, a respectable life-time in itself.

"Old Bonaparte," says Sir R. Broun, (*Memorabilia*, p. 42.) "who flourished cir. 1750 and downwards, was the first who had a regular formed polished Curling-stone upon our ice."

We do not hear of any earlier; while specimens linger on upon the field of battle—antiquated and doomed—till the formation of the Grand Club in 1838. It may be said, however, as marking the transition, that, at the beginning of the last quarter of the eighteenth century, the circular stones were *novelties*, and by the end of the first quarter of this century the boulder-stones were *antiquities* on the ice. Cairnie says:—

"About the year 1770, in many parts of Scotland, where the game is now almost brought to perfection, the curling-stones were in their natural state as taken from the fields, or from the beds of rivers, many of them in use wanting handles, some of them having merely a hole made for the thumb, and a few only having the benefit of a polished bottom: at that time too, the stones were variously shaped, few of them so perfectly rounded as to be admissible on the rink of 1833, and some of them of a triangular form, one of which we ourselves well remember, 'ycelpt the cocked hat, truly formidable on the ice: for, unless it was hit full, it often happened that it was not moved far from the spot, but made the rotatory motion in great perfection. At the present day, the shape of all curling-stones is, or rather must be, circular; but in some places their shape, although circular, is very uncouth; and we have a pair in our possession made at the Bridge of Allan, that from their shape and handles are known by the name of the Water Stoups."*

Cairnie's correspondents at that time gave similar testimony. Thus C. D., from Neilston:—

"Forty years ago the stones were generally selected from dykes in the neighbourhood; but on one occasion a player borrowed a shoemaker's lap or beating-stone, which gave him such an advantage in playing that the others declined playing with him unless it was laid aside."

And A. Crawford, Lochwinnoch:—

"Mr Cunningham of Craigends played in 1779 with his grandfather's *stane*. His grandfather must have lived in the beginning of the last century; the stane was natural, without polishing, except the plain iron handle. It was *three-neukit*."

As an exquisite specimen of the roughness of the old game, even under the auspices of a Laird, and of the reception the new-fangled "circulars" got on their first appearance, we may give an incident in the match played in 1783, between Beith and Lochwinnoch, the latter club being led as usual by Garthland mentioned above.

"One Gavin Gibson, a Beith man, had a fine Osmund Stone, and towards the gloaming it began to snow; Gibson let go his stone, James Riddell sprung upon the cramps, followed the wake of Gavin's stone through the snow and knocked it to flinders. Garthland *hotched* and *leuch*, and *held his sides*, as Riddell expressed it."

---

* *Essay on Curling*, p. 2.

So much for Garthland, but the elegance and embellishment of such horse-play have happily disappeared with the Lochwinnoch boulders, and fine Ailsas are in no such danger as "fine Osmunds" were on their first appearance in the time of Gavin Gibson and the *hotchin'*, *lauchin'* laird of Garthland. The circular stone, in its career, has itself run into several types before becoming that "thing of beauty" which makes it "a joy for ever" in the hands of curlers. Our Kays and Thorburns were not yet at work, and the mason and blacksmith were not up to the art of polishing.

The old boulders were not without a polish of a kind. Mr Wilson of Chapelhill tells us that the old curlers, when they got a likely stone from the sea-shore, dug a place for it in the stable entry, and after the horses' hoofs had polished the stone sufficiently, they took it out to do duty on the ice. Not more brilliant was the polish of the circular stone in its early days. Its advantage lay simply in its rough circularity. For a long time it remained one-sided. Pennant speaks of the stone that came under his notice in 1772 as *hemispherical*, but one of the earliest developments was the conical stone, as we find it in one of the earliest illustrations we have of the game— a woodcut in the *Winter-Season* of James Fisher, the Blind Fiddler of Ochiltree—(pub. 1810). The stone (Fig. 23), though circular, very much resembles in appearance an ordinary mason's mallet.*

FIG. 23.
FROM FISHER'S "WINTER-SEASON."

---

* In this connection it is interesting to add the experience of John Pearson, now a builder in Sheffield, which shews the true spirit of a curler, and the possibility of a good game out of the ordinary mason's mallet—"In the winter of 1844-45 a number of Scotch masons were engaged, along with others, in the erection of Worsley Hall, the seat of the Earl of Ellesmere, near Manchester. The winter being severe, and all work at a standstill owing to the frost, it became difficult to know how to pass the time. There happened to be a good pond in front of the Hall, on which we slided and skated until we got tired. At last some one proposed that we should try Curling, but the question arose, How could we get curling-stones? My father suggested that we should try our mallets. No sooner said than done. The ice was swept, the rink marked out, and each selected a pair of mallets and commenced play. I can assure you they made a very good substitute, the

A STUDY OF STONES.

Even as late as 1830, according to Sir R. Broun:—*

FIG. 24.

"Conical shaped stones, *i.e.*, stones made like a sugar-loaf, broad below and tapering up, prevail at Dunblane: they are," he says, "very secure runners, and have handles let into the stone at both ends, so that in delivery it is swung off the fingers. They are also of great height, so as to prevent the player stooping when throwing them. They are certainly more fanciful than elegant."

Extremes meet—and we find some again flattened down like flukes, and between the two a great variety of high types of stone, some of which are still popular with modern players.

FIG. 25. FIG. 26. FIG. 27.
DIAGRAMS FROM BROUN'S "MEMORABILIA CURLIANA."

A tendency to favour *weight* was still to be found for a long time after the round stone was introduced. Pennant, we have seen, puts the limit at 70 lbs. as far as his observation went, but a good many were above that weight. We have no "Jubilee Stones," "Saut Backets," or "Sows,"— no circulars that balance a boll of meal, but we have many beyond the "comprehension" of the modern curler among the relics of the early circular age. William Gourlay, in the end of the century had a pair weighing

---

games being as keenly contested as if we had been playing with the best Crawfordjohns or Burnocks. We were never afterwards at a loss to know how to pass the time, and many of us, indeed, were sorry when the frost went, and we had to give up our play. I have played in many games, both in Scotland and in England, since then, but never enjoyed Curling more than I did with the ordinary mason's mallet on the pond at Worsley. The names of the players who took part in the games, as far as I can remember, were D. Readdie, P. Whitten, R. Kirk, J. Burt, my father and myself, from Kinross; H. Russel, Kettle; J. Clark, Colinsburgh; John Hare, a member of a well-known family of curlers, from Sanquhar; W. Blake and J. Scott, Dumfries; and J. Tait, Jedburgh. My uncle, then superintendent of Worsley Yard for the Bridgewater Trust, joined us occasionally, John Hare and my father generally acting as skips.

* *Memorabilia Curliana*, p. 46.

70 lbs. each, which he played—as we have seen—to great purpose, on the Drumlie meadow, near Denny.

"Till lately" (1830), says a celebrated curler of the Duddingston Society,[*] "the stone which I played was 72½ lbs.—'the stone of my might!'"

A Kilmarnock authority[†] says:—

"For forehand playing some have heavy stones. We know of one pair as heavy as 75 lbs. each. In some of the neighbouring parishes few stones are used lighter than 53, and many are of 60 lbs."

FIG. 28. "THE CHEESE,"
FROM EAST KILBRIDE, LANARKSHIRE.

With the circular stone the necessity of illustration—even of the very earliest specimens is done away; and "The Cheese" (Fig. 28) here presented, may simply stand for all its neighbours—only it has its history, and acquires a certain importance from having been present with the curlers at their Banquet in commemoration of the Royal Club's Jubilee.

"The Cheese" was one of a rink of stones made about sixty years ago from a block of whinstone out of Thornton Hall quarry in the parish of East Kilbride, Lanarkshire. It weighs 70 lbs., and was played for a considerable time by Mr James Smith, then of Thornton Hall. The last parish match at which it was played was about forty-five years ago (1843), when Mr James Strang of the Peel, Busby, played it as first stone for the Carmunnock Club against the Mearns Club, Renfrewshire, on the Brother Loch. On that occasion Mr Strang was the only curler on the ice who could play "The Cheese" to the tee. On many occasions after matches it was used as a test of strength, and at certain times of the year it was used for the purpose of weighing oatmeal and cheese.

This is one immediate result of the circular development —the *individuality* of the stones dies away—just as we lose the character of the old days—the bedesman, the packman, the daft Davie, through the civilising work of "Puffing Billie." Stones, like human beings, are so far monotonised by being civilised—they all become "cheeses." In some cases a certain distinction attaches to the stones as

---

[*] Broun, *Memorabilia*, p. 45. [†] *Ibid*, p. 69.

memorials of their owners, as in the case of two still preserved in Penicuick House, which were played by Sir James Clerk in the latter half of the last century, the one having a Star (Fig. 29), and the other the family Horn ("Free for a blast") (Fig. 30), hewn out in the upper side.

FIG. 29.
"THE STAR," FROM PENICUICK HOUSE.

FIG. 30.
"THE HORN," FROM PENICUICK HOUSE.

In the keeping of the Ardgowan Club is one of the stones (Fig. 31) said to have been played by "the king o' a' the core"—Tam Samson, immortalised by Burns; and it is interesting—not only as a memorial of the curling "king," but as a good example of the earlier type of the circular stone. The stone is only used in the initiation of members.

FIG 31. TAM SAMSON'S STONE.

It has a silver plate fixed into it, with the inscription, "Tam Samson's Stane. Presented by Peter Morrison to Ardgowan Curling Club, 1857." Its weight is $54\frac{1}{2}$ lbs., circumference $35\frac{3}{4}$ inches, height $6\frac{1}{5}$ inches. Handle of iron—clear of stone 1 inch, extreme height $1\frac{3}{4}$ inches.

An interesting set of stones (Fig. 32), with a certain remnant of individuality about them, is that here represented by the kindness of their possessor, J. M. Thomson, Vice-President of the Holyrood Club. From the situation in which they were discovered it is more than likely that they belonged to the old Canonmills Club, and probably they are as ancient specimens of the round stone as are anywhere to be found. One is specially noticeable as having a *ring* handle, by which it was swung on the first middle finger. They are marked by quaint lettering, typical of old Scots figures.

FIG. 32. FROM THE OLD CANONMILLS CLUB.

Cairnie tried to preserve the individual nomenclature with his stock of stones which he provided for his little club; but there is nothing in the names—they are all of the *lucus a non lucendo* description, and he might as well have numbered them 1, 2, 3, &c. In 1820, some years after a club had been formed at Largs, one bold member challenges all his fellows—

> "I, with *the Driver* and *John Bull*,
>   The *Glasgow* and far-famed *Secunder*,
> With *Caledonia* and *Belle Poule*,
>   Shall beat the Club, or shall knock under.
> And just that we may wet our throttle,
> I'll lay of rum a single bottle."

The challenge from Parnassus was reducible thus—"I, with six stones, will play any member of the club for a bottle of rum." Cairnie's own attempt[*] at immortalising the stock of "circulars" provided for his friends is just as meaningless, but it is interesting as the final attempt of this keenest of curlers to preserve the *individuality* of the channel-stane.

[*] *Essay*, p. 49.

LOQUITUR RECTOR.*

"No party politics around our Tee,
For Whig and Tory on the ice agree ;
Glory we play for, may it be our lot,
To gain the Bonspiel by a single shot.
Nisus, we trust, will do as he is bid,
And young *Euryalus* oft lie patiid,
Guarded by *Venus*, he will rest secure,
And, *Mars* behind them, close the barrier door ;
The *Rose* and *Thistle* vis-à-vis shall be,
To ward off wickers that would reach the *Tee ;*
To break their line our *Nelson* cannot fail,
Napoleon's there, have at them in detail ;
La Liberté triumphantly shall ride,
Conserro and *Reform* keep near her side ;
Largs, as a player, doubtless will excel,
To move their winner we have *William Tell ;*
Of marksmen good we many have to spare,
And *Robin Hood* and *Little John* are there ;
The game shall end before that it is late ;
The winning stone, he shall be named *Tam Pate.*†
In friendship we shall pass a jovial night,
And fix the day we may renew the fight."

A glance at this set of stones from Cairnie's own *Essay* (Plate II.), will illustrate the loss of individuality in the new curling era, and, at the same time, the enormous change for good that had come about by roundness and polish at the end of the first quarter of this century. These bring us, in fact, to the modern stone and the modern game.

 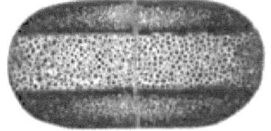

FIGS. 33, 34, 35.

---
* Skip.
† The Warlock player, on the Hamilton side, against Castle Semple.

Our Study of Stones has, we hope, given such information as may be useful and interesting alike to the historian and the curler. It will be noticed that we have counted of great importance the introduction of the circular stone. If it be held to be discreditable to our country that curling existed, as we have shewn it must have done, in some form or other for upwards of two centuries before our ancestors thought of using round stones, it ought, on the other hand, to be acknowledged that as long as curling remained in its imperfect form, it never attained to the rank of a national game—obscurity was the consequence of imperfect development. But when, in addition to its being a game of chance and a test of strength, it became a social force, bringing genial fellowship and kindly intercourse between man and man as its results, and when it finally developed, through the round weapon, into something that required scientific skill on the part of those who engaged in it—then it rushed forward into nationality; and, ever since, it has been recognised as the most truly national of our amusements. The discredit of delay is surely atoned for by the readiness with which it was adopted and cherished when it became worthy of such treatment. In all national games it will be found that these elements—*chance, force, fellowship,* and *skill,* have their place in greater or less degree. It is so in football, cricket, golf, and other really national games; and we hope never to be found depreciating any of them that we may glorify Scotland's ain game of curling. In none of them, however, will the necessary elements of a truly national and popular amusement be found more harmoniously blended. From the special danger of them all— viz., to develop scientific skill at the expense of all other things—we are protected by the weather, which is the all-potent regulator of the conditions of our game. At the same time our *skill,* in comparison with that of our ancestors, ought to be infinitely superior with the improvements we have inherited. Their force, their enthusiasm, as they battled long ago on the arena of the icy plain, were not wasted; their happy evenings over "beef and greens," and a tumbler or two afterwards, were not mere selfish indulgences, but their play and their brotherly fellowship made them better men, and *that betterness* is our inheritance to-day. No man lives to play—not even to curl—keen, keen though he be; but the man who knows how to temper duty with pleasure, and feels that his amusements, as truly as his serious employments, are worthy of attention, will best discharge what he owes to those who lived before him, and to those who are to come after him.

"Thae wild days are gane, but their memories call us,
    So we'll stand by langsyne, and the guid ancient use."

It is our duty, as it is our privilege, to guard the honour, to increase the glory, to deepen the enthusiasm of curling: it is our inheritance—handed down for improvement while we have the use of it, and to be handed on with added interest and value to those who succeed us.

"Let ilka true-born Scottish son,
    When cranreuch cleeds the snawy grun',
'Mang curling cores seek harmless fun,
    And gar his heart's blude tingle."

NOTE.—While these sheets were passing through the press, two stones (Figs. 36 and 37) were sent to us by the kindness of Mr A. Gow, having been found on the Fala Estate by him in 1885, and are now in the possession of Lord Stair at Oxenfoord Castle. A number of others of the same period have also been found on this estate.

FIG. 36.

FIG. 37.

" In ancient days fame tells the fact
 That Scotland's heroes were na slack
 The heads o' stubborn foes to crack,
   An' mak the feckless flee, boys !
 Wi' brave hearts beating true and warm,
 They aften tried the curling charm,
 To cheer the heart an' nerve the arm ;
   The roarin' rink for me, boys !"
              Alexander Maclagan.

" It boots not whence the curler hails,
   If curler keen an' staunch he be,
 Frae Scotland, England, Ireland, Wales,
   Or Colonies ayont the sea ;
   A social britherhood are we,
 An' after we are deid an' gane,
 We'll live in literature an' lair,
 In annals o' the channel-stane."
              J. Usher.

" Our fathers in the days of yore,
 Bravely themselves in battle bore,
 And dearly loved the friendly splore.
   .   .   .   .   .   .
 To give and take be ready still,
 To strike a foe still have the will,
 Still guard a friend with all your skill."
              Rev. G. Murray (Balmaclellan).

CHAPTER III.

HISTORICAL AND POETICAL REFERENCES.

O "leave no stone unturned" that might illustrate the History of Ancient Curling has been our endeavour in the foregoing chapter. By a study of the different types thus brought under notice, the development of the game may be distinctly traced. The testimony of the rocks is not, however, to be too much depended on. Curlers who worship antiquity may hesitate before making Stirling their *Mecca*, because of the venerable black *Caaba-stone* that is enshrined in the Macfarlane Museum there. The stone itself is old, but the date (1511) inserted in it seems comparatively new; and this may be the case with other specimens that put in claims to great antiquity. We must now look beyond words of doubtful origin that are used in play, and stones of doubtful age that are preserved in museums, to historians and poets, whose works may be expected slowly but surely to reflect the customs and amusements of the people. Such information as these convey cannot but prove valuable, and we are therefore dealing with the records of the game in the order of their importance, when we proceed to notice the evidences of its origin and progress that are found in our literature. Supposing that what we have stated as to the obscurity of this form of winter amusement before the invention of the circular-stone is correct, we do not expect to find much notice taken of it in its earlier stages. In this we are not disappointed, for

No mention is made of the game of curling by any of our Scottish historians and poets previous to the year 1600.

So far our present chapter must prove a case of "snakes in Iceland." Its negative nature cannot be satisfactory to curlers, who believe that their favourite amusement was one at which our monarchs—when we had them all to ourselves—"disdained not to play," and that curling was a national game perhaps before we in Scotland were a nation. We are sorry, for their sakes, that we cannot go further back; but as for curling, we see nothing to be gained by pushing its claim to antiquity, nationality, and Royal patronage too far. The popularity of the game rests on its merits. It has the future before it, as the winter game of this and other countries; and in our present inquiry it is better to clear the ground, though it may not please our antiquarian brethren to find their pet traditions destroyed. We have already stated that curling of a kind was engaged in, during the sixteenth century, when the kuting-stone, or piltycock, was in use. No allusion is however made to it, in the history or poetry of that period; and before the sixteenth century we have no evidence either from ancient stones, or from ancient writers, that such a game or the germ of it was in existence. This the *keen* historian does not wish to believe. He is determined to force the testimony, and so we find him "owre a' ice," in his wild pursuit of references. Here is a passage from Sir Richard Broun,* one of the best and most enthusiastic of early writers on curling :—

---

* *Memorabilia*, p. 61.

"Of the remote antiquity of the game of curling, we have the most legitimate proof from Ossian:—'Fly, son of Morven, fly! Amid the circle of stones, Swaran bends at the stone of might.' Either the game then is much more ancient than has hitherto been dreamed of—or else Macpherson has been most unhappy in his allusion!"

We have looked in vain for this interesting passage as quoted by Broun, but "the stone of might" is a common expression in Ossian's Poems. The words of Starno and Swaran (Ca-lodin, Duan I.) are "not in vain, by Loda's stone of power." In Fingal (Duan III.) we read of the "gray-haired Snivan that often sang round the circle of Loda; when the stone of power heard his voice, and battle turned in the field of the valiant." These references, it appears, are to acts of worship performed by the Fingalian heroes.* Broun need not have been at the trouble of transforming Scandinavian crom-lecs into Caledonian channel-stanes. Is it not plain that Swaran was a curler— "Swaran of lakes," who, "slowly stalking over the stream, whistled as he went"? Was it not a signal for a curling match to begin when "Launderg rolled a stone the sign of war"? Why did the son of Maben not penetrate further into ancient literature, and find in the *Fall* a proof that our first parents tried the "slippery game" in the garden of Eden?† All supposed references

* Clerk's *Ossian*, Vol. I. p. 78; Vol. II. p. 156. Blackwood, 1870. Clerk's translation has "stone of spectres" for Macpherson's "stone of power."
† Broun should have been credited with a joke, had we not found from a MS. note to a proposed second edition of his work, that he prepared to enlarge on the point, and to add some remarks on the popularity of the poems of Ossian with Napoleon Bonaparte and Lord Byron. Since his time, "the stone of might," and "the circles of Loda," are often found doing duty in curling songs. The Rev. Mr Muir of Beith, in the following spirited lines, gives a happy account of another transformation of "the stone of might." The lines were published in Broun's work with the motto from Ossian prefixed.

"In the days o' lang syne, as some auld stories tell us,
  At Yule when the fiel's are a' kiver'd wi' snaw;
Nae bonspiel was ken'd but the horn brightly sparkling,
  And wild bursts o' joy *sounding loud thro' the ha'*.

"But the watch-fire blazed red on the high top o' Gaitfel,
  The signal weel kenn'd to prepare for dread fight,
For Norseman had sworn, 'mid the circles of Loda,
  He would force us to bend *at the stone of his might*.

"But wi' braid sword and targues we met them at Largs,
  And our laddies bare aff the big stane o' his might!

to curling, previous to the seventeenth century, may be treated like this mythical allusion from Ossian—they are unworthy of serious attention. Had the game been of any great importance in the century previous, then it is more than likely that we should have heard of it, as we hear of archery, golf, football, and other games.

Archery is the oldest of our national amusements. In early times it could scarcely, however, be regarded as a sport, for it was practised by the people, at the command of Parliament, as the chief method of defence against our enemies before gunpowder came into use. Football is next in antiquity, being prohibited in favour of the practice of archery before we hear of golf.* Then, along therewith, the game of golf is "cryed downe" as interfering with archery—both being denounced as "unproffitable sportes."† Curling is not so ancient as these; and, if it did exist as an amusement in the fifteenth century, it never came under the ban of Parliament. Curlers need not be sorry to find that their game is later in the field. Archery was a

---

"To the ice of Loch Tankard our buirdly braw callans
    First bare the big whin-stane, and marked out the tee,
Syne drew the dread hog-score, the hack and the circle
    Around which our fathers *oft sported wi' glee.*

"And ilk year sin syne in the dark dreary winter,
    When the snell blasts o' Boreas begin first to bite,
Wi' loud roaring noise round the circles of Loda
    We bend, but in sport *at the stone of his might.*

"While our stones loudly rattle we are ready for battle,
    If the foe dare to try the dread force of our might."

The words in italics are repeated as the song is sung to the air of *Spanking Jack. Gaitfel* is the highest mountain in the Isle of Arran. *Loch Tankard* is the ancient name of Kilbirnie Loch.—*Memorabilia*, 84-85.

* *James I. Parl.* 1. cap. 17, A.D. 1424.
† "It is decreeted and ordained that the Weapon-schawinges be halden be the Lordes and Baronnes, Spiritual and Temporal, four times in the yeir. And that the Fute-ball and Golfe be utterly cryed downe, and not to be used. And that the bow-markes be maid at ilk Parish Kirk a pair of Buttes and schutting be used. . . . . And that all men that is within fiftie, and past twelve yeires, sall use schutting."—*James II. Parl.* 14. *cap.* 64 (1457).

"It is thought expedient . . . . . that the Fute-ball and Golfe be abused in time cumming."—*James III. Parl.* 6. *cap.* 44 (1471).

"It is statute and ordained that in na place of the Realme there be used Fute-ball, Golfe, or uther sik unproffitable sportes."—*James IV. Parl.* 3. c. 32 (1491).

game of war; its practice on the part of the people, by Act of Parliament, did not make it popular, and now it has almost died out. Football has not escaped connection with bloodshed and crime.* Golf and football were both, in their days of ancient popularity, "cryed downe" by the Lords, spiritual and temporal, and prohibited as interfering with the duty of the people to practise the art of national self-defence. But curling, "the child of day, of honour, and of sociality," has no antecedents like these to be ashamed of, and we ought to be proud that it has come down to us with no stain upon its character. The little loss of antiquity which some are so eager to deny, is really a gain of dignity, for which curlers ought to feel thankful. We are better without "historical references" when these are blots upon our good name.

The traditions as to the *Royal patronage* of ancient curling require a little attention. It is generally supposed that several of the Stuart kings were "keen curlers." The wish, we fear, has been father to the thought. For the sake of those monarchs, as much as for the glory of the game, we would gladly believe that they knew the virtue of the channel-stane, but our investigations scarcely permit us to do so.

James I. (1394-1437)—in whose time, it is said by some, the game of curling was introduced from Flanders—was not only an accomplished poet and musician, but he also excelled in all manly exercises—such as archery, wrestling, throwing the stone and the hammer, walking, running, and horsemanship, and "in all honest sports and solace that could enliven the spirits of his followers"† We have no

---

* The game of football was much indulged in by the Border youth, but, unfortunately, at the assemblies held for such purpose, many of their most daring exploits were planned, and crimes which might otherwise never have been perpetrated, owe their origin to the meetings of the hot-blooded Borderers for this apparently innocent amusement. The murder of Sir John Carmichael of that Ilk, Warden of the West Marches, by the Armstrongs, was agreed to at a football match at which they were present, on Sunday, June 15, 1600.—*Armstrong's History of Liddesdale, Eskdale, etc.*, Vol. I. p. 83; Douglas, Edin., 1883. *Pitcairn's Criminal Trials*, Vol. II. p. 364.

† *Bower Scotichronicon.* Bk. xvi. ch. 28, 30.

account of his prowess on the ice. "Feasting, games, tournaments, and every species of feudal revelry," marked the great occasions of his reign, and the Christmas festivities that were closed in gloom by the dark and cruel deed which deprived Scotland of one of the best of rulers "were unusually splendid."* Not a word, however, is heard of curling among all the "gamyn and gle."

As far as we are aware, no suggestion has been made that James II. or James III. knew anything of the game. Tradition is, however, determined to have it that James IV. (1472-1513) was a curler, and, no doubt, if the game had been in any degree popular in his reign, James would have been found enjoying it, in its season, as he enjoyed other popular games. That the King curled, and that he left a silver curling-stone to be played for annually by the parishes in the Carse of Gowrie as a token of his appreciation of the game, are common traditions. We can find no evidence to warrant belief in their truth. Curling was cheap, and even His Majesty may have been able to play a game free of expense when the principal implements were of nature's own making; but a silver stone as a trophy for the Carse of Gowrie curlers could not have got through the meshes of the Lord High Treasurer's net, and we find no mention of it, or of any curling outlay, alongside the items of the King's expenditure on golf, archery, and the like.† Broun, in referring to this tradition (*Memorabilia*, p. 62), speaks of the Gowrie trophy as if it were then (1830) in existence. If so, it must since have disappeared. In its absence we may be pardoned for calling it a myth; and without it we have no evidence to prove that James IV. curled anywhere else than in the imagination of Sir Richard Broun, or some early writer on the game.

In a second edition of the *Memorabilia*, this writer had in view a supposed allusion to curling in the time of James V.

---

* Tytler's *Scottish Worthies*, III. 44.
† Archery and shooting at the butts, shooting with the cross-bow, and culveryng, playing at the golf and football, not only occur continually, but in all of them the King himself appears to have been no mean proficient.—Tytler's *Scottish Worthies*, III. 342.

(1511-1542) in Pitscottie's *Cronicles of Scotland*. The chronicler, referring to some sports which were held at St Andrews in 1530, when the King received an embassy from his uncle, Henry VIII., says (II. 347-8):—

"In this yeir came an Inglisch ambassadour out of Ingland, callit lord Williame, ane bischope, and vther gentlmen to the number of thrie scoir horss, quhilkis war all able, wailled gentlmen, for all kynd of pastime, as schotting, louping, wrastling, runing, and casting of the stone. Bot they war weill assayed in all these or they went home; and that be thair awin provocatioun, and almost evir tint, quhill at the last the kingis mother favoured the Inglismen, becaus shoe was the king of Inglandis sister: and thairfoir shoe tuik ane waigeour of archerie vpoun the Inglischmanis handis, contrair the king hir sone, and any half duzoun Scottismen, aither noblmen, gentlmen, or yeamanes; that so many Inglisch men sould schott againes thame at riveris, buttis, or prick bonnett. The king, heiring of this *bonspeill* of his mother, was weill content. So thair was laid an hundreth crounes, and ane tun of wyne pandit on everie syd."

Broun's argument from the above passage is:—

"If *bonspiel* was a word applied to curling in the sixteenth century, as in the nineteenth, it carries the antiquity of the game 130 years further back than the notice of it by Gibson in his edition of *Cambden's Brittannia*."*

The word was not, however, applied to curling, as a reference to Jamieson's Dictionary, where the passage is given, might have shewn. It was applied to a match of archery, and the use of it in this connection may be handed over for consideration by those who think that the word *bonspiel*, now almost invariably applied to great curling matches, helps to prove the foreign origin of our national game. If that is all that can be advanced to prove that the "King of the Commons" was a curler, then he also must be given up. Besides, had curling been played by the Court in the time of James V., or in that of his father James IV., we should most undoubtedly have found some reference to it in the poems of Sir David Lindsay (1490-1555), one of whose duties was to arrange and superintend the Royal sports. But the good old poet says nothing about it, and it does not appear that he had found the secret,

---

* Broun had by this time (1832) evidently found that his statement on p. 10 of his book—"The earliest notice of curling is by Cambden in his *Brittannia* (published 1607)"—was incorrect. To this mistake reference is made in a later note, p. 90.

known only to curlers, of warding off the severities of winter, and making the season of frost the most delightful in the whole circle of the year, for it is thus he complains pathetically in his Prologue to the *Dreme* (1528)*:—

> "Quhar art thow May, with June thy syster schene
> Weill bordourit with dasyis of delyte ?
> And gentyll Julie, with thy mantyll grene,
> Enamilit with rosis red and quhyte /
> Now auld and cauld Januar, in dispyte,
> Reiffis from us all pastyme and plesour ;
> Allace! quhat gentyll hart may this indure?"

What curler would give "auld Januar," were it only "cauld" enough, for all the other months of the year?

Of James VI. (1567-1625) golfers may well be proud. He is their own peculiar patron, and some of their clubs are named after him. He appointed a club-maker † for himself, and a ball-maker ‡ for the nation, and did much for the "Royal and ancient game." He also has been credited with a knowledge of curling. In the year 1844, when a large company met to do honour to the worthy representative of one of the best old Jacobite families— Sir Patrick Murray Thriepland of Fingask—the president of the meeting (C. Robertson), in proposing the health of the Prince of Wales—then a boy little over two years of age—thus forcibly commended to His Royal Highness's tutors the example of James VI.:—

"He [the Prince] has scarcely begun his education, but you will all agree with me in maintaining that if, in the progress of that education, he is not made a 'keen, keen curler'—if he is not thoroughly initiated into all the mysteries of that health-restoring, strength-renovating, nerve-bracing, blue-devil-expelling, incomparable game of curling—his education will be entirely bungled and neglected. I think that the Royal Grand Club should take that subject into its earliest and most serious consideration. We would all deprecate Royal degeneracy. His ancestors were distinguished for the countenance they gave to the manly and ennobling exercises and pastimes peculiar to Scotland. It is true that some of them—such as James III., James IV., and James V.—for some time discountenanced some of the amusements, for the purpose of encouraging the practice of archery when the country was at war ; but James VI. rose in all the glory of curling, as well as golfing, grandeur, and greatness ; he was not only a distinguished golfer, but a

---

* Laing's Edition of *Lindsay*. 2 vols., 1871. I. 7.
† William Mayne, 1603.   ‡ James Melvill, 1618.

'keen, keen curler.' He knew how to keep his own side of the rink, to sweep the rink, his neighbour's stone from the score to the tee, his adversary's past it. Let the young Prince go and do likewise."

Most excellent advice! Every curler hopes that the time may come when the education of our princes shall include their initiation into the mysteries of curling, and when no monarch who cannot "gie the curler's grip" shall be allowed to ascend the throne. Scotland ought to insist on this, in these days when national wrongs are all being righted. It would be well, however, not to rest our demand on the example of James VI., put forward with true Jacobite feeling at the Feast of Fingask. There may be poetry in the statement, but there are no historical facts to support it.

"Henry Darnley," says Broun,* "during the severe winter he was forced to spend at Peebles, was much employed in curling, chiefly on a meadow—now, we understand, part of the glebe."

This is the last tradition of the Royal patronage of ancient curling (if we may include the silly young lord in our list, because of his unfortunate marriage). There is such a circumstantial air about it that there may perhaps be more in it than in some of the other traditions. By those who had no good to report of Queen Mary, it was said that, a few days after Darnley's murder, she "was seen playing Golf and Pallmall in the fields beside Seton." † That her husband had been a curler, and—like many curling husbands—neglectful of his spouse during the frost, may have been the fair widow's excuse for such conduct. Let all curlers be warned! But Darnley's curling is perhaps more mythical than Queen Mary's golf; and we have no proof to shew that Peebles was at the play as far back as 1565, though the roaring game has been known and practised in that ancient town for a long time.

Curlers are, of all men, most loyal. The first and last lesson on the rink is obedience to the "ruling monarch," and such training makes them obedient to the powers that

---

* *Memorabilia*, p. 62.
† *Inventories of Mary Queen of Scots.* Pref. p. 70. 1863.

be. They are proud of the Royal patronage now extended to the game; but it will be as well for them to abandon those doubtful traditions as to the kingly countenance given to curling by the Stuarts. Curling owes nothing, as far as we can see, to any Royal support given to it in its infancy. That many of the gentry were keen curlers in the early days of the game is abundantly evident from our present chapter. In curling they were, however, following their cottars rather than their kings, for curling at the first was the game of the poor: it cost little or nothing. Golf, on the other hand, was expensive; it was the game of the rich.* Let us only hope that while golf has been so cheapened by the use of guttapercha, that it is spreading far and wide, curling is not, by expensive ponds and exclusive clubs, getting beyond the reach of the poorer classes. If this shall ever be the case then the glory shall have departed from the game, for it shall have lost the grand power it now possesses of uniting in the closest brotherhood the different classes of the community.

Between the years 1600 and 1700, we have here and there references to curling-stones, and to persons who were curlers, but no account of the game.

When we do come to find from historical and poetical allusions, that curling existed in the seventeenth century, we have to be content with small mercies. The references are like angels' visits, "short and far between." Dissertations, songs, and even sermons, on the subject are in these days "as plentiful as blackberries," and their authors, however sanguine, do not expect more than a passing notice for their productions; but those precious little blinks that show us—though but dimly—our forefathers on the curling-rink must not be so lightly esteemed. They are valuable because they are so ancient and so rare. So far as we can

---

* James VI., in giving James Melvill the monopoly of ball-making, stipulated "that the said patentaris exceed not the pryce of four schillingis money of this realm." It is remarkable to find that so expensive a game was so popular, even among the poorer classes, in ancient times.

judge, the earliest reference to curling is to be found in a "quaint and curious" work, which was written in 1620, and published eighteen years later, entitled *The Muses Threnodie, or, Mirthfull Mournings, on the death of Master Gall. Containing varietie of pleasant poeticall descriptions, morall instructions, historical narrations, and divine observations, with the most remarkable antiquities of Scotland, especially at Perth. By Mr H. Adamson. Printed at Edinburgh in King James Colleg̣e, by George Anderson, 1638.* This poem is an old Scottish *In Memoriam*, differing in more ways than in the exuberant verbosity of its title from that of Tennyson. In our laureate's long lament over the loss of his friend Arthur Henry Hallam, we have a poetical account of modern ideas in religion and philosophy. In Henry Adamson's *Threnodie* over the death of his friend James Gall, we have a history of Perth more practical than poetical. The earlier is to the later work "as moonlight unto sunlight, and as water unto wine," but the similarity of their mode of sorrowing associates the two in one's mind.

When Henry Adamson dedicated his *Recreations* to his native town of Perth and its civic rulers in the year 1637, he styles himself "*Student in Divine, and Humane Learning.*" This, at the age of 56, was a modest estimate of his position, though it should never be too late for any one to use the designation. Modesty, however, does not altogether explain its use by the poet. He was destined for the ministry, and was a good classical scholar as his work shews, but he got no further than the office of *Reader* in the kirk of Perth. From this office he seems to have been suspended for a time, owing to an unfortunate love-affair. By his future conduct he was able, however, to redeem his reputation,

* An edition of this work, with valuable notes by James Cant, was published at Perth in 1774. The main portion of the poem is also to be found in *Perth: its Annals and its Archives*, by David Peacock. Richardson, Perth, 1849.

The celebrated Drummond of Hawthornden was an intimate friend of Henry Adamson's, and in 1636 he urged the publication of the poem in a letter to the author, in which he says:—"These papers . . . . appear unto me as *Alcibiadis Sileni*, which ridiculously look with the faces of Sphinges, Chimæras, Centaurs, on their outsides; but inwardlie containe rare artifice, and rich jewels of all sorts for the delight and weal of man."

and when he died in 1637—a year before his poem was published—his loss was deeply lamented by his friends, who all "held him in high esteem for his wit, learning, and amenity of manners and disposition." George Ruthven (1546-1638), physician and surgeon in Perth (a relative of the Earl of Gowrie, who was murdered there in 1600 for alleged treason), was one of Adamson's dearest friends. He seems to have been a prototype of Captain Grose, with "a fouth o' auld nick-nackets," which he called his *Gabions*, some useful, some ornamental, and all inseparable from his personality. James Gall (1595(?)-1620), the friend of both, was a merchant in the town, well-connected—like Adamson—an accomplished scholar, and a pleasant companion. He shared the fate of those who are beloved by the gods, and died of consumption at an early age, though his dear old friend the physician tried all he could to save him, by the special skill of *Apollonian arts*, collecting herbs on Kinnoull and Moredun hills, and administering them to his patient without any good result. It was a "doleful day" to Adamson and Ruthven when they lost James Gall. The *Muses Threnodie* is their united lamentation over his death, but Ruthven is made to appear as chief mourner, and, of course, his *Gabions* must share his grief.

"Of Master George Ruthven the teares and mournings,
Amids the giddie course of Fortunes turnings,
Upon his dear friends death, Master James Gall,
Where his rare ornaments bear a part, and wretched Gabions all."

This is the superscription of the chief poem which, as we have noticed, develops into a rhyming account of Perth—the story being interrupted now and then by the old doctor's wail—

"Gall, sweetest Gall, what ailed thee to die?"

As the gabions are so important, our poet, however, before entering on the larger theme, devotes a brief introductory poem to a description of them. It is "The Inventarie of the *Gabions, in* M. George, *his Cabinet*,"* and as we read the

---

* Adamson's work is generally called *Gall's Gabions*, but this is a misnomer for *Ruthven's Gabions*. "The curiosities of all kinds with which Ruthven's closet was stocked he called his gabions, a quaint word peculiar to himself."—*Cant.*

list, which seems to be collected from all parts of heaven, earth, and elsewhere, we come upon the following :—

> "His cougs, his dishes, and his caps,
> A Totum, and some bairnes taps ;
> A gadareilie, and a whisle,
> A trumpe, an Abercorne mussell,
> His hats, his hoods, his bels, his bones,
> His allay bowles, and *curling-stones*,
> The sacred games to celebrat,
> Which to the Gods are consecrat."*

When Ruthven addresses himself to his task, he calls upon his gabions to help him "to mone;" and when he enters his closet and shuts the door, he singles out *three* from among all the others as specially fitted to give him "dolefull comfort" while he sits and echoes their lamentations.

Bowes.
> "Now first my *Bowes* begin this dolefull song,
> No more with clangors let your shafts be flung
> In fields abroad, but in my cabine stay,
> And help me for to mourn till dying day.
> With dust and cobwebs cover all your heads,
> And take you to your matins and your beads,
> *A requiem* sing unto that sweetest soul,
> Which shines now, sancted, above either pole.

Clubs.
> And yee my *Clubs*, you must no more prepare
> To make your bals flee whistling in the aire,
> But hing your heads, and bow your crooked crags,
> And dresse you all in sackcloth and in rags,
> No more to see the Sun, nor fertile fields,
> But closely keep you mourning in your bields,
> And for your part the trible to you take,
> And when you cry make all your crags to crake,
> And shiver when you sing alace for *Gall!*
> Ah if our mourning might thee now recall !

Curling Stones.
> And yee my *Loadstones* of *Lidnochian* lakes,†
> Collected from the loughs, where watrie snakes
> Do much abound, take unto you a part,
> And mourn for *Gall*, who lov'd you with his heart :
> In this sad dump and melancholick mood
> The *Burdown* yee must bear, not on the flood,

In *Harper's Magazine* (April 1889) we notice an account of *Gabions of Abbotsford*, the word having been applied by Sir Walter Scott to "curiosities of small intrinsic value, whether rare books, antiquities, or small articles of the fine or useful arts."

* Adamson's poem, as originally printed, consists of xx. and 87 pages, the xx. being devoted to the "Inventarie," and not numbered. This quotation is from page x. ; that which follows is from pp. 2 and 3.

† "Lednoch is situated about four computed miles north from Perth, on the banks of Almond River ; about this place the best curling-stones were found. The gentlemen of Perth, fond of this athletic winter diversion on the frozen river, sent and brought from Lednoch their curling-stones."—*Cant's Note* (1774).

F

> Or frosen watrie plaines, but let your tuning
> Come help me for to weep by mournfull cruning.
> And yee, the rest, my *Gabions* lesse and more
> Of noble kinde, come help me for to roare,
> And of my wofull weeping take a part,
> Help to declare the dolour of mine heart.
> How can I choose but mourn? when I think on
> Our games Olympike-like, in times agone."

Three games were thus popular with those three ancient worthies of Perth, who were *cronies* there in the beginning of the seventeenth century. Curling is mentioned last of the three, but it may not have been least in their estimation. Owing to its brief and fickle season compared with the unlimited time given for the enjoyment of the others, it would naturally fall to be mentioned last. It is interesting to find the *loadstones* or kuting-stones from the Lake of Lednoch so far *ben* at this early period. Ruthven evidently kept a selection in the closet for himself and his friends, and carefully protected them till John Frost called forth the cronies and their loadstones to the "frosen watrie plaines." Gall loved the ice-gabions with his whole heart like a true curler, and Adamson's affection for them can easily be read between the lines of his poem. George Ruthven may be singled out from the trio as the most ancient curler of whom we have any record. He was ninety-two years of age when the *Muses Threnodie* was published. He was already an old man of seventy-four when Adamson made him and his "Loadstones of Lidnochian lakes" mourn over the death of Gall in 1620. He remembered John Knox's visit to Perth in 1559, and the appearance of Saint Johnstown* before the rabble had destroyed its many noble ecclesiastical buildings†—

> "then all our quires
> And convents richly stood . . . . . .
> Most sumptuously adorn'd with steples, bels,
> Church ornaments, and what belongeth else." ‡

---

* The name of Perth in the days of Popery, when it was supposed to be under the protection of John the Baptist.

† Though Knox's preaching and teaching were made the occasion of the demolition of so many beautiful structures at Perth and elsewhere, the Reformer himself condemned such deplorable conduct as the work not of "thame that war ernest professours, bot of the rascall multitude."—*Knox's Historie*, p. 128. Edinburgh, 1732.

‡ *Threnodie*, p. 53.

There were brave men before Agamemnon, and no doubt
there were heroes on the "watrie plaines" before George
Ruthven, but to him let curlers doff their Tam o' Shanters
as the first of the brotherhood, until some older hero shall
dispute his claim to the honour. Perth has much to be
proud of in the part she has played in the history of our
country. It is not the least of her distinctions that three
hundred years ago George Ruthven taught her citizens,
both by precept and example, what neither the sons of
Æsculapius nor their patients yet fully understand, how
much curling and such healthy recreations can do to make
men cheerful workers and "jolly good fellows;" and
how the "grassy links" and the "frosen watrie plaines"
must be visited by us with our gabions if we are to do any
good in the world and attain to a venerable old age.*

The names of two divines follow that of the Perth
doctor in the early references to curling. This will not
surprise curlers, who are aware of the weakness of the
"cloth." "Frae Maidenkirk to John o' Groat's," says an
old proverb, "nae curlers like the clergy." Their keenness
seems to be a matter of apostolical succession, and that of
a kind which does not cause strife, but which unites them in
brotherhood. It seems to have done this from the very
first, for at the head of the long line of clerical curlers we
find an Episcopalian bishop and a Covenanting minister—

"The lawn-robed Prelate and plain Presbyter
Erewhile that stood apart"

shaking hands on the ice, which bridges over the great
religious gulf that lies between them. Henry Adamson's
volume, with its reference to Ruthven and his curling
friends, was published in 1638. This was a memorable
year in the see-saw conflict between Prelacy and Presbytery
which so long kept the country in misery. The Presbyterians,
in the famous Assembly which then met at Glasgow, under
the guidance of Alexander Henderson, set the King, Charles I.,

---

* In case the Fair City should ever think of making itself fairer by a
statue in Ailsa of Ruthven, it may be of advantage to state that "M.
George was a bonnie little man."—*P. Threnodie*, p. 26.

and the Marquis of Hamilton, His Majesty's Commissioner, at defiance, and determined to make a clean sweep of the bishops. Instead, however, of sweeping them away because they were bishops, the Assembly put them to mock trial upon charges that in most cases affected their moral character. The proceedings were all faithfully recorded at the time by Robert Baillie (1599-1662), minister of Kilwinning, a member of the House. In his *Letters**
we read, under date 11th December 1638:—

"Orkney's process came first before us: he was *a curler on the ice on the Sabbath day*: a setter of tacks to his sones and grandsones for the prejudice of the Church: he oversaw adulterie, slighted charming, neglected preaching and doing of any good there; held portions of ministers' stipends for building his cathedrall."

Not a good account this of a bishop or of any other man, but it must be taken with a grain of salt. George Grahame,† for such was "Orkney's" other name, does not give a very good impression of himself in his Vicar-of-Bray-like willingness to renounce his Episcopacy that he might retain his property. But he was not so bad as his neighbours, for the charges against him were light compared with many that were preferred against other prelates in that Assembly. It sounds strange to hear of a bishop curling on the ice on the Sabbath day, but, even if the charge had been true, it did not follow that "Orkney" had a double dose of original sin. The rigid observance of the day of rest, which has been such a strong feature of Scotland since that time (though happily modified of late),

---

* *Letters and Journals containing an Impartial Account of Public Transactions, Civil, Ecclesiastical, and Military, in England and Scotland, from the beginning of the Civil Wars in 1637 to the year 1662.* These were first published in 1775. Laing's edition, from which we quote (Vol. I. pp. 163-164) was published in 3 vols., 1841-42. Buckle (*Miscellaneous and Posthumous Works*, II. 241) calls Baillie "the most learned and one of the most moderate of the Presbyterian clergy," and this seems a just account. In 1661 Baillie was elected Principal of Glasgow University.

† George Grahame, A.M., translated from See of Dunblane to Orkney 1615. Member of Court of High Commission, 1615, 1619, 1634. He voted in Parliament 4th August 1621, for confirming the five articles of Perth; was deposed by the General Assembly 11th December 1638, and disclaimed Episcopal government 11th February following, prudently preserving his estate of Gorthie and other property. Died between 1644 and 1647. . . . From the bishop are descended the families of Blair-Drummond, Methven, and Watt of Skaill.—Dr Hew Scott's *Fasti Eccles. Scot.*, 1870. V. 458.

was only beginning then to show its horns. It was an importation of English Puritanism, and not known to Knox and the early reformers. The day was more of a festival than a fast, and after attending church people were free to amuse themselves. The bishops shared this freedom,* and Grahame on some stray visit to his former See of Dunblane, where the game had even then been long known, as the old stone of "1551" testifies, may have had a fling with some of his friends on a Sabbath afternoon, without losing their respect or his own peace of conscience. To the "soft impeachment" brought against him we should suppose a good many members of that stern Assembly might have pled guilty. Most likely "the lads frae Kilwinnin wad send the stanes spinnin" even in those times, for curling reputations are not made in a day, and if Robert Baillie was the good minister we take him to have been, he would himself be a curler, and charitably disposed to this curling prelate. We shall suppose, for the sake both of the Assembly and of the bishops, that the charge was departed from as not heinous, rather than from want of proof. At any rate it came to nothing.

William Guthrie of Pitforthy (1620-1665) is one of the most honoured in the list of our Scottish worthies. Covenanting ministers are generally supposed to have been grim, sour, narrow, and totally opposed to worldly recreations and amusements. The description does not apply to Guthrie. He was a devoted pastor, giving up his paternal estate to a younger brother, that he might more freely devote himself to his work. He was a successful and able preacher, whom people flocked from great distances to hear, and so beloved by the people of Fenwick, of which parish he was the first minister, that

---

* "They had not that respect for the sanctity of the Sabbath which has always been characteristic of Presbyterian Scotland. They aped the greater laxity of Episcopal England. They saw no evil in a ride on horseback, or a hand at whist, on the Sabbath; *the Bishop of Orkney indulged in curling*, and the minister of Glassford encouraged his parishioners to dance and play at the football when the sermon was done."—Cunningham's *Church History* (1859), Vol. II. chap. iii. p. 104.

"They turned the corn-field of his glebe to a little town: every one building a house for his family upon it, that they might live under the drop of his ministry."

(Would that all glebes were so populated in these degenerate glebe-feuing times!) But Guthrie was also fond of all manly exercises and amusements, and these he made subservient to the nobler ends of his ministry.

"He made them," says his biographer,* "the occasions of familiarizing his people to him, and introducing himself to their affections; and, in the disguise of a sportsman he gained some to a religious life, whom he could have little influence upon in a minister's gown; of which there happened several memorable examples."

That Guthrie included curling among his athletic accomplishments is well attested by the veritable kuting-stone which he used, and which is still preserved at Craufurdland Castle. This curious potato-like specimen we have sketched at p. 36, and it will always be looked upon as one of the most interesting relics of ancient curling. Later on in the *Memoir* from which we have quoted it is said (p. xxv.):—

"He used the innocent recreations and exercises which then prevailed, fishing, fowling, and *playing upon the ice*, which at the same time contributed to preserve a vigorous health, and while in frequent conversation with the best of the neighbouring gentry, as these occasions gave him access, to bear in upon them reproofs and instructions with an inoffensive familiarity."

The popularity of this old curling Covenanter, not only with the poor, but with the rich, is shewn by the fact that he was allowed to remain in Fenwick, at the urgent entreaty of "some of the greatest in the kingdom," long after his brethren had been driven from their parishes, but he had at last to turn out by the relentless order of the Archbishop of Glasgow. His people would have fought for him, but like a Christian and a curler, he counselled peace and submission to fate; and when the soldiers came upon the scene, he "called for a glass of ale, and craving a blessing himself, drank to the commander." Within a year after he died. Let his memory live for ever among us, for a worthier than he never lifted the channel-stane; and

---

* Dunlop, in Memoir prefixed to Guthrie's work, *The Christian's Great Interest*. Glasgow, 1755, p. xii.

from William Guthrie may many in this and coming generations learn how to sweeten their religion by the "innocent recreation" of "playing upon the ice."

The next brief reference to curling in the seventeenth century gives us a glimpse of some lairds enjoying the game together in the Border district in the year 1684. It is found in Fountainhall's *Decisions*,* under date December 30, 1684:—

"A party of the forces having been sent out to apprehend Sir William Scot of Harden, younger, because Tarras and Philiphaugh deponed that they communicated remotely their design to him, as a man of good fortune; and one William Scott in Langhope, getting notice of their coming, by the cadgers or others, he went and acquainted Harden with it, as *he was playing at the Curling with Riddel of Haining, and others;* who instantly pretending there were some friends at his house, left them and fled. Haining having related this, the said William Scot, and James Scot of Thirlstone, old Harden's brother, are brought in this day to Edinburgh. Thirlstone is liberate, as finding nothing to say to him, but William is put in the irons, because he declined to tell who gave him advertisement of the party's coming."

Curling lairds had thus their share of troubles in these weary times as well as the curling clergy. Scot of Harden would relish his Hogmanay "in the irons" as little as Grahame and Guthrie did their deposition. Unlike his successor *Beardie* (the great-great-grandfather of Sir Walter Scott), who is said to have taken a vow never to shave his beard till the exiled family of Stuart was restored, and who lost his all in the Jacobite cause, Sir William Scot, the curler of the seventeenth century, seems to have been a supporter of the Earl of Argyll in his rebellion against Charles II. Sir John Riddell of Haining was also disaffected, but both appear to have got remission after James VI. ascended the throne. Very soon after this and we come to the hog-line of Scottish history—the Revolution of 1688, to which all these troubles of the seventeenth century

---

* *The Decisions of the Lords of Council and Session, from June 6, 1678, to July 30, 1712, collected by the Honourable Sir John Lauder of Fountainhall, one of the Senators of the College of Justice,* Edinburgh, 1759; Vol. I. p. 328. Lauder was counsel for the Earl of Argyll at his trial in 1681, and a zealous supporter of the Protestant religion. He was appointed Lord of Session (Lord Fountainhall) after the Revolution.

led—and then there opens up a brighter era for curlers, and for those who did not curl. Those ancient worthies, who in the dark days cultivated the curling art under difficulties now unknown to us—and who faithfully upheld the cause of curling till the day of freedom, peace, and brotherhood saw its recognition as a national game—will ever deserve honour from succeeding generations of curlers; and none, we are sure, will grudge the little space we have devoted to their memory.

In the same year in which allusion is thus made to curling by Lord Fountainhall, we find a reference to the stone used in the game, by Sir Robert Sibbald, M.D. (1639-1722), in his *Scotia Illustrata Sive Prodromus Historiæ Naturalis*, published at Edinburgh in 1684. In Part II. Book IV. Cap. III., p. 46, under the heading *De Marmoribus*, there occurs the following in a list of different kinds of stone or marble to be found in Scotland[*]:—

"Lapis niger, quo super Glaciem luditur, nostratibus *a Curling stone*."

The last reference of the seventeenth century which falls to be noticed is found in an interesting and now very rare little work, published by John Reid, Edinburgh, in 1693, and entitled—"*A Description of the Isles of Orkney, by Master James Wallace, late Minister of Kirkwall. Published after his death by his son.*" At pp. 9-10[†] it is said—

"To the East of the Mainland lyes Copinsha, a little isle but very conspicuous to seamen, in which and in severell other places of this Countrey are to be found in great plentie excellent stones for the game called Curling."

In his *Account of the Game of Curling* (p. 23), Ramsay gave this statement from Wallace's work as from Camden's *Brittannia*, which was published as far back as 1607, and up

---

[*] It is not unlikely that this refers to the stone noticed by Wallace in his work on Orkney, the reference to which comes next on our list. Wallace's work was dedicated "To the much-honoured Sir Robert Sibbald of Kipps, M.D.," etc., and in the dedication Wallace's son says, "It was in compliance with your desire (when you were composing your *Atlas*) that my father made this description, to give you an account of that countrey."

[†] In the excellent reprint of this work, edited with notes by Dr Small, and published by Brown, Edinburgh, in 1883. *V*. Chap. I. p. 11.

till the year 1840 * it was regarded by all writers on curling as the very earliest historical reference to the game. This mistake seems to have arisen from the fact that in 1695 an edition of Camden was published by Bishop Gibson (Queen's College, Oxford), in which the statement occurs under "Additions to the Orcades" (p. 1076), after the following explanation by the bishop (p. 1073) :—

"The isles of Orkney are generally so little known, and yet withal so lightly touched upon by our author [Camden], that the curious must needs be well pleased to see a further description of them. Mr James Wallace is our authority—a person very well versed in antiquities, and particularly in such as belong to those parts, where his station gave him an opportunity of informing himself more exactly."

Camden himself had no notice of the curling-stones of Copinsha, and their testimony to the game has therefore to remain in the background as belonging to the close of the century. Mr Wallace does not tell us how far the "great plentie" availed to supply curlers in these early times, when they did not think of rounding or polishing the stones; but as doubts have been thrown upon the fitness of such sea-boulders as were found at Copinsha, for use on the ice,†

---

* Dr Walker-Arnott of Arlary was the first to point out this mistake, in a communication published by him in the *Annual* of 1840, though he also makes a mistake in giving 1675 as the date of Gibson's translation of Camden, instead of 1695. In the *Annual* of 1842 a Historical Sketch, drawn up at the instance of the Committee of the Grand Club, appeared, and in this—notwithstanding Dr Arnott's note—the old error is repeated (Ramsay, at the Annual Dinner in 1844, also repeats the statement as to the mention of the game by Camden in 1607). Dr Arnott complained to the Committee, and an investigation into the subject was made. The Report of the investigation is found in the *Annual* of 1847, signed by Professor Ferguson, and is decisive as proving that Camden never mentioned the subject, but that, as noted above, the passage was taken from Wallace's work, and inserted by Gibson in his folio edition of Camden (1695), p. 1076. This incident in its early history testifies to the usefulness of the Royal Club as a Court of Appeal on all matters of interest to curlers.

In *The Channelstane*, Ser. III. pp. 58-62, Captain Macnair has also very clearly pointed out the error regarding Camden.

† In the minutes of the Clunie Curling Club, under date 5th Jan. 1830, we find that in recognition of their kindness in presenting him with a "fluted kettle," Principal Baird, had presented the members with a pair of the "Copinsha stones," to be played for as a prize. In doing so he writes (Ap. 5, 1829)—

"A book printed 150 years ago, says that the best curling-stones were to be got at Copinsha, an island in Orkney. I passed near it last summer on a calm day, and sent a boat on shore for fourteen suitable blocks. They were brought on board accordingly, and were landed here. From two of the best blocks I have got a pair of curling-stones (and they are very we are not warranted in supposing that the Isle of Copinsha was the Ailsa Craig of ancient curling, or that supplies were forwarded from thence, to any great extent, to curlers in the South. Wallace's statement may, however, be held to prove that the game was known as far north as Orkney in the end of the seventeenth century.

> *Between 1700 and 1800 the literary references to curling shew that it was generally practised in Scotland. Several accounts of the game and of interesting bonspiels are given; curling societies are formed; and curling is by the end of the century entitled to be regarded as the great national winter game.*

Ramsay, writing in 1811,* says:—

"At Edinburgh, where curlers are collected from all the counties of Scotland, this amusement has been long enjoyed. And in so great repute was it towards the beginning of the last century, that the magistrates are said to have gone to it and returned in a body, with a band of music before them, playing tunes adapted to the occasion. Then it was practised chiefly on the North Loch, before it was drained, and at Canonmills."

We find this statement repeated in all succeeding accounts of the game, and it is highly creditable to the civic dignitaries of the period to find that they gave such

---

beautiful) made and handled. I shall beg the club to accept of them as a present from me to be competed for on the ice, and to become the prize of the best player."

How it fared with these prize stones in the Clunie Club—whether they were *useful* as they were *beautiful*, we do not discover, but the notices that here follow are not in their favour.

"We also saw lately a pair of curling-stones, belonging to Principal Baird, which he brought from the Isle of Copinsha, interesting to curlers as being associated with the first historical notice of the game. Camden is mistaken, however, in calling them 'excellent'—for upon trial, according to a well-known connoisseur, they are found to be 'not worth a rap.'"—*Memor. Curl. Maben.* p. 62.

"The ancient sports and pastimes of Scotland are frequently referred to by our old historians and poets; but among these we find no notice of curling till 1607, when Camden, in his *Brittannia*, in reference to the Isle of Copinsha, as it were, incidentally alludes to the game, from the circumstance of a peculiar species of rock found in that place being, as he states, used in making stones to play the game, but which rock has since been found to be useless for any such purpose—a circumstance which satisfactorily shews that the people knew nothing about curling-stones, or of the right metal required for the foundation of a weapon of tough but friendly warfare."—*Curler's Magazine*, Dumfries, 1842, p. 6.

* *Account of the Game of Curling*, p. 26.

official patronage to such an excellent and profitable
amusement. It is a pity the old custom has ceased. A
minute search of the Town Council Records has given
us no proof that the magistrates gave such formal
countenance to the game, but we see no reason to dis-
believe the statement. Up till the time of the Reform
Bill of 1832, the Council Records, it seems, are very
meagre. Processions on the part of the Council were also
commoner in those days than they are now, and the Nor'
Loch was a popular resort of the citizens in the time of
frost. Sir Richard Broun (*Memorabilia*, p. 62) supplements
Ramsay's statement by saying that on the occasion of the
magisterial procession "the air played was *The Curlers
March*, since known by the name of *The Princess Royal*.
In *Songs for the Curling Club held at Canonmills*, to which
we shall refer later on, the first place is given to *The
Curlers March*. Tune, *Princess Royal*. The *March* is
rather ponderous, but the enthusiasm of the "curling core"
gives it considerable animation, and it cannot fail to be
interesting, as the earliest curling song we meet with. The
air *Princess Royal* may be recognised as that to which the
well-known naval song *The Arethusa* is sung. The music of
this song is generally ascribed to Shield, but as he was not
born till 1748 it is plain that this conflicts with Broun's
statement that the air is that to which the magistrates of
Edinburgh marched in the beginning of last century. The
words of *The Arethusa* fix its date as not earlier than
the end of last century, as it describes a naval encounter
with the French. We have come to the conclusion that
Shield was not the author of the tune, that he simply
adapted it as he did in other cases (for in the operas which
he wrote he was in the habit of introducing ancient or
national melodies), and that the music of *The Princess Royal*
was really the property of the curlers, and the accompani-
ment of their *March*. That it is the tune to which Broun
referred is proved by the fact that *The Curlers March* is
suitable to it, and probably to no other. Shield, as far as
we can learn, never claimed it as his. It is found in

M'Glashan's *Collection*, published in 1782. It is also in Gow's *Repository*,* published in 1802, and as Shield was then alive it is very improbable that a few years after the publication of *The Arethusa* he would have allowed Neil Gow to make use of an air composed by him, and to give it under a different name in a collection of the *Dance Music of Scotland*.† It is only an act of justice, and one for which the brotherhood ought to be grateful, that the tune should now be restored to its rightful owners, and that the alliance between *The Curlers March* and *The Princess Royal*, for a long time broken, should here be renewed. There is no difference between this version from Gow and that of Shield, except that in the latter a change of key is necessary to adapt it to the pitch of the human voice, and some slight simplification of the notes is needed to make it more suitable for singing.

THE CURLERS MARCH.

* Gow's *Repository of the Dance Music of Scotland*, Popular Edition (Book II. p. 45). Published by John Purdie, Edinburgh. Dedicated to the Duchess of Buccleuch by Neil Gow & Sons.
† In the recollection of many persons living the tune as given in Gow was often played as a country dance.

"Tho' Sol now looks shyly, and Flora is gone
  To Mother Root's lodgings, of turf, mud, and stone,
      Where they two together,
      Throughout the hard weather,
  Unsocial as Vestals, keep house quite unknown.
  Unlike are the curlers, now more social grown—
  Unlike to recluses who winter alone--
  With mutual friendship glowing, to action prone,
      Forth come they
      Brisk and gay,
  All in flocks like sons of the spray,
  Inspired by the sound of the curling-stone!

"Tho' hedges around us, and trees everywhere,
  Their hoary heads shaking o'er their arms quite bare,
      Are all in a quiver,
      As cold made them shiver.
  We curlers are sportive, and youthful our air.
  Since Pan has afforded abundance of clothes,
  And Ceres vouchsafes acquavitæ and brose,
  Who cannot very well, with the help of those,
      On ice stay
      All the day—
  Cold and care both driving away
  The name of a curler unwarily chose.

" Tho' quitting, and shaking her cold northern nest
  Of feather'd snows, where she long lay at rest ;
      Her pinions awaiting —
      Mischief meditating—
  With hostile intent comes the full-fledg'd tempest.
  To curlers determin'd their posts to maintain
  And bravely resolv'd thro' a winter campaign
  With hard fifty-pounders to answer again.

>   And to treat
>   Ev'ry threat
> With smart repulse and contempt meet ;
> Such impotent bluster seems perfectly vain !
>
> " Then sally out boldly, and form round our ring,
> Like waters in frost we together will cling,
>   To combat proud Boreas,
>   Or who else may shore us,
> Until we shall meet the return of the spring.
> Now mark the dread sound as our columns move on—
> So solemn, so awful, so martial's the tone,
> The clouds resound afar whilst the waters groan !
>   Stable rock
>   Feels our shock,
> As if stern Mars in transport spoke—
> Such the thunder and crash of the curling-stone !
>
> " Our exercise o'er, to headquarters away,
> Where old sullen Night seems young, cheerful, and gay ;
>   Full-handed approaching,
>   Her rival reproaching,
> Cries, eat, drink, laugh dead, my young brother scrub Day.
> The squint-ey'd churl now no longer is seen
> Obey the command of the sable-clad queen—
> Profusion's preceded by beef and green.
>   And the bowl,
>   Highland soul !
> Does all our cares and fears controul,
> Whilst gleefully we drink—'To all Curlers keen !' "

This ponderous *March*, as an argument in favour of the creditable custom of the civic rulers of Edinburgh in the early part of the seventeenth century, has pushed itself forward among the references now under notice. In the strict order of time, the earliest allusion of the writers of this century to curling is that of " the Laird of Romanno—a quaint physician named Pennecuik, who wrote verses," and published them in 1715.* Alexander Pennecuik, M.D. (1652-1722), was evidently—like George Ruthven, that ancient curling doctor of happy memory—a supporter of the game from a medical point of view. He prescribes it for himself and his patients in these words :—

---

* *A Geographical, Historical Description of the shire of Tweeddale. With a Miscellany and Curious Collection of Select Scotish Poems.* By *A.P. M.D. Edin. 1715.* The lines quoted are at p. 59 in *The Author's Answer to his brother J P's many Letters, disswading him from staying longer in the Country, and inviteing him to come and settle his residence in Edinburgh* (Old Reekie).

"To Curle on the Ice, does greatly please,
Being a Manly *Scotish* Exercise,
It Clears the Brains, stirrs up the Native Heat,
And gives a gallant Appetite for Meat."

There we have the praise of curling in a nutshell. "Curl," says the doctor, "and throw physic to the dogs." If Peebles was not at the play in the time of Darnley, the folks of the district evidently knew well the virtues of the game when the quaint poet-physician lived among them two centuries ago. It is to be hoped that they have not forgotten the old doctor's prescription, for it is a good one.

Allan Ramsay (1686-1758) clearly indicates that curling in his time was recognised as the popular national winter game. Allan spent his boyhood in a curling district —Craufurd Moor. When he comes to Edinburgh he makes archery his favourite amusement, and composes several songs in its honour, but in the winter season he must have found time after curling the wigs of the citizens, to have a curl with some of them on the ice. It is more than likely that the poet knew the virtues of "Whirlie" (p. 38-9), for he must often have visited Sir John Clerk at Penicuik,* when curling was being keenly carried on by the baronet and his neighbours. When he retired from the Luckenbooths in 1755, to spend his declining years in the curious octagonal mansion, which he had built on the Castle-hill, he must have heard the roar of the curling core as they played on the Nor' Loch beneath, and he was not a curler if he kept the house on such occasions. It is true we find the poet, after the magistrates have prohibited his playhouse in Carrubbers' Close, in a metrical complaint to Lord President Forbes, saying:—

"When ice and snaw o'ercleads the isle,
Wha now will think it worth their while

---

* Ramsay spent much of his time during his latter years with Sir John Clerk of Pennycuik, and Sir Alexander Dick of Prestonfield, who courted his company; because they were delighted by his facetiousness. Sir John, who admired his genius and knew his worth, erected at his family-seat of Pennycuik an obelisk to the memory of Ramsay.—*Vide Life of Allan Ramsay.* Preface to *Poems*, 2 vols. Camden, Cadell, and Davies, 1880.

> To leave their gowsty country bowers,
> For the anes blythsome Edinburgh's towers,
> Where there's no glee to give delight,
> And ward frae spleen the langsome night!
> For which they'll now have nae relief,
> But sonk at hame, and cleck mischief." *

Curling might, for all that, have been the "glee" that gave delight to day: it was the dulness of the evening that vexed the heart of honest Allan. There was then no Northern Club in the city, with the electric light turning night into day for curlers, or Ramsay might have been comforted by the curling-pond, when the theatre was denied him.

In his *Epistle to Robert Yarde of Devonshire*,† the poet pursues quite a different strain. He writes to his friend:—

> "Frae northern mountains clad with snaw,
> Where whistling winds incessant blaw,
> In time now when *the curling-stane*
> *Slides murmuring o'er the icy plain.*"

The dulness of the evenings is forgotten. With curling bonspiels, and the happy feasts of fellowship that follow them, winter in Scotland loses all its bitterness, and we can "laugh in our sleeve" at the "gowks" who think that we are in misery during the frost, or at any other time; indeed—

> "We wanted nought at a'
> To make us as content a nation
> As any is in the creation."

So it is now: so may it continue to be! Our Scottish winter is delightful when we have our Scottish winter game. Allan Ramsay was the first to celebrate the happy union, and we thank him for it.

In his poem on *Health*, dedicated to the Earl of Stair in 1724, Ramsay has a good word to say of curling, as of other manly games. Lethargus, the slothful, who "snotters, nods, and yawns" in his easy chair close by the fire, is contrasted with Hilaris, the active, whose constitution is braced by exercise, and made proof against the winter's cold:—

---

* *Gentleman's Magazine*, 1737, p. 507.
† *Poems*, Vol. II. p. 383. London, 1800.

> " Free air he dreads as his most dangerous foe,
> And trembles at the sight of ice or snow.
> The warming-pan each night glows o'er his sheets,
> Then he beneath a load of blankets sweats;
> The which, instead of shutting, opes the door,
> And lets in cold at each dilated pore—
> Thus does the sluggard health and vigour waste.
> * * * * *
> " But active Hilaris much rather loves,
> With eager stride, to trace the wilds and groves;
> To start the covey or the bounding roe,
> Or work destructive Reynard's overthrow:
> The race delights him, horses are his care,
> And a stout ambling pad his easiest chair.
> Sometimes to firm his nerves, he'll plunge the deep,
> And with expanded arms the billows sweep:
> Then on the links, or in the estler * walls,
> He drives the gowff or strikes the tennis-balls.
> *From ice with pleasure he can brush the snow,*
> *And run rejoicing with his curling throw;*
> Or send the whizzing arrow from the string—
> A manly game, which by itself I sing.
> Thus cheerfully he'll walk, ride, dance, or game,
> Nor mind the northern blast or southern flame.
> East winds may blow, and sudden fogs may fall,
> But his hale constitution's proof to all.
> He knows no change of weather by a corn,
> Nor minds the black, the blue, or ruddy morn."

The poet's ideal of a healthy life is not, however, complete. " Bodily exercise profiteth little " without the culture of the mind, and so he wisely adds:—

> " Here let no youth, extravagantly given,
> Who values neither gold, nor health, nor heaven,
> Think that our song encourages the crime
> Of setting deep, or wasting too much time
> On furious game, which makes the passions boil,
> And the fair mean of health a weak'ning toil,
> By violence excessive, or the pain
> Which ruin'd losers ever must sustain.
>
> " Our Hilaris despises wealth so won,
> Nor does he love to be himself undone;
> But from his sport can with a smile retire,
> And warm his genius at Apollo's fire;
> Find useful learning in the inspired strains,
> And bless the generous poet for his pains.
> Thus he by lit'rature and exercise
> Improves his soul, and wards off each disease."

This complimentary reference by Ramsay to the beneficial effect of the curling throw occurs at the close of the first

---
* Ashler.

quarter of the century. It is close upon the beginning of the last quarter before we find any other allusion to the game in our literature. Then, as we have stated, curling was fairly installed as our Scottish national winter game, and ever since its progress has been remarkable. This long interval of silence does not, however, imply that the amusement was neglected. We know that it was not. It was a transition period in which the rough block was gradually discarded, and the round stone brought into use. No mention is made of it in the reign of George II. (1727–1760), but it must be remembered that at that time the country was still disturbed by "civil disorder, and political disaffections and antagonisms." With the final crushing of the Jacobite Rebellion at Culloden, in 1746, the condition of the country admits of the development of the game, which above all others is symbolic of brotherhood, prosperity, and peace. The second and third quarters of the eighteenth century may therefore be regarded as important in the history of curling, though we hear so little of it at that time. John Frost seems to have done all he could to advance the game, if we are to believe Andrew Crauford's communication to Dr Cairnie,* about a remarkable visitation of His Majesty at Lochwinnoch and elsewhere.

"There was an extraordinary and tedious frost in 1745 or 1746. The inhabitants of the south side of the Loch walked over the ice to the kirk on thirteen Sundays successively. The wells, fountains and burns were dried up by hard frost. The people suffered great hardships. The ice was bent, and *bowed* down to the bottom, because no water entered into the Loch. The Curling ceased on account of the curve of the ice. James Buntin of Triarne, Beith Parish (son of the Laird of Ardoch, Cardross Parish, Dumbartonshire), was the father of Nicol Buntin, who lived in Beith, and whose burial happened in this remarkable frost. The attendants at this funeral had the drops from their noses frozen like *shuchles* (Anglice, *icicles*). All events, through all the parishes surrounding Beith, for many years subsequent to that frost, were dated from *Nicol Buntin's burial.*"

It makes our teeth water to read of days like these, and we may be sure that even in the most disturbed districts, curlers would find times and opportunities for indulging in

* Cairnie's *Essay*, p. 88.

their amusement. Sir Walter Scott, when he depicts the social life of this period in *Guy Mannering*, does not omit to notice that even then curling matches were common in Galloway, and the south of Scotland, in the age of Jacobites, gipsies, and smugglers. Julia Mannering, as she confides the story of her love to Matilda Marchmont, suddenly introduces us to "a small lake at some distance from Woodbourne now frozen over," and "occupied by skaters and curlers, as they call those who play a particular sort of game upon the ice"—

"The scene upon the lake was beautiful. One side of it is bordered by a steep crag, from which hung a thousand enormous icicles, all glittering in the sun; on the other side was a little wood, now exhibiting that fantastic appearance which the pine-trees present when their branches are loaded with snow. On the frozen bosom of the lake itself were a multitude of moving figures—some flitting along with the velocity of swallows, some sweeping in the most graceful circles, and others deeply interested in a less active pastime—crowding round the spot where *the inhabitants of two rival parishes contended for the prize at curling:* an honour of no small importance, if we were to judge from the anxiety expressed both by the players and bystanders."

In the next chapter Jock Jabos informs us, at the instance of Glossin, that auld Jock Stevenson was at the "cock" —*i.e.*, was skip of one of the rinks—and that "there was the finest fun among the curlers ever was seen" (though Harry Bertram was too concerned about the said Julia to pay any attention to the bonspiel). In this pleasant peep of a curling match in the middle of last century, Scott writes with the knowledge that makes his romances as valuable for historical information as they are interesting in themselves. The conditions were not yet such as permitted of curling making extensive progress; but the game was generally practised, and matches between rival barons, or between neighbouring parishes, were becoming common. As will be seen in our next chapter, a good many clubs had also by this time been formed, with the object of uniting curlers in brotherhood, and advancing the progress of the game.

When Pennant passed through Eskdale and Liddesdale— the country of Dandie Dinmont—in the year 1772, gathering information about the manners and customs of the different districts of Scotland, and "takin' notes" with a view to "prent them," he must have fallen in with some keen curlers, for it is here he remarks, "Of the sports of these parts, that of curling is a favorite."* Cattle-lifting had given way before curling, and the district was none the worse for the change.

Pennant's description (*vide* p. 56) has generally been quoted as the earliest, but this however appears to belong to an account of the game found in the *Poems*† of James Graeme (1749–1772). Graeme, who was a student of divinity, and a native of Carnwath, Lanarkshire, died of consumption at the age of 23, in the same season in which Pennant made his tour; and the poems, which were written during his University holidays, were published by his friend Dr Anderson in 1773,‡ while Pennant's work was not published till 1774. The poetical merit of this account of curling is not of the highest order, but the picture of the brawny youth tugging the old channel-stane from the side of the loch illustrates the ancient game, and the "hoary hero" fighting his battles over again after the bonspiel, is too faithful to be omitted. We therefore give this earliest account as it is found at pp. 37–39 of Graeme's volume:—

CURLING: A POEM.

" Fretted to atoms by the poignant air,
  Frigid and Hyperborean flies the snow,
In many a vortex of monades, wind-wing'd,
Hostile to naked noses, dripping oft
A crystal humour, which as oft is wip'd
From the blue lip wide-gash'd: the hanging sleeve
That covers all the wrist, uncover'd else,
The peasant's only handkerchief, I wot,
Is glaz'd with blue-brown ice. But reckless still
Of cold, or drifted snow, that might appal
The city coxcomb, arm'd with besoms, pour
The village youngsters forth, jocund and loud,

---

* For remarks relating to Eskdale, Pennant was indebted to John Maxwell, Esq. of Broomholme, and Mr Little of Langholme.—*Pennant's Tour*, Vol. II. p. 4.

† *Poems on Several Occasions.* By James Graeme. Edinburgh, 1773.

‡ Graeme's Poem on curling had also been published anonymously in Ruddiman's *Weekly Magazine.* February 1771.

And cover all the loch : With many a tug,
The pond'rous stone, that all the Summer lay
Unoccupy'd along its oozy side,
Now to the mud fast frozen, scarcely yields
The wish'd-for vict'ry to the brawny youth,
Who, braggart of his strength, a circling crowd
Has drawn around him, to avouch the feat :
Short is his triumph, fortune so decrees ;
Applause is chang'd to ridicule, at once
The loosen'd stone gives way, supine he falls,
And prints his members on the pliant snow.

The goals are marked out ; the centre each
Of a large random circle ; *distance scores*
Are drawn between, the dread of weakly arms.
Firm on his *cramp-bits* stands the steady youth,
Who leads the game : Low o'er the weighty stone
He bends incumbent, and with nicest eye
Surveys the further goal, and in his mind
Measures the distance ; careful to bestow
Just force enough ; then, balanc'd in his hand,
He flings it on direct ; it glides along
Hoarse murmuring, while, plying hard before,
Full many a besom sweeps away the snow,
Or icicle, that might obstruct its course.

But cease, my muse ! what numbers can describe
The various game ? Say, can'st thou paint the blush
Impurpled deep, that veils the stripling's cheek,
When, wand'ring wide, the stone neglects the *rank*,
And stops midway ? His opponent is glad,
Yet fears a sim'lar fate, while ev'ry mouth
Cries *off the hog*, and TINTO joins the cry.
Or could'st thou follow the experienc'd play'r
Thro' all the myst'ries of his art ? or teach
The undisciplin'd how to *wick*, to *guard*,
Or *ride full out* the stone that blocks the pass ?

The *bonspeel* oer, hungry and cold, they hie
To the next ale-house ; where the game is play'd
Again, and yet again, over the jug ;
Until some hoary hero, haply he
Whose sage direction won the doubtful day,
To his attentive juniors tedious talks
Of former times ;—of many a *bonspeel* gain'd,
Against opposing parishes ; and *shots*,
To human likelihood secure, yet storm'd :
With liquor on the table, he pourtrays
The situation of each stone. Convinc'd
Of their superior skill, all join, and hail
Their grandsires steadier, and of surer hand."

Robert Burns (1759-1796) does not say much about curling. To the everlasting regret of the brotherhood of the rink, our national bard has not dedicated any special song of praise to our national game. A *bonspiel* has not secured a place among his inimitable pictures of rural life. There is a great deal about winter in Burns: the season seems to have had a strong effect on his mind. It is not, however, the crisp frosty day—so dear to curlers, when the air is clear and the ice is keen, that delights the poet's heart: it is the wilder aspect of winter that affects him, and this because it answers to his feelings—

> "Come winter, with thine angry howl,
> And raging bend the naked tree :
> Thy gloom will soothe my cheerless soul,
> When nature all is sad like me!"

At the sound of "chill November's surly blast," he sings the dirge *Man was made to mourn*; and in the same tender strain of sympathy the "winter-night"—

> "When biting Boreas, fell and doure,
> Sharp shivers through the leafless bower,"

hears him lamenting over the sufferings of beasts and birds, and the sorrows of the poor and the oppressed. A peculiar lustre has been shed on our national game by the sympathy and charity that have always attended on it. Curlers in their winter amusement remember the needs of the suffering poor. It is therefore the more surprising to find that Burns in his tenderness of heart did not give its meed of praise to the game which so happily combines benevolence with enjoyment. Curling does not, however, pass unnoticed by our national bard. That it was the common game of winter may be inferred from the first two lines of *The Vision* (1786):—

> "The sun had clos'd the winter day,
> The curlers quat their roarin' play."

That Burns knew the game, and that he understood the value set by curlers on a good skip, may in the same way be inferred from his *Elegy on Tam Samson* (1786). Thomas was "one of the poet's Kilmarnock friends—a nursery and seedsman of good credit, a zealous sportsman, and a good fellow." He was still in the flesh when the poet, following the example of Allan Ramsay and others, when they wished to honour their friends, celebrated his virtues in an elegy. Among other virtues Samson's prowess and reputation as a curler are thus referred to—

> "When winter muffles up his cloak,
> And binds the mire like a rock;
> When to the loughs the curlers flock
>   Wi' gleesome speed,
> Wha will they station at the cock?
>   Tam Samson's dead!
>
> He was the king o' a' the core,
> To guard, or draw, or wick a bore,
> Or up the rink like Jehu roar
>   In time o' need;
> But now he lags on Death's 'hog-score'
>   Tam Samson's dead!"

In his *Thoughts on the Seasons* (pp. 157-173) published at London in 1789, David Davidson, a Kirkcudbright poet, has under *Winter* done special honour to curling. He shews a thorough knowledge of the game as it was practised in Galloway in his time, and his contribution to its early literature is perhaps the most valuable handed down to us. Among a great variety of amusements on the ice, some quite unknown in our time, in which the Gallovidians then indulged, Davidson gives curling the first place—

> "Forth to the frozen lake, on frolic keen,
> The youthfu' swains repair—A motley *throng*,
> On various sports intent, ...
> Some shoot the icy fragments.—To the goal,
> Some hurl the polish'd pebble.—Some the top,
> Fast whirling frae their thumbs, whip dext'rously—
> An' some, bold, frae the crushed bank dart on,
> String after string, the sleek well-polish'd *slide*.
> Hither, the manly *youth*, in jovial bands,
> Frae every hamlet swarm.—Swift as the wind
> Some sweep, on sounding skates, smoothly along,
> In dinsome clang, circling a thousand ways,
> Till the wide crystal pavement, bending, rairs,
> Frae shore to shore, by th' rush o' madden'd joy.
> On sledges some hurl rapidly along,
> Eager, an' turning oft' to 'scape the flaws,
> An' dang'rous chinks, the wind an' sun have made.
> But manliest of all! the vig'rous *youth*,
> In bold contention met, the channelstane,
> The bracing engine of a Scottish arm,
> To shoot wi' might an' skill.—Now, to the lake,

> At rising sun, with hopes of conquest flush'd,
> The armed heroes meet.—Frae dale to doon
> The salutation echoes—and, amain,
> The baubee toss'd, wha shall wi' ither fight,
> The cap'ring combatants the war commence—
> Hence, loud, throughout the vale, the noise is heard,
> Of thumping rocks, an' loud bravadoes' roar."

In a parody of *Chevy Chase* (pp. 160-170), there follows after this prelude an account of a bonspiel on Loch Carlingwark, near Castle Douglas, between two rival chiefs, from opposite ends of the county, Ben o' Tudor and Gordon of Kenmure, than which nothing better has ever been written in the annals of the national game.

God prosper long the hearty friends
  Of honest pleasures all ;
A mighty *curling* match once did
  At C***** w**k befal.

To hurl the channelstane wi' skill,
  Lanfloddan took his way ;
The child that's yet unborn will sing
  The curling of that day.

The champion of Ullisdale
  A broad rash aith did make,
His pleasure, near the Cam'ron isle,
  Ae winter's day to take.

Bold Ben o' Tudor sent him word
  He'd match him at the sport.
The Chief o' Ken, on hearing this,
  Did to the ice resort.

Wi' channelstanes baith glib an' strong,
  His army did advance—
Their *crampets* o' the trusty steel,
  Like bucklers broad did glance.

A band, wi' besoms, high uprear'd,
  Weel made o' broom the best,
Before them, like a moving wood
  Unto the combat press'd.

The gallant gamesters briskly mov'd,
  To meet the daring fae—
On Monday they had reach'd the lake,
  By breaking of the day.

The chieftains muster'd on the ice,
  Right eager to begin—
Their channelstanes, by special care,
  Were a' baith stout and keen.

Their rocks they hurled up the rink—
  Ilk to *bring in* his hand—
An' hill an' valley, dale an' doon,
  Rang wi' the ardent band.

Glenbuck upo' the *cockee* stood—
  His merry men drew near--
Quoth he, Bentudor promised
  This morn' to meet me here.

But if I thought he would not come—
  We'd join in social play.
With that the *leader* of the ice,
  Unto Glenbuck did say

Lo, yonder does Bentudor come—
  His men wi' crampets bright--
Twelve channelstanes, baith hard an' smooth,
  Come rolling in our sight.

All chosen rocks of Mulloch heugh,
  Fast by the tow'ring Screel—
Then tye your *crampets*, Glenbuck cries—
  Prepare ye for the speal.

And now with me, choice men of Ken,
  Your curling skill display—
For never was their *curler* yet,
  Of village or of brae,

That e'er wi' channelstane did come,
  But if he would submit
To *hand* to *nieve* I'd pledge this crag,
  I should his *winner* hit.

Bentudor, like a warrior bold,
  Came foremost o' them a'—
A besom on his shouther slung ;
  On's hans twa mittens bra'.

An' with him forth came Tullochfern ;
  An' Tom o' Broomyshaw—
Stout Robert o' Heston, Ratcliff, and
  Young John o' Fotheringhaw.

An' wi' the laird o' Cairnyhowes,
   A *curler* guid an' true,
Good Ralph o' Titherbore, an' Slacks,
   Their *marrows* there are few.

Of Fernybank needs must I speak,
   As ane of aged skill.
Simon of Shots, the nephew bold
   Of Cairny on the hill.

With brave Glenbuck came *curlers* twelve—
   All dext'rous men of Dee.
Robin o' Mains, Clim o' the Cleugh,
   An' famd Montgomery.

Gamewell the brisk, of Napplehowes,
   A valiant blade is he.
Harry o' Thorn, Gib o' the Glen,
   The stoutest o' the three.

An' the young heir of Birnyholm,
   Park, Craigs, Lamb o' the lin—
Allan of Airds, a *sweeper* good;
   An' Charley o' Lochfin.

Bentudor a Riscarrel crag,
   Twice up the ice hurl'd he,
Good sixty cloth-yards and a span,
   Saying, "so long let it be."

It pleas'd them a'—Ilk then wi' speed,
   Unto his weapon flew—
First, Allan o' Airds his whinstane rock
   Straight up the *white ice* drew.

"*A good beginning!*" cries Glenbuck—
   Slacks fidging at the sight,
Wi's bra' *blue-cap*, lent Airds a smack;
   Then roared out, "*good-night!*"

Next Robin o' Mains, a *leader* good,
   Close to the witter drew—
Ratcliff went by, an' 'cause he miss'd,
   Pronounc'd the ice untrue.

Gib o' the Glen, a noble *herd*,
   Behind the *winner* laid—
Then Fotheringhaw, a sidelin shot,
   Close to the *circle* play'd.

Montgom'ry, mettlefu', an' fain,
   A rackless stroke did draw;
But miss'd his aim, an' 'gainst the *herd*,
   Dang frae his *clint* a flaw.

With that stepp'd forward Tullochfern,
   An' (saying to hit, he'd try)
A leal shot ettled at the cock,
   Which shov'd the *winner* by.

Clim o' the Cleugh, on seeing that,
   Sten'd forth, an' frae his knee,
A slow shot drew, wi' muckle care,
   Which settled on the *tee*.

Ralph, vexed at the fruitless play,
   The cockee butted fast—
His stane being glib, to the loch-en',
   Close by the witter past.

Stout Robert o' Heston, wi' his broom,
   Came stepping up wi' might—
Quoth he, "My *Abbey-burn-fit*
   Shall win the *speal* this night."

With that brisk Gamewell, up the rink,
   His well *mill'd* rock did hurl—
Which, rubbing Ratcliff on the *cheek*,
   Around the cock did twirl.

Now stepp'd a noted gamester forth,
   Fernybank was his name—
Wha said, he would not have it told
   At C * * * * * w * * k, for shame;

That e'er the chief o' Ken should bear
   The palm of victory—
Then heezing his Kilmarnock hood,
   Unto the *cock* drew he.

The *stanes*, wi' muckle martial din,
   Rebounding frae ilk shore,
Now thick, thick, thick, each other chas'd,
   An' up the rink did roar.

They closed fast on every side—
   A *port* could scarce be found—
An' many a broken channelstane
   Lay scatter'd up an' down,

"Shew me the winner," crys Glenbuck;
   "An' a' behind stan' aff":
Then rattled up the rocking crag,
   An' ran the port wi' *life*.

Bentudor flung his bonnet by,
   An' took his stane wi' speed—
Quoth he, "my lads, the day is ours"—
   Their chance is past remead.

Syne hurlin' through the crags o' Ken,
   Wi' *inrings*, nice an' fair,
He struck the *winner* frae the cock,
   A lang claith-yard an' mair.

The speal did last frae nine forenoon,
   Till setting o' the sun—
For when the hern scraich'd to her tree,
   The combat scarce was done.

Thus did Bentudor an' Glenbuck,
   Their curling contest end.
They met baith merry i' the morn'—
   At night they parted friends.

After this spirited ballad there follows (p. 171) an account of the social gathering of the curlers in the evening, which in these early times was quite as important a part of the game as it is now.

> "The sportive *field* is o'er.—Now, friendly, all
> Conveened o'er a bowl of nect'rous juice,
> Recount the fam'd achievements o' the day—
> The song goes round.—Among the jovial sons
> O' health an' peace, true mirth is melody.
> Regardless of, or consonance or voice, the catch, the glee,
> The martial tale is sung—an' frae the mouths
> O' the concording company, applause abounds.
> The laugh, the roar, the mirthfu' story, round
> The wakefu' table spread.—The banter too,
> For eminence in curling pow'r an' skill
> Rings through the lighted dome.—Again, the hard,
> The well-contested *speal* is called up—
> The wide-spread *table* to the rink is turn'd;
> An' bowls an' bottles, implements of *war*.
> Here stands the *winner* by a bottle hid,
> Inmoveable, save by a nice *inring*—
> *There* stands the *tee*—up through the *port* he came,
> Wi' a' his might—on *this* he gently rubb'd—
> On *that* he brak an *egg*—from *that* to *this*,
> From *this* to *that*, thump, thump, amidst the thrang,
> At length the winner struck, wi' mettled smack;
> An' sent *him* birling up aboon the *fire*."

The poem finishes with this pious wish, in which every true curler will join—

> "Since jovial thus, the social sons of mirth,
> The wint'ry minutes pass—be it *my* lot,
> In some snug corner of my native land,
> Unknowing, or *servility* or *wealth*,
> Far frae the busy world, remote to dwell;
> Where, loud the sounding skate, upo' the lake,
> Re-echoes frae ilk shore—where hurling sledge,
> Upo' the icy pavement, boundeth far;
> An' where the channelstane loud roaring, makes
> The hamlet hyud depress'd wi' pensive cares,
> Forget his every trouble in his joy.
> There in some quiet retirement, would I-pass
> The Winter's gloomy days, wi' social friends
> O' sterling wit an' jest.—With them I'd join
> In a' the various scenes o' rural mirth,
> An' rural joy.—With them o' pliant soul,
> I would of Nature's boundless province sing—
> Admiring still the season's gradual change;
> An' each fair object through the varied year."

In the year 1792 there was published a small volume

entitled, *Songs for the Curling Club held at Canonmills.* To this we shall refer in our next chapter, but it comes under our notice here as the first volume dedicated to the game of curling.

In the *Statistical Account of Scotland*, which was prepared by ministers of the Church of Scotland, under the editorship of Sir John Sinclair, and which dealt with the country and the manners and amusements of the Scottish people at the close of the century (1790-1799), we have several notices of curling. These we give in their order.

CRAWFORDJOHN.—"Curling is a favourite diversion among the commonalty; and even the gentlemen sometimes join in it." Vol. vi. No. 32, p. 277. Rev. W. Miller.

MUIRKIRK.—"Their [the people's] chief amusement in winter is curling, or playing stones on smooth ice: they eagerly vie with one another who shall come nearest the mark, and one part of the parish against another, one description of men against another, one trade or occupation against another, and often one whole parish against another —earnestly contend for the *palm* which is generally all the prize; except perhaps the victors claim from the vanquished, the dinner, and bowl of toddy which, to do them justice, both commonly take together with great cordiality, and generally without any grudge at the fortune of the day, or remembrance of their late combat with one another, wisely reflecting no doubt that defeat as well as victory is the fate of war. Those accustomed to this amusement or that have acquired dexterity at the game are extremely fond of it. The amusement itself is healthy: it is innocent: it does nobody harm: let them enjoy it." Vol. vii. No. 54, p. 612. Rev. J. Sheppard.

DRYFESDALE.—"The principal diversion or amusement is curling on the ice in the winter, when sometimes scores of people assemble on the waters, and in the most keen yet friendly manner engage against one another, and usually conclude the game and day with a good dinner, drink and songs." Vol. ix. No. 28, p. 432. Rev. T. Henderson.

WAMPHRAY.—"We have but one general amusement, that of curling on the ice: and the parishioners of Wamphray take much credit to themselves for their superior skill in this engaging exercise. After the play is over it is usual to make a common hearty meal upon beef and greens, in the nearest public-house." Vol. xii. No. 41, p. 602.* Rev. W. Lingers.

BOTHWELL.—"Curling is their chief amusement in winter." Vol. xvi. No. 17, p. 314. Rev. M. Macculloch.

It is strange that these are all the notices of the game of curling in such an excellent publication as the old *Statistical Account*. We know for certain that it was

---

* Inserted in vol. xxi. at p. 441.

extensively practised in many of the parishes whose ministers are silent on the subject, and it is a matter of regret that so few references are made to it. The deficiency is a further illustration of the slowness of historians to recognise the importance of such things in parochial and national life. Now that the time has come for a new publication* setting forth the condition, socially and otherwise, more especially of our landward parishes, it is to be hoped that greater justice will be done to our national game and its influence in our rural districts.

Our endeavour in this chapter has been to give an exhaustive account of Historical and Poetical References to curling up till the close of the eighteenth century. The nineteenth century is the period of the modern game; and the references in our literature, since the publication of Ramsay's *Account* in the year 1811, would require a volume or volumes to themselves. To complete our statement we may, however, include two notices which occur previous to Ramsay's publication, and which refer to curling as practised in the end of the eighteenth and the beginning of the present century. One is from *A Winter Season*, by James Fisher, published in 1810. Additional interest is given to this description by a woodcut representing the early game as played with stones shaped like masons' mallets (*vide* p. 60). In a curious kind of blank verse prose, Fisher (though blind) thus vividly depicts the curlers at their play :—

"With tramps, and brooms, and stones, a crowd now comes, with jocund glee, the long-projected speel to play, for beef and greens, in manly sport; the rink now chosen out, and distance fixed, the tees both made, and hog-scores justly drawn, the best of three, 9 or 11 shot games; agreed upon, the dinner to decide; a piece of coin is then tossed high in air, to show which side shall first begin the sport; or not so heathenish this to know, a stone is played by one on either side, and now the keen contested curling match begins; stones roar from tee to tee the ice along—lye here; strike this; well done; guard that; well played, alternate cry those who the game direct: soon as a stone the hog-score o'er has got, and judged by those concerned to stop too short, sweep, sweep ! then's all the cry ; how then the brooms are plied to sweep it on ; but when the distant score one does not reach, 'tis hog

* This was pressed on the attention of the public some years ago, by Messrs Cochran-Patrick, .E. J. G. Mackay, and others, but nothing has yet been done.

it off with laughter much and loud, and still the healthful sport goes on, till three huzzas declare the victor side; now off they go with appetite to dine, and drink, and spend in social glee the evening all."

The following footnote to Fisher's notice of the game gives a good account of the earlier style of play :—

"For the information of those of our southern neighbours who may not be acquainted with the game of *curling*, so much practised in many parts of Scotland, it may not be amiss to observe that the tramps are made of iron to go upon the feet, something after the form of stirrup irons, with sharp prominences at the bottom to prevent the curler from sliding while engaged in play. The curling-stones are of different forms and various weights, but always uniformly flat and smooth on the bottom, with a handle of iron or wood affixed in the top: the tee is of a circular form, with a small hole cut in the middle; the rink is the distance betwixt the two tees, and is shorter or longer according as the ice will admit; the hog-score is drawn at the distance of about four or five yards from each of the tees."

The other notice of the early part of this century, with which we close our chapter, is from *British Georgics* (1809) (pp. 22-26), by James Grahame, the author of *The Sabbath*. Under *January*, the poet in elegant strains sings of the winter delights of Duddingston Loch, and then favours us with what will ever be regarded as one of the finest descriptions of the *bonspiel* * :—

"But chiefly is the power of frost displayed
Upon the lake's crystalline broad expanse,
Wherein the whole reflected hemisphere
Majestically glows, and the full sweep,
From pole to pole, of shooting star is seen:
Or when the noon-day sun illumes the scene,
And mountain hoar, tree, bush, and margin reed,
Are imaged in the deep. At such a time,
How beautiful, O Duddingston! thy smooth
And dazzling gleam, o'er which the skaiter skims
From side to side, leaning with easy bend,
And motion fleet, yet graceful: wheeling now
In many a curve fantastic; forward now,
Without apparent impulse, shooting swift,
And thridding, with unerring aim, the throng
That all around enjoy the mazy sport:

* "Though I am no friend to idleness, I am humbly of opinion that innocent recreations ought to be encouraged: that festivals, holidays, customary sports, and every institution which adds an hour of importance, or of harmless enjoyment, to the poor man's heart, ought to be religiously observed. To draw a picture of rural life, so truly and at the same time so pleasingly as to render the original an object of higher interest than it was before, is no easy task. The merit to which I lay claim is that merely of fidelity."—*Grahame, Prefix to Georgics*, pp. ii.-iii.

Every one who reads these lines will feel that the poet has done justice to his opinion, and that the merit he claims is richly deserved.

Dunedin's nymphs the while the season brave,
And, every charm enhanced,—the blooming cheek,
The eye beaming delight, the breathing lips
Like rosebuds wreathed in mist,—the nameless grace
Of beauty venturing on the slippery path,—
Heighten the joy, and make stern winter smile.
Scared from her reedy citadel, the swan,
Beneath whose breast, when summer gales blew soft,
The water-lily dipped its lovely flower,
Spreads her broad pinions mounting to the sky,
Then stretches o'er Craigmillar's ruined towers,
And seeks some lonely lake remote from man.

Now rival parishes and shrievedoms, keep,
On upland lochs, the long expected tryst *
To play their yearly bonspiel.† Aged men,
Smit with the eagerness of youth, are there,
While love of conquest lights their beamless eyes,
New-nerves their arms, and makes them young once more.

The sides when ranged, the distance meted out,
And duly traced the tees,‡ some younger hand
Begins, with throbbing heart, and far o'ershoots,
Or sideward leaves, the mark ; in vain he bends
His waist, and winds his hand, as if it still
Retained the power to guide the devious stone,
Which, onward hurling, makes the circling groupe
Quick start aside, to shun its reckless force.
But more and still more skilful arms succeed,
And near and nearer still around the tee,
This side, now that, approaches ; till at last,
Two seeming equidistant, straws or twigs
Decide as umpires 'tween contending coits.§

Keen, keener still, as life itself were staked,
Kindles the friendly strife : one points the line
To him who, poising, aims and aims again ;
Another runs and sweeps where nothing lies.
Success alternately, from side to side,
Changes ; and quick the hours un-noted fly,
Till light begins to fail, and deep below,
The player, as he stoops to lift his coit,
Sees, half incredulous, the rising moon.
But now the final, the decisive spell,
Begins ; near and more near the sounding stones,
Some winding in, some bearing straight along,
Crowd justling all around the mark, while one,
Just slightly touching, victory depends

---

* Appointment.
† A match at the game of *curling* on the ice.
‡ The marks.
§ In some parts of Scotland the stones with which curlers play are called *cooting* or *coiting stones.*

Upon the final aim : long swings the stone,
Then with full force, careering furious on,
Rattling, it strikes aside both friend and foe,
Maintains its course, and takes the victor's place.

The social meal succeeds, and social glass ;
In words the fight renewed is fought again,
While festive mirth forgets the winged hours—
Some quit betimes the scene, and find that home
Is still the place where genuine pleasure dwells."

" Now mony a club, jocose and free,
  Gi'e a' to merriment and glee;
  Wi' sang and glass, they fley the pow'r
  O' care, that wad harass the hour."
Robert Fergusson.

" Then to the inn they a' repair,
  To feast on curlers' hamely fare—
  On beef and greens and haggis rare,
  And spend the nicht wi' glee, O !

And there owre tumblers twa or three,
  Brewed o' the best o' barley bree,
  They sing and jest while moments flee,
  Around that social tee, O ! "
T. S. Aitchison.

" True feelings waken in their hearts
  And thrill frae heart to han';
  O peerless game that feeds the flame
  O' fellowship in man ! "
Rev. T. Rain.

" The Pillars o' the Bonspiel—Rivalry and Good Fellowship."
Old Toast.

CHAPTER IV.

ANCIENT CURLING SOCIETIES.

URLING—the game of rivalry and good-fellowship—has naturally made great progress by the institution of societies or clubs.* The principle of association could not readily be taken advantage of in troublous times, and it is not till the eighteenth century that we find it used for the development of the game. Societies were then formed in those districts where it had previously been popular. Curlers in such districts were prepared to appreciate the advantage of societies in promoting social fellowship and scientific skill. Experience also fitted them to frame such conditions of membership as would best secure these ends. It is with the written records of the early curling societies that we have now to deal in tracing the history of the national game.

The dividing-line which we have already drawn between ancient and modern curling, forces us also in this chapter to confine our attention to the records of such societies as

---

* The word *club* occurs very rarely in the records of last century. Excepting Dunfermline and Duddingston, the designation invariably used is *society*.

existed in the last century. Curling societies which claim to be ancient, but whose records go no further back than the present century, must not expect from us more than a passing notice. This is the only course open when we wish to tread the sure ground of history. As illustrative cases we may give Linlithgow and Lochleven, where, as we have already said, there are traces and traditions as to curling "from time immemorial." That a club existed at the former place in the last century may be gathered from a chance entry which we have discovered in the minute-book of the Dunfermline Club, where the sederunt of the annual meeting in the house of James Cupar, 2nd February, 1792, includes

"Mr John Gibson, a visiting brother from Linlithgow Club."

John Gibson and his brother members at Linlithgow do not appear to have written down their doings, and by their negligence we have lost a good deal, for curling at Linlithgow in Gibson's day must have been carried on in the light of long experience. In the case of Lochleven, the members of the Kinross Club, as faithful guardians of its curling fame, after a careful inquiry by Sheriff Skelton and a committee in 1818, decided to carry the existence of a curling society there as far back as 1668. That there was curling on Lochleven long before that need not be doubted, and that the Kinross Club deserves highest honour for the careful preservation of the traditional mysteries of the game will be apparent when these come to be considered; but the want of written records prior to the year 1818 leaves us, as in the case of Linlithgow, without that information as to the early game on Lochleven, which would here have been of the greatest interest.

On the present list of the Royal Caledonian Club we have twenty-eight affiliated clubs entitled to attention as having been formed in the eighteenth century. We give them in the order of their institution, with the counties to which they belong, as it is of importance to note the geographical area of ancient curling.

"CURLERS," PAINTED BY SIR GEORGE HARVEY, R.S.A.

See yon enthusiastic band!
  All crowding round the Tee,
With bosoms in uplifted hand,
  And faces full of glee!
And see, at further end one stoop
  With earnest noting eye—
Then follow up his roaring stone
  With eager ecstacy.

See how it nods in conscious pride!
  "They cheer it moving on—
"He's ragin' mad," one besom cries
  "No, no, she's a rare stone."
Soop—oop,—no, no,—it has it all.
  It takes their guard away—
It strikes—it cannons—wins the end—
  Hurra, hurra, hurra!

W. GRAHAM.

ANCIENT CURLING SOCIETIES. 115

Kilsyth	(Stirling)	1716.
Kirkintilloch	(Dumbarton)	1716.
Dolvine	(Perth)	1732.
Doune	(Perth)	1732.
Strathallan, Meath Moss }	(Perth)	1736.
Dunfermline	(Fife)	1738.
Muthill	(Perth)	1739.
Ardoch	(Perth)	1750.
Borestone	(Stirling)	1750.
Earlston	(Berwick) *ante*	1756.
Coupar-Angus and Kettins }	(Perth)	1772.
Saline	(Fife)	1772.
Balyarrow	(Fife)	1775.
Cupar	(Fife)	1775.
Hamilton	(Lanark)	1777.
Blairgowrie	(Perth)	1783.
Lasswade	(Midlothian)	1785.
Cambusnethan	(Lanark)	1789.
Jedburgh	(Roxburgh)	1790.
Kelso	(Roxburgh)	1790.
Bridge-of-Allan	(Stirling)	1790.
Gargunnock	(Stirling)	1790.
Douglas	(Lanark)	1792.
Cumbernauld	(Dumbarton)	1796.
Yoker	(Dumbarton)	1796.
Forfar	(Forfar)	1797.
Camelon	(Stirling)	1800.
Dundee	(Forfar)	1800.

In addition to these, the following clubs existed in the last century, though their names are not found in the list of the Royal Club:—

Govan	(Lanark)	1725.
Grahamston	(Stirling)	1740.
Canonmills (Midlothian)	*circa*	1760.
Lesmahagow	(Lanark)	1770.
Anderston	(Lanark)	1773.
Sanquhar	(Dumfries)	1774.
Wanlockhead	(Dumfries)	1777.
Grougar	(Ayr)	1781.
Muirkirk	(Ayr)	1784.
Fenwick	(Ayr)	1789.
Newliston	(Linlithgow)	1789.
Linlithgow (Linlithgow) }	*ante*	1792.
Sandholes	(Renfrew)	1795.
Duddingston	(Midlothian)	1795.

Of the forty-two societies thus enumerated, only ten possess written records of the last century, and in a few cases these do not extend back to the dates at which the societies are said to have been formed. Through the kindness of the various secretaries, all the available records have been placed in our hands, and we have perused them "at some expense of eyesight, and with no small exertion of patience." In what follows we have tried, as far as possible, to make the different minute-books speak for themselves, and tell us what they know about the manners and customs of eighteenth-century curlers and curling clubs.

MUTHILL (1739).—The honour of possessing the most ancient records falls to Muthill. It is awarded, however, with some hesitation, for the minute-book of the Muthill Society, though a neat and interesting record, is evidently not so old as the society itself. At a general meeting of the society, held in the house of John Bennet, vintner, on 14th January, 1823,* there was

"Voted to William Gentle, clerk, for books and drawing out Records and Laws of this society since its formation as contained in this book, £1 5s."

The minutes are, therefore, William Gentle's work. This is borne out by the first set of rules entered in the volume, which bears to have been revised in 1820 and 1821; but it is evident that William Gentle had documents in his hands which were written at the formation of the society, and that other parts of the volume are transcribed from these. The antiquity of the records may thus be allowed to pass. The list of members of the society, as "constitute in the year 1739," begins thus:—

	No.		£	s.	d.
"1739.	1.	The Rev. Mr William Hally, Minister, Muthill	-	-	6
	2.	Mr William Lanson, Mill of Machany		-	6
1740.	3.	{ The Rev. Mr William Erskine, Episcopal Minister, Muthill		-	6"

At first the society was not a large one, and Mr Hally seems to have been its leading spirit.† By the end of the century, however, we find that 187 members had been enrolled. A kindly custom on the part of the brethren was to allow members of other societies to "initiate" into Muthill Society for 3d., being half the annual fee of ordinary members. Since they are the most ancient regulations that have come down to us, we may here give the

"RULES AND STATUTES to be observed by the SOCIETY OF CURLERS in MUTHILL, November the 17th, 1739.

1. That each Member shall attend the Precess of any Quorum of the Society when called, unless they have a reasonable excuse, under the penalty of Six Shillings Scots.

2. That no match of curling shall be taken up with another Parish untill five of the Members of the Society be previously acquainted therewith, and those that shall be chosen to play in any such match

---

* There had been no ice in the two previous years, 1821 and 1822.

† A drawing of the stone supposed to have been used by Mr Hally is given at p. 40. The parishioners of Muthill were so opposed to Mr Hally at his ordination in 1704 that they refused to allow the Presbytery to enter the church; but he was afterwards much esteemed by them for his good qualities. He died in 1754. Dr Rankin, his able successor, informs us that "Mr Hally was a man of great physical strength, and a good wrestler as well as curler and preacher."

are not to absent themselves therefrom, under the penalty of Five Shillings Sterling, and being extruded the Society till payment.

3. That the annual election of all the officers of the Society shall be upon the first Tuesday of ——

4. That there shall be no wagers, cursing or swearing, during the time of game, under the penalty of Two Shillings Scots for each oath, and the fines for by wagers to be at the discretion of the Precess and the other members present, and the wagers in themselves void and null.

5. That every residing Member of the Society betwixt and the next annual election shall provide himself in a curling stone, to be kept in this place under the penalty of One Shilling Sterling.

6. That all the money received by the Society for the entry of new Members or Fynes be kept for the use of the Society in general.

7. That every Member shall pay yearly to the Treasurer Four Shillings Scots, for the use foresaid.

8. That after this date at taking up any matches betwixt any two parties they are only to have choice about.

9. That there shall be no addition or alteration made of the above Rules but at the yearly meetings.

And its recommended to the Society in general to provide four right leading stones to be equally divided in all matches, etc., etc., and the Committee to draw up the men for the match."

There is little information in these as to the manner of playing the game at Muthill in ancient times, and we have no record in the old minutes of any bonspiel, but sundry charges for carting stones imply that the society had frequent matches with Ardoch, Monzie, and other parishes. Under date February 7, 1789, we have this curious entry:—

"To Isabel White for whiskey for cleaning the ice, £0 1s. 8d."

How the whisky was applied to such a useful purpose the minutes do not state. At the annual meeting, December 26, 1789, it was agreed

"That every stone handed or mended at the expence of the box is common to all the brethren, or them who puts on more than one stone if they shall choose to hold it up shall have liberty to do with it as they please."

Drawings of some of these old stones may be seen at p. 46. One stone sufficed for each player, but the records state nothing about the rinks, or the numbers composing them. It is interesting to notice the prohibition of *wagering, cursing*, and *swearing* (Rule 4). Such a rule is common to most of the old societies, and it shews how jealously the early players protected the reputation of the game, and how anxious they were to exalt its position.

CANONMILLS (1760).—Ramsay, when writing his account

of curling in 1811, and referring to the tradition regarding the Town Council's patronage of the game (vide p. 91) in the beginning of last century, says:—

"Then it was practised chiefly on the North Loch, before it was drained, and at Canonmills. At which latter place a society was formed about fifty years ago, and continued to flourish a considerable time. Of late, however, it has dwindled away to nothing."

We have given illustrations (p. 64) of stones of the earlier circular type which are supposed to have belonged to this club, but no trace can be found of any written records of its transactions. Certain songs composed for the club were, however, printed in a small volume* in 1792, and as some of these appear to have been written soon after its formation, they entitle it to notice here. These songs are more interesting than dry minutes, and give us useful information as to the words in use at the game, and as to the social habits of the players.

"The Canonmills Loch," says Captain Macnair,† "on which the members of the club were wont to assemble, has long since disappeared, having been drained and built over many years ago. In his plan of the city of Edinburgh and its vicinity, published in 1837, Hunter places it in the angle formed by the junction of the roads leading down from Bellevue Crescent and Eyre Place, adjoining the ground occupied by the Gymnasium, but better known in those days as 'the Meadow.'"

This situation must have been very convenient for Edinburgh curlers when deprived of the use of the Nor' Loch for their favourite sport, and in those days of clubs, they would naturally form themselves into a company that they might more effectually enjoy the game and its attendant socialities. In many respects Canonmills was better suited than Duddingston Loch for the townsmen, and we are not surprised to find in one of the minutes of the Duddingston Club (8th December, 1824) this entry:—

"The meeting thought that a piece of ground might be obtained about Canonmills, which might be occasionally used, as more convenient for many members than Duddingston."

As regards the membership we are left to conjecture—

---

* *Songs for the Curling Club held at Canonmills.* By a Member. Edin. Printed by J. Robertson, 39 South Bridge.

† Preface to *Curling, Ye Glorious Pastime,* an excellent reprint of the *Account of Curling* by Ramsay, and the Canonmills *Songs,* in one volume, published in 1882.

we have not even the name of the author or authors of the songs; but while it existed the club could not fail to be an important one, and as the song set to the *March* of the magistrates comes first in the collection, it is probable that the patronage of the Town Council was bestowed on the Canonmills curlers. The songs are such as could not fail to be appreciated by citizens of wit and learning who inclined to unbend the bow at the curlers' feasts, and they are full of that enthusiasm which always animates the votaries of the game. The *Curlers March* is succeeded by *The Blast*, which calls upon the brethren, now that Phœbus has wandered south, to rear the "broom standard," for it is only fools that dread the wintry death of Nature: curlers smile at such fears

"As we mark our gog,
And measure off our hog,
To sport on her cold grave stone."

We are next favoured with a song in which the singer* pokes fun alike at the pride of the city and the antiquity of the national game, and it is easy to imagine the hilarious mirth with which the Canonmills curlers would receive this account of

THE ORIGIN OF EDINBURGH CASTLE.

Tune—"AULD LANG SYNE."

I. "On Calton-Hill and Aurthur-Seat,
  Great Boreas plac'd his feet,
  And hurled like a curling-stane
  The Castle wast the street.
    "But that was lang syne, dear sir,
      That was lang syne,
    Whan curling was in infancy,
      An' stanes war no fine.

II. "An' lest it should be mov'd or stole,
  (Tho' strange it seems to tell),
  The handle loos'd, and left the hole
  Which now serves for a well.
    "But that was lang syne, dear sir,
      That was lang syne,
    Whan curling was in infancy,
      An' handles no fine.

---

* Sir Richard Broun has, among the notes prepared for a second edition of his *Memorabilia*, which never "came off," appended the name of Dr Bairnsfather to this song—on what authority we know not. The title implies that the songs are by one author, but the internal evidence is against this.

III. "Next, as a hint he meant a fort,
　　　Which Northerns might defend,
　　He like a flag-staff prap'd up,
　　　His besom shaft on end.

　　"But that was lang syne, dear sir,
　　　That was lang syne,
　　Whan curling was in infancy,
　　　And besoms no fine.

IV. "Wha thinks it's fase that we alledge,
　　　May carefu' search the hole ;
　　If he finds not the handle-wedge,
　　　He then may doubt the whole.

　　"For 'twas there lang syne, dear sir,
　　　'Twas there lang syne ;
　　An' what needs fo'k dispute about
　　　What happened lang syne."

The song which follows this humorous sally is a melancholy one, and bemoans the long absence of frost :—

I. "I've mony winter seen an' spring,
　　　But like o' this did I ne'er see—
　　Three open winters in a string—
　　　An' may the like again ne'er be.

Chorus—" Alake my walie curling-stanes
　　　Ha'e no' been budg'd thir winters three ;
　　'Tween the rain's plish-plash an' a fireside's fash
　　　They have dreary winters been to me.

V. "When I on former winters think
　　　How on the ice we met wi' glee,
　　And cheerfu' swat to clear a rink,
　　　It gars me sigh right heavylie.
　　　　" Alake, &c.

VI. "When we had mark'd our gog an' hog,
　　　And parties form'd o' four or three,*
　　Ilk ane wi' crampits an' broom scrog,
　　　How anxious yet how blythe played we.
　　　　" Alake, &c.

VII. "When we had keenly played a while,
　　　Brose comes, an' whisky, cawld to flee,
　　We Sol and Boreas to beguile,
　　　'Tween shots wi' spoon or glass make free.
　　　　" Alake, &c.

VIII. "When anes our game or light was done,
　　　We marched to dinner merrylie,
　　Wi' saul an' body baith in tune,
　　　Wha shu'd be blythest a' our plea.
　　　　" Alake, &c.

---

* This seems to imply that the number on a rink was less than in other clubs of the early times.

IX. "When comes the bowl we drink an' sing,
　　　An' crack o' bonspales till ha'f ree,
　　Syne part in peace—a happy thing;
　　　Sic times again I fain wad see.
　　　　　"Alake, &c.

X. "May Boreas hasten frae the north,
　　　Gi' silver lokes to bush and tree;
　　I'd rather he wad plank the Forth
　　　Than Thetis ever on us be.
　　　　　"Alake, &c."

The lament over *Three Open Winters* is followed by *The Welcome Hame*, sung to the chorus—

"There's nae luck about the house,
　There's nae luck at a';
What luck can winter days produce
　Whan curlers are awa'."

Now that the loch is bearing, the "deam" is ordered to set her wheel aside and put the house in order; to "ram the chimley fu'," and "get on the muckle pat," while "mine host" himself hastens to the "bot" and wails a "breast" to make fat brose for the curlers, who will readily be recognised as "kin" to the moderns by this touch of nature—

"Gae, ladie, seek their crampits out,
　For they will a' be here
To get a dram, without a doubt,
　Afore the ice be clear."

When everything has been set in order against their coming—the "substantials" ready, the "muckle room" dusted, and the tables placed—the anxious host breathes a sigh of relief, as well he might.

"Hech, now I think the warst o'ts o'er,
　Sae they may come their wa';
May this frost staun thir fortnights four,
　Gar beef and whisky fa'."

In the last song of this ancient and interesting collection, the praises of the game as a health-giving, innocent, and social amusement are quaintly set forth, and it would be difficult to find among the thousands of poetical panegyrics of this century anything better than *The Choise* of the old Canonmills Club.

"This curlers' weather is, I trow—
　O weels me on the clinking o't;

Fo'k may good ale and whisky brew,
  We'll hae fun at the drinking o't.
For now we'll meet upon the ice,
  An' in the e'ening blythly splice,
To drink an' feast on a' that's nice,
  My heart loups light wi' thinking o't.

" By Boreas baud in icy chain,
  Fu' weel we loo the linking o't,
Nor wish't to be soon loos'd again,
  But rather fear the shrinking o't.
United by his potent hand,
  In gleesom friendly social band,
We eith obey his high command,
  Nor ever think o' slinking o't.

" The lover doats on Menie's eye,
  His life lies in the blinking o't,
For if it's languid he mawn die,
  He canno' bear the winking o't.
But curlers wi' unfettered souls,
  That ane another's cares controuls,
On ice conveen like winter fowls,
  An' please them wi' the rinking o't.

" The sportsman may poor mawkin trace
  Thro' snaw, tir'd wi' the sinking o't ;
Or if his gray-hound gi' her chase,
  He's charmed wi' the jinking o't.
But curlers chase upon the rink,
  An' learn dead stanes wi' art to jink ;
When tir'd wi' that, gae in an' drink,
  An' please them wi' the skinking o't."

COUPAR-ANGUS AND KETTINS (1772).—The record-book (as it is entitled) of this club begins rather abruptly with a genuine sheet of antique writing, which informs us that—

"The silver medal or curling ston was challanged, played for and gained by the following persons in Bendochie and Blairgowrie."

Eight names follow, and as a ninth there comes that of Isack Low, "the *brandey* or oversman." This is the first designation of a skip which we have found in the old records. The rink evidently consisted of nine men. David Campbell was "brandey or oversman" in the losing (Coupar) team, which also included nine names. The victors on this occasion were challenged by the parishes of "Alith and Rattray," and were beaten on 14th February, 1772. The following challenge is then issued from Coupar-Angus, 11th January, 1774 :—

"I take the Liberty to address you as the Head of a Partie of Curlers who chalanged our silver medall or Curling Stone upon the

14th Feby. 1772, when you were fortunate enough to wine it from the united Pairishes of Blairgowrie and Bendochie, then the Holders of the medall. In hopes of your having complied with the terms contain'd in the 7th Article of our Table of Regulations, upon which this medall can and only can be play'd for by this Society, I hereby am impowered to signifie to you a resolution of our meeting you and the other curlers in the Pairishes of Alyth and Ratrey, upon Saturday the 15th current, by nine o'clock forenoon, leaveing you to fix the place anywhere in our Pairishes, in order to do our best to regain our medall. Your answer is expected on Thursday by twelve o'clock."

This challenge was accepted and the match played, at Welton of Balbrogie, on 22nd January, 1774, Peter Constable being "brandey" for Coupar, with seven other players on his rink, against Charles Rae and seven players of Alyth and Rattray. The latter were victorious, and thus retained the medal.

In the *Annual* of 1843, p. 122, we are informed that the silver medal thus competed for from 1772 to the end of the eighteenth century was the gift of Colonel Hallyburton of Pitcur, and that it resembled "an old-fashioned iron crusie." The winners of it attached each year a silver plate to the "medal" recording their victory; but when Coupar was victorious nothing was added, so that these plates recorded the defeats of the society in place of heralding its victories. In 1836 a fine of one guinea was imposed on David Davidson for having lost the ancient trophy, but it does not appear from the minutes that the fine was ever paid or the trophy recovered.

The articles of this society, like those of Muthill, give little or no light regarding the method of playing the game. They provide for the annual election of a president with "the powers which commonly belonged to the presidents of other courts," and a clerk, whose duty is "to keep a book containing the regulations of the society, a list of the members, and such transactions as they shall judge proper to be recorded." There were no other offices, the *brandeys* or *oversmen* in matches being elected for the occasion. Each member was taken bound under a penalty of ten shillings sterling to supply two "proper curling-stones" within a year after his admission, and (Rule 7)

"He is likewise to take care never to appear on the ice with a design of playing without being furnished with a sufficient broom, under such a penalty as the first Curling Court having received information shall think proper to inflict."

If a member left the parish his stones became the property of the club; and in matches he was not to be accepted as an antagonist after his removal "out of the Parishes of Coupar or Ketins." The fine for not providing stones seems to have been rigidly enforced, and many "brothers" suffered for their neglect. It was quite out of proportion to the value of stones in these days, as this is given in the following items of expenditure:—

"1794. Jan. 2. Pd. W. Mitchell for 8 curling stones £0 18 0
              Pd. for a stone   .   .   .   0 1 9"

The articles of this old club, like those of Muthill, impose certain fines upon their unruly and gambling members. It is enacted:—

"Rule 14. That if any brother in the course of play, or at society meetings, shall be guilty of swearing or giving bad names to any member, he shall pay two pence for the first offence, and be at the mercy of the court for repeated acts of said crimes.

"Rule 15. That no brother shall engage to play with any other brother in this society for above the value of one shilling sterling for one game, under the penalty of five shillings, to be paid in to the Clerk of the Court."

Few offences against these moral laws are recorded in the old minutes, but that such offences were not uncommon in the end of the century is evident from the following entries in the treasurer's account:—

"1795. Jan. 30. Cash for Oaths .   .   .   £0 0 9
           Feb. 2.   do.   .   .   .   0 0 9
             ,, ,,   do.   .   .   .   0 3 2
             ,, 16.   do.   .   .   .   0 1 4"

In one case, occurring some twelve years before this, the cash was not received without some trouble, as these extracts shew:—

"COUPAR-ANGUS, 30*th December* 1783.

"At a meeting of the Curling Society held here this day—Jno. Bett, Esq., Preses, and James Campbell, junr., Clerk—it was reported by some of the members that Jno. Crockett, one of the members, was this day on the ice curling, and had been guilty of swearing several times, also had lost one sixpence at play, therefor he should be called to court and make payment of the usual fines in like cases; that after being several times sent for to appear for the above crimes and make payment of the fines, and never appearing, a party of the members, consisting of Chas. Ducatt, Jno. Edward, Jno. Bruce, and Alex. Henderson, was accordingly sent to bring him; and after having gone to his house and asked him to come, he presented a gunn to them, and swore that he would shoot the first person who should attempt to lay hands on him, and struck Chas. Ducatt on the breast.

"The Preses, considering the conduct of the above Jno. Crockett, hereby dismisses him from being a member of this society, and hereby secludes and debarrs any of the members from hereafter curling upon the ice with him until he shall in a full meeting hereafter acknowledge his faults, and make such compensation to the society as they shall think the nature of the crime above requires, and appoint the members present to intimate the above resolution to their absent brethren.

"(Signed) JNO. BETT."

"COUPAR-ANGUS, 12*th January* 1786.

"The within-designed Jno. Crockett appeared before the meeting, and made full and ample satisfaction to them for the faults he committed against their rules; therefore they, in consideration thereof, hereby admit him again as their brother, to enjoy the haill priviledges of a member of this society as formerly.

"(Signed) CHAS. DUCATT."

On the *ex-pede-Herculem* principle, the curlers of Coupar and Kettins, accustomed to use such stones as we have before described (Ch. II. p. 42), must have been men of great strength: it was creditable to themselves, and fortunate for their offending brother, that they did not "sit upon" him more heavily.

SANQUHAR.—The minutes of this club carry us back to the year 1774, when the society was formed, and with the exception of blanks between 1809–17, 1819–1829, and 1832–1841, they contain a careful record of the doings of the society for the long period of one hundred years. They supply us with more information as to the ancient game than any we have previously noticed, and as this information has for some time been available in a little volume which holds a worthy place in the literature of curling,* Sanquhar has hitherto held an advantage over the clubs of the last century, and has been better known than most of its contemporaries. The first minute runs thus:—

* *History of the Sanquhar Curling Society.* By James Brown, Secretary. Published on the occasion of the centenary of the society, 21st January, 1874.

"SANQUHAR, 21st *January* 1774.

"This day the married and unmarried men in this parish had an engagement at curling upon Sanquhar Loch, twenty-seven on each side. The unmarried men gained the victory in both dinner and drink. In the evening they dined all together at the Duke of Queensberry's Arms in Sanquhar. After dinner it was proposed and agreed to, that they should form themselves into a society under the name of the Sanquhar Society of Curlers, and that a master should be chosen annually, with several other regulations. Accordingly one of the oldest curlers present being chosen preses appointed a committee of the best qualifyed to examine and try all the rest concerning the curler word and grip. Those who pretended to have them, and were found defective, were fined, and those who were ignorant, and made no pretentions, were instructed. John Wilson, Schoolmaster in Sanquhar, was chosen clerk to the society, and Mr Alexander Broadfoot in Southmains, was chosen master for the present year. The terms and prices of admission into the society were submission and obedience to the master, discretion and civility to all the members of the society, and secrecy. Fourpence sterling to be paid by every one in the parish, and sixpence sterling to be paid by every one without the parish at their admission. And liberty was granted to the clerk and some other members to add what new incmbers, where (*sic*), and to report them to the society at their next election of a master."

The Freemasonry of ancient curling is here for the first time clearly indicated, but we still look in vain for rules by which curlers were then guided at play. They seem to have been very chary of committing these to writing—perhaps they had no hard and fast rules by which they could act. The omission is at any rate a noticeable feature in all the older records. The Sanquhar Society had, however, a system of organisation worthy of notice. On the 16th January, 1776, according to their second minute,

"The society agreed to form themselves into six rinks of eight players each, and to appoint some of their number as commanders over them, these six rinks to be kept up as a standing veteran army; and also to have some of those that remained over above these six rinks as a *corps-de-reserve* with a proper commander over them. Into this seventh rink or *corps-de-reserve* the young men are first to be admitted, to be preferred to the veteran rinks as their merit deserves and occasion requires. These rinks are to be called after the names of their respective commanders."

It was the duty of the commander of the youths' rink to instruct those under him in the art of the game, and we believe this kindly interest in the initiation of the young is still kept up in Sanquhar and surrounding districts. It is a custom, we fear, "more honoured in the breach than in the observance," but Sanquhar deserves honour from all who love the game for instituting it. With such excellent organisation we are not surprised to find that the members of the Sanquhar Society entered into the game with enthusiasm, and enjoyed the social intercourse which pleasant matches with other parishes brought about.

"In former times," says Mr Brown (p. 12), "the periodical bonspiels that took place between parishes were the source of much pleasure apart from the game itself. In these days there was little intercommunication, particularly in winter, in country districts. Every little country town was shut up as it were in itself, and out from the rest of the world, social intercourse being confined to the inhabitants of the place. A spiel between two parishes, therefore, was looked forward to with much interest as affording the opportunity of seeing new faces, gathering up some scraps of news, and forming new friendships. They were the subject of much joyful anticipation, and great preparations were made for its advent. So great was the flurry and excitement into which the curlers were thrown that a certain wag used to say of Crawick Mill, then a spirited and happy little place, 'It was an unco nicht in Crawick Mill. They were running wi' teapots and razors the haill nicht.'"

Among the regulations of this old society there are only two which may be quoted as interesting:—

"Article V.—The masters are to give due warning to the players at all times when any game is to be played either among the rinks, or with a different parish, and in case of neglect to be liable to pay the sum of One Shilling: and any player so warned either refusing to come forward, or not giving a plausible reason for his non-attendance, shall forfeit the sum of Sixpence. The masters are to have the principal charge of their respective rinks, assisted by such of their own rinks as they shall appoint, not exceeding two, and every player is to submit without murmur, complaint or reluctance, to the master's judgment, or those nominated by him. The masters are to use their endeavour to suppress swearing or abusive language on the ice among their players, and every person offending shall be fined of a sum not exceeding Twopence.

"Article IX.—At any play among the rinks the reckoning not to exceed Sixpence each player."

In the former of these "articles" the right of a master or skip to appoint two assistants on his rink, and his responsibility for the good behaviour of his players are worthy of notice. Regarding the latter Mr Brown in his *History* (p. 19) writes:—

"The ninth Article, dealing with the subject of 'reckonings,' points to a custom prevalent at one time of meeting in the evening at the end of an important play, such as the playing for the Parish Medal, in a social capacity. In connection with inter-parochial games, again, this social entertainment took the form of a dinner with a liberal supply of toddy. These 'dinners and drinks,' as they were called, were for long the stake played for between parishes, and were grand affairs, the ticket being Five Shillings. This is a rather startling figure, as money went in those days, and considering that the members of the societies were, for the most part working men. Still it was so, and it came to be regarded as a point of honour with every curler to attend these dinners. Many were reduced to the direst shifts ; frequently borrowing had to be resorted to by way of concealing their poverty from all but the lender. . . . The practice of playing for dinner and drink appears to have prevailed more or less down to 1830, when at the annual meeting of that year a resolution was passed on the motion of Mr Hislop, weaver :—'That at all parish spiels there should be no dinners, which being put to the vote, it was agreed that dinners should be done away with in a general way, but that any member or rink may dine with the challenging party if they agree to it.'"

The two brief notes that here follow prove that the ancient curlers of Sanquhar were not behind their brethren at Coupar in the exercise of charity towards offenders :—

"*Jany.* 1782.

"Walter M'Turk, surgeon, was expelled the society for offering a gross insult in calling them a parcel of d——d scoundrels."

"*17th Dec.* 1788.

"The meeting proceeded to chuse officers for the ensuing year, when Mr Walter M'Turk, surgeon, was chosen Preses."

Besides covering a multitude of sins, the charity of the old curlers of Sanquhar soothed the sorrows of those to whom the frosty season brought misery, when it brought happiness to the curler's heart. Games were played for oatmeal and for coals to be distributed among the poor, and this laudable practice is kept up in the district to this day. Long may it continue ! In many parts of the country the same custom has for a long time prevailed. It is one of the brightest and best features in the history of our national game, and if it should happily become universal, curling shall then take even a higher place than it does now as "a sweetener of life and solder of society."

HAMILTON (1777).—The minute-book of the old curling club of Hamilton—a neat octavo—begins with this manifesto :—

"We, Subscribers—curlers in Hamilton, considering that the lovers of the sport of curling have never yet incorporated themselves into a society, and are still labouring under the want of many valuable advantages which might be attained thereby.

"The accumulated benefits which accrue from an united body, and which are enjoyed by each individual are priviledges which every social spirit longs to be possessed of.

"Partly animated with the hopes of attaining those invaluable ends, but more especially excited thereto by the following circumstance (having formerly each of us severally contributed to the forming and maintaining of a canal for the purpose of curling, in the Muir of Hamilton, upon a liberty being granted by the magistrates of the said place so to do, and having done the same at a considerable expense. The honorable magistrates in consideration of which have been pleased again to confirm the same priviledges to us as a society by honorary promise, investing us with the exclusive power of managing, supporting, and employing that canal in all respects as we shall find necessary for enjoying the sport of curling, and by their authority to maintain these powers granted to us when occasion requires).

"Actuated by these flattering inducements we do now hereby constitute and form ourselves into a regular society for the purpose of managing the above mentioned canal, and likewise ordering ourselves in other respects as becomes a company of curlers."

The "Articles of Regulation" that follow the manifesto, like others we have noticed, refer chiefly to the conduct of business. A Preses and four "managers" are appointed, to whom are "committed the executive powers of the society to act agreeable to their resolution, and in every other respect as they may find necessary for the interest thereof": the entry-money is fixed at one shilling and sixpence sterling, to be paid "by way of annual supply," to keep up the canal and meet other expenses. Members are to be admitted by ballot or general consent, and in all games they are to be "preferred in the draught before strangers." In the list of original members some are marked "dead" and others "run awa'," a distinction which we may safely presume is not now necessary. The society was evidently more cosmopolitan than its neighbours, for we have under date 1796, December 27, the following admissions:—

John Robison of London.
Wm. Rowe of London.
John Torrance of Hampstead.
Robt. Walkenshaw of Glasgow.

All entered at London and made honourary members here.

The magistrates and the curlers of Hamilton seem to have worked very amicably together, and some of the council must not only have been patrons of the society, but proficients at the play, for several bailies in the early times held office as *masters*. Magisterial protection does not seem

I

however, to have extended to the loch, for we find frequent payments for "publishing with the drum," offering rewards for information as to parties who destroyed the ice and the bank of the loch; while the "watching" of the loch by the officer is an expensive item in the yearly accounts. This personage, destined in the future to be one of the "institutions" of every well-regulated society, meets us for the first time in the following minute:—

"14 Nov. 1781. The curlers met at John Eglinton's, and," *inter alia*, "appointed Robert Bruce as their officer, to warn the meetings and attend on the ice, etc., for which he is to have a pair of shoes annually at Candelmas."

The cost of the shoes was 5s. 9d., rising gradually to 10s. towards the end of the century, and this leather salary seems to have been regularly paid. To supply plenty of "cows for the curlers" was one of the duties included in it, besides those mentioned above! In 1788 an officer's widow gets 6s. by way of a solatium, as she was doubtless unable to fill her husband's shoes; and in 1792 another widow (the office must have had some fatality about it) is paid one guinea. The officer's inner man was not neglected, as several entries of the following kind show:—

"To drink to the officer when cutting the loch, 1s."

In the hour of disgrace the poor fellow is also allowed a "consideration" in which apparently to drown his feelings, for we read:—

"HAMILTON, 8th Nov. 1791.

". . . The meeting dismissed their officer, and the managers appoint to meet this day fortnight at Humphrey Crearrer's in order to make choise of a new officer. Every member that chooses is desired to attend, and dinner to be on the table precisely at 3 o'clock. The meeting agree that *the clerk when dismissing the officer give him 2s. 6d. to drink for warning extra meetings.*"

It is only indirectly that the Hamilton records furnish any information about the game as it was then played.

FIG. 38. HAMILTON CRISP.

Each rink, or *rack*, as it is called, consisted of seven, sometimes of eight players, and up till 1836 one stone was used by each player. The Hamilton player, in delivering his stone, did not use the *hack* in the ice as he now does, but steadied himself on the *crisp*, an iron cross with prongs for fastening it in the ice, of which we have here a specimen said to be 200 years old. The article was certainly not costly, as appears from this entry in the accounts :—

"1782. April 16. By cash paid for crisps . £0 2 0."

Some years later there occurs the following reference to some mechanical appliance for describing the *broughs* not unlike that now in use :—

"To Thomas Miller for making the wood with pricks for marking the toesee and circles on the ice . . . . £0 1 0."

The earliest notice of a bonspiel occurs in 1792, January 21, when—

"Five racks [rinks], four out of the town and one of the parish, met with five racks from Cambusnethan on the Dead Waters and played a bonspele, 155 game."

The "box" of this ancient club was not replenished, as in the clubs we have noticed, by any extensive system of fines, though fining was at times resorted to, and that even in the case of members of the High Court.

"12 Nov. 1793. James Mack never having attended during the whole last year as a manager, it was unanimously agreed he should be fined. The vote carried 5s."

No rule against profane and insulting language seems to have been needed. These good old curlers were evidently true to their original bond of union, and able without the force of fear to order themselves in all respects "as became a company of curlers." They had meetings for business and social enjoyment twice a year, and the different hostelries in the town—"John Eglinton's," "The Fox and Hounds," and about a dozen others—were all patronised in turn, the evenings being spent, as the records relate, "with the greatest possible conviviality and hilarity," and "with all the mirth and glee of curlers." Nor was the sympathy that sweetens the curler's cup of enjoyment unknown to them, as the following proves :—

"HAMILTON, *Jan.* 29, 1795.

"This night a quorum of curlers met in the house of Wm. Clark, and," *inter alia,* "appointed a general meeting of the society to-morrow night to take into consideration to give something to the poor, as a subscription is opened for that purpose in the town."

New members were formally initiated by the society at these meetings, and had the "word" and the "grip" communicated to them, the secrecy and correctness of which they were held bound to preserve.

John Frost in these days, as in ours, was a fickle friend; he would take offence and not visit Cadzow for a season, and all the arts of the warlock Tam Pate, and the prayers of Tam's contemporaries, could not avail to bring him out of the sulks. This will shew how they acted then:—

"HAMILTON, 5th April 1791.

"This night met in the house of John Eglinton, by desire of the Preses, the following persons, and took their dinner, as they had no bonspel this season, there being no frost."

Were not these ancients wise? Why should they lose their dinner because they had lost their play?

BLAIRGOWRIE (1783).—The earliest records of this old club are found in a small volume which covers the period 1796-1811. The story of its first thirteen years cannot therefore be told. In the next minute-book of the club, which has been very carefully kept by the different secretaries from the time of James Duffus to that of John Bridie, we find, however, an old document that gives indisputable evidence of the club's earlier existence. This is a reply to a challenge which had evidently been sent from Coupar-Angus to Blairgowrie, and is as follows:—

"*To the* Reverend Mr THOMAS HILL, C. Angus.

"The curling society of Blairgowrie present their respectful compliments to Mr Hill, and will do themselves the pleasure of meeting eight of the Coupar Society on the Loch Bog in terms of their challenge.

"BLAIRGOWRIE, *Thursday forenoon, ten o'clock*, 1784."

A minute-book of the club, containing records previous to 1783, is said to have been lost; and there is one amusing tradition which would lead us to believe that the Blairgowrie curlers played for beef and greens as far back as the Rebellion of 1745. Both sides on that occasion lost the prize, and the landlord more than likely lost the reckoning. In an "ode" written by Mr Bridie, and recited at the centenary celebration of the society in 1883, we have, in the style of the *Address to a Mummy*, a history of the Blairgowrie Club, in which a certain incident of the Rebellion is thus detailed :—

> "Tradition tells a story of the village,
> About the 'forty-five' or still more early,
> Of rude invasion, foraging, and pillage
> By some bold soldiers following Prince Charlie
> Who on a winter evening came to Blair,
> And greedily ate up the curlers' fare.
>
> "Ah, who can faithfully depict the scenes,
> How these marauders rallied in a body,
> And made a mess of all the beef and greens,
> And swallowed rather than discussed the toddy,
> And put the innkeeper in consternation,
> Awed by the military occupation !
>
> "What could he do ? Though in himself 'an host'
> He was confronted by an armed band
> Of hungry fighting men, each at his post,
> Obeying his superior in command ;
> What wonder if he got a little nervous,
> So cavalierly pressed into 'the service.'
>
> "Then who can realise the blank despair
> Of all the curlers, tired and hungry too ?
> Winners and losers of the game were there,
> Prepared to dine as curlers always do,
> And round the festive board to meet, and sink
> Their petty quarrels in a friendly drink."

The rules of the Blairgowrie Club were framed in 1796 by the Rev. Mr Johnstone, minister of the parish—the president, and a committee. An annual dinner is the first thing to receive attention in the rules, and this seems to have been of great importance. Members who sent an apology and did not dine were fined sixpence. Those who neither sent an apology nor came to dinner were afterwards fined one shilling; and as this did not secure a full attendance, a fine of two shillings and sixpence was imposed on all absentees. "The utmost harmony and conviviality,' according to the common entry in the minutes, prevailed at these gatherings. Tom, Dick, and Harry were not eligible, for the rule as to membership was this :—

> "No person can be admitted a member of the society unless recommended by one of the members as a person of good character, who has formerly played on the ice."

But notwithstanding this protecting clause, it was still thought necessary to enact the following

"RULES FOR THE REGULATION OF THE MEMBERS WHILE ON THE ICE AND IN SOCIETY.

"No member, while on the ice and in society, shall utter an oath of any kind, under the penalty of twopence *toties quoties*.

"No brother curler shall give another abusive or ungentlemanlike language when on the ice and in society, or use any gestures or utter insinuations tending to promote quarrels: otherwise he shall be liable to be fined for the same at the discretion of the members then present."

The *utmost conviviality* mentioned above was scarcely consistent with the following rules as to the quantity of drink to be consumed on special occasions:—

"The members, when playing among themselves in a *birled* game, shall not spend more in a publick-house upon drink than sixpence each for one day. If, however, a regular challenge is given and accepted by one class of curlers to another, the expense on such an occasion may amount to but not exceed three shillings each to the losers, and the gainers half that sum."

Most of the earlier minutes record sundry fines for failing to observe the rule that each person

"Shall be bound within three months from the date of his admission to provide himself with two curling-stones, which must be approved of by the society; or in case he fail to do this within the above period he forfeits five shillings that the society may therewith provide stones for him, and he shall not be at liberty to carry them away, as they are understood to belong to the society."

A supply of stones, "not less than three dozen," was also provided and kept in repair at the expense of the club. These were got from the Ericht when it was "in ply," and the work of finding them does not seem to have been very easy, for we read on 15th July 1799, that a committee at the command of the Preses

"Proceeded up the water of Ericht, and they have to report that they found and laid aside a considerable number of stones out of which eighteen or twenty very excellent curling-stones may be picked, and the committee request, as they have been at considerable pains in searching out the stones, that another committee should be named to bring them home."

The cost of "handling" them after their home-coming may be reckoned from the following account:—

"To boring 24 stones, ... £0 9 0
  „ handling „ with iron . . . 1 4 0
  „ lead 0 2 6
  „ sorting the Jumpers for boring . . 0 2 0"

An inventory of these stones (of some of which drawings are to be found at p. 41) is now and then entered in the record, and at one time their number is put down at "fourteen dozen." They would appear for a long time to have been protected by no covering, but simply to have been kept together by a chain. In the beginning of this century, however, a house was erected for them at a cost of twelve shillings and elevenpence, from which cost four shillings fell to be deducted as "the price of the old chain sold!"*

No information is given in the earlier minutes as to the form of play. But in this, as in other old clubs, the rink generally consisted of eight, and was presided over by a *director*. *Grips* were used for footing in delivering the stone, and Rule 8 prescribed that

"No member shall be seen on the ice as a player without a broom, under the penalty of twopence stg."

Members would appear to have been "initiated," though the tradition† as to "white-headed Jamie Cammell" and the Coupar-Angus Club having been the means of communicating the sign and secret to Blairgowrie (*Annual*, 1842, p. 60), finds no support in the records. Prompted by that sympathetic spirit to which we have had to refer in the case of other old clubs, the Blairgowrie curlers in the early part of this century organised a "charitable fund" for the benefit of members requiring occasional relief, and for "any other charitable purpose." The "fund" only continued for a few years, but while it lasted it seems to have done good service.

MUIRKIRK (1784).—The Rev. Mr Sheppard, in his *Account of Muirkirk*, written about the end of last century, informs us (*vide* p. 107) that curling was the people's chief amusement in winter, but he makes no reference to any society of curlers which may then have existed in the parish. As the minute-book of this society has recently gone amissing we are unable to do justice to its antiquity, or to give therefrom extracts illustrative of eighteenth-century manners and customs. That the Muirkirk people are proud of their old club, and ready to do honour to its age, is sufficiently proved by an account of the centenary cele-

---

* In 1819 a stone and lime house was built for £7. In 1881 a brick one cost £50. Such is the benefit of civilisation.

† This is further referred to at Part II. chap. 4.

bration in the *Cumnock Express* of date February 16, 1884. At this happy and enthusiastic gathering, which was presided over by J. G. A. Baird of Muirkirk and Adamton, the secretary, Alexander Donald, schoolmaster, gave an interesting account of the history of the society, from which, in the absence of the records, we may be allowed to quote :—

"The celebration of the centenary of a society wakens up imagination, and is a particularly suggestive occasion. In the first decade of the eighteenth century all Scotland was in agitation over the loss of the Edinburgh Parliament ; and as debate followed debate the fury of the people grew more intense, till at length the Duke of Hamilton summoned all the Lowlanders to muster to the fray. Muirkirk made a brave response, and raised a large volunteer corps, which only awaited the signal to march to Edinburgh. Now, it was the sons of these patriots who met in 1784 and founded the Muirkirk Curling Club. Henceforth they believed that 'peace hath her victories no less renowned than war'; they beat their fathers' swords into curling-stone handles, and studied war no more. Men with such blood in their veins could never sit through the long dreary winter by the cheerless ingle-cheek in

'The auld clay biggin';
An' hear the restless rattons squeak
About the riggin'.'

. . . . . These old farmers were public-spirited, and beguiled the tedium of winter by playing at the *knyting stane*. A stone was obtained in the channel of the river ; a niche was chipped out for the forefinger and thumb, the stone being partly *cuist* or *cuited* along the ice. Then came large hemispherical blocks, the handle being fixed at one side.
. . . . The earliest historical document I can get my hands on is of date 1791, when reference is made to a match between Douglas and Muirkirk, and it is added that nearly thirty years had elapsed since the two clubs had met, thus carrying the existence of a curling society back to 1760. . . . . The regular minutes begin in 1783, and continue up till date."

DOUGLAS (1792).—A neat little quarto volume, entitled *Minute-Book, Douglas St Bride's Curling Club*, gives us a good many interesting notes about the early days of curling, of some of which we shall defer making use until we come to deal with subsequent chapters. The organisation of the club, as set forth in the rules adopted by the ice-players in the parish of Douglas on 25th January 1792, does not differ much from that of other societies already noticed. The office-bearers were president, vice-president, six directors, and a treasurer and clerk, all of which " must execute their respective offices without any salary or gratuity whatsoever"; and of the two first-named one "must always reside within a mile of the town." An officer was also appointed "to warn all the players whenever desired by the president or any of the directors"; his salary to be five shillings yearly. The entry-money of members (who were duly initiated on entry by receiving the word and grip) was sixpence, and the annual subscription threepence. This was a small sum, but it seems to have been amply sufficient for the society's wants in those days, for the only expenditure we hear of in the earlier record is at a meeting in the house of Douglas Sleigh, vintner, on 25th January 1793, when

"Thomas Brown presented his account for carrying stones to Muirkirk, amounting to six shillings, which, being examined and approved, orders were given to the treasurer to pay the same—also five shillings to the officer as his salary. And two shillings and sixpence to John Brown's daughter at Claydubs, as a small recompense for the trouble he is at with the curling-stones belonging to the society."

In regard to the arrangement of players in rinks, Rule 4 thereanent was to this effect:—

"The players shall be divided by the office-bearers into racks, and places in these racks in all parish games, and any person refusing to play in the place allotted to him shall be fined in the sum of sixpence."

The Douglas Society seems to have kept up a series of matches with certain parishes in the neighbourhood, such as Muirkirk, Carmichael, Lesmahagow, Lanark, and Crawfordjohn, the results of which are faithfully recorded in the minute-book. These seem to have been looked upon as of the very greatest importance, for it was enacted in Rule 6 that

"Any person refusing to play a parish game, when warned by the officer (unless he can give such an excuse as the majority of his rack shall approve of) shall be fined in the sum of one shilling."

Previous to such matches coming off, the racks (eight players each) practised carefully at home among themselves. It was wisely stipulated that these matches should not cost any of the players more than two shillings sterling.

The jubilee of the St Bride's Club was celebrated in 1842 by a dinner presided over by James Paterson, president.

"On the right of the chair," says the minute, "was Thomas Haddow, the senior member of the society, being then in the 80th year of his age, and 63rd as a player: he was a member at the first constituting of the society in the year 1792, and from recollection could relate many of the most eventful circumstances that had occurred in curling during the bygone half century."

In a poem* written by Captain Paterson about the beginning of this century are duly celebrated the deeds of Thomas Haddow (who is said to have been the prototype of *Lazarus Powhead* in Scott's *Castle Dangerous*), and of other ancient worthies among the curlers "of that loved place called Douglasdale." Skipper Tam (Haddow) draws the broughs with "knife and string." Another hero is described as glancing up the rink

> "With stone in hand and foot in natch
> In attitude of dire despatch;"

while of Bailie Hamilton it is said

> "A better drawer ne'er clapped foot in natch;
> He once, near Bothwell Brig, with dext'rous cunning,
> Drew through a ten inch port for three times running;
> The rink in length was forty yards and nine,
> As measured by Tom Haddow with his line;
> And when the stone they in the port did place,
> On neither side was there an inch of space;
> The ice in length was forty-two yards good,
> Down from the pass to where the bailie stood;
> The plaudits loud from lookers-on and all,
> Alarmed 'The Douglas' in his castle hall."

Darkness descends on the players, and when "the fun" is thus ended,

> "Reluctantly they think upon their homes,
> And now in Flecky's barn they lodge their stones;
> Then future matches made—wi' muckle sorrow
> They all depart, resolved to meet to-morrow."

DUNFERMLINE (1784).—The minutes of the old curling club of Dunfermline extend from 2nd February 1784 to 2nd February 1808. After the latter date the club seems for a time to have been inactive till 1827, when a new club was formed, into which the few surviving members of the old club were admitted. The old minute-book was then handed over to the united club. From the list of members we infer that the club existed for some time previous to the date of the first minute in the volume, for we

---

* *The Douglas Bonspiel:* A Poem. Though written in 1806 the poem was not published till 1842.

find Adam Paterson and five others entered as members in 1778, and the first meeting recorded is called the "Anniversary Meeting of the Curlers." The designation of *club* is used in 1785, and as far as we can judge this is the earliest use of the word among the old curling societies. This club ought in our estimation to be held in honourable remembrance because it was the earliest to recognise the necessity of having a *chaplain* among the office-bearers, and to "William Peebles" belongs the honour of having been the first spiritual adviser of any curling club. The other office-bearers were president, vice-president, clerk, and treasurer. It would appear that these offices were objects of ambition among the members, for in the first minute we find it declared

"That if any member in the society shall at, or preceding any future election, either ask or solicit, or employ for them to ask or solicit, a vote for any office herein [the member] that shall so solicit or employ any for him so to do, shall not only be declared incapable of any office, but shall be expelled from the society for so doing, and this regulation shall be a standing rule in future."

The entry-money of members was fixed at two shillings and sixpence, of which one shilling only was applied to the society's use, and one shilling and sixpence was spent by the meeting *as usuall*—*i.e.*, we presume in enabling members to drink "a few toasts suitable to the occasion," as they seem always to have done at their anniversary gathering. While the office-bearers were not allowed to canvass, they seem to have been allowed to pay *cann* (a donation to the funds, which we hear of in no other society), for we have under date February 2, 1795, the following appended to the minute:—

"N.B.—Præses cann 2s. 6d., vice do., 1s., secretary, 6d., chaplain, 6d. Treasurer being always contd. pays no cann."

Penalties were inflicted on those who did not respect the sociality of the club, and any person who did not attend the anniversary meeting was fined two shillings and sixpence, unless he had a valid excuse.

In 1784—

"The meeting unanimously declared their displeasure at so many new entrants neglecting to attend the anniversary meeting, lays them under the bane of the society, and shall admit none of them without a satisfactory excuse, or repeating their entry."

Twenty years later we have the society dealing smartly with three members who had promised to dine, but did not appear—they were fined "five shillings each, being their proportion of the bill." Like their contemporaries, these Dunfermline men as they dined did not forget the needy, for it is stated that after dinner on February 2, 1785, the meeting

"Distributed five shillings to the poor and other necessary uses."

We look in vain in this old record for any news about the method of play. Each "entered curler" was bound to have two curling-stones of his own property upon the ice, but we cannot determine whether at that early date these two stones were—contrary to the custom of the time—used by their owner in the practice of the game. There is no mention of directors or rinks, or of any "word" or "grip" in use, and it is not till the minute of 2nd February 1804, that any notice is found of the implements of war. Then, after passing an account of six shillings for crampets and for preserving the stones,

"The meeting authorize the Preses to get the stair on the south side of the pond taken down and enlarged, and door and lock put upon it to hold the curling-stones, crampets, brooms, &c., and that the expense be defrayed by the club."

DUDDINGSTON (1795).—No records have been preserved of a curling society which is said to have been instituted at Duddingston about the middle of last century. The later society, instituted in 1795, and the minutes of which, with a few blanks, extend onward from that date to 1853, is by far the most important of all the eighteenth-century curling societies. Dr Cairnie, writing in 1833, says:—

"In mentioning societies of curlers, the Duddingston certainly merits to be placed the first on the list as containing many members who are highly eminent for scientific knowledge, wealth, respectability, and worth."

In the strict order of time, Duddingston, however, falls into the last place in this chapter, though we cordially agree with Cairnie's verdict. This is not unfortunate, as the transition from ancient to modern curling is distinctly connected with the formation of the Duddingston Society. The regulations drawn up in 1795 differ but little from those we have already described; the ideas of our forefathers as to the high character of the game, and its power to promote health, mental vivacity, loyalty, and religion, are well expressed in the Resolutions; while the *Laws* of Curling adopted by the club are the embodiment of the collective wisdom and experience of the earlier societies. These Regulations, Resolutions, and Laws, while shedding light on the bygone century, open up at the same time a new era in curling, and their influence is manifest in all the societies which were formed between the time of the Duddingston decrees and the formation of the Grand Club in 1838, when a greater than Duddingston arose to guide the destinies of the national game. The Duddingston Club was, in the end of the last and the earlier part of the present century, a kind of Grand Club. Its name went far beyond its local habitation, and it numbered among its members distinguished curlers from all parts of Scotland. Besides, the old Duddingston curlers did more than exercise themselves on the ice during the day and meet for dinner and drink at night— they turned attention to the past, and sought to collect all available information as to the origin and progress of the game, and under their auspices the first history* of it was published. Like their brethren at Canonmills, they also had songs specially written for their annual meetings, some of which have perhaps done more than all the rules and regulations to popularise the national game. As the precursor of the Grand Club, at whose instance we write, we may therefore well award the place of honour among last century clubs to the Duddingston Society.

The minutes open with this formal document :—

"DUDDINGSTON, 24*th January* 1795.

"Curling hath long been a favourite amusement in many parts of Scotland for many ages past. It is an exercise very conducive to health, tends to promote society, and often unites its votaries, who come from north, south, east, and west, in the strongest bonds of friendship.

* Ramsay's *Account of the Game of Curling*, 1811. The work was read and approved of by a Committee of the Society before it was put into the publisher's hands, and on being published its sale was promoted by the members. Songs and all documents in the society's possession were handed over to **Ramsay** for use in the volume.

"The inhabitants of the small parish of Duddingston have long been famed for their attachment to the manly exercise of curling; this was greatly promoted by their having a large loch conveniently situated and near to the Metropiles. Some years ago a society was formed to keep up the spirit of this diversion, which seemed to be fast falling into decay. Of late several gentlemen who have already joined the society, and others who wish to do so, have expressed a desire that a few rules might be drawn out and laid before them to be inspected by the society, and, if approved of by the majority of the members, would be adopted for regulating the future conduct of the society. A committee of their number was appointed for the purpose of drawing up the rules—viz., Messrs Thomas M'Kill, Michael Linning, David Scott, and John Edgar—which they accordingly did, and were approven off by all the members present, and is here inserted as follows, viz.:—

"'RESOLUTIONS AND REGULATIONS OF THE CURLING CLUB OF DUDDINGSTON.

"'1. Resolved that the sole object of this institution is the enjoyment of the game of curling, which, while it adds vigour to the body, contributes to vivacity of mind and the promotion of the social and generous feelings.'

"'2. Resolved that peace and unanimity, the great ornaments of society, shall reign among them, and that virtue, without which no accomplishment is truely valuable and no enjoyment really satisfactory, shall be the aim of all their actions.'

"'3. Resolved that to be virtuous is to reverence our God, religion, laws, and king, and they hereby do declare their reverence for and attachment to the same.'

"The said curling club, in order to the permanent and regular existence of their institution, have adopted the following regulations."

The "regulations" which then follow are, as we have remarked, very like those which have been given from other clubs. We have our old friend protesting against "strong language" in No. 4:—

"He who utters an oath or imprecation shall be fined in the sum of threepence."

To this is added a new and salutary prohibition in rule 5:

"Any member introducing a political subject of conversation shall be fined in a penalty of sixpence, to be paid immediately."

Besides president, vice-president, and secretary (the last-named receiving remuneration for his trouble, and having his fees as a member remitted), Duddingston Club created quite a number of ornamental and useful offices. They had a *chaplain* as at Dunfermline, the first being the Rev. Mr Bennet, minister of Duddingston, who seems to have been very liberal toward the club in giving a site on the glebe for a curling-house, and otherwise doing a great deal for its prosperity. Their "officer" was an important personage, and had, besides his salary, "a coat with suitable uniform" provided for him. When assessments and fines were imposed, the officer was sent to "the respective lodgings" of those who had not paid, to collect the same, and he had to see to the safety both of curlers and skaters; the skating club, which seems to have worked amicably with the curlers, having provided a ladder and ropes, which, in case of accidents, were under the officer's care. One of the members was elected "Master of Stones," and his duty was to see that each member on entry lodged a pair of stones in the curling-house, which, in the event of the member's removal, remained the property of the club. There was also a *surgeon* to the society (Mr Bairnsfather, Liberton, being the first elected to that office); a *poet-laureate*, a *medalist*, and a body of *counsellors* composed of "gentlemen permanently residing in Edinburgh," whose duty it was to assist the president and judge as to applications for admission to the club.

Parties who wished for admission had to apply in writing, and on being approved by the council their names were submitted to the general meeting. The entry-money was at first three shillings sterling, and if the entrant did not bring along with him two curling-stones he had to "pay down five shillings in lieu thereof." There does not appear to have been any ceremony of initiation, but in 1802 a motion was carried that a silver medal, "with proper insignia as a badge, to distinguish the members from any other gentlemen," should be worn, and the entry-money was thereupon raised to one guinea, which covered the extra expense of the medal. This badge, under the penalty of one shilling, had to be worn on the ice and also at the anniversary dinner. Mr M'George having given the "dye" for the same gratis, "in the most polite manner," was appointed medalist to the society. Some years after, the price of admission was raised to three guineas, and as there were frequent extra assessments, the membership of the society must have been rather an expensive luxury. In the course of its existence the Duddingston Society seems to have become very much a *legal* one, for we find that on one occasion, when no fewer than seventy new members were admitted, there were in the number twenty-nine advocates, twenty-two writers to the signet, nine writers, and two accountants. No society of the kind, notwithstanding this preponderance of "wig and gown," ever numbered in its ranks such a company of peers, baronets, judges, and representatives of the different learned professions, as these names prove :—

"Marquis of Queensberry, Marquis of Abercorn, Sir Thos. Kirkpatrick of Closeburn, Sir George Mackenzie of Coull, Sir Alexander Boswell of Auchinleck, Sir Alex. Muir Mackenzie, Sir George Clerk of Penicuick, Sir Patrick Walker of Coats, Sir Chas. G. S. Menteath of Closeburn, Sir Wm. Gibson-Craig of Riccarton, Sir Charles Gordon, Sir Charles Douglas, Sir John Hay, Sir William Hamilton, Sir John Dick, Sir Alex. Macdonald Lockhart, Sir Patrick Walker, Sir Robert Burnett, Sir John Gillespie.

"Lords Murray, Cockburn, Ivory, Colonsay, Moncreiff, Fullarton, Cunningham, Jeffrey, and Gillies.

"Major Hamilton Dundas of Duddingston, Colonel Macdonald of Powderhall, Lieut.-Col. White.

"Henry Fergusson of Craigdarroch, John Clerk Maxwell of Middlebie, Lauderdale Maitland of Eccles, Robert Dundas of Arniston, James Maidment, Cosmo Innes.

"Principal Baird, Professor Dunbar, Professor Ritchie.

"Revs. John Ramsay of Gladsmuir, John Thomson of Duddingston, Dick of Currie, James Muir of Beith, John Somerville of Currie, James Macfarlane of Duddingston, G. S. Smith, Tolbooth, Wm. Proudfoot, Strathaven.

"Drs Cairney, Berry, Dymock, Bairnsfather, Dumbreck, Mackenzie, and Stewart."

"In order to prevent disputes and ensure harmony among the members," it was resolved by the society in 1803 to prepare a Code of Laws by which the play should be regulated. Messrs Home, David Scott, Millar, Linning, M'George, Edgar, Trotter, Ewart, and Muir were the committee appointed to do this work. In presenting their report they stated that

"The rules had been prepared with the greatest care, most of which are strictly observed in those counties in which the game of curling prevails."

When we meet with this first Code of Curling Laws we have crossed the border line of the beginning of the century, for they were not finally adopted till January 6, 1806; but as the outcome of the experience of the eighteenth-century clubs and the basis of our present code, these rules will ever be historically interesting to curlers, and they are therefore given *in extenso*:—

"Rules in Curling to be observed by the Duddingston Curling Society.

"I. The usual length of a rink is from thirty-six to forty-four yards inclusive; but this will be regulated by circumstances and the agreement of parties. When a game is begun the rink is not to be changed or altered, unless by the consent of the majority of players; nor is it to be shortened, unless it clearly appears that the majority are unable to make up.

"II. The hog score to be one-sixth part of the length of the rink distant from the tee, and every stone to be deemed a hog the sole of which does not clear the score.

"III. Each player to foot in such a manner that, in delivering his stone, he bring it over the tee.

"IV. The order of playing adopted at the beginning must be observed during the whole course of a game.

"V. All curling-stones to be of a circular shape. No stone is to be changed throughout a game, unless it happens to be broken; and the largest fragment of such stone to count, without any necessity of playing with it more. If a stone rolls or is upset, it must be placed upon its sole where it stops. Should the handle quit a stone in the delivery, the player must keep hold of it, otherwise he will not be entitled to replay the shot.

"VI. A player may sweep his own stone the whole length of the rink; his party not to sweep until it has passed the hog score at the farther end, and his adversaries not to sweep until it has passed the tee. The sweeping to be always to a side.

"VII. None of the players, upon any occasion, to cross or go upon the middle of the rink.

"VIII. If in sweeping or otherwise a running stone is marred by any of the party to which it belongs, it must be put off the ice; if by any of the adverse party, it must be placed agreeable to the direction which was given to the player; and if it is marred by any other means, the player may take his shot again. Should a stone at rest be accidentally displaced, it must be put as nearly as possible to its former situation.

"IX. Every player to be ready when his turn comes, and to take no more than a reasonable time to play his shot. Should he, by mistake, play with a wrong stone, it must be replaced where it stops by the one with which he ought to have played.

"X. A doubtful shot is to be measured by some neutral person, whose determination shall be final.

"XI. Before beginning to play, each party must name one of their number for directing their game. The players of his party may give their advice to the one so named, but they cannot control his direction, nor are they to address themselves to the person who is about to play. Each director, when it is his turn to play, to name one of his party to take the charge for him. Every player to follow the direction given to him.

"XII. Should any question arise the determination of which may not be provided for by the words and spirit of the rules now established, each party to choose one of their number in order to determine it. If the two so chosen differ in opinion, they are to name an umpire, whose decision shall be final."

Three years after the passing of the above Code of Laws we find the Duddingston curlers moving quite away from the past, and originating point competitions, about which nothing is heard in the eighteenth century. This was done in 1809, on the ground that

"As no sport was more deserving of encouragement, and as none seemed to offer a juster or more interesting competition than curling, it would be proper to the society to institute a prize medal, which should be played for once every winter."

A gold medal, "with proper inscriptions and embellishments," was accordingly secured, the winner of which was

"To have his success announced in the newspapers, and to be allowed, if he chooses, to append a small badge thereto, expressive of his having been victor for the year."

It is notable that only three *points* were at this time thought worthy of being played—viz., *Drawing*, *Striking*, and *Inwicking*—at each of which competitors had four chances.

The point medal day seems to have been popular, and Sir Alexander Boswell of Auchinleck, a member of the club, dedicated a poem to its honour, the first three stanzas of which may be given as indicating the enthusiasm aroused by the annual battle of the *Points*:—

"Let lads dam the water in ilka how trough,
  For cheerin' frost comes wi' December ;
And curlers o' Scotland on Duddingston Loch
  The glorious MEDAL remember.
       Chorus—"Duddingston Loch !
           Duddingston Loch !
     Strain ilka nerve, shouther, back-bane, and hough.

"Let rogues and let fools rin to cards and to dice,
  And gamblin', sit girnin' and gurlin' ;
But honest men ken that tho' slipp'ry the ice,
  Still fair play an' fun gang wi' curlin'.
       Chorus.

"Then ring it round Reekie, our auld bizzin' byke,
  That the rinks are a' measured an' soopit ;
And out flee the lads, to draw, inwick, and strike,
  Frae plough, counter, desk, bar, and pu'pit."
       Chorus.

The Duddingston curlers seem to have had many of their meetings enlivened by the muse of Sir Alexander Boswell. These meetings were at first held at the Curlers' Hall, Duddingston, but they seem to have been removed to Edinburgh, and in the minute of 11th December 1816, written at *M'Ewan's Tavern*, we have the following entry:—

"A duet composed by Mr Boswell was sung to the meeting by that gentleman, and received with unbounded applause; [the duet] was ordered to be recorded in the minute-book of the society, and the thanks of the meeting were voted to Mr Boswell."

This is the first we hear of Boswell's famous duet between *Lochside and Damback*—one of our classic curling pieces, the first verse of which, in the best o' braid Scotch, is enough to justify the "unbounded applause" with which the song was received by the Duddingston Society.

"Let feckless chiels like cricket weans,
Gae blaw their thums wi' pechs and granes,
Or thaw their fushionless shank banes,
And hurkle at an ingle.

"But lads o' smeddum croose and bauld,
Whase bluid can thole a nip o' cauld,
Your ice stanes in your grey plaids fauld
And try on lochs a pingle.

Chorus—"When snaw lies white on ilka knowe,
The ice stane and the guid broom kowe,
Can warm us like a bleezin' lowe,
Fair fa' the ice and curlin'!"

One name among the members of this old society deserves especial honour—that of James Millar, advocate. At the meeting in

"Archers' Hall,* *8th Dec.* 1824,

"The secretary stated that since the last meeting the society had suffered a severe loss by the death of Mr James Millar, advocate, one of the presidents. The secretary felt it a duty incumbent upon him, and due to the memory of a gentleman highly esteemed by the members, to mention a few of the many services rendered by their late friend to the Duddingston Curling Society.

"Mr Millar had been a member for upwards of twenty-three years, during which period he laboured incessantly to promote the welfare and prosperity of the society. To his exertions, chiefly, the society is indebted for the excellent rules now adopted and observed by the members when on the ice. He was among the first, if not the first,

---

* The meetings were held there after the society had secured a piece of ground adjoining for playing the games of quoits and bowls in the summer season.

who suggested the idea of a medal to be worn by each member and furnished the motto for that medal [*Sic Scoti*, &c.] He it was also who first suggested the idea of instituting a gold prize medal to be played for annually, which has excited a keen spirit of emulation among the players. The secretary from his official situation had occasion to witness the unwearied endeavours of the late Mr Millar to have the society established on the most respectable footing, and he lived to see these endeavours crowned with success. On the ice it is well known to us all that he was the life of the curlers."

This statement of the secretary was approved of by the meeting, who joined "with Mr Ewart in lamenting Mr Millar's death." From the account above given of Mr Millar's work in the Duddingston Society, it is evident that he must ever be regarded as one of the greatest benefactors of the national game.

On the same evening on which "Mr Boswell" sang to the society his duet of *Lochside and Dunbuck*, we find that

"A poem composed by Mr James Millar was read to the meeting and received with unbounded applause, and ordered to be recorded in their minute-book, and the thanks of the society were voted to that gentleman."

For "feast of reason and flow of soul" that night must surely have been a memorable one in the history of the club. A short time afterwards Mr Millar was elected to the high position of poet-laureate. As a memorial of one who did so much for the game as a member of the Duddingston Society, we give the words in which Mr Millar himself, after recounting the various joys of *The Scottish Sportsman* as shooter, fisher, archer, and golfer, exalts the joy of the curler above them all:—

"Such, such are my joys, yet one dearer unsung
    The bold Caledonian claims for his own ;
'Tis when winter her white robe o'er Arthur* has flung,
    And the loch at its base under icy chains thrown.

"Then eager we haste, with the slow-rising sun,
    To enter the lists on the slippery vale ;
Where defiance to combat, or prize to be won,
    Prolongs the fond strife until darkness assail.

"How ardent the conflict when curlers engage !
    The keen piercing north wind unheeded may blow ;
Let the cit or the coxcomb fly trembling his rage ;
    No feeling have those but to vanquish the foe."

---

* Arthur's Seat.

"Nor inglorious the wreath that the victors entwine ;
　'Tis the meed of sage counsel which brilliant deeds crown ;
Just eye, steady nerves, active strength must combine
　With devotion to toil and a love of renown.
"Now the well-polished whin-stone wins calmly its way
　With nicest 'momentum' in the ring to repose ;
Now strikes like the bolt, as resistless its sway,
　Yet, the guidance so sure, it strikes only its foes.
"But who can describe the still varying game?
　New efforts, new schemes, every movement demands,
Tho' each change but augments the enthusiast's flame,
　And each crisis loud praise or censure commands.
"And oft it will chance, as the doubtful war burns,
　That victory rests on one high-fated blow ;
Hope and fear fill the combatants' bosoms by turns ;
　These pray it may hit ; those, that erring it go.
"All eyes bend on him who decides the great stake :
　Dread pause! the stone's sped. Hark! 'He has it!' they cry.
'He has it!' resounds throughout Duddingston Lake,
　And the rocks of proud Arthur, 'He has it,' reply.
"Thus passes the day ; ah! too brief. Yet belong
　Other charms to the eve ; then the feast and the bowl,
Feats recounted or threatened, the laugh and the song,
　Till social delights pervade every soul."

It must ever be a matter of regret that the Duddingston Society, which to Ramsay, when he wrote in 1811, seemed "to be fast rising to a degree of celebrity unexampled in the history of curling," should have been allowed to perish. The success of its efforts to extend the game and make it more than ever national became, however, the society's ruin. The Grand Caledonian Club took up the duty which the society had so nobly tried to perform, and with the formation of other clubs in Edinburgh, affording greater facilities to the curling citizens, the pond at Duddingston was gradually deserted.*

The records which we have thus noticed may be held to indicate the nature of those other curling societies of last century, whose minutes have not been preserved, and of

---

* We would venture to suggest to the Coates Club, which is now the careful guardian of the minutes of this society, that when the centenary year—1895—comes round, the literature of curling might be enriched by a small volume containing an account of the society, and some extracts from its valuable records. Such a publication would give pleasant glimpses of the social life of bygone times, and illustrate the development of our national game.

many other societies which, without any formal constitution, are known to have existed in the south and west of Scotland, and more especially in Galloway, where the game is of great antiquity, and where memories of famous *bonspiels* in olden times are still fresh. There is a family likeness about them which proves that curling had been long practised in Scotland, for in districts widely separated, when intercommunication was difficult, such general agreement could only have come about very slowly.

The formation of societies in the last century had much to do with the development of curling and its promotion to the dignity of a national game. Curling-stones, to begin with, were improved. They might be natural boulders from the channel of the river, but as we see in the case of those taken from the Ericht at Blairgowrie, they had to pass examinations in which the fittest only survived, while the huge cairn and the three-neukit specimens were " plucked " and went to the wall. The circular type thus gradually came into fashion, and with it scientific skill became of more importance than mere physical force—a change which, as we have noted, did much to popularise the game. Kindlier feelings were shewn to the stone when its character was thus improved, and greater care was taken of it. Instead of being left on the margin of the loch to be tugged out, as Graeme describes, when frost came, it was comfortably housed at the expense of the society. Duddingston was not the first to shew such humanity, but the better feeling of the time is reflected in this minute :—

"CURLERS' HALL, *7th Feby.* 1795.
" .... The meeting taking into consideration the reduced situation of their curling-stones, owing to their being left in a destitute state in the open field, and no person to look after them when the game is over, they therefore crave the sympathy of the members ; which being considered by the meeting, they unanimously resolve and agree to build a house for the stones at the expense of the society."

Curlers themselves were also improved by the societies. There were " rough blocks " among them also, if this sketch of Cairnie's (*Essay*, p. 89) be true :—

"The Laird of Barr (Hamilton of Barr) was a curler too. He was a middling player ; but he was fond of hearing himself swear ! He was a grand banner [swearer], not from anger, but out of amusement. He used the following usual form of expression : 'Lard, Gad, conscience, that is a gran' shot.' The curlers felt joy when they heard the jolly and uproarious laird swear."

In the societies all such coarse conduct was, as we have seen, punished severely, and the Laird of Barr would have had to atone for the looseness of his manners by the loss of his money. The Rev. Dr Somerville of Currie, a distinguished curler, says in 1830, in a letter to Sir Richard Broun :—

"Among those who are truly imbued with the spirit of the game there exists a degree of punctilio and etiquette, even among the commonest artizans, which would reflect credit upon many in a far superior station ; and though it is confessedly somewhat of a boisterous game— a ' roarin' play,' as Burns has it—yet I can honestly aver, to the best of my recollection, I never heard an oath or an indecent expression made use of upon the ice."

If there are any "blocks" among us nowadays whose tongues are not so polished as their Ailsas, they may "niblins tak' a thocht and mend" as they read the early laws which, to their credit be it said, were generally framed and adopted by working men ; for in the lists of membership the names of noblemen and gentlemen are at the first conspicuous by their absence.

Decorum in speech and behaviour, respect toward authority, obedience to law, and the duty of each to contribute to the happiness of others were all enforced by a system of fines which had no respect of persons. Into the pocket of every offender the brethren put their hands, and took out sufficient to satisfy their regulations and quench their thirst ; and if any one demurred, they simply extracted more or expelled him from the society. It is a wonder there were not more John Crocketts in such times ; but "heaven's first law" is often enforced with penalties to the ultimate advantage of the sufferer, and by such stern enactments curling and curlers had a character given to them which they have never lost.

By the formation of societies not only the stones and the manners but also the style of play was improved. The society when formed was generally parochial, and if the nobility were not to the front there was sufficient scope for emulation among the " ministers, surgeons, writers, butchers, fishers, weavers, masons, wrights, grocers, farmers, smiths, tailors, shoemakers, *publicans, and sinners*," who, with a few others that might be added to Cairnie's list, usually made up the roll of membership. It was then, as it is now, an object of ambition to be elected a master or director; and unlike the feudal baron who, when he made a bonspiel with a rival, stuck himself at the head of his vassals, who could generally curl better than himself, or the *cock-lairds*, at whose curling *broolzies*

> "Their farming slaves a han' maun lend,
> And neither whinge nor swither,"

the society acted on the *detur digniori* principle, and elected the best man to direct them. The haughty big-wig and the reckless stone-breaker were set aside, and skilful players like Deacon Jardine* and Tam Haddow took command of the rink, and kept it as long as they kept their reputation. Promotion in the *ranks* was thus the reward of true merit, as it should always be in well-regulated societies; and when this was the case the members played their best, that they might attain honour among their fellows.

While the pillar of *rivalry* was thus satisfactorily adjusted in its position, that of *good fellowship* was securely and happily set up in the social gatherings that were convened on the ice and ended in the inn, when the frost paid a visit to the parish, and in the anniversary meetings of the society, which took place "fither or no." They might have their political and religious differences and their social distinctions, but the lines of Norman Macleod were as true then as they are now :—

---

* Deacon Jardine, according to Sir R. Broun, " 'flourished' from the beginning of the eighteenth century downwards, and was the oldest Preses of the Lochmaben rinks, whose name has survived the lapse of an hundred and thirty years." . . . . " Of Deacon Jardine's *forte*, it was said that he could with his stone *birse a needle*—i.e., he could wick a bore so scientifically that he would undertake, having first attached, with a piece of shoemaker's wax, two needles in the side of two curling-stones, just the width of the one he played with apart, and upon two stones in front, similarly apart, and in the line of direction, having affixed two birses, to play his stone so accurately that, in grazing through the port, it should impel the birses forward through the eyes of the needles!" (*Memorabilia*, pp. 25 and 60).

> "In fine **frosty** weather, let a' meet thegither,
> Wi' brooms in their haun's, an' a stane near the **'T'**;
> Then, ha! ha! by my certies, ye'll see hoo a' parties
> Like brithers will love and like brithers agree!"

In the *High Jinks* of the Curling Court, which were then, perhaps, more common than they are now, members were all *brothered*, and in a rough-and-tumble way they were jumbled together, and all distinctions forgotten in the presence of "My lord" and his "officer," and amid the excitement of "the roupin' o' the stoup."

An honest countryman, when he was once asked if he was a total abstainer, is reported to have answered in pious indignation, "'Deed no, sir, 'am the *verra opposite*." Society gatherings in the olden time were not cold water conventions, but it would be defamation of character to say they were the very opposite. Excessive drinking was prohibited, as many of the records have shewn. The eighteenth century was the age of clubs, and the vice of intemperance was then common in clubs and outside of them, but intemperance was not encouraged by the clubs of the curlers. The reverse was rather the case. They certainly loved curling more than drinking. Over their *pap-in*, their *cappie-ale*, or their bowl of whisky-punch, they recited the adventures of the day's healthy amusement and cemented the ties of friendship, and by the song and sentiment and sociality that graced them, their meetings were redeemed from the sottish self-indulgence and debauchery that disgraced the period.

If these old curlers did not quite conduct themselves as their descendants do in this cultured and enlightened age, they were certainly better employed than in cracking skulls and shedding blood as their ancestors had been accustomed to do. Nor must it ever be forgotten how benevolence mingled with their conviviality, and how they often caused the hearts of the widow and the orphan to sing for joy by their kindly distributions of food and *eldin*, thus making curling what we hope it will ever be—a trusted ally of "the charities that soothe, and heal, and bless."

We are now in a position to conclude our History of Ancient Curling by a summary account of the conditions and customs that have come under our notice as we proceeded with the divisions under which we have seen fit to arrange the subject. In no separate chapter have we found it possible to detail accurately such conditions and customs, but from a conjunct view we may, with the aid of some additional light, present them in outline that they may be compared and contrasted with those which now prevail.

Nature is so faithful to us that she never changes her methods, and by breaking the connection between the present and the past renders useless the little knowledge we have gained of her ways. So the original patent granted by her to John Frost, by which to "bind the mire like a rock," has never been improved upon. We may therefore premise that our forefathers curled on ice similar to ours, with variations of crunklie and clean, dour and gleg, drug and keen, laugh and smooth, dauchie and clear, slagie and crisp, according to the weather—sufficient to test the versatility of the players. But if the quality was similar, the quantity was greater. When drainage had not sucked the life away from pits, ponds, dubs, dams, tarns, and pools, and water as a motive power had not been converted into steam, curlers were, when frost came, literally beset with glittering temptations of "crystal brigs." And frost came oftener then than it does now, though wise men tell us that poor old Sol is growing feebler like ourselves with age. When his rays come forth no longer and heat is uniformly diffused, we frigid nations will be on a level with our less fortunate torrid neighbours, and there will then be no curling and "no nothing." We could reconcile ourselves to the consummation if only in our little day the lessening of the sun's heat gave us more ice, but what with gulf-streams, sun-spots, and other "new inventions," we have a poor time of it compared with our great-great-grandfathers, and never once in our lifetime have we had such a luxury as the Beith curlers had at Nicol Buntin's burial, when they "had the drops from their noses frozen like *shuchles*." Let us hope that John Frost will see it to be his duty to work his patent more effectively, or else hand it over to the Royal Club to make better use of it.

The portion of ice set apart for a curling *spiel* was called the *lead*, *rank*, or *rink* (by which last name it is still described), and as it was then shorter than it is now—its ordinary length being 30 yards—this partly explains how early curlers were able to play such heavy stones.

At each end of the rink was the *tee, toe-see, cock, cockee, wittyr, gog*, or *gogsee*, as it was variously called. Then, as now, it was what all aimed at, the centre of attraction, the cynosure of every eye. A bawbee, a pinch of snuff, or a plain button inserted in the ice was enough to mark the interesting spot, but a later improvement was "a circular piece of iron with a hole drilled in the centre and having a small prong immediately opposite, which is pressed down into the ice to keep it fixed" (Fig. 39).

FIG. 39.

We have a relic of antiquity in the form of a wooden pin about a foot high, which was used the better to indicate the tee from a distance. It is rather a dowdy edition of the fairy form which artists are accustomed to sketch hovering over the *gog*, and looks not unlike a champagne bottle dying of consumption; but though its intentions might be good, its existence need not be prolonged, as its purpose is sufficiently served by a "besom shank."*

Round the toe-see were drawn several concentric circles, called the *broughs*, varying in diameter from 2 to 12 feet. The space about the tee and the broughs

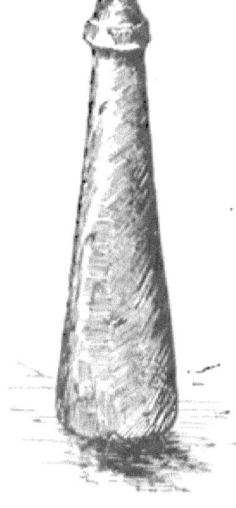

FIG. 40.
ROSLIN TEE-MARKER.

---

* Movable indicators of this kind are still in use in several places. That of the Alloa Club is described as *made of wood, in the shape of a quart bottle*.

was called the *boardhead*. The *coal, collie score, hog*, or *hog-score*, a line (generally *wavy* or *serpentine*, so as to

Fig. 41.

distinguish it from an accidental crack in the ice) was drawn at a distance from the tee of one-fifth or one-sixth part of the whole rink, so that when the rink was 30 yards the hog was either 6 or 5 yards distant from the gog. The dread Rubicon was therefore easier crossed when the rink was shorter.

FIG. 42.

Rink or *rack* was the term applied to a team of players. This was generally composed of eight men, though the number varied from three to nine, and was presided over by a *brandey, director, master, oversman, kin-hawn, leader,* or *douper*,* as he is variously called, whose duty it was to direct the game and to play the last stone.

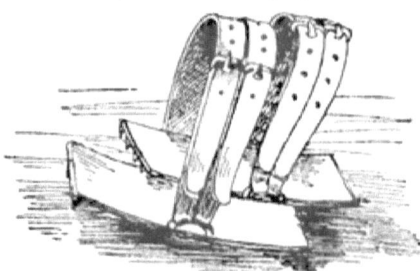

FIG. 43. CRAMPITS.

Sir George Harvey's picture of the *Curlers* in the beginning of this chapter, and the figures † on the two foregoing pages give a good idea of their ordinary *accoutrements* in the end of the last and the beginning of the present century. The *kowe, cowe,* or *broom,* without which no player was allowed to appear on the ice, is conspicuous,

and there is a picturesqueness in the ancient article that we miss in our modern besom. Of the stones used we need add nothing to what has already been said. The one which has left the hand of the player‡ in Harvey's illustration, and which "nods in conscious pride" as it moves along the *kowe,* attended by the excited dog, who

FIG. 44. CURRIE CRAMPITS.

is no doubt on his master's side, and by the faithful sweepers, has, it may be noticed, a ring-handle, and is rather more antique in appearance than those which are at rest around the tee.

The oldest type of foot-hold used by the curler for delivering the stone and attending to the sweeping was the *crampbit, crampet, cramp,* or *tramp*—a piece of iron

---

* The designation *skipper* or *skip* is not found in the last century records examined by us.

† From drawings by the late James Drummond, R.S.A. (1842), in the possession of Captain Macnair. While the drawings are in many respects interesting, the "brethren" will detect some deficiencies which lead us to infer that the artist was not a curler.

‡ The player is said to be the Rev. Dr Aiton of Dolphinton.

or steel with prongs on the under-surface, which was usually bound to the foot with straps.

James Riddel seems, however, to have had a simpler mode of attaching himself to this *understanding* when he *sprang upon* the cramps, and knocked to flinders the fine Osmund stone of Gavin Gibson (p. 59).

FIG. 45. CURRIE CRAMPIT.

So late as 1833 we find Sir Richard Broun defending the use of these articles, and he gives an illustration of an improved form of crampits, invented by the Rev. Dr Somerville,

"Which consists of two separate pieces of iron, connected with a screw, and which, by the key or screw-nail, can be fixed upon the boot or shoe, under the ball of the great toe—its best position being that where the spring of the foot is made—with a degree of firmness equal to that held by a vice" (Figs. 44 and 45).

Dr Cairnie, however, condemned the use of them as "almost barbarous," and by his invention of the foot-iron, now generally used in an improved form, they were gradually displaced.

FIG. 46. CAIRNIE'S FOOT-IRON.

The *trickers* or *triggers*, *grippers* or *crisps*, were a later type of the foothold, giving less latitude to the player in delivering the stone, as they were fixed in the ice and not bound to the feet. The trickers were pieces of iron, generally of a triangular shape, with sharp pikes below and a hold above to prevent the foot from slipping, one being sometimes set for the heel of the right, the other for the toe of the left foot. Their use marked an improvement in the game, as they confined the curler to a certain spot in delivering his stone, but it was quite permissible, we believe, to shift the tricker a yard or two to the right or to the left as best suited the player when he wanted to get past the guard or

160 ANCIENT CURLING.

OLD TRICKERS.

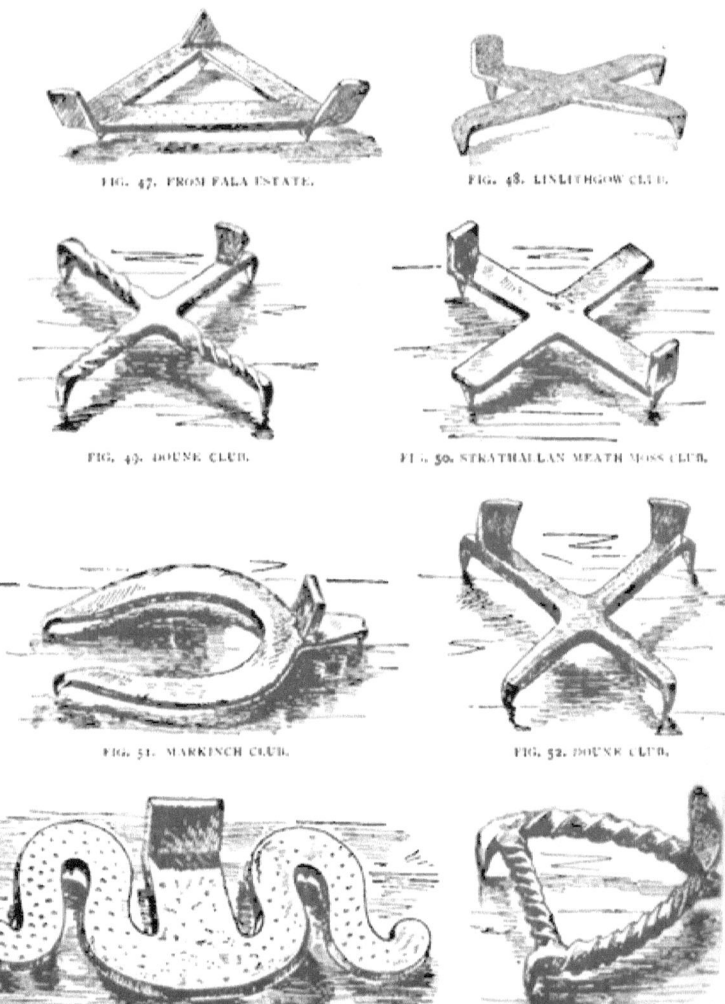

FIG. 47. FROM FALA ESTATE.
FIG. 48. LINLITHGOW CLUB.
FIG. 49. DOUNE CLUB.
FIG. 50. STRATHALLAN MEATH MOSS CLUB.
FIG. 51. MARKINCH CLUB.
FIG. 52. DOUNE CLUB.
FIG. 53. STRATHALLAN MEATH MOSS CLUB (*front*).
FIG. 54. STRATHALLAN MEATH MOSS CLUB.

take some particular shot. Sketches of a few of these *gabions* now in the possession of some of our older clubs are here furnished, from which it will be seen that their variety of form was extensive.

The *hack* or *notch* in the ice, which some of the best clubs and most skilful players still prefer before any other, is a later style of foothold. With a strong knife a longitudinal hollow is made in the ice in which one foot is fixed as shewn in Fig. 55, which also indicates the relative position of the other foot. The hack is so simple and so natural that it might be supposed to be the most ancient form of foothold, but it is really an indication of further improvement in the mode of play. While

> "The trimling player stell'd his tramp
> Wi' mony a stumping stog,"

and moved about "like a hen on a het girdle" till he got into suitable position to take the shot he wanted, or adjusted the trickers with the same uncertainty, the use of the hack permitted no such liberties, and the "capering combatants" had to play from one position and deliver the stones so as to make them cross the *tee*. The hack is, however, liable to weaken the ice and let up the water, and it is unsuitable for the artificial ponds now so common, so that for sake of uniformity it would be better for curlers generally to adopt the foot-iron.

FIG. 55.

The game in early times generally consisted of a certain number of shots, "31" being a common number, and the *bonspiel*, which was generally played between five rinks of eight men each, was in such a case only decided when one side reached the score of "155," and unless a majority of rinks on one side were uppermost, a mere majority of numbers did not secure a victory. This anomalous custom has been discontinued, but in the south of Scotland the game of numbers has not given place to the game of time, as it ought to have done.*

---

* "27" (instead of "31") was the old number in Galloway. Later it was "21." Now the game generally consists of a certain number of "heads" or "ends."

L

The great "field-day of the ice campaign" was the *bonspiel*, in which parish met to measure strength with parish and decide which was to look up to the other, for a year at least, as superior. The curling society, where it was formed, carried out the preparations for the great event, and took the honour of the parish into its keeping. Mimic battles were previously fought on the home ice, that the generals who had been chosen to do battle in name of the parish might discipline their forces and test their efficiency before the struggle came off.

With "the neb o' the morning" all were astir when the eventful day came which was to decide for another year their curling fate. The stones had been carted off at midnight, and after a hurried breakfast the warriors sped over the hills to the scene of action followed by the good wishes of the whole parish. The gudewives had done their part in preparing a good supply of *vivres*.

"These consisted of bread and cheese with porter *ad libitum*, and such of the company as chose had hot pints prepared, consisting of porter, eggs, biscuit, sugar and whisky, of a consistence as thick as ordinary porridge, and well might be called meat and drink." *

These were safely deposited at the side of the pond, as Harvey's picture does not fail to indicate, and the artist has not forgotten to assist Dr Cairnie's memory by putting the "*Grey Beardie*" at the side of them. With appetites whetted by their early drive in the crisp morning air, the curlers might have been excused for falling upon their stores at once, but they must first open war and test the enemy's mettle with the aid of "only a thimblefu."

> "An' ere they did the play begin,
>   Ilk stamock got a cauker,
> For nane did think it was a sin
>   Most bonnily to tak' her.
> Ahin' the quickly toomed glass
>   How the wee finger twirled,
> Then up in air a bawbee was
>   For heads or tails hie birled
>   To lead that day."

Not more keenly did their forefathers fight for civil and religious liberty than did the "glorious congregation of

---

* Cairnie's *Essay*, p. 63.

incomparable curlers" for the honour of their parish, with channel-stanes for swords and kowes for spears. Supple-sinewed, broad-chested, brawny-armed young fellows and "aged men smit with the eagerness of youth" alike nerved with the love of conquest, and fired with a desire for glory, put forth every energy they could command, as if the struggle were one of life and death. Uncouth and clumsy as their stone-weapons were, they *drew*, they *guarded*, they *ported*, they *brittled*, they *chuckled* with a dexterity which was simply marvellous. A brief pause hurriedly to despatch the said *rivres* by the loch-side; then faster and more furious grew the fray—the one side anxious to regain what they had lost, the other determined to retain what they had won. They ran, they soopit, they roared till they were hoarse; yet with all the uproar there was no disorder, each rink moving with the precision of a tried regiment under a skilful general. Their ponderous granites "growled" along the rink; and though the ice "rairded" under their crampeted tread, they heeded not, as they watched with eagerness the effect of each shot on the enemy, and plied their brooms and played their stones as their commander directed. Often, as it happened, fate hung upon the last shot of all, and as the stone of destiny left the hand of the *cideat* director, every nerve of every player quivered with excitement till the deed was done which decided the fortune of the day. Besoms and Kilmarnock bonnets "cuist" high into the air, with "hollas loud and lang," proclaimed the joy of a victory more important than Waterloo to its victors; while Edinburgh after Flodden was no sadder spectacle than the village of the vanquished parish, when the stragglers came back from the scene to tell in tears the story of defeat. Thus closed the day of rivalry; but the evening had to succeed, with its merry gathering around the table in the "muckle room," and its finishing touches of mirth and fellowship, without which no bonspiel was considered perfect in the olden time. In the steam of "beef and greens," and the flowing cup of kindness, all unpleasant remembrances of the day's feud melted away. Heart opened out to heart under the genial glow of sympathy, and with song and sentiment the winged hours flew past; the old ties of brotherhood were strengthened, and new friendships were formed, as the curling heroes of two parishes met, no longer in rivalry but in good-fellowship; and thus the pillars of the bonspiel were established more firmly than ever.

These parish bonspiels and their attendant festivities marked the dawn of Scotland's better day. They were only possible among a free, loyal, and independent people, and so they brighten up the landscape of Scottish history when religious wars, clan quarrels, border lawlessness, and Jacobite risings no longer trouble the land. We have been a fighting nation, and such we are, and will be to the last; but if we could only give up the war-cries that cause strife and bitterness among us, and confine our energy to such healthy conflicts as curlers engage in, our fighting would be good for us; it would brace our nerves and strengthen our sinews, and bring us into a condition of healthy equality and fraternity.

This story of Ancient Curling has taken up more time and more space than our first intentions had allotted to it. When so many old documents and relics were handed over to us by various clubs, and when fresh interest was aroused in the past by the great commemorative gathering of curlers on November 28, 1888, it seemed to us that we should in the circumstances best discharge our duty by preparing such an account of the game as would embrace all the new information furnished to us, and all that writers on the subject since Ramsay's time had set down. Our desire has been to make as clear as possible the history of curling up to the beginning of this century. There is for those who come after us a rich and wide field in the records of later clubs, into which we shall only enter to take a rapid survey of the ground. Others will no doubt take up and complete the story of curling, and perhaps by fresh investigation supplement what we have written about ancient times. It is enough for us now if, by what we have written, curlers at home and abroad are brought into closer fellowship with those who, from the time of George Ruthven to that of James Millar, did such good pioneer work, and even in far-off times, established for curling the reputation it has ever held as the best, the healthiest, and the manliest of all games. Truly, they were a set of noble fellows, and we cannot give them the " word " and the " grip," as they look out upon us from the dim past, without having our enthusiasm warmed and our devotion to curling increased. As the game increases in popularity, and finds for itself a home, as we trust it shall, in lands even more suited for its development than our own, we may look for many further improvements in the method of play. One thing, however, is certain—and it is sufficient excuse for the time and space we have given to the subject of Ancient Curling—we shall never improve upon the good-fellowship of the curlers in the old times on the ice and by the social board, and we shall never give a better account of ourselves than did the founders of the Duddingston Society, when in the name of the brotherhood of the last century they resolved that " to be virtuous is to reverence our God, religion, laws, and king "; that " virtue, without which no accomplishment is truly valuable, and no enjoyment really satisfactory, shall be the aim of their actions "; and that " peace and unanimity, the great ornaments of society, shall reign among them." It seems to us that the best we can do is simply to uphold these ancient traditions of the game, and to be true to the spirit of them.

That we have lifted the veil of obscurity from the origin of the game, and settled the question in favour of Scotland, we do not profess. Perhaps it may never be possible to do this; but that Scotland has been the chosen guardian of curling from infancy to manhood can never be doubted or denied. Nor can it be denied that the child of our adoption in its every feature proclaims its parentage. "That sport," as Christopher North once truly said, "stirs the heart of auld Scotland till you hear it beating in her bosom." Our pawky humour, our canniness, our keenness, our love of independence, our sociality, our *perfervidum ingenium*, are all reflected in our curling, and all at their best—for curlers are the "wale" of their countrymen, and the truest exponents of our national character. What it gives of insight into our inner life is, however, not so important as what it does in return for our fostering care, in mitigating for us the ills of life, and ministering to us sympathy, strength, and joy. Curling converts what would otherwise be the bitterest into the most delightful part of the whole year, and at the very time when no stranger would think of visiting our bleak shores, in the seemingly inhospitable season of frost and snow, we are found amusing ourselves together, and pitying those who have no enjoyments like ours. In curling our youth have an outlet for their enthusiasm and energy, and a means of cultivating strength of body and vigour of mind, by an amusement which is in no way associated with vicious temptations: while from age it wards off disease and infirmity, and gives new life to the stiffening limbs. It comes to the labourer at the time he most needs relief, when the fields are at rest and he does not require to work; it makes him forget the burden of toil, and cheers his heart, and makes his life more worth living. It draws the professional man and the man of business away from care and worry, and removes the wrinkles of anxiety from the troubled brow. It brings rich and poor together in a way that nothing else does or can do, and without taking from the one his dignity or from the other his self-respect, it makes them feel that they are "a' John Tamson's bairns," and that beneath and above all social distinctions there is a deeper, higher relationship—that of sympathy and common humanity.

As something more than "a mere amusement;" as, in fact, an important force in the development of our national character, the student of Scottish history may find much instruction in the history of the national game. The lover of humankind may also watch with interest its progress and seek its prosperity, and from what it has done in this country in the past he may infer how much it is possible for curling to do in helping on the time

"When man to man the world o'er
Shall brithers be an' a' that."

We in Scotland may well be thankful, as we are, for our inheritance, and proud, as we are, of our game. Our pride and thankfulness will, however, only be complete when every country under the dominion of the ice-king shares the inheritance with ourselves. Wherever Scotchmen go (and where on earth do they not go?) let them therefore carry with them their brooms and their channel-stanes, and give the blessing of curling to every country of their adoption where the old friend of their fatherland—John Frost—is permitted to visit them. They can take from auld Scotland no better gift, and keen, keen will be our delight when the brotherhood is as wide as nature will allow it to be. With those who remain at home the future of curling is in safe keeping. Not till Scotland herself passes into oblivion shall any true son of hers allow the noble game to be forgotten. Together they have prospered and together we wish them prosperity—the Land o' Cakes and her ain game o' curlin'.

> "Lang wave the thistle on the lea,
>   Lang live this northern land,
> Lang rowe her burnies to the sea,
>   Lang live her curling band!
>
> "O Scotsmen, aye be Scotsmen true,
>   And on the icy plain
> Still joyful swing and bravely fling
>   The roaring channel-stane!"

PART II.

MODERN CURLING.

THE CHANNEL-STANE.

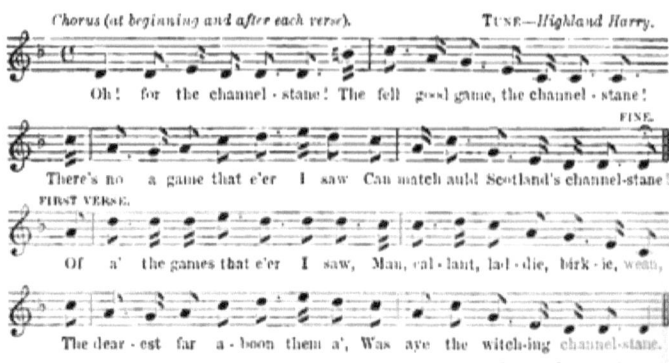

Chorus (at beginning and after each verse).   TUNE—*Highland Harry.*

Oh! for the channel-stane! The fell good game, the channel-stane!
There's no a game that e'er I saw Can match auld Scotland's channel-stane!

FIRST VERSE.

Of a' the games that e'er I saw, Man, callant, laddie, birkie, wean,
The dearest far aboon them a', Was aye the witching channel-stane.

Repeat Chorus to FINE.

I've been at bridals unco glad,
  Wi' courting lasses wondrous fain,
But what is a' the fun I've had—
  Compare it wi' the channel-stane?
    Oh! for, &c.

I've played at quoiting in my day,
  And maybe I may do't again,
But still unto myself I'd say,
  This is no the channel-stane.
    Oh! for, &c.

Were I a sprite in yonder sky,
  Never to come back again,
I'd sweep the moon and starlets by,
  And beat them at the channel-stane
    Oh! for, &c.

We'd boom across the Milky Way—
  One tee should be the Northern Wa
Another, bright Orion's ray,
  A comet for a channel-stane!
    Oh! for, &c.

CHAPTER I.

THE TRANSITION PERIOD—1800-1838.

THREE words describe the curling of the period now to be considered—progress, enthusiasm, confusion. What with excitement caused by fear of French invasion up to the peace of 1815, political agitations previous to the Reform Bill of 1832, and the introduction of Free Trade, and with the bitter conflict within the Scottish Church on the question of Church and State which led to the Disruption of 1843, the country was anything but quiet. John Frost, however, did his best to draw all classes and conditions together on the ice by giving them many fine hard winters, and if beyond the Grampians the people did not yet pay him much attention, the Gallovidian poet's words were true of his own and of the southern districts of the country—

"In Auld Scotlan' whan winter snell
Bin's up the fosey yirth,
Then jolly curlers ha'e a spell,
O' manly fun and mirth ;
Whane'er the ice can har'ly bear
A hame lie hurkling nane,
Wha liketh independent cheer,
And can a channel-stane
Owr hog that day."

In most parishes the curling club became a recognised necessity. Masons, weavers, and workpeople generally were never more devoted to the game, and the nobility and gentry gave it their heartiest support. Literary men extolled its praises in song and story, and at last we get one genuine blink of Royal patronage in the fact that His Majesty King William IV.,

"Through Sir Andrew Halliday, gave a commission to Principal Baird to send several pairs of curling-stones to Bushy Park."

With all this progress and enthusiasm there was, however, much confusion. Curlers are conservative, and the advanced methods and rules of Duddingston were only slowly adopted: the barbarous tribe of natural boulders, crunching crampits, and movable triggers lingered on. The local mason did his best to nidge the local block, but there was neither beauty nor uniformity among the stones. Many players still used only one stone, and the number in a rink ranged from 4 to 16. The style of play was altogether more varied than in the previous century, and before parish battles could be fought a number of questions had generally to be settled, and numerous conditions made by which to regulate the play.

The progress of curling in the period and its distribution throughout Scotland may be understood from the following list:—

AYR.†

Ardrossan Castle (1830).	*Kilmarnock Junior (1820).	*Largs Gogoside.
Auchinleck.	*Kilmarnock Morning Star.	„ *Thistle (1813).
Ayr (1820).		„ Noddle (1814).
Ayr Victoria (1838).		Loudon.
Beith (2 clubs).	Kilmarnock Netherton-hall.	*Mauchline Senior (1838).
Cumnock.		
*Dalry (1814).	Kilmarnock Senior (1810).	Maybole.
Dreghorn.		Rowallan (1832).
Dundonald (1820).	Kilmarnock Social.	Sorn.
Fenwick.	„ *Townend (1810).	Stewarton Heather (1835).
Fenwick Waterside.		
Galston.	Kilmarnock Union (1838).	Stewarton Friendly.
Irvine Senior (1838).		„ Social.
Kilmarnock Friendly.	Kilmaurs.	Tarbolton.
„ *Holm.	Kirkmichael & Water of Girvan (1815).	

† Clubs printed in ordinary type either are or have been affiliated with the Royal Club, and an asterisk distinguishes those that joined the Royal at its formation in 1838. Clubs in italics have not been so affiliated.

THE TRANSITION PERIOD.   173

BERWICK.
Duns (1801).

BUTE.
*Millport.

CLACKMANNAN.
Dollar and Devonvale (1828).   Tullibody (1830).

DUMBARTON.
Dumbarton (1815).   Duntocher (1838).   Lennox (1821).
                                                  Waterside (1820).

DUMFRIES.†
Border, Langholm.   *Irongray.*   Moffat (King Robert
Closeburn.   *Johnstone.*   Bruce) (1831).
Dalton St Bridget's   *Kirkbean.*   *Newabbey.*
  (1837).   *Kirkmahoe.*   *Ruthwell.*
Dumfries (Rowley Pow-   *Kirkmichael.*   Springkell and Middle-
  ley) (1831).   *Lochmaben* (1823).   bie (1827).
Dunscore.   *Lockerby.*   *Terregles.*
Glencairn.   *Tinwald.*
                                                  *Thornhill.

EDINBURGH.
Bellsquarry and Living- *Edinburgh Clydesdale.* *Newton.*
  stone (1831).   Glencorse (1830).   *Penicuick (1815).
*Corstorphine (1830).   *Kirknewton (1825).   Redhall (1838).
*Currie (1830).   *Merchiston (1809).   Rosslyn (1816).
Dalkeith.   Midcalder (1830).   *Stow.*
*Drum (1814).   *Musselburgh (1816).   West Calder (1823).
Edinburgh (1830).

FIFE.
Abbotshall (1833).   *Dunfermline Mechan-   *Leuchars (1837).
*Abdie (1831).   ics (1830).   Leven (1838).
Aberdour and Dalgety‡   Hercules (Colinsburgh)   Lochgelly (1831).
  (1818).   (1835).   Stratheden (1838).
Airth.   Kilconquhar.   St Margaret's (Inver-
Ballingry (1838).   Kirkcaldy (1838).   keithing) (1834).
                                                  Torry (1837).

FORFAR.
Kirriemuir (1809).

HADDINGTON.
Dunglass and Cock-   *East Linton (1838).   Gladsmuir (1835).
  burnspath (1831).

---

† Sir R. Broun states that the game "flourished" (though clubs do not then appear to have been formed) at *Annan, Applegarth, Cummertrees, Ecclefechan, Eskdalemuir, Hutton and Corrie, Johnstone, Kirkpatrick-Juxta, Mouswald, Penpont, Torthorwald, Wamphray.*

‡ Then the Otterston Club.

KINROSS.
*Kinross† (1818)   Orwell (1826).

KIRKCUDBRIGHT.
Buittle (1838).   Kelton (1831).
Crossmichael (1838). Kirkbean (1830).

LANARK.
Anderston.   Dalziel (1820).   *North   Woodside
*Avondale (1818).   *Dolphinton.   (1819).
Bishopbriggs.   East Kilbride (1830).   *Partick*.
Cathcart.   *Gorbals*.   Port Dundas.
Carnwath.   Kelvindock (1813).   Shotts (1829).
*Chryston (1831).   *Willowbank (1837).

LINLITHGOW.
*Bathgate (1811).   *Linlithgow Junior   Uphall (1833).
*Buchan (1838).   (1830).   *Whitburn and Fauld-
Linlithgow (1820).   Torphichen (1831)   house (1829).

PEEBLES.
Broughton United   Eddleston (1830).   Peebles‡ (1821).
   (1816).

PERTH.
Abercairney (1811). *Crieff*.   Meikleour (1814).
Alyth (1815).   *Dunblane (1816).   *Methven (1831).
Auchterarder (1830). Dunkeld (1830).   Monzie (1810).
Bendochy (1832).   *Kilmadock*.   Rohallion and Birnam
*Carnie (1838).   Kinfauns (1834).   (1837).
Cairney and Dupplin *Kinnoughtry (1838).   St Madoes (1826).
   (1832).   Maderty (1814).   *Scone and Perth.
Clunie (1825).   Meigle (1814).   Strathmore (1826).
Coldoch (1828).

RENFREW.
Barrhead (1807).   *Levern* (1828).   Paisley *Sneddon* (1815).
Eaglesham (1821).   Lochwinnoch (1827).   „   *United* (1829).
Greenock (1830).   *Neilston* (1824).   „   *Storrie St*.
Houston (1835).   *Nitshill* (1829).   Pollokshaws (1801).
Hurlet and Nitshill Paisley Iceland.   Port-Glasgow (1818).
   (1822).   „   Union.   Renfrew King's Inch
Kilbarchan (1829).   (1830).

ROXBURGH.
Hawick (1803).

SELKIRK.
Ettrick.   Galashiels (1823).   *Selkirk*.

---

† The club then regularly constituted is said to have existed " from
time immemorial."
‡ The game flourished also at Newlands, Traquair, Linton, and Hartree.

STIRLING.
Banknock (1831).   Larbert (1838).   Slamannan (1838).
*Denny (1830).   Laurieston and Zetland   Stirling (1820).
Drymen (1830).   (1838).   West Quarter and Pol-
Falkirk (1816).   Logie.   mont (1836).
Kippen (1830).   Milton of Campsie (1830).

WIGTON.
Loch Connel (1838).   Penninghame (1828).   *Wigtown.*

A great many of these were no doubt *soi-disant* clubs, without any regular constitution, or stated business to transact, but they fairly indicate the popularity of curling in their several counties. Most of the old clubs of last century continued their work, and of these the minutes of Doune, Strathallan Meath Moss, Ardoch, Jedburgh, Bridge of Allan, which were formerly silent, begin at this period to give us their news. Their imperfect organisation no doubt accounts for the fact that among the numerous clubs in the above list we have only been able to find the records of twenty-four, viz. :—

Abdie.	Dumfries.	North Woodside.
Aberdour (Otterston).	Dunblane.	Orwell.
Alyth.	Duns.	Peebles.
Auchterarder.	Gladsmuir.	Penicuick.
Ayr.	Hawick.	Penninghame.
Clunie.	Kelton.	Rosslyn.
Currie.	Kinross.	Strathmore.
Dumbarton.	Meigle.	Willowbank.

With such information as these various records furnish, and the added light of the curling literature of the time, we may arrange the various counties into groups, where they appear to have some bond of connection, and in this way we may survey the curling of what we have called the transition period in the history of the game.

I. WESTERN GROUP.—*Ayr, Renfrew, Lanark, Dumbarton.*

Curlers may well keep their eye upon AYR, as the county that contains within itself the chief storehouse to which future generations must come for their implements of war. Besides, no other county is richer in curling literature or more honourably associated with the development of the national game. Of its three divisions, Cunningham had the lead, with its memories of Covenanter Guthrie, who as far back as 1644 used the "innocent recreation," and of Tam Samson, who with his retainers kept court in Sandy Patrick's a century later. Tam was now "deid," but Tam the second was the honoured preses of one of the many clubs that bound the curlers of *Kilmarnock* together at this period. Their curling made them long-lived—so their historian * tells us. And no wonder, for the young men of the *Morning Star* met on the ice at 7 A.M., and had two hours' play before they began work. Keen as they were, they spared some of their time to the literary side of their game, and from the Kilmarnock press a collection of curling songs, with a treatise on the game based on the work of Ramsay, was issued in 1828.† Most of the songs are by Ayrshire bards, and though all the singers are not *deacons* at the business, even Solomon might have been a wiser and a better man if he had been privileged to hearken to such experience as one of them gives in these anonymous lines:—

> "I ha'e tried love, I ha'e tried war,
> I've tried to play the warldling,
> But, 'boon a' crafts or joys, to me,
> Is winter's darling—curling.
>
> "There's aye sic glee around the tee,
> Ilk man's a social brither,
> Blyth morn and e'en, a curler keen
> In snell, snell, frosty weather."

The Craufurds of Craufurdland have always done their utmost to keep alive the enthusiasm of the Kilmarnock players, and a silver trophy given by the lady of the castle in 1829 brought Kilmarnock into competition with *Fenwick*, whose players were then in possession of the scientific secret which has made them famous. *Mauchline, Galston, Sorn, Loudon*, and such parishes could at this time each turn out a quota of 130 or 150 players. From these and the other

---

* Archibald M'Kay. *History of Kilmarnock*, third edition, p. 114.
† *A Descriptive and Historical Sketch of Curling; also, Rules, Practical Directions, Songs, Toasts, and a Glossary.* Kilmarnock: Crawford, Bookseller.

One of the compilers of this publication also contributes an interesting account of Kilmarnock curling to Cairnie's *Essay*, pp. 68-77.

Ayr parishes we have no written records, but the minutes of the *Ayr* Club formed in 1820 are before us, and may be held to illustrate the customs of the county clubs. Here the rules were those of Duddingston, but the usual number of players was eight in a rink—it was never to exceed ten. The use of crampits attached to the feet was forbidden, as they injured the ice, but a pair was placed at each end to be used there, and in order to perform his sweeping duties with safety, the player was to have "carpet shoes or something similar." The Ayr Club had its court for initiation—new members receiving the "word," and old ones being examined in their knowledge of it. The Earl of Cassillis was a member, and the number of members being limited to fifty there was consequently keen competition for admission. The Ayr curlers—"honest men"—remembered the "bonnie lasses," as the Kilmarnock and other clubs were wont to do, and annually gave a ball which made them and their club popular in the "auld toun." It is to them also that the Barns Club owes its existence—they having resolved themselves in 1821 into "a club to commemorate the birth of Burns, that the stigma of their having no such club, while almost every other place in Scotland had one, might be removed from Ayr."

Auchinleck—the parish of Sir Alexander Boswell (1775-1822)—had its club, and here the distinguished patriot and song-writer celebrated the praises of the game with as much applause as he did at Duddingston, till he was slain in a duel by a Fifeshire curler—James Stuart—an event which is one of the saddest in our annals. Pity indeed that political hatred overcame curling fellowship, and that Ayrshire and Scotland lost so early one of the most amiable and accomplished of men.

That patron of all manly sports, the Earl of Eglinton, was by this time leading *Kilwinning* curlers with his redoubtable henchman, Hugh Conn. In *Beith* there were then, as there are now, many keen and good curlers who flocked down to Kilbirnie when the "icy chain" was safely thrown over it. Another member of the Duddingston Club—the Rev. James

Muir—was minister here. His song, *When chitterin' birds on flichterin' wing,* is one of the best we have, and Beith may ever be proud of its author. *Dalmellington,* too, had its poet—Robert Hetrick, who wrote some good verses.

"From the lochs at Straiton to the flushes at Largs," curling was as popular then as "Rockwood" found it at a later day, and among the Ayrshire curlers there were many noted names. Chief among them all, and even among the curlers of Scotland at this period, we place John Cairnie, the inventor of the system of artificial pond-making which has done so much for curling, and of the foot-iron now in common use. A native of Neilston, Cairnie served a period of faithful duty as surgeon in the H.E.I.C.S., and in 1813 he settled down at Largs —"the Montpelier of the North," as he called it—where he built Curling Hall. (He had no wife and children to whom he might have attached curling names.) From this time he threw aside his doctor's toga and made curling his hobby. He introduced it at Largs and other places, and at the annual dinners of the Duddingston Club, of which club he also was a member, his new pavement-pond system was first explained and discussed. In 1833 he published his *Essay on Curling,* which was written to vindicate his claim as an inventor against that of Dr Somerville of Currie, but the work will remain valuable for its information about the game as it was then practised in different districts of Scotland, and for the pleasant glimpses it gives us of the writer and his friends in the west, on the ice, and by the social board. Here is his account of one of the dinners of the *Noddle* Club (so called from the Noddle Burn on which they curled).

FIG. 56.
DR CAIRNIE, FIRST PRESIDENT OF THE ROYAL CALEDONIAN CURLING CLUB.
(Photographed from a picture by Mr John Fergus, Largs.)

"On 10th December 1823 the gentlemen of the club dined at the King's Arms Inn, when they were honoured with the company of no less than 11 visitors. The bill of fare is mentioned in the club-book, consisting of hare soup, fried whitings, a large turbot, a joint of corned beef, roasted beef, corned pork, two tongues, chickens, a fine goose, four grouse, and vegetables, dumpling, pudding, custard, jam, and jellies; a moderate proportion of wine was given, and the charge to each person present amounted to 7s. 8½d., including ale, porter, and a modicum of drams; the dinner was excellent."

Like George Ruthven of happy memory, Cairnie was "a bonnie little man," keen to win, and difficult to beat; kind to the poor, and a favourite with all his friends. He had lost his left arm by a gunpowder explosion, but what his right arm found to do was done with all its might, and whether on his yacht or on the paved pond at Curling Hall, he was always happiest when making others happy. An elegy written in 1844 by his friend Captain Paterson makes fitting reference to his worth and to the sense of grief occasioned by his death.

"Why droops the banner half-mast high,
And curlers heave the bitter sigh?
Why throughout Largs the tearful eye,
So blear'd and red?
Oh! listen to the poor man's cry!
'John Cairnie's dead!'

"While winter's breath as waters freeze,
Lays waste the fields and bares the trees,
Or well-rigged yachts in joyous breeze
For prizes ply,
Cairnie! thy name by land or seas
Shall never die."*

* The banner referred to is the flag which used to be hoisted on a high mast when the ice on Cairnie's pond was ready for sport. One room in Curling Hall was decorated with the numerous trophies Cairnie had carried off by flood or field, yacht or curling-stone. The initials "J. C." at once attracted our attention when we lately visited the place, but they turned out to be those of Mr John Clark, Anchor Mills, Paisley, who has made of Curling Hall a palatial residence, and whose splendid steam yacht was lying where Cairnie's cutter appears in the frontispiece to the *Essay*. The pond has disappeared, but the ship's bell and figurehead of the *Semiramis*, on which Cairnie was surgeon, are to be seen in the beautiful grounds adjoining the Hall, and the stone pillar erected in the garden by Cairnie, on the spot where Haco is said to have fallen in the battle between the Scots and the Norwegians in 1263, is still there. It has a Latin inscription, of which we give a translation: "Here took place the fury of the Goths. Here lies buried Haco of Denmark, and everywhere around the earth covers his Norwegian comrades. Hither they came seeking a kingdom. Here victorious Scotland gave to her enemies—graves, their just reward, on the 4th day after the nones of October, A.D. 1263. Largs, on the very kalends of June 1823, John Cairney set me up and commanded me to commemorate that event to thee. Commemorate thou it to others."

In the county of RENFREW, the chosen home of curling has always been the safe and beautiful loch of Castle Semple or *Lochwinnoch*, as it is usually called. The famous match[*] between the Duke of Hamilton and M'Dowall of Garthland popularised curling here, and led to its introduction by Mr Cunningham of Craigends into the district of Strathgryffe, *Kilbarchan, Houston,* and *Bridge of Weir.* From the time of that laird, who in the end of last century was constantly with the curlers, and in Strand's Inn "paid all their *drink, baiks, buns, &c.,*" and who was "beloved and even adored at Lochwinnoch," the curlers there have always enjoyed the patronage and support of the M'Dowall family. They have also, it appears, a supernatural patron and friend of whom we have some account in Dr Crawford's *Crune of the Warlock of the Peil* (1838). This was auld Ringan Sempill, "a camsheuch and capernoytit carl," who, when he was in the flesh, dwelt in a "wee isle" in the loch called the Peil. The Peil was destroyed, and its occupier died of grief, but auld Ringan's wraith thereafter "haunts his lanelie abode," and when the curlers linger too long on the loch, now that the "thow is cum," and "the snaw is meltin' on Mistilaw," the oracle *crunes* to them this salutary counsel :—

"Curlers, gae hame to your spedds or your plews,
  To your pens, to your spules, or your thummills ;
Curlers, gae hame or the ice ye'se faw throu',
  Tak' your ellwands, your elsins or wummills."

At *Greenock* a flourishing club existed which no doubt owed its origin to Sir Michael Shaw-Stewart, who was

---

[*] An account of this match is given by Dr Andrew Crawford, the eminent antiquary, in Cairnie's work (pp. 91-93). On the first day the game was all even, and "the ladies tried to raise his Grace's thoughts in vain ;" his mind was so chained on his fate next day, that he could not "keep his spirits up within the limits of courtesy at Castle Semple, where a large party of the neighbouring gentry were present to meet him." The Duke won—thanks chiefly to the warlock Tam Pate, "who never missed a single shot," and never gave a smile or uttered a *cheep* in the general joy after the victory was won by his solitary shot. The Duke, for all that, should have lost, but one Dalgliesh, draper and douper, who had laid a bet of 1000 guineas on the match, is said to have missed a shot which lay open, "by the private hint of Garthland, that his Grace might gain the game." If the match did good to curling in the district, it was not because of its commendable features, and the Paisley manufacturer who vented his indignation against the Duke was not untrue to his curling principles when he said, "It wad be weil dune to gar his feet meet the lift."

always promoting the best interests of the citizens of Sugaropolis, and whose curling inclinations are evident in the dedication to him of Cairnie's *Essay*, and in the fact that an artificial pond was formed by him at Ardgowan on Cairnie's system.

In *Paisley* the game must have been popular in those days, for John Good, weaver (Johnny Gude), had in his time —he had curled for fifty years—supplied the curlers with no less than 200 pairs of stones. Garthland selected some *Heigh Linn* curlers to play against the Duke of Hamilton— a sufficient proof of their reputation. A club also existed in the town whose members went into the game "keenly and scientifically." They had ten rinks of seven players each, and their watchword was the worthy and appropriate one—"Meet friends and part friends."

In the county of LANARK, where Graeme described the game so early as 1771 (*vide* p. 100), we have few literary productions of this period by which to judge of its progress. The poem of Captain Paterson already referred to, and some songs by Walter Watson, *Chryston*, of average merit, are all that we can discover. The list of clubs is small for the population, but it must be remembered that those strongholds, *Douglas, Lesmahagow, Cambusnethan,* and *Hamilton*, still existed and manfully upheld the cause. Inventive genius must at this time have been very busy in this district improving or trying to improve the stones. An advanced type of stone seems to have been used at Hamilton as far back as the *Hamilton* v. *Garthland* bonspiel in 1784, for Dr Crawford says that at Lochwinnoch they took to improving their stones after the Duke's visit

"*In imitation of the Hamilton fashion*, for Lanarkshire stones were bored through the centre admitting a screw. Hence these stones were called at this village *Duke-hand* for many years afterwards."

The hollowed-bottom, now so common in Canada and at home, was here introduced, and at Wishaw they tried a peculiar style of stone, one sole of which ran on three projecting points, and the other on a circle of about one inch. Some of the stones had steel bottoms (a *Dalry* invention, for a time popular also at *Beith*), and some stones were of cast-iron (if the Irishism may be pardoned), made with bottoms of steel or of brass by the *Shotts* Iron Co. No wonder, indeed, that the men of Bathgate—as their poet relates—quailed at the sight of the Cam'nethan men's artillery when they came against them in 1831.

> "Before the icy war began
> Our hearts had well-nigh failed us
> As we surveyed their famous stanes
> Prepared to assail us.
>
> "For some were big as ony cheese,
> And some had bright steel bottoms,
> Some ran on feet, some ran on nane,
> Ours looked like bits o' totums."

It will be seen from the list that many clubs existed in the proximity of the city of Glasgow. *Anderston*, one of the oldest, was formed "for the healthful, cheering amusement of curling; no cursing or swearing was allowed, and the club required of all the members polite, kindly behaviour as brothers." The others were doubtless quite as sound in their constitution. We meet our friend Cairnie in the records of the *Willowbank* Club, disposing of *Conserve* and *Radical*, and other Largs worthies (*vide* p. 65) to the members, and arranging a match. A pond constructed by this club cost £287, and when it had to be abandoned soon after as insufficient, the society nearly "lagged on the hog-score," but some financial "soopin" put matters right, and it is now strong and flourishing. The records of *North Woodside*,[*] published at the instance of Colonel Menzies, the present popular president, introduce us to the makers of Glasgow in the first quarter of this century, setting an example to future generations of the citizens by playing on the ice. Such names as Napier, Baird, Edington, Lumsden, Dalgliesh, Graham, Orr, Crum, Fleming, and Henderson are found on the list, and we watch with interest the movements of the club from the time they curled on the Kelvin, then a clear and unpolluted stream, when the revenue of the Clyde was

---

[*] *Sixty-six Years of Curling: Being the Records of the North Woodside Curling Club from 1820-1886, with Biographical Notes and List of the Members.* Glasgow, 1886.

only £6000, and the city of Glasgow, with its then population of 147,000, did not extend beyond Jamaica Street, till after shifting their rendezvous from time to time before the city's advancing strides, they pitch their tents at Frankfield in the Glasgow of to-day, with its river revenue of £300,000, and its population of well-nigh one million inhabitants— the second city of the empire. Let Glasgow flourish, but do not let her forget the example of the curlers to whom she owes so much of her success, and who owed so much of their success to the curling by which they lightened the burdens of civic and commercial care.

When we cross from the county of Lanark into DUMBARTON, we find the ancient *Kirkintilloch* Club, still farther up the reaches of the Kelvin, uniting lairds, farmers, shopkeepers, and wabsters at the roaring game. The old records of the club were unfortunately burnt some years ago. A club was also formed at *Waterside* in 1820. It seems to have been the custom for curlers to resort to that quiet little stream the *Luggie*, which poor David Gray has made classic by his beautiful poem. There are no finer lines in curling literature than those in which the amiable poet describes the ways of the Waterside curlers of his day, and as we read them and revert to those of Graeme, we see the features that are common to curlers and curling in every generation, and which never cease to touch the poet's heart.

" Now underneath the ice the Luggie growls,
And to the polished smoothness curlers come
Keenly ambitious. Then for happy hours
The clinking stones are slid from wary hands,
And *Barleycorn*, best wine for surly airs,
Bites i' th' mouth, and ancient jokes are crack'd.
And oh, the journey homeward, when the sun,
Low-rounding to the west, in ruddy glow
Sinks large, and all the amber-skirted clouds,
His flaming retinue, with dark'ning glow
Diverge ! The broom is brandished as the sign
Of conquest, and impetuously they boast
Of how this shot was played—with what a bend
Peculiar—the perfection of all art —
That stone came rolling grandly to the *Tee*
With victory crowned, and flinging wide the rest
In loudly crash ! Within the village inn,
What time the stars are sown in ether keen,

Clear and acute with brightness; and the moon
Sharpens her semicircle; and the air
With bleakly shivering sough cuts like a scythe,
They by the roaring chimney sit, and quaff
The beaded '*Usquebu*' with sugar dash'd.
Oh, when the precious liquid fires the brain
To joy, and every heart beats fast with mirth
And ancient fellowship, what nervy grasps
Of horny hands o'er tables of rough oak!
What singing of *Lang Syne* till teardrops shine
And friendships brighten as the evening wanes!"*

The rules of a club which then existed at the town of *Dumbarton* were the Duddingston set with a few unimportant changes. Their social meetings were usually held in the Hammerman's Tavern, when "excellent songs were sung, and toasts *apropos* and eloquent were delivered"—so the minutes relate, and on one occasion their secretary bursts into verse, which for amusement may be compared with the lines above:—

"The dinner was good
And the club right hearty,
And altogether 'twas
An excellent party."

When the Dumbarton curlers lost a match they did what was next best—praised their conquerors, and this extract of minute after they had been beaten by Glasgow is not the worst inheritance that Glasgow curlers have handed down to them.

"DUMBARTON, 29*th January* 1838.

"*Inter alia.*—The curlers from Dumbarton are very happy to speak as to the politeness and gentlemanly conduct of their [Glasgow] opponents."

A great bonspiel took place between Dumbarton and two rinks from Bonhill and Kilmarnock, on Loch Lomond, 16th February 1837, an account of which, from the *Glasgow Herald*, as inserted in their minutes, describes the scene as

"Beyond measure grand; such, indeed, as we are sure was never before seen, and may perhaps never again be displayed. For besides the roaring curlers and their numerous admirers, there was a crowd of skaters and sliders, whirling, frisking, and moving about in all directions on the crystal bosom of the loch—some of them visiting Inchmurrin and the neighbouring islands—some calling at Balmahed, and others walking across from the Cameron shore to Balloch, Aber, and the vicinity, and *vice versa*, even for many miles."

---

* *The Poetical Works of David Gray.* Edited by Henry Glassford Bell. Maclehose, 1874. Pp. 16-17.

II. SOUTHERN GROUP.—*Dumfries, Kirkcudbright, Wigton.*

In the county of DUMFRIES curling was as popular at this period as in 1772, when Pennant crossed the border and found it a favourite sport in "these parts." No county in Scotland—we may safely say—had so many curlers in proportion to its population. From Criffel to Queensberry when the ice held the roar of the channel-stane was everywhere heard. For the number of clubs and curlers the written records are, however, few. *Sanquhar*, which helped us so much in the last century, is silent most of this time, and the Queen of the South has no message till 1831, when the *Dumfries* Club (afterwards called *Rowley Powley*) was formed, with William Thomson, Sheriff-Clerk, president, and Alexander Young, Procurator-Fiscal (father of the present Lord Young), vice-president. None of the others have anything to say. At Dumfries the rules of the game cannot have been very well defined, for in 1833 it was resolved—

"That the mode of play in the choice of skips and other matters respecting the game shall be settled by a majority of those present on the ice-board at commencing the play."

Parish bonspiels in the frost season were everywhere the order of the day. Nearly every parish had a contingent of 100 or 130 players ready to go to battle, but the 40 best were usually picked, and the play was "*jist perfection*," if such accounts as we have before us are true—*e.g.*,

"*Moffat* v. *Kirkpatrick-Juxta at Loch Hoppar*, 5th February 1831. The skips on both sides displayed excellent generalship, and the men executed their orders to a nicety."

Nothing can go beyond that, and as these parishes were no better than their neighbours our conclusion is easily formed. *Closeburn* was particularly favoured by having as president Sir Thomas Kirkpatrick, who had been president of the Duddingston Club, and after him Sir C. S. Menteath, another Duddingstonian, who in 1831 presented the club with what is described as "the most splendid silver medal of the kind extant, with a superb design of the loch crowded with curlers, and the old baronial tower in the distance amid surrounding scenery." *Terregles*, too, had its medal—a gift from the president, the Rev. G. M. Burnside, with the excellent motto, *Palmam qui meruit ferat*. A letter from William Brown to his brother at Coalstoun, which has not before seen the light, gives a most graphic account of a match between this club and the county town, and of the evening of rollicking mirth that succeeded. The Terregles "character" is sketched with inimitable humour.

"1st *February* 1831.

"On Saturday an annual match betwixt 15 Dumfries choice players and 15 Terregles was played on Maxwelltown Loch. I was one of the former. It was a close canter—a rink on either side gained, and the receding one was 20 all. Dumfries had in the winning shot, invincibly guarded, when the last stone on the opposite side was, through desperation, dashed up, and miraculously displaced it by hammering one stone against another until it was reached. We afterwards all dined together, and had a great deal of fun. There was a curious character amongst us from Terregles—a tall thin fellow, more than six feet—his face like a cheese-cutter, and an enormous nose about four inches long and one and a half deep, which formed the segment of a circle. After a tumbler or two, it was the richest treat I ever saw to see him. He was an elder, and serious withal, yet liked a joke. Had you seen him when Murray began to tell one, stretching out his neck—his mouth beginning gradually to widen and open—till at last he shook his head and grinned like open day—his mouth reaching from ear to ear, and his nose completely curved. I laughed till my shirt stuck to my back. Some were asking for respite, as they were quite done out. Big Kerr sat near me—I saw the sweat hailing off him!"

If written records are scarce, the literature of this period, which adorns the story of curling in Dumfries county, is plentiful and interesting. What many deem the finest of all our curling songs, *The Music o' the Year is Hushed*, was composed about the beginning of the second decade of the century by the Rev. Henry Duncan, D.D. (1774-1846), president of *Ruthwell* Curling Club, whose name is known far and wide as the founder of Savings Banks. What curler does not know and love that song, and especially the final stanza, into which the *word* has been so deftly woven?

"Now fill a bumper to the brim,
    And drink wi' three times three, man,*
May curlers on life's slippery rink
    Frae cruel rubs be free, man.

---

* Dr Duncan signed himself "A Curler in all Weathers," but he did not give temperance lectures out of season, and his reputation for good sense has been wounded in the house of its friends by these lines being thus transformed—

"Now fill a bumper—fill but ane—
    And drink wi' social glee, man."

In his *Sacred Philosophy of the Seasons* Duncan also refers to curling as "a game peculiarly prized."

> "Or should a treach'rous bias lead
> Their erring course agee, man,
> Some friendly inwick may they get
> To guide them to the tee, man."

John M'Diarmid (1790-1852), who, after assisting to start the *Scotsman*, returned to Dumfries to conduct the *Courier* newspaper at Dr Duncan's desire, contributed to that paper from time to time interesting notes on curling, and his essay on the subject in his *Sketches from Nature* (pp. 250-261) (1830) is able and interesting. It contains a good account of Cairnie's rink, to which attention was then being directed.

So much was Dumfries imbued with a desire to advance "the manly and exhilarating game," that a cheap *Curler's Magazine* was actually about the close of this period started in the town. Its first number seems to have been its last, but the worthy venture deserved a longer life.

In the February number of *Blackwood's Magazine* for 1820, under the title *Horæ Scoticæ*, No. I., a clever *jeu d'esprit* from the pen of Professor Gillespie of St Andrews (an old Closeburnian) appeared, giving an account of an imaginary bonspiel between the curling clubs of Closeburn and Lochmaben in which the Ettrick Shepherd plays the part of the Prince in "Hamlet." The article is full of rollicking mischief, but it displays, at the same time, an intimate knowledge of the game. This highly humorous production had something to do with the publication in 1830 of Sir Richard Broun's *Memorabilia Curliana Mabenensia*. Sir Richard, after having been absent from Lochmaben (his birthplace) for fifteen years, was fortunate, on his return, to have a long, memorable, and successful campaign with his curling *confrères* during the winter 1829-1830, and it then occurred to him to put into shape "the feats of the *Lochmaben* ice, where curling was practised in all its proficiency and enthusiasm." With unpardonable want of judgment, Broun took up the Professor's article as a serious publication, and attacked its author most fiercely as "the anonymous vilifier and traducer of a whole population." Gillespie, according to his friend Christopher North, "was one of the warmest and kindest hearted of men that ever lived, with a heart as full of benignity as an egg's full of meat, and not a drop of rancour in his whole composition." Broun's attack upon him was therefore, and must ever be, an ugly blot on the *Memorabilia*. There is also a forbidding amount of confusion in the volume ; it is in many respects like a dictionary of adjectives favourable to the game jumbled together without alphabetical arrangement ; but spite of unworthy invective and annoying disorder, it is a work by the reading of which every curler must profit. It may be because it recalls the scenes of our youthful years, when the enthusiasm of Dumfriesshire curlers first inspired us with a love for the game, but we must certainly confess to our high admiration of the *Memorabilia*, and award its author the first place in the temple of literary curling fame. "Marjory o' the mony lochs," as Burns called *Lochmaben*, has no need of other chronicler than Broun to exalt the fame of such old heroes as Deacon Jardine, Captain Clapperton, " Buonoparte," and " The Tutor." Her *souters* and her " invincible board " are for ever associated with her fame as truly as the illustrious Bruce ; and when shall *Mouswald* wipe out the stain of her defeat when, after twenty-eight years of victory, she in an evil hour challenged Lochmaben ?

"They were as nothing in our hands ; and would have been soutered outright, but for one of our party who was bribed by the promise of goose for dinner, and a black lamb for his daughter, to let them get a shot or two. One of our party encountered at the commencement of the spiel a huge red crag, which he struck with such force that he sent it 20 yards distance from the tee, and made it tumble over the dam-dyke (the ice played upon being a temporary pond). This bold stroke quite discomfited them. Another of our players incurred the displeasure of the worthy clergyman, who upon the occasion headed his parishioners, by the cant phrase *concert ye boys, soop!* and by asking, with a peculiar gravity of countenance, when the aspect of the day was completely overcast for Mouswald, how the game went. The dinner cost 5d. per head. These were the good old beef-and-greens times ; but the drink was (shame fa' them !) in the proportion of Falstaff's gallon of sack to the pennyworth of bread !"

The Lochmaben rules, which were drawn up by Broun, are based upon the rules of the Duddingston Society. Unlike Cairnie, Broun of course orders crampits, but in other respects the Lochmaben and Largs lists are much alike, and when they deviate from Duddingston it is not to much advantage.*

It cannot be from any Bœotian defects in the curlers of GALLOWAY that the world hears so little about their doings in this as in other periods. We must ascribe their silence to the fact that they are too intensely devoted to the game to spare time for talking about it, or for giving to future generations documentary evidence of their doings. We are not, however, helplessly ignorant of the condition of matters in that district at the period now under review. A short journey from Dumfries brings us to *Kirkbean*, in the Stewartry of KIRKCUDBRIGHT, where a club existed which could then turn out forty picked players to give a good account of themselves in a bonspiel with any neighbouring parish. The Rev. Thomas Grierson,† minister of the parish, employed his pen in praise of the game and composed a few songs ‡ which are still popular, in one of which we have a spirited address to Kirkbean curlers on their way to meet *Newabbey*—

"Come, cheer up, my lads, to Loch Kindar we steer,
To strive for those laurels we all hold so dear,
'Tis to glory we call you, where curlers are seen,
With their tramps all so bright, and their besoms so green.

---

* Of Sir Richard Broun's life—his defence of his own and other baronetcies, his many Utopian projects, and the "real service" he rendered to the nation by establishing a national mausoleum and a necropolis at Woking in 1849—a full account is given in the *Dictionary of National Biography;* but why does our college friend, who writes the same, omit all notice of the "real service" Sir Richard rendered to our national game? To our regret we have been unable to secure a portrait of Sir Richard in time for insertion here, but we promise it in our second edition, so that curlers who with ourselves lament this defect in our work have the remedy in their own hands!

† This gentleman, like many other brethren of the cloth, must have had curling on the brain. He was an ardent pedestrian and mountain-climber, and in his *Autumnal Rambles* (p. 108), as he bids adieu to the Coolins, he remarks that curling clubs "might engage in a worse speculation than establishing a manufactory at Loch Scavaig for furnishing the heroes of the broom with their implements of war. *Hypersthene* is so renowned for hardness, closeness of texture, and specific gravity, that there can be no doubt of its capabilities: the only fear is that, if it does not belie its name, the weapons may last for ever and thus injure the stone-market. Joking apart, might not some wind-bound vessels lay in a store of good sound blocks, and establish a curling-stone mart at the Broomielaw?"

‡ Afterwards published under the title *Four New Curling Songs, with a Dissertation on the Game of Curling.* By an Old and Keen Curler. James Hogg, Edinburgh.

> Hearts of oak are our skips, light and sure are our men;
> We always are ready—steady, boys, steady!
> We'll *draw* and we'll guard, boys, again and again."

Crossmichael parish had a strong and formidable club, which was in the habit of challenging its neighbours to frequent combat. This habit was an inheritance from the Rev. Nathan M'Kie, an eccentric divine and a keen curler of pugilistic taste, between whom and Lord Kenmure an amusing system of challenge and counter-challenge in metrical form was kept up, a specimen of which is given in the *Memorabilia* (pp. 95-97).

A copy of one of M'Kie's declarations of war has just come into our hands, which, though of older date than our present period, may here be given; for the spirit of it lives on among the Galloway clubs as fresh and strong as in the days of Nathan.

"CROSSMICHAEL MANSE, 17*th January* 1767.

"DEAR SIR,—We make no doubt but your bosom glows with ambition, and we take this opportunity of challenging you and all your brave icy warriors in the parish of Balmaghie to engage the parish of Crossmichael against Tuesday first to come to the Boat of Livingston. For your encouragement we shall tell you that the last time you appeared on the field your army happened to work wonders, and to do more in a single year than for anything known to us they could boast of for ages. If you have true skill and valour, we expect a discovery of them at the determinate season; otherwise it is but fair to be silent for ever. If you shrink back from the field and value yourselves in a single victory, the impartial and unprejudiced world will conclude that you have no confidence in your own strength and that you tremble to think of the military glory of Crossmichael.

"If you refuse to accept a new challenge we will regard it as a defeat, and publish it to the world, that you are all made up of cowardice, cunning, and pusillanimity. So far as we can judge we think we have the power, and it is our firm design, to adorn our heads with laurels, and to reduce you to your former state of littleness, insignificancy, and obscurity. We will bring twelve warriors to the field, and let it be your care to have the same number, such as your great Goliath, Alexander Smith, James M'Millan, Slogairie, the M'Lellans, the Carsons—in a word, the best you can choose for your arduous enterprise. We are to fight under the banner of a brave young general, Mr David Gordon of Drumrash, and we will do what we can in order to secure to him and ourselves an immortal fame and glory.

"We design to dine at Bridgestone, and at your cost if our hands serve us.—We are, with due regard,

"Yours sincerely,
(Signed) "NATHAN M'KIE."

"*P.S.*—We are to meet you at the aforementioned place precisely at 10 o'clock forenoon."

Mactaggart in his *Galloridian Encyclopædia* (1824), to which we have before referred, gives us (in a *raither coorse* style) valuable information about the curling of the period in the south of Scotland. *Borgue*, *Sorby*, and *Closeburn*, according to him, were then "among the first of curling communities." Compared with the curlers of Borgue (his native parish), those of "*Kirkcudbric*, *Twinholm*, and *Girthon*" were "a shilpit crew," "pewtring bodies at bonspiels." This was just another way of challenging them to fight in the style of the famous Nathan M'Kie, and we are not to suppose that bounce would save Borgue from the fury of these clubs when the day of icy vengeance arrived.

By far the worthiest successor of the Kirkcudbright poet Davidson was the minister of *Balmaclellan* and laird of Troquhain—the Rev. George Murray, who began in this period to celebrate in song his love of the game and the deeds of his curling compeers. Let us have part of the biography of "Dean Swift," the name he gave to his channel-stane. It gives us a good account of the preparation of the curling-stone of the period, when *Rabs* had it all to do, and the fine poetic feeling in which, as a true curler, his affection for his friend the "Dean" is expressed is beyond praise.

> "Where lone Penkiln, mid foam and spray,
>   O'er many a linn leaps on his way,
>   A thousand years and mair ye lay
>   Far out of sight :
>   My blessings on the blythesome day
>   Brought thee to light.
>
> "Though ye were slippery as an eel,
>   Rab fished ye frae the salmon wiel,
>   And on his back the brawny chiel
>   Has ta'en ye hame,
>   Destined to figure at the spiel
>   And roaring game.
>
> "Wi' mony a crack he cloured your croun,
>   Wi' mony a chap he chipped ye doun,
>   Fu' aft he turned ye roun' and roun',
>   And aye he sang
>   A' ither stanes ye'll be aboon
>   And that ere lang.
>
> "Guided by many a mould and line,
>   He laboured next with polish fine,

> To make your mirrored surface shine
>   With lustre rare—
> Like lake, reflect the forms divine
>   Of nature fair.
>
> " A handle next did Rab prepare,
> And fixed it with consummate care—
> The wood of ebony so rare,
>   The screw of steel—
> Ye were a channel-stane right fair,
>   Fit for a spiel.
>
> " Ye had nae name for icy war—
> Nae strange device, nor crest, nor star—
> Only a thread of silver spar
>   Ran through your blue ;
> Ilk curler kenned your flinty scar
>   And running true.
>   .   .   .   .   .
>
> " A time will come when I no more
> May fling thee free from shore to shore ;
> With saddened heart I'll hand thee o'er
>   To some brave chiel,
> That future times may hear thy roar
>   At ilka spiel."

From the minutes of *Kelton* Club—the only written records which we can discover in the Stewartry at this period—we infer that Dumfries and Kirkcudbright had here a bond of connection, the Lochmaben rules being adopted and entered *verbatim* in the Kelton records. Duddingston, through Lochmaben, was therefore making its influence felt in Galloway as in other districts. When a county bonspiel with Dumfries was proposed, Kelton issued circulars to the other parish clubs to gauge their playing strength and their sentiments. Mr Sinclair of Redcastle, the Kelton president, gave in 1832 a medal to the club, as a proof of " his great anxiety that the ancient and truly manly amusement ought to be encouraged and kept up in this his native parish." If curlers throughout Galloway were at this time as strict and exemplary as they were at Kelton, no Early Closing Act was required in those parts ; the evening's diversion must have borne the morning's reflection in triumph, and neither secret nor open sin can have marred the beauty of their brotherhood. Who thinks this impossible may carefully read the Kelton bye-laws.

"1. The convivial meetings of the club shall on every occasion be dissolved at 10 o'clock P.M., and the chairman shall leave the chair at that hour.

"2. At any club dinner the expense shall not exceed 2s. 6d.—viz., dinner, 1s. 6d.; spirits, 8d.; beer, 3d.; waiter, 1d.

"3. As this club has been formed to promote the manly game of curling, and to unite the members in a social bond of union and good fellowship, any member who shall, either secretly or openly, create disunion among the members or disturb the harmony of the club in any manner of way, shall be instantly expelled and declared incapable of being again admitted a member of the club."

The favourite meeting-place of this and other clubs seems to have been Carlingwark Loch, the most beautiful sheet of water in the south of Scotland, on which Ben o' Tudor and Glenbuck "met merry" in Davidson's day; but at Milton Loch, Glen Too, Loch Brack, Loch Ken, and Mossroddoch, many famous bonspiels were fought of which the Gallovidians in time to come may read with delight in Murray's Poems.*

Of curling in WIGTONSHIRE at this time we hear little, and therefore cannot say much. Between *Wigtown* and *Loch Connel* many clubs must have flourished, and of the renown of Sorbie we have already heard, but of none of these have we any authentic records. At *Penninghame* a club was formed in 1828, at the instance of Captain (afterwards Admiral) Sir Houston Stewart, R.N., who resided for a time at Penninghame House, and who constructed there an artificial pond to which he was in the habit of inviting some of the keenest curlers. After the day's play he entertained them all to a beef-and-greens dinner with plenty of grog, and sent them home happy. In the Penninghame Club the number in each rink was fourteen, and *seconds* were appointed to assist the skips in managing such large squads of players. Like the Ayr curlers, the members propitiated the favour of the fair sex (a wise thing to do) by an annual ball, which must have been a grand affair as they usually ordered "150 cards of invitation, 100 ball tickets, and 4 sets of contra dances," and made elaborate provision in the way

---

* *Sarah Rae, and other Poems.* By the Rev. George Murray of Troqubain, J.P., Minister of Balmaclellan. Greenock, 1883.

Vide also *The Bards of Galloway.* Fraser, Dalbeattie, 1889.

of music and "refreshments for the ladies." This club had a serious crisis to come through. Their dam burst on one occasion and flooded a tannery in the valley below, the owner of which insisted on *skinning* them to the extent of £176, 10s. 10d. damages. His claim was eventually settled for £50, but the Penninghame experience was not dearly bought if all clubs see to it that in the annals of curling such an accident shall never occur again. With apologies to their clever countryman Mactaggart, we leave our southern brethren to follow the game which has become endeared to them by so many pleasant associations, with this parting wish—"Heaven ever smile on the *curlers* of the south of Scotland, for a better race of beings is nowhere to be found between the sea and the sun."

III. EASTERN GROUP.—*Edinburgh, Linlithgow, Peebles, Selkirk, Haddington, Berwick, and Roxburgh.*

In the city of EDINBURGH the national game has always been recognised and encouraged in a manner worthy of the Scottish capital. The magistrates, as we have seen, graced the opening of the winter sport on the Nor' Loch, and if the curlers had not the support of a civic procession when they afterwards moved to Canonmills and thence to Duddingston, as the development of the city forced them, many of the most distinguished citizens were found among their ranks as they gathered round the tee. In Curlers' Ha' the "wit and wisdom" of the capital, and men of mark in every profession and from every district of Scotland, united by their devotion to the national game, celebrated its praises and helped its progress. Duddingston was at this time a centre of light, and to this remarkable club the transition of curling from the imperfect methods and ungainly implements of the past century to the better and more scientific style of the modern game was mainly due. Of the influence of Duddingston at this period we shall have further proof as we proceed. It is at this stage that we must award honour to the Rev. John Ramsay, at that time minister of Ormiston, who in 1811 wrote the first historical account of curling. We have had to differ from some of Ramsay's views, and to correct some of his statements, but we cannot too highly value the work he did in collecting all that was then known about the past, and publishing it with the rules of the Duddingston Club and the songs that enlivened the club's social meetings. The influence of that club can never be estimated apart from Ramsay's book, which for nearly twenty years acted as "guide, philosopher, and friend" to the curlers of Scotland.*

Curling had the benefit of some attention at this period on the part of journalistic writers. *Johnston's Edinburgh Magazine* (Vol. I., 1834) has a long review of Cairnie's *Essay* from a Lochwinnoch point of view. When the *Memorabilia* appeared, Professor Wilson took an opportunity of recommending it to the Moral Philosophy Class in the University of Edinburgh as an excellent work on the subject! He also gave the substance of it in an article in *Blackwood* (December 1831). Christopher, "like Grey Goshawk, stared wild" when he read Broun's attack on Gillespie's *jeu d'esprit* of 1820—he had been dreaming that "the early sins of Maga had passed into oblivion, and that her reputation was pure as a vestal virgin," but he soon recovers himself, and before proceeding to praise the better part of the book, soundly rates the Baronet for his foolishness. We have said much about clubs and curlers, but let Christopher North give us his description of the curlers' dinner of the period. Our tastes are surely simpler nowadays, for it is only in fractions that we get a feast of the kind. Listen to the learned Professor of Moral Philosophy :—

"Look at that dinner!

"The table is all alive with hot animal food. A steam of rich distilled perfumes reaches the roof, at the lowest measurement seven feet high. A savoury vapour! The feast takes all its name and most of its nature from—beef and greens. The one corned, the other crisp —the two combined, the glory of Martinmas. The beef consists almost entirely of lean fat—rather than of fat lean—and the same may be said of that bacon. See! how the beef cuts long-ways with the bone—if it be not indeed a sort of sappy gristle. Along the edges of each plate, as

---

* Any one who desires to hear more about Ramsay may refer to our account of his life in *The Channel-stane*, Vol. IV., pp. 27-32.

it falls over from the knife-edge among the gravy-greens, your mouth waters at the fringe of fat, and you look for 'the mustard.' Of such beef and greens there are four trenchers, each like a tea-tray; and yet you hope that there is a *corps-de-reserve* in the kitchen. Saw you ever anywhere else, except before a barn-door where flail or fanners were at work, such a muster of how-towdies! And how rich the rarer roasted among the frequent boiled! As we are Christians—that is an incredible goose—yet still that turkey is not put out of countenance—and 'as what seems his head the likeness of a kingly crown has on' he must be no less than the bubbly. Black and brown grouse are not eatable—till they have *packed*; and these have been shot on the snow out of a cottage window, by a man in his shirt taking vizzy with the 'lang gun' by starry moonlight. Yea—pies. Some fruit—and some flesh—that veal—and this aipples. Cod's head and shoulders, twenty miles from the sea, is at all times a luxury—and often has that monster lain like a ship at anchor off the Doggerbank—supposed by some to have been a small whale. Potatoes always look well in the crumbling candour of that heaped-up mealiness, like a raised pyramid. As for mashed turnips, for our life when each is excellent of its kind we might not decide whether the palm should be awarded to the white or the yellow; but perhaps on your plate with the butter-mixed bloodiness of steak, cutlet, or mere slice of rump, to a nicety underdone, both are best—a most sympathetic mixture, in which the peculiar taste of each is intensely elicited, while a new flavour or absolute *tertium quid* is impressed upon the palate, which, for the nonce, is not only invigorated but refined."

Beyond Duddingston we have no written records of any of the city curling clubs formed about this time, though Merchiston figures favourably in several county bonspiels. The minutes of the *Penicuick* Club, transcribed in beautiful style by John M'Lean, a boy of thirteen, and carefully preserved at Penicuick House, extend onward from 1812. The secretary must have been a man of many superlatives, for in nearly every minute it is difficult to say which subject he praises most—the game of curling, the Penicuick curlers, or the patron of the curling club, Sir George Clerk, Bart, M.P. for Edinburgh. Perhaps Sir George gets the largest allowance: and no wonder, for he was not only a keen, keen curler like his ancestor Sir John, the friend of Allan Ramsay and Dr Penicuick of Newhall, but he took such an active interest in the curlers, who had been so "bad that nobody would play with them," that in time they received from Merchiston, over which they had triumphed, the title "Champions of the icy world." Every year Sir George gives them a silver medal, and, as if the gratitude of adjectives were insufficient to express their feelings, they present him in turn with "a pair of brass crampits," and, later on, their distinguished president, Dr Renton, is commissioned to convey to Sir George a silver horn.* As may be supposed, the Duddingston rules were obeyed at Penicuick, Mr Clerk Maxwell having been one of the counsellors, and Sir George Clerk a president of the Duddingston Club. At their annual dinner they were examined in the "word," and, if deficient, fined; "two bowls of punch" were drunk; the reckoning was then called, and every member allowed to depart.

The rule of some other clubs of the period which prohibited the introduction of political subjects does not appear to have been part of the constitution of the Penicuick Club. A few years after Waterloo had been fought and won, we find in the club minutes an indication of the social discontent and disorder which prevailed among certain classes at this time, and which threatened revolution. The curlers, who were all tenants and feuars of Sir George Clerk, could not fail to see how the agitation affected the position of their patron, and, "faithful among the faithless," they determined to comfort him with the confession of their loyalty. When Mr Maxwell, Sir George's brother, was doing duty as one of the gentleman volunteer corps which was then stationed in the Castle of Edinburgh—the regular troops being called to Glasgow owing to the disorder of the time—the club adopted "with rapturous applause" the following letter to Sir George Clerk, which is interesting as a specimen of their secretary's power of language, if it is not valuable as a unique document among curling records of the period:—

"PENICUICK, 14*th December* 1819.

"To Sir George Clerk, Bart., M.P.

"We are inclined to believe that a practical attachment to the manners and amusements of our native country has a moral effect of retaining in our minds a reverential regard for those envied institutions,

---

* The Penicuick family hold their estate from the Crown by a charter, which obliges the heir to repair to Buckstane, parish of Colinton, Midlothian, and to blow a horn when the king passes that way a-hunting; hence the motto of their crest, "Free for a blast." Reference is made to old curling-stones at Penicuick, p. 63.

sacred and civil, which the patriotism and valour of our ancestors has transmitted to us, and that those days which the nature of our climate has devoted to a secession from rural labour are much more rationally spent in that innocent rivalry of manual exertion and mathematical nicety which our national pastime affords, than in poring over imaginary wrongs and studying the blasphemous and treasonable publications of the disappointed, the intention and tendency of which is to subvert that national spirit of loyalty, patriotism, and prowess which embellishes the pages of our national history and in the late tremendous contest has so eminently exalted our national character."

Sir George in his reply, dated 22nd December 1819, promises "to encourage and promote our national amusement," and proceeds:—

"I trust that it is a more innocent mode of spending any leisure hours than in reading or listening to the seditious and blasphemous publications that have been so industriously circulated by wicked and designing men, who for their own ends endeavour by exciting a spirit of discontent to excite those who suffer themselves to be led by them to acts which must inevitably plunge them and their families into the greatest miseries. The period would, by undermining their religious principles, deprive them of all hope hereafter. I hope that none such are to be found in our neighbourhood, and that every man there will exert himself as far as his influence extends to check their progress."

The minutes of the *Rosslyn* Club cover the period 1820–1836, but do not contain much of general interest. Along with Penicuick, the club gained distinction in a great bonspiel between Midlothian and the Upper Ward of Lanarkshire in 1831, which was played on Slipperfield Loch, Peeblesshire, an account of which is found in their minutes, with a testimony added in favour of such matches:—

"As they tend to strengthen the rivalry which is peculiar to the game, promote dexterity in the art, and enlarge the sphere of social intercourse by bringing together kindred spirits that but for such occasions would never meet."

The Rosslyn Club have been fortunate in the support of the Wedderburn family. The mother of Colonel Wedderburn, a thorough enthusiast, knitted worsted vests and presented them to the members of the five rinks of the club. *O si sic omnia!*

The *Currie* Club, formed in 1830 "in order to promote and keep alive the genuine spirit of the most ancient, manly, and exhilarating game of curling," at the very outset of its career took up a prominent position among contemporary clubs. The ability of its founders entitled it to distinction.

The Rev. Dr Somerville, first president of the club, the inventor of what was called the safety gun, was one of the most enthusiastic curlers that ever lived. In the controversy with Dr Cairnie as to the invention of artificial ponds, the Ayrshire curler had the best of it, and Sir Richard Broun, who acted as arbiter in the matter, awarded to Cairnie the merit of the discovery, the difference between the doctors amounting to this, that Cairnie had made *clay* and Somerville *pavement* the basis of the shallow-level pond, the one holding that the water froze from its surface downward to the clay, the other that it froze upward from the surface of the pavement. The shallow-level principle seems, however, to have first suggested itself to Cairnie. There can, however, be no doubt that Somerville conducted a series of long and expensive experiments with the object of obtaining for curlers greater facilities for play than were available on water-borne ice, and it is even said that he carried his experiments so far as to have practised on his drawing-room floor the effect of soft soap and other slippery materials as a substitute for ice. His *crampits* and *toe-see* we have already noticed. *The Justice* and *The Counter* we notice later on. Dr Somerville is also said to have suggested the alteration of handles from the old rectangular to the present form. He had much to do with the improvement of curling and its implements at this period, and was regarded as an authority on all matters connected with the game, while none ever extolled it more highly than he did.*

Another of the founders of the Currie Club—Robert Palmer, schoolmaster—was a typical curler of the period. Of great force of character, full of enthusiasm, and possessing abilities that would have made him in any profession a man of mark, he was one of the most noted parish teachers of his time. His leisure hours he gave to the advancement of

---

* Poor Dr Somerville! Life's burden became too much for him to bear, notwithstanding his curling enthusiasm, and his end was sad; but surely it is not worthy of our brotherhood to leave his grave (as we were lately surprised to find it) unmarked by any memorial stone. We should be glad to be the means of raising, with the help of the fraternity, a simple monument to one who so much loved and improved the national game.

curling, and his fame as a skip is indicated in Lees' painting of the Grand Match, where Palmer is seen anxiously welcoming with outstretched arm the stone that makes its way to the tee. He was the inventor of the *teeringer*, one of the most useful of curling appliances. His literary power, combined with the most thorough knowledge of the game, fitted him to be, as he afterwards was, one of

FIG. 57. ROBERT PALMER.
(*Enlarged from a miniature photograph.*)

the most efficient office-bearers of the Grand Club. Before us is a set of diagrams for the point game drawn up by Dr Somerville, Mr Palmer, and Mr Cunningham of Harlaw, in 1836. All the points now played are there illustrated, and while we occasionally meet with additions by other clubs to the Duddingston three points, we must assign to Currie the honour of completing the present system of point competition. The families of Scott of Malleny and Gibson-Craig of Riccarton have done much for the prosperity of this important club.

In the county of LINLITHGOW many a merry bonspiel was fought on the grand old Castle Loch, but of the two clubs which then existed in the historic town of *Linlithgow* we cannot give any account. Under the care of Sir William Baillie of Polkemmet, "a noble specimen of the good old county gentleman," the *Whitburn* Club was noted for its prowess. About the close of this period five Duddingston rinks made a bet of 100 guineas to 50 against any that dared to meet them. Major Hamilton Dundas (uncle of the present popular Baronet of Polkemmet), then of Duddingston, and a member of the challenging club, brought forward five rinks of Whitburn players, who knew nothing about the bet, and the gallant Major saw with satisfaction his venturesome Duddingston friends "gently let down" at Drumshoreland Pond, 155 to 56. He had, of course, much pleasure in entertaining both losers and winners to beef and greens, &c., in Uphall Inn.

The life and soul of the *Bathgate* Club was Thomas Durham Weir of Boghead, under whom the club was, in 1829, roused from a dormant state, and made "the champion club of the whole surrounding country." Accomplished, active, and of a most generous and unselfish disposition, the Laird of Boghead was always at his best at the head of the curlers, and with his enthusiastic "bravissimo" he led them on to many a gallant victory. A celebrated rink of the club, under the best skip, William Gordon, builder and stonemason, is said never to have been beaten.*

When we turn to the county of PEEBLES to see what they are doing at this time with the "manly *Scotish* exercise" of their ancient Laird of Romanno, we find a club in existence at the county town in 1821. At a meeting on 24th December, in that year, Mr James Turnbull laid before

---

* An interesting account of the Bathgate Club is found in *The Channelstane*, Vol. IV., pp. 1-26. A neat little volume, privately printed, gives an account of the presentation to Mr Weir of his portrait in 1862 by the Bathgate curlers.

the club a set of regulations which was unanimously adopted. The regulations are introduced by a preamble or "whereas," in which Mr Turnbull (he must have been a limb of the law) does the part of devil's advocate before introducing us to the good character of the game. As the Peebles regulations are unique of their kind, we give them as they stand in the sederunt-book of the club :—

"None of the pastimes in which Scotchmen indulge have given occasion to such a diversity of opinion as our national manly game of curling. By some it has been reprobated as an encouragement to idleness, a temptation to profane swearing, an incitement to quarrelling, and an inducement to dissipation. By others it has been extolled in the language of unqualified panegyric, and declared to be friendly to innocence, conducive to health, favourable to temperance, and contributive to social intercourse.

"For our part, without minutely discussing its merits or demerits, but weighing them in a strict balance, we can state from experience that curling, so far from promoting idleness, is an active and laborious recreation, an enemy to every spirit of sensual indulgence, debarring those who engage in it for the time being from tippling in taverns, lounging lazily and effeminately at a fireside, or devoting themselves to worse employments; peculiarly adapted also to the preservation of a sound constitution by favouring its votaries with these two grand preventatives of disease and restoratives of health—air and exercise.

"At a season of the year when the plough is arrested in the furrow, when masonic and many other handicraft employments are laid aside, and when the mill-wheel refuses to revolve on its axis, what can be more harmless, what more salubrious, what more social, than for those who are in possession of health, endowed with muscular strength, blessed with a keen eye and a steady hand, to repair to the still river, Cuddies pool, or the flooded gytes, the waters whereof are bound in icy fetters, and the surface smooth as the polished mirror, and transparent as the crystalian cup, and there give a display of strength, dexterity, and skill, united in a game the darling of our forefathers!

"Viewing the game of curling as completely legal, taxation having not yet reached her stones, as bracing to the nerves by keeping the muscles in natural play, as diffusing brotherly kindness by bringing friends and neighbours together, and as promoting a spirit of honourable emulation by an energetic competition for the prize of victory, we the members have agreed to form ourselves into a society by the name, style, and title of the Peebles Curling Club, and to adopt the following regulations :—

"1. Every member shall be able to prove himself the lawful owner of at least one stone.

"2. The number of stones to be played with at any particular time shall be determined by the whole body when the members are all standing ready for the game near by the gog-see.

"3. When ladies come near the rink and are disposed to play, the skips shall have the privilege of instructing them to handle the stones agreeable to the rules of the game.

"4. When a member falls and is hurt, the rest shall not laugh, but render him every assistance to enable him to regain his former erect position.
"5. When the club, according to use and wont, beat their opponents they shall not exult too much so as to wound the feelings of a fallen foe, but consider the victory merely as the chance of war.
"6. Every member shall also provide himself with a broom or besom and a pair of trickers.
"7. The club to dine annually by subscription on the 13th day of January, the expense of the dinner and drink not to exceed 2s. or 2s. 6d., and any member subscribing and not attending the dinner he is to forfeit one shilling.
"8. The club dinner shall be restricted to beef and greens, and whisky toddy."

In 1823 (January 13), Tweeddale met Midlothian at Penicuick with fifteen rinks, each with fourteen players. Tweeddale won by ninety-two shots. According to the Peebles minutes this was the largest meeting of the kind that had then taken place, and " was attended by many of the gentlemen and others of the two counties and city of Edinburgh, anxiously awaiting the fate of the day." Dr Renton of Penicuick had the burden of carrying out arrangements for this bonspiel, and the doctor some years after proceeded to Peebles to arrange a return match. His experience, as recorded in the Penicuick minute-book, shews that the Peeblesians were as careful of their laurels as the doctor was original in his resources—

"He found them more anxious to start obstacles to retard it than arrangements to forward the match. In order to obviate all objections started, Dr Renton, in the pure spirit of gallantry, proposed for the accommodation of all parties to commission a steam-packet to convey the whole curlers to Iceland, where, unless they were disturbed with a shower of fire and sulphur from the burning Mt. Hecla, they would find ice 4000 years old in readiness for them, and they might return with the pillars of a former world for curling stones—viz., the fine stupendous basaltic columns of Iceland."

When we cross over into the county of SELKIRK, we do not escape from the shadow of Duddingston, for there we find a member of that distinguished club president of the *Ettrick* Curling Club. This is no other than the Ettrick Shepherd himself. James Hogg (1772-1835) was as devoted to the channel-stane as he was to the fiddle. " So uniformly smooth," he says, " has my married life been, that on a retrospect I cannot distinguish one part from another, save by some remarkably good days of fishing, shooting, and curling on the ice."* Up till 1823 the curlers in the district used to meet on the Loch o' the Lowes. In that year the stones were all thrown into the loch by some wicked boys, and they were never recovered. James Hogg, however, made a pond at Altrive Lake, and another at Mount Benger. He was a ubiquitous curler, for, besides Duddingston, Peebles had his name on her roll, and on one occasion there is added to a minute—"The meeting was enlivened by the Ettrick Shepherd telling his queerest stories and singing his drollest songs." Then we hear of him among the Tynron curlers, when he had a farm "up the Skarr." "Skin them, skin them," was his only remark, as his shepherd kept coming with news of fresh disasters among the sheep, and on he went with his game, " always happiest when he was most unfortunate." Doubtless Selkirk had many other curlers at that day, but it was enough for one county to give us such a man.†

In the county of HADDINGTON it is likely that curling was known previous to this period (*vide* p. 45), but it seems to have been for a time forgotten. The sons of Anak at *Cockburnspath* had a club, but they said nothing till the day of jubilee arrived, and then they silenced the world with their stone of might. The farmers in the neighbourhood formed a club at *Gladsmuir*, and the historian Ramsay, being now minister of the parish, naturally prescribed for them the Duddingston rules, with the addition that Somerville's *Justice* was to be used in measuring disputed shots, and that "the stones produced by each new

---

* *Poetical Works of the Ettrick Shepherd*, Vol. II., p. 84. Blackie & Sons.

† That most popular of all curling songs, *O for the Channel-stane*, is generally ascribed to Hogg. No doubt he could have written it, but we are inclined to think it was written, not by Hogg, but by his friend Professor Gillespie. The Shepherd, with his knee-breeches, blue coat, and plaid transformed into a sprite in yonder sky, and curling with a comet against the moon and starlets, is a companion-portrait to that in the Professor's *jeu d'esprit*, *Closeburn* v. *Lochmaben*; and to put the song above Hogg's own name was quite in keeping with the usual treatment the Shepherd received from the *Ebony* writers, who, according to his own account, made it a principle "never to deny a thing that they had not written, and never to acknowledge one that they had."

member were to be examined, and admitted or excluded by
a majority." This club was not altogether in bondage to
curling. If the feelings of the members when they met
preferred the dinner-table to the icy-board, that alternative
was open, and they went for it, seeing they had enacted
that the president, or secretary, or any three members shall
have power "to call a meeting of the club either to curl
or to dine, as the weather may permit or the members
incline." *

When we cross the Lammermuirs to survey the curling
of BERWICK, we find as usual that "Duns dings a'," and in
our list stands "alone with its glory," though, doubtless,
there were other clubs of which we hear nothing. It is
only in 1822 that the *Duns* Club gives heed to its ways by
writing, and then we find them agreeing to drink William
Hay of Drummelzier's health at every meeting of the club
for indulging it with the use of the Hen-poo Pond. The
Duns curlers had a philosophy of clothes, for we find that
a certain match was lost because Mr M'Watt, one of the
players, "wore a pea-jacket," and another because one of the
losers "wore a greatcoat." For not appearing on the ice
"at least once in a season" members were fined 1s. In
some cases they had better have paid the fine than have
made the appearance they did—*e.g.*,

"Ice tried by Messrs Bell and Jamieson, the welter weights of the
club. The former made an attempt to bathe by diving through the ice,
but only succeeded in getting his extremities, &c., immersed, while the
latter was so amused at the attempt that he failed to make one."

Of a musical friend from Edinburgh who "tried his hand"
it is recorded—

"He had evidently been accustomed to play quoits, as the first
stone he tried he *pitched into the ice*, instead of along the rink, and
terminated the play."

One of the old Duns players (James Cunningham), in
far-off Queensland, recalls in these stanzas the pleasant

---

* This club has in its possession a curious snuff-box, in the shape of a
curling-stone, presented by Alex. Bruce. The stone is of Peterhead
granite; the box of wood from the old pulpit of the ruined kirk of Gladsmuir; the sides of the box of oak from the *Royal George*, sunk at Spithead;
and the wood of the handle from the room in which the Gowrie conspiracy
is alleged to have been attempted to be carried out in the year 1600.

memories of happy meetings on "the Hen-poo" in the bygone times:—

"The auld Hen-poo', the auld Hen-poo',
  Eh! man, I mind it weel,
The Brunton Well, the Witches' Knowe,
  The Law, the Sergeants' Shiel.
The Mains Gate, wi' its lime-trees grey,
  And geans sae white wi' bloom,
The Skartin Kames abune the brae,
  Whar grows the yellow broom.

"The auld Hen-poo', I lo'ed it best
  When cauld the wintry blast,
Wi' drivin' snaw an' bauld Jock Frost,
  Had lock't her waters fast.
E'en yet I hear the birrin' stane
  Row roarin' to the tee;
The Poo's the same, the men are gane,
  And changed are you an' me.

.   .   .   .   .

"Now fare ye weel, thou auld Hen-poo'
  Whar happy we hae been,
An fare ye weel, ye curlers a',
  Wha aye were true and keen.
My channel-stane's owre the hog-score,
  'Twill sune be owre the tee,
Hen-poo, Duns Law, an curlers a',
  Farewell, farewell to thee."

In the county of ROXBURGH there were, as we have noticed, curling clubs established at *Kelso* and at *Jedburgh* in the end of last century. Of the former we have no records, and in the case of Jedburgh the records are very meagre. Curlers seem up till then to have played with natural boulders from the River Jed: a pair of cramps cost 2s. 8d.; five common brooms, 1s. 3d.; and a big heather broom for cleaning the ice reached the figure of 5d. We are here first introduced to a system of little matches and little bets, which we do not meet with in any other early records, and which seems to have been common among the curlers in the Borderland from the time of the introduction of the game. A little match of eleven or thirteen points having been made up for beef and greens, or a mutchkin of toddy, the members not engaged in it began to put some "dross" on the event—2s. to 1s., 1s. per stone, or a level shilling, as the case might be.

This system of little matches and little bets seems to have been carried to its height at *Hawick*. Indeed, one of the old written records of that club, beginning in 1812, appears to have been used for the sole purpose of registering the bets of the Hawick curlers and their results. The transactions of the "deil's dizzen" begin with this minute :—

"HAWICK, 14*th December* 1812.

"The curling club having met this evening, *being a full club of 13 members*, resolved that all wagers in future shall be paid to the clerk of the club as soon as they are played for, and to be expended when the preses shall think proper, it being understood that he (the preses) shall make it known to all concerned with said wagers and as many more of the club as the preses shall think proper—*play or pay*."

Some years after this we find the club enacting that on and after that date " no bet shall be taken under a mutchkin of whisky toddy." Not for imitation (for our ideas of Border curling are not exalted by these records), but to shew how not to do it, we take a leaf out of the Hawick book :—

BEE-HIVE, *Dec.* 14, 1812.

A game of 13 shots for 3 shillings.
Charles Scott, jun., and Thos. Potts
against
John Kyle and John Graham.

J. K. and J. G. lost.

To be decided to-morrow morning if the preses finds it proper.

On Kyle and Graham's head
Wm. Richardson gives C. Armstrong
Two half-mutchkins to one.

W. R. lost 1 mⁿ.

A game of 9 shots for 1s. 6d. each.
James Oliver against Thos. Potts.
The former to throw 3 stones against the latter's 6 stones. James Oliver always to throw the first stone and the two last, independent of the winner of the end. To be played on Wednesday morning at half-past 8 o'clock. *Play or pay.*

J. O. lost.

On Mr James Oliver's head John Hume gives
Sergt. Dalgetty 2 half-mutchkins to one.

J. H. lost.

On Thos. Pott's head, William Richardson gives
Wm. Millar an equal bet of a half-mutchkin that
Thos. Potts will gain.

W. M. lost.

Moreover, Joseph Peacock wagers a half-mutchkin against Adam Elliot that Thos. Potts will lose.

J. P. lost.

In various other forms the "ruling passion" manifests itself. Two curlers, "whose united ages amount to 115 years," challenge any other two " for a bottle of whisky made into punch," and " the old boys gained." James Oliver bets William Millar " a mutchkin of whisky toddy " that he will throw a stone further—the best of three throws—and on this there are several side bets. Then—

"10*th January* 1826.

"R. Wilson bet Jas. Millar that the Dove Mount Well is 20 feet higher than Hassendean Pond. R. W. lost. Thereafter Millar bet Wilson that the Dove Mount Well is no higher than Hassendean Pond, but Mr Thomson (who decided the former bet offhand) could not decide this without a great deal of trouble."

Beyond this dark circle there seems to have been a club of much larger proportions—there were in all sixty members, who enjoyed the roaring game without any speculation in their eyes, Elliots, Olivers, Rutherfords, and Scotts being numerous, and the Duke of Buccleuch,* himself a curler, and ever the generous friend of Hawick, gave them a pond and encouraged them in every way he could.

IV. NORTHERN GROUP.—*Stirling, Fife, Kinross, Perth, Forfar.*

STIRLING county, true to her ancient traditions, kept careful watch over the progress of curling. It was meet that the game of freedom and independence should be played at Bannockburn. A part of the Serbonian bog, where the English cavalry were ensnared and defeated, was accordingly transformed into a curling pond, and the *Borestone*, in which Bruce planted his standard before the battle, was the name under which the oldest club in Stirling continued to " curl the channel-stane." In many a keen encounter did the old *Bridge of Allan* test the mettle of the newer clubs on Airthrey Loch. When Cairnie got his queer *Waterstoups* at *Falkirk*, that place could turn out a hundred good curlers for a bonspiel, and it is said (*Annual*, 1843, pp. 136–138) that about the dawn of the present period the farmers of the Carse and the tradespeople of the town got into a curling feud which could not be settled for days and days, and was only ended by

* One of the best contests we ever engaged in was on a rink made up at Newbattle Abbey against a rink from Dalkeith Palace, skipped by the late Duke, who entered into the fight with the utmost keenness, and came out of it better than we desired.

"the thow." The bitter combatants have all "ta'en their gate," but here is the picture of one good old soul whose memory is worth preserving in our pages :—

"Regularly as nine o'clock came round was 'Meg Weir,' the worthy old housekeeper of a bachelor of the party, whose residence was at a short distance from the scene, seen threading her way through the snow, with her coffee-kettle in one hand, and the other necessaries of a curler's breakfast in a basket over the other arm ; and loath they frequently were to stop their game even for so necessary a duty, and many a time was Meg's voice raised in angry expostulation at their pertinacity in continuing to play till the coffee, as she said, would be 'as cauld as the ice they were staunin' on.' Roused by her entreaties, they at length formed a circle on the ice, and discussed a hasty meal, with noble appetites and small ceremony, grudging every moment which it kept them from the play, Meg bustling about meanwhile, helping each to the contents of her well-filled basket, and entertaining them with shrewd and caustic remarks, for she was a privileged character among the band of friends. 'My certy,' she would say, 'gentlemen, but it's a pity ye canna get curlin' a' the year through : had ye no better tak' a passage in ane o' the whale-ships to Greenland, whar they say they hae ice a' simmer, an' finish out yer game there when this frost lifts ?' and, turning to her employer, would ask, 'Is your side winnin' the day, maister ? Stick till them,' she would add ; for Meg took almost as keen an interest in the success of her master's party as they did themselves. Occasionally, too, would Meg vary their repast with a 'cog o' the kail-brose o' auld Scotland,' and a right good and fitting breakfast it is for those who are to engage in 'Scotland's ain game.'"

Of the old clubs at *Kilsyth, Grahamston, Gargunnock,* and *Camelon* we have no information, and the same has to be said of the *Stirling* Club, formed in 1820 ; but a memorable bonspiel seems to have been fought about the close of this period (25th January 1838) on Airthrey Loch, in which the Banknock Club, which had then existed for seven years, figures to disadvantage. This club, in its brief course, had often been on the warpath, and after challenging and beating Stenhousemuir, *Larbert, Kilsyth, Falkirk,* and *Denny,* it could find nothing better to do than to "divide itself" and enjoy the luxury of civil war to keep its curling blood in circulation. This was better than sitting down, like Alexander, to cry for want of something to do, but it became tiresome, and so the Banknock heroes issued a final challenge to "any club in the county of Stirling for thirty players, as also the Dunblane Club, in the county of Perth."* Dunblane took

* The formal challenge appeared in the *Stirling Journal,* 26th January 1838.

up the challenge and won—121 to 69. This battle of Airthrey excited the greatest interest in the whole district, and its incidents are not forgotten to this day.

In the kingdom of FIFE the first club to attract our attention is the *Otterston*, so called from Otterston Loch where the members played. The minutes open with the motto :—

"Interpone tuis interdum gaudia curis
Ut possis animo quemvis sufferre laborem,"

and their dry record of annual meetings is relieved by a selection of curling songs inserted in the blank spaces by a later hand. Dr William Bryce, minister of the parish, was long secretary, and among the early members were the Earls of Moray and Morton, Admiral Sir Philip Durham (who was one of the few rescued from the *Royal George*), the Marquis de Riario Sforza, a friend of the preceding, Mr John Philip, Commissioner for Lord Moray, Mr Stuart of Dunearn, in a duel with whom Sir Alexander Boswell was fatally wounded,* Captain Mowbray of Otterston, Mr Wemyss of Wemyss Castle, and Captain Bogle, who fought in the Peninsular war, and was five years confined in a French prison. The social meetings of these worthies seem to have been conducted in great style, for we find a professional singer receiving one guinea for "singing a variety of songs during the sederunt." Here is one of the dinner bills thus set to music, the responsible parties being two earls, one honourable, one captain, two ministers, two doctors, and seven esquires.

Red Lion Inn, Aberdour, Dec. 23, 1822.

To 15 gentlemen's dinners,		£2 10 0
„ Beer,		0 1 6
„ Porter and ale,		0 3 0
„ Whisky,		0 3 0
„ Wine, 5 bottles,		1 2 6
„ Toddy,		1 5 0
„ Officer's dinner,		0 3 0
		£5 8 0

---

* Mr Stuart was tried for murder before the High Court of Justiciary, Jeffrey and Cockburn appearing for his defence. The jury acquitted him on the ground that he could not have acted otherwise than he did. He survived his acquittal fifty-two years.

At *Dunfermline, Markinch, Leven,* and *Kilconquhar* curling
was then popular, and at the last-named place we are told
(*Annual,* 1843) " it was no uncommon thing for the curlers
after playing a whole day on the ice to retire at twilight for
a little refreshment, then start to it again quite fresh, and play
by the aid of lanthorns until the crowing of the cock warned
them to stop."

"Though curling ne'er *in* Eden was essay'd,
Yet glorious *spiels,* no great way off, are played."

This couplet introduces a "Recitative" by Professor
Gillespie, called *The Jolly Curlers,* which appeared in 1821
in *The Caledonian,* a quarterly journal published at Dundee.
Gillespie was then minister of Cults, in succession to the
father of Sir David Wilkie. Along with Mr Dingwall of
Ramornie and some neighbouring farmers, he used to enjoy
the game on the same spot as that now played on by the
Pitlessie Club. In the evening the party met in rotation at
each other's houses, and it was a rule that if any hostess put
more on the table than the orthodox beef and greens, she had
to provide the next dinner. The "Recitative" gives the
songs sung by the individual members of the company after
dinner, but before the song goes round the bowl has to be
produced, and as the Edinburgh Professor of Moral Philosophy has described the beef and greens, we may now ask
the Professor of Humanity at St Andrews to tell us how
our curling fathers prepared their toddy.

Now comes *the bowl,*—an heirloom old,
Which three good quarts of punch can hold.
We hate your *tumblers,* brittle ware—
They want the jolly social air ;
And jugs are our abhorrence too—
They hide the beverage from our view.
Show me the man of heart and soul,
And I'll produce his three-quart bowl.
A horse looks bare without a saddle—
A bowl looks *cow'd* without a *ladle :*
So, from his den of deep recess,
The twisted serpent seems to hiss ;
His tongue all brandish'd for the fight—
All rampant he—beware the bite !
The water smokes ; the whisky-bottle
Emits his soul, through gurgling throttle :

> Amidst the board he takes his place—
> Vast 'moderator' of his race:
> The spoon is motion'd knowingly;
> The punch is ready—taste and try;
> The smack is o'er; the sentence passed—
> 'We've *hit the very thing*' at last.
> And now, around the fire we gather—
> A fire looks well in frosty weather.
> Our half-moon table suits our numbers;
> And neither wife nor care encumbers.
> Lolling at ease, with haunch on high,
> We hatlins sit and hatlins lie:
> Our eyes all beaming full of glee
> The happiest of the happy we." *

On the beautiful Loch of Lindores the *Abdie* Club, a revival in 1830 of an old club which had long been dormant, kept up the sport, and their amusing and profitable use of the licence of the Curling Court must be noticed later on. The first president of the revived club was Admiral Sir Frederick Lewis Maitland of Rankeillour, K.C.B., who, as commander of the *Bellerophon*, frustrated the attempt of Napoleon to escape by sea after Waterloo, and to whom the defeated Emperor yielded up his sword, 15th July 1815. The gallant admiral was a keen curler, and took a personal interest in the success of the club. Mr Ogilvie Dalgleish, of whom we shall hear again, was also prominent among its early friends and supporters. By a decree of this society, every member (the chaplain excepted) was bound to wear the club uniform at play, the coat thereof being blue, the vest buff. Sixteen large buttons were to figure on the coat, eight small ones on the vest; the cost of buttons and die being £5, 2s., which the members had to pay. Dr Burton, the first secretary of the club, who afterwards practised for a time at Haddington, is still alive, aged ninety, a splendid testimony to the medical effect of that game which the little Perth doctor so long ago recommended to the faculty.

---

* The half-moon table that was used by the jolly curlers, the ladle with spirally grooved handle (likened in these lines to a serpent), and the punch-bowl, are still preserved as heirlooms by the present Mr Dingwall of Ramornie. The "Laird" of the company in the "Recitative" is not gifted with musical power, and Brother Clapper sings for him *The Channel-stane*. From the presence of the popular song here, and its absence from the Ettrick Shepherd's works, we incline to think it was Gillespie's and not Hogg's (*vide* p. 204).

In the county of CLACKMANNAN we have no less than two clubs on our list at this time—a respectable number for a county of such small dimensions. If they were good players they were like Tam Pate—they did not give a single *cheep*; and we cannot say of what stuff the *Dollar and Devonvale* and the *Tullibody* clubs were made. We can only infer from the prowess of such modern clubs as the Alloa and Alloa Prince of Wales that the curlers of old were worthy sires of such sons; and Clackmannan has sufficiently atoned for her silence by giving us in our day Lord Balfour of Burleigh, whose eloquence has more than once exalted the praise of the game, and whose devotion to the highest interests of his country has led him to advocate and befriend the curling cause. It is to such men we look to extend the popularity of our national winter sport.

In the small and compact county of KINROSS we have two most efficient clubs, both with interesting records, to guide us in tracing the history of curling and finding out the nature of its secrets. *Kinross* Club was the creation of an awakened conscience among the Lochleven curlers of the time, who felt that they had not been doing their duty toward their ancient and valuable inheritance. Since it was started in 1818 it has, under faithful rulers from the time of Sheriff Skelton to that of Mr Burns Begg, its present enthusiastic president, made its influence felt in the curling world, and done much to uphold the best traditions of the national game. In its minute-book in " pristine purity " the sacred Eleusinian mysteries of the Curling Court are carefully guarded by the warning voice, " *Procul, oh procul este profani!* " and much that is interesting and valuable about the curling of the past is there treasured up.

A fine type of the keen Kinross curler of this period was John Wright Williamson, writer and banker, who, from the time he settled at Kinross in 1818 till the day of his death,* never ceased to take an interest in the Kinross Club, and in all that concerned the game. It was the

---

* Mr Williamson died in 1879, at the advanced age of eighty-six. His portrait is given in a subsequent chapter of our volume.

delight of his life to curl, and among the Lochleven band there was no better player. When infirmity forced him to lay down his channel-stane, he would still trudge many a weary mile against a blinding snowstorm to follow the fortunes of his club; and to the very last he appeared at their social meetings, enlivening them by his sprightliness and humour. "Nothing," says Mr Begg, "could have been more enjoyable than the spirit and effect with which *The Channel-stane* was sung by this veteran curler, even after the touch of extreme old age had woefully impaired his power of expression."

In the *Orwell* Club, which is also honourably identified with the progress of curling, Mr Black of Tillywhally, with the gift of a pond, appears as the friend of its youth. The most notable name, however, is that of George Walker Arnott, LL.D., who resided at his estate of Arlary from 1831 till 1846, when he was called to Glasgow as Professor of Botany in the University. Dr Arnott's hand is everywhere visible in the early records of Orwell Club, of which he was for a time president. He seems to have found in curling a pleasant pastime amid severe application to his professional studies, and with all that earnestness and vigour which characterised his life and work * he played the game, investigated its history, and studied its science. His *Laws of Curling*, published in 1838, succeeds the publications of Ramsay, Broun, and Cairnie in their order. The *Laws* of Arnott are " principally founded on those framed by Lochmaben," but they contain some inter-

FIG. 58.
G. A. WALKER ARNOTT, LL.D.
(*From a photograph.*)

---

* A notice of Dr Arnott's life and his distinguished career as a botanist, written by Dr Hugh Cleghorn, F.L.S., is found in the *Transactions of the Botanical Society*, Vol. IX., 1867-68.

esting amendments; and, as winding up the story of the diversities and differences among the clubs of this period, and suggesting the new tale of order and uniformity, the little volume will always be worthy of attention.

For the number of clubs existing there in the last century, and the great extent of the county, the clubs of PERTH which come under our notice at this period are, in proportion, very few. Of the renown of the *Dunblane* Club we have already had proof. Patrick Stirling of Kippendavie and several others had been " brothered and entered " as far back as 1815, but we have no minute previous to 1820. Ramsay's account of the game is then inserted almost *verbatim* as an introduction to the records of the club, so the influence of Duddingston must have been felt here as elsewhere. Entrance to the club was obtained for 2s. 6d., 1s. of which went " to the bowl " and 1s. 6d. to the funds; for the earlier race of curlers always insisted on drinking a new member's health at his own expense. If a member did not appear on the ice once in a season he was fined 2s., and if he did appear he must have his "besom neatly tied." Every oath cost 1d. If repeated, the price was doubled; and the doubling process went on with each new offence, so that an ill-tongued member might swear himself out of a large fortune in a small space of time. If a member refused to pay he was not allowed to play, and if he appeared in a state of intoxication he was at once expelled the club as a disgrace to the company. Long live Dunblane!

The *Doune* Club, with 1732 as the year of its nativity, does not begin to speak till 1812, when seven masons, two slaters, and a cattle-dealer draw up an elaborate set of rules. These gentlemen were more drouthy than their friends at Dunblane, for of the new member's entry-money 2s. 6d. went to the bowl and 1s. to the funds. They had a yearly examination of all their members in the knowledge of the "word," and each member found deficient received the diploma of *rusty*, and was charged 1s. for his ignorance. The accounts of their social gatherings are brief but pointed, as—*e.g.*,

"Rustys were condemned, and over a jug or two of toddy natural goodwill and harmony prevailed, and a pleasant evening was spent.

"The snuff, the sang, the cup gaed roun',
 The crack, the joke, an' a', man."

On match days the usual refreshment was "pyes and porter;" but they must have had a *corps-de-reserve* of a stronger liquor, for we find in 1831, when they meet Dunblane, and the contest could not be proceeded with owing to a blinding snowstorm—

"The respective clubs pledged each other's health in a bumper of mountain dew, and hoped to meet again on some more favourable day."

The patronage of the Earls of Moray has been of great benefit to the club, and though they themselves have said it, the Dounites were keen and good curlers from the time their forefathers frightened the followers of Prince Charlie, who mistook their stones for cannon-balls and their besoms for swords, till the present day.

"The lads o' Doune are ill to beat,
 Their stanes they handle weel,
 And aye among the best o' clubs
 They're ranked as true as steel."

Of equal antiquity with Doune, the *Ardoch* Club is a good deal older before it has anything to say. Up till 1828 they curled with natural boulders, each with one stone, and nine players on a rink. From tee to tee the distance was 30 yards. The two foremost players *barleyed* the others. At the above date the stones were improved by being nidged into roundness, the usual size being 10 inches diameter by 5 in depth. Two "brothering masters" were appointed annually to look after the initiation of new members. Here are some interesting rules from the records which illustrate the ways of this club:—

"1. Only one member shall speak at a time, and in addressing the president the speaker shall rise to his feet.

"2. Whisky punch to be the usual drink of the club in order to encourage the growth of barley.

"3. No politics of Church or State to be discussed.

"4. No member to speak of the faults of another member in curling, nor deride the office-bearers, nor disobey the order of the day.

"5. Any member convicted of robbery or reset of theft shall have his name erased from the roll of members.

"6. Any member appearing at a meeting the worse of liquor shall be obliged to leave immediately for the day.

"7. Any member who swears, dictates to another how to vote, or persists in trifling motions without being supported, shall be fined.

"8. The amount of each fine to be 6d."

The *Auchterarder* Club was formed in 1830, and was open to "all the male inhabitants of the parish," while "none but those of good character were admitted." Once admitted, "members were accountable to the club for their conduct, not only upon the ice, but while going to or returning from a game." It was a graceful custom in this club to exact no annual dues "from members who had attained to the age of sixty years, unless it were their own pleasure to pay them." Each rink of five players was presided over by a *leader*, who determined the length of the rink and directed the game. It was the leader's duty to fix the grips so that players sent their stones over the tee. The front grip was to remain fixed, but the "hinder grip" might be shifted after one player had sent up his stone. With all our keenness, it is quite possible to have "too much of a good thing" in the way of frost, as this experience of the curlers of Auchterarder, dated 31st October 1836, clearly shews:—

"The fields adjacent to the pond being then covered with corn, uncut or in the stook, it will readily be supposed that there was little taste for curling in any member of the club."

One of the oldest and most interesting clubs in Perthshire is the *Strathallan Meath Moss*, but it is only near the close of this period that its records begin, when we find the factor on the Strathallan estate drawing up rules and regulations for the club. Through all its course the Strathallan family have treated the club as a darling child, and the annual meetings are like pleasant family gatherings, with Viscount Strathallan, the Master of Strathallan, or some member of the house generally presiding—laird, tenant, and cottar meeting together in mutual confidence and esteem. The annual dinners seem to have been held in the *Boo-hall*. Sometimes "Lady Strathallan sent sundry viands that are not included in ordinary curlers' fare," but usually the dinners were models of simplicity. The bills are carefully preserved in the minutes, and every detail is entered. In one we find "mustard, 6d.; pepper, 3d.; salt, 1s.; dram-glasses broke, 1s. 2d." But we shall give one of the oldest in full, that our brethren may see how in the days of old forty-seven curlers dined sumptuously and drank plentifully at a cost of 1s. 6d. per head, *eteceteras* included, and handed over a surplus to the funds of the club. *O tempora! O mores!* Here is the bill:—

NOTE OF CURLING DINNER FOR 49 MEMBERS, 18TH FEBRUARY 1831.

CASH RECEIVED.		CASH PAID.	
47 members paid 1/6 each,	£3 10 6	67 lb. beef @ 4½d.,	£1 5 0
Fines of Curling Court,	0 1 7	Whisky, 3½ gallons (being 21 bottles @ 1/3 and 1/7 each) or 7/6 p. Gⁿ.,	1 6 6
From Mr Thomson, David Erskine Robertson sent his dinner money a few days after, he being not present on the dinner evening,	0 2 8	10 lb. sugar at 11d.,	0 9 2
		Bread,	0 5 0
		2½ lb. candle,	0 2 0
	0 1 6	Women for cleaning the room and preparing the dinner,	0 5 6
			£3 13 2
		Paid balance to the treasurer to go to the fund,	0 3 1
	£3 16 3		£3 16 3

The youngest knight of the broom we have heard of crosses our path in Strathallan Meath Moss, when a son of the Master of Strathallan is "entered" at three years of age. His initiation and subscription were, however, judiciously postponed till the young idea could send a channel-stane over the hog. The Strathallan players seem to have stuck out longer than others against fitting their tee, and as long as they used grips it was permitted, as at Auchterarder, that the foremost grip might "be turned but not moved out of its place after the first leader has sent his stone up." In their point game they added *guarding* to the Duddingston list, and in a competition for a pair of curling-stones presented by the Hon. W. H. Drummond,

31st October 1836, out of four shots at the four points, John Houston won the coveted prize with *one* point. For each rink a leader and a skipper (or *principal*) were appointed to direct the play—" no other being allowed to say one word," and any person " finding fault with the direction " was liable to be fined one shilling—a rule that is worthy of universal adoption. As we shall see, the ancient mysteries of curling were here carefully preserved, and no member was allowed to play who was not brothered. The late Lord Strathallan used to relate at the curling dinners that in the early part of this century, and in the previous period of its existence, the Strathallan Club was never known to be beaten, for if losing at the curling they "called out" their enemies on the bank of the pond, where they never failed to come off victorious at *fisticuffs*. It was not thought advisable to continue this habit after the close of the first quarter of the century, and it is now quite safe for southerners to meet his Lordship's retainers at a Grand Match and beat them on their curling merits—a difficult thing, we believe, to do.

The ancient club at *Muthill* was still to the fore, and we hear of a club at *Crieff*, but of curling at this time in George Ruthven's Perth we hear nothing, though we have no reason to suppose that it had been forgotten there. At *Methven* the game had been carried on for a century, and there was a club there in 1831 which kept records. These were lost forty years ago. The great patron and friend of this club was Robert Smythe of Methven, a gentleman much beloved and respected by all in that district. His enthusiasm for the national game, and his generous disposition toward the curlers and their club, will ever be remembered.

When we come to the *Clunie* Club we again find the influence of the Duddingston Club strongly manifesting itself. One of the presidents of Duddingston, Principal Baird, had formerly been minister at *Dunkeld*, where he introduced the game, and when he removed south he still kept up an intimate friendship with the curlers. In recognition of his kindness we find him receiving from " his friends in the Stormont " a fluted silver tea-kettle, and in return the Principal sends them the Kilmarnock Treatise on Curling, and a pair of Copinsha stones (*vide* p. 89) to be competed for according to Duddingston point rules. It is only in 1831 that we find this club giving up the use of natural boulders and agreeing to play in future with made stones. They had continued the boulders for a while to accommodate other clubs, but owing to the trouble of collecting them, in consequence of the quantity of water in the burns and rivers, they determined to do this no longer, and to play no matches with clubs that did not use "made stones." The Doune Club had an official peculiar to itself—a *handlemaker*, who was no doubt useful. One entry describes a match between the chaplain and the president for a bottle of whisky, which the chaplain lost, as he deserved to do. Two charity matches during this period took place with Dunkeld, the losing side paying five shillings *per* player for the poor of the parish of the winners. Little is said about the club's festive gatherings, except that "the evening was as usual spent in true curler fashion." This covers a good deal—curlers all know how much.

Coupar-Angus and *Blairgowrie*, as in the previous century, keep faithful records of their doings, and remain true to the old traditions of the game. The latter was a special centre of light and leading in the north, to which pilgrims came from far and near for illumination in the "word" and the mysteries, and for instruction in the art.

Farther north, again, the Duke of Athole was setting an example to the Scottish nobility, as his successors have continued to do, by taking a personal and sincere interest in our national game. His Grace, it seems, was the inventor of a new style of curling which is thus described by Sir R. Broun in 1830:—

"The late Duke of Athole suggested a new mode of curling—viz., upon skates, and with long poles forked at the end. The player fixes this upon the handle of the stone, and then retires ten or twelve yards from the tee. He next swiftly pushes it forward, humouring its motion, and having his eye fixed upon the object to be aimed for at the further end. When the stone reaches the tee he gives it the requisite impulse. This is described as an elegant mode, and makes a highly interesting game."[*]

[*] Cairnie remarks on this (*Essay*, p. 59): "Wanting the skates, and with firm footing, this contrivance may be introduced with advantage, if

This new plan does not seem to have been accepted to any great extent by curlers, who do not generally care for fanciful deviations from the orthodox methods, but we are inclined to think that the bent-down handles on many of the old stones that have come under our notice, as in the collection at present to be seen at Blair Castle, indicate that the Duke's plan had been tried in a good many places, and more especially with the old implements that were at the time falling into disuse.

In the year 1815, Thomas Dick and William Patullo, two pilgrims from *Alyth*, got the "word" from Blairgowrie, and on their return home they initiated thirteen others and formed the Alyth Club. Grateful for its creation, the Alyth Club soon after entertained the twelve Blairgowrie curlers who had received their deputation to a dinner, which cost £4, 3s. This was, no doubt, a special feast of fat things, and its nature is not recorded; but at Alyth, as at Strathallan, the ordinary annual dinners of the curling club are all preserved, and we may give the two first for comparison with those which we have already noticed, and with the "reckoning" that awaits us nowadays after an evening's enjoyment:—

27th *January* 1815.

FIRST ANNUAL DINNER OF THE ALYTH CURLING SOCIETY IN MR A. HENRY'S.

To dinner for 15 gent. @ 1/6,	. .	£1 2 6
„ 1 chopin whiskie toddy,	. .	0 4 0
„ 3 chopin double strong whiskie toddy,		1 4 0
		£2 10 6

---

a little modified. The missiles, perhaps, might be formed of hardwood, with steel-plate bottoms; and were it possible, by means of a pole of wood, which might be called the ice-mace, to move the stones in every direction, and to disengage it from them when the aim was taken and the propelling power applied; in that case we conceive the improvement might be considerable, for we should be able to take better aim, and there would be no necessity for stooping; the curling-mace would operate in the same way as a mace on a billiard ball, and, perhaps, could give a more forcible impetus to the projected *material* than could be done by the present mode of throwing it."

4th January 1816.
SECOND ANNUAL DINNER AT MR LEMAN'S.

		£	s.	d.
To dinner for 20 gent. @ 1 6,	.	1	10	0
„ 10 mutch. whisky toddy,	.	1	10	0
„ 2 mutch. gin,	.	0	6	0
„ 2 bottles porter,	.	0	1	0
„ 20 bottles beer,	.	0	3	4
		£3	10	4
Allowances for waiter,	.	0	3	0
		£3	13	4

The society at Alyth seems to have been particular in the matter of securing suitable stones, and, like others, it had an examining committee. At one meeting in 1822 four suitable pairs were purchased at 6s. per pair; six pairs that were found unserviceable were "broke, and the handles laid up for future use;" one pair, belonging to David Ogilvy, was condemned as unfit for service. In 1825 two pairs were approved of "only on condition that the owners of said stones shall give the bottoms of them a better polish, and dress the upper part of them with a hammer as curling-stones ought to be." George Crocket, for not providing proper stones as required by the regulations, was given "a charge before the Baron Bailie of Alyth;" if he appealed by reclaiming petition against the bailie's decision, answers were to be presented to the Supreme Court of Scotland—all this to be at the instance and expense of the society. If the said George Crocket appealed to a higher court, "Mr Moncur shall then bear the expense as a private individual."

So much disappointment was caused by the committee's decisions, and so much trouble brought upon the society, that it was at last decided that the society should provide all stones required by the members, each member thereafter to pay 15s. per annum to cover costs, and to be left with Hobson's choice. Here is a brief minute extracted from the Alyth record which gives a delightful little picture, from one of the most northern points that curling had then reached, of that gentle, genial, brotherly fellowship which always attends the game.

"ALYTH, 17th December 1827.
"The society having now discussed the several matters which came under their consideration and got all the important business settled, spent the remainder of the night in that kind, social, and orderly manner which ought to distinguish all keen curlers, and by the hour of 12 settled their tavern bill and departed, much delighted with one another's company, and taking an affectionate good-night of each other."

The last Perthshire club which falls to be noticed is the *Strathmore*, established in 1826. This club met at Meigle, the annual gathering being held on Auld Handsel Monday—a day on which several other clubs in the north were accustomed to meet. For a long period the Rev. Patrick Barty acted as secretary of the club, and David Nairn of Drumkilbo as president—the latter securing the gratitude of the curlers by making a pond for them at his own expense. The rules and regulations at Strathmore were like many which we have already noticed. "Giving bad names to any member" was held to be as bad as swearing, and the same fee was charged for both, viz., 2d.; the *morale* of the game being further protected by a rule (No. 12) which was to this effect:—

"No political toasts nor discussions, and no improper toasts whatever to be permitted."

Though there was a Strathmore Club in the county of Perth, we do not hear much of curling in the Strathmore of FORFARSHIRE when we cross into that county. This was one of the counties where, in fact, curling was only partially known in the period now under review. At the town of Forfar a club was instituted in 1797. In that year the club played on a natural pond at Carseburn, with stones of a very rough description, and two-legged iron handles. The two leading skips were the Rev. John Skinner, D.D., Episcopal minister, Forfar, and the Rev. Mr Eadie, Secession minister, who uniformly skipped the opposing rinks. They both played with stones weighing 65 lbs. each, which were known by the name of "The Jannies." The club has had to shift its curling tent several times since it was first pitched on Carseburn—playing at Cow-loch, Southmuir, and Loch of Forfar in succession; but under the kindly patronage of the

Earl of Strathmore, a keen supporter of the ancient game, they have finally found a place of rest where they may curl undisturbed. The *Dundee* Club dates back to the last year of last century. *Kirriemuir* had also a club in 1809, and the game appears to have been known at *Brechin* in early times, but from none of them all have we any written records till we come to a later stage. The secretary of the

FIG. 55. SIR JOHN OGILVY.
(From a photograph by Messrs Maull & Fox, London.)

Strathmartine Club informs us that up till 1867, when his club was formed, the game was quite unknown in the district comprised in Mains and Strathmartine, Auchterhouse and Tealing parishes. Sir John Ogilvy, Bart., one of the most respected landlords of this county, who was Member of Parliament for Dundee during four Parliaments, 1859–1874 deserves gratitude and honour from curlers in the North, and from all who love the game. He became, as we shall see, one of the wisest counsellors and staunchest supporters of the Royal Club, of which he was president more than once. At this period he was a keen curler, and doing what he could to strengthen the cause in his native county. Even now, at the advanced age of eighty-six, Sir John's heart is in the game, and in the progress of our work we have had from his lips and from his pen—for he is still "clear and keen"—interesting reminiscences of curling and curlers in days so long gone by that few besides himself are able to tell their story. Between the present and the past we have no more interesting link of connection to-day than this good old Baronet of Baldovan. His last letter to us (October 10, 1889) contained these words—"The pleasantest days of my life have been spent on the ice." We receive them as the benediction of a venerable patriarch, and hand them on to the brotherhood of the future as the legacy of a long and honourable life.

It appears from the survey we have thus given of the curling of Scotland during the period 1800–1838, that the game was most popular in the counties of the western and southern districts—such as Ayr, Renfrew, Lanark, Dumfries, and Kirkcudbright. In the eastern counties—such as Haddington, Berwick, and Roxburgh—it had not yet made great progress. In such counties as Edinburgh, Fife, Kinross, and Perth, we hear of many notable clubs and players at this time; but among the people generally the game cannot be said to have been so popular as in the counties we have mentioned. Beyond Perth and Forfar curling appears to have been at this time little known. Its benign influence had not extended to the Highlands. The fact that the clergy of the period were not able to employ themselves like the minister of Tibbermore accounts for many things that have happened since then.* When some Ayrshire sheep-farmers started a curling club at Laggan, in Inverness county, about 1855, the shinty-players — finding, like

* *Vide* Mrs Oliphant's *Life of Principal Tulloch*, third edition, p. 18.

P

Othello, that their occupation was gone—did all they could to oppose the game; and some of them actually carried off the club-house of the curlers, which has not since been heard of. Perhaps the shinty had to do with the expulsion of curling from some places in the North where it had been known in a previous century; for Scotia's darling must some time or other, with her broom on her shoulder and her crampits bound on her snowy feet, have taken a Highland trip; and if she then failed to gain the affection of the lovers of shinty, there were some among the North men who were won by her loving countenance, and yielded to her charms. There are memories of curling in the *Buchan* district 150 years ago. It is certain the game was played on the loch of Kininmonth towards the close of last century. The late Dean Ranken, Old Deer, used to relate that the Rev. Mr Cumming, Longside (born 1770), the grandson and successor of the Rev. Mr Skinner (Tullochgorum), once described to him how farmers from all quarters assembled together on the ice day after day when the frost lasted, and specimens of old curling-stones since found in this and other Highland districts are proof of the fact that curling was not unknown in the North at an earlier time.

Explain it as we may, the game had, however, been forgotten, and there are no reminiscences of its presence north of Perth and Forfar at this time. It was even in danger of languishing in the South, if we are to believe Christopher North in this eloquent passage of his *Winter Rhapsody* :*

"A change has come over the spirit of the curler's dream. They seem to our ears indeed to have 'quat their roaring play.' The cry of 'swoop, swoop' is heard still—but oh! a faint, feeble, and unimpassioned cry, compared with that that used on the Mearns Brother Loch to make the welkin ring, and for a moment to startle the moon and stars—those in the sky as well as those below the ice—till again the tumult subsided—and lo! all the host of heaven above and beneath serene as a world of dreams. Is it not even so, Shepherd! Oh! what is a rink now on a pond in Duddingston policy, to the rinks that rang and roared of old on the Loch o' the Lowes, when every stone, circled in a glorious halo of spray, seemed instinct with spirit to obey, along all its flight, the voice of him that launched it on its unerring aim, and sometimes in spite of his awkward skill-lessness, when the

---

* *Blackwood's Magazine*, Vol. XXIX., February 1831, pp. 303-4.

fate of the game hung on its own single crank, went cannonading through all obstacles till it fell asleep, like a beauty as it was, just as it kissed the Tee!"

The Professor was unnecessarily alarmed. Scotland stood where she did in her devotion to the game. But it is not easy for curlers to keep up enthusiasm when the winters are damp, as they had so often been in the decade that preceded the Professor's wail. A few fine frosty winters, and then there came a rush of clubs, the war-cry was keener and clearer than ever, and the old enthusiasm returned like a giant refreshed, to make Scotland's game more truly national than it had been before. How this was done we shall see in our next chapter.

AN SGUABAG BHEALAIDH.

Air fonn—"*So mar theid an gun a dheanamh.*"

Seisd—'S i mo luaidh an sguabag bhealaidh,
    Chuireas snuadh an gruaidh nam fearaibh,
'S i mo luaidh an sguabag bhealaidh,
'S àlag mhear nan cuairteag.

Ged thig oirnne reoth' 'us gaillionn,
Chuireas gròiceanaich do 'n teallach
Theid na cròlaich mach le farum
Thun a chàth bu dual daibh.
    'S i mo luaidh, &c.

Gur e 'n cròladh gaol nam bairean,
Bheireas cail 'us ceol 'us carthan,
Slainte crè 'us speiread aigne
Nach bi lag no truaillte.
    'S i mo luaidh, &c.

Thig an t-aodhair thig am baran,
Thig an t-aosda thig an gallan,
Dh' ionnsuidh éire ghlas na carraid,
'Thogas tlachd mu 'n cuairt di.
    'S i mo luaidh, &c.

"Sios am bacan," cluinn an sgiobair.
"Seol dhomh clach ri taobh na bioraid."
Sid air falbh, an eiteag bhinneach,
'S i air chrith 'na gluasad.
    'S i mo luaidh, &c.

'S ann an sin tha 'n horo-gheallaidh,
Ga toirt suas thar Sgor-na-caillich,
Rang a dàimh le stri ga faire,
'S laigh i 'm barr na cuairteig.
    'S i mo luaidh, &c.

Eadar "togail" agus "dionadh,"
"Sgram an geard" no "sgaile a cliathach,"
Cha 'n eil sean no og nach iniannaich,
Bhi fo riar do bhuaireis.
    'S i mo luaidh, &c.

'S lionar cuach de dh' fhuarag Adhal,
Nitear òl do Bhròd Dhunchaillionn,
Buaidh 'us cliu do 'n Diuc tha againn,
Sar chul-taic na sguabaig.
    'S i mo luaidh, &c.

Pol. Camshron.

Blar an' Adhal.

CHAPTER II.

THE VICTORIAN ERA—ROYAL CALEDONIAN CURLING CLUB.

THE ORIGIN OF THE GRAND CLUB.

HE history of curling, from the end of the period with which the last chapter deals till the present time, is very much the history of the Royal Caledonian Curling Club: and as this club began its career soon after Her Most Gracious Majesty's accession to the throne, its history may be called the Victorian era of the game.

The institution in 1838 of a Grand National Club, with its headquarters in the Scottish capital, and having for its object the regulation of the laws and methods of curling by the united deliberations of representatives from all the clubs of the country, is the most important and far-reaching event in the whole history of curling.

The necessity for such an institution arose out of the confusion to which we have referred in the last chapter. Although the famous and powerful Duddingston Club had done much to improve the science and the style of play, the confusion among curling communities still continued, and unless something were done to improve matters, it became evident to all concerned that progress was impossible. In arranging the first county match in the century—that between Midlothian and Peebles in 1823—Dr Renton of Penicuick had found the greatest difficulty, owing to differences among the clubs as to the rules of the game, the number and size of stones, and the number on each rink; and as far back as 1824 he had urged on the secretaries of various clubs the formation of a National Curling Association, on the principle of the Highland and Agricultural Society. But nothing was done; and in the match between Midlothian and Lanarkshire in 1831, the difficulties of arrangement were felt as much as ever.

With Sir Richard Broun and Dr Cairnie—the two great curling authorities of the time, the idea of a National Curling Association had also been discussed. Cairnie, in 1833, in the Addenda to his *Essay* (p. 139) says:—

"The author of the *Mem. Cur.* has suggested to us a scheme for the formation of an Amateur Curling Club for Scotland; and we trust he will soon, in a second edition of his work, furnish the curlers of this country with the particulars. He has been so kind as to suggest to us some of the items connected with the plan of formation; and we sincerely wish the talented gentleman's views of the subject may be realised. We think it would be a very desirable matter that, connected with this Curling Club, it should be recommended that every curling society in Scotland should correspond, and give in a list of their office-bearers, the number of curlers, matches played, and any matter connected with the game that is interesting."

The author of the *Memorabilia* does not seem to have pursued his suggestion. For two years after the publication of his book he collected notes for a second edition, but he went off to London and left the *Memorabilia* and the suggested amateur society in the hands of others. In the old minute-book of the *Douglas St Bride's Curling Society* we meet with them both. This society, at one of its meetings, received a communication from Captain John Paterson, Crofton Hill, near Lanark, announcing a new edition of the *Memorabilia*,* and along with this the following:—

---

* Broun seems to have concealed his authorship of the *Memorabilia* for a considerable time. Cairnie evidently knew the author, though he did not divulge his name, but Captain Paterson, in his communication to the

PROSPECTUS.

AMATEUR CURLING CLUB OF SCOTLAND,

INSTITUTED 1834,

For Promoting and Cherishing the Noble National Game of Curling.

"RESOLUTION.—That the Amateur Curling Club shall be entirely *exclusive*, embracing the name of such curlers alone as are entitled to be handed down to posterity, as associated *par excellence* with the ice of the nineteenth century. Members shall be admitted—

"1. *Ex-officio.*—From being presidents or office-bearers of any curling society throughout Scotland.

"2. *Ex-merito.*—From being *distingué* either from literary productions upon the subject of curling, or from inventions of some kind practically connected with the game.

"3. *Ex-suffragio.*—From very high scientific skill: gaining a society's medal, or a recommendation from the office-bearers of the local society to which the candidate belongs, shall be necessary for admission under this head."

This society of *distingués*, as further appears from Paterson's circular, was to be under the patronage of the Duke of Hamilton and the Duke of Athole; the Presidents were to be—Earl of Moray, Earl of Elgin, Lord Elcho, and Lord Torphichen. Vice-Presidents—Hay and Clerk, baronets. Chaplains—Drs Baird, Bryce, Duncan, &c. Secretaries—The Ettrick Shepherd, Captain Paterson, Adam Wilson, Robert Brown. Then follows the list of members. *Ex-officio*—Earl of Moray, and 150 others. *Ex-merito*—Drs Cairnie and Gillespie, Hogg, Captain Paterson, and about twenty others. *Ex-suffragio* — John Linning, and fifty others. Paterson's communication to the Douglas Society closed with the request that the preses should

"Furnish him with the names of such curlers as he may consider entitled to be admitted as members of the Amateur Curling Club of Scotland, stating the nature of their claims to such distinction," and "in compliance with this request the secretary is directed to prepare the necessary returns and forward them without delay."

If the members of this mutual admiration amateur society intended to advance the national game, they certainly went

---

Douglas Club, refers to the volume as written by "Robert Brown, Esq., Secretary of the Lochmaben Club." The name, it will be noticed, is also erroneously entered in the prospectus of the proposed amateur society. It is not easy to account for Paterson's ignorance of Broun's authorship, especially as he announces that he is to be a contributor to the new edition of the *Memorabilia*, and takes such liberties with the book. Halket & Laing's *Dictionary of Anonymous Literature* does not include the *Memorabilia*.

the wrong way about it. The society, as might be expected, came to nothing.

Dr Arnott, in his *Laws of Curling* (1838), after doing his best to reduce the various methods to uniformity, left many points to be settled by curlers before a match began. In the pamphlet, however, he made a practical suggestion regarding the necessity of abolishing all variations on the curling "word," which led to important results. Arnott's suggestion was to this effect (*Laws of Curling*, p. 11):—

> "All brothers have probably the same *grip*, but there appears to be considerable variation as to the *word*: this last is to be regretted, and might be easily remedied by a convention formed of the secretaries, or some accredited office-bearers of the principal initiated clubs of Scotland."

Some person, following up this suggestion, inserted in the *North British Advertiser* of May 26, 1838, the following advertisement:—

> "TO CURLERS.—In consequence of what is suggested at p. 11 of the '*Laws in Curling*' (a pamphlet just published by Maclachlan & Stewart, Edinburgh), it is hoped that the *Initiated Curling Clubs* in Scotland will depute one of the Brethren of their Court to meet in the Waterloo Hotel, Edinburgh, on Wednesday, the 20th June next, at 11 o'clock A.M., for the purpose of making the mysteries more uniform in future, and, if requisite, to form a Grand Court, to which all provincial ones shall be subject, and to elect a Grand President, with other Office-bearers. It is hoped that all Brethren who see this notice will direct the attention of their President or Secretary to it without delay.—16th May 1838."

Who inserted this advertisement?

Soon after the Grand Club's institution the question was raised, but it was found that the origin of the club, like the origin of curling itself, was surrounded with mystery. The claimants for the distinction were as numerous as the cities of Greece which competed, after his death, for the honour of "blind Homer's birth." We have a letter before us, written by John M'George, in which he distinctly states that the late Dr Cairnie, Mr Ogilvie Dalgleish, and himself were the "projectors" of the club. Cairnie had certainly most votes among those who gave their opinion on the subject. Charles Cowan, without any hesitation, ascribed the honour to Dr Renton. Mr Burns Begg declares that the club really "emanated from the little county of Kinross;" and as the "suggestion" which led to the preliminary advertisement was avowedly taken from Dr Walker Arnott's *Laws in Curling*, printed by the secretary of the Kinross Club (James Whitehead), and published by that gentleman, in conjunction with Maclachlan & Stewart, there seems to be some grounds for this pretension.

It does not appear that any one of those gentlemen ever directly claimed to have inserted the famous advertisement. Dr Cairnie openly stated that he had not done so, just when it had come to be tacitly understood that he had; and Dr Renton confined his claim to the naming of the club after its birth. There the matter had to rest until now, the only definite information about the said advertisement being that given in an "account of the origin of the club" in the *Annual* for 1844, in which the writer stated that,

"On inquiry at the office of the newspaper, he learned that a gentleman called with the advertisement, paid 10s. 6d. for it, but gave no name, and left no reference."

While we were busy investigating the records of the old curling societies, we came upon some entries in the Auchterarder minute-book, from which new light is thrown on the subject. The advertisement, it appears, was brought under the notice of the secretary, for the time being, of the Auchterarder Club, who took the opinion of several "brethren of the Court" as to the propriety of sending a deputy to the proposed meeting in the Waterloo Hotel. With true Scottish caution, it was decided to ascertain by whose authority the meeting had been called, the Auchterarder Court being convinced

"That the success or failure of the measure would depend upon the station and character of the individual by whom it had been concocted."

A request was accordingly sent to William Murray, writer in Edinburgh, to do the club the favour to ascertain by whom the Waterloo Hotel had been engaged for the meeting of curlers on 20th June, and by whom the advertisement was inserted. Mr Murray was at the same time requested to forward a copy of the pamphlet referred to in the advertisement to the secretary of the Auchterarder Club; and in the event of his being satisfied with the respectability of the person by whom the meeting was called, he was commissioned to act as the representative of their Court at the Curling Conference. Mr Murray evidently went about the business in lawyer-like style, and this is his reply :—

"EDINBURGH, 14*th June* 1838.

"MY DEAR SIR,—Your letter of 'high import,' dated the 11th, did not reach me until yesterday at mid-day. I cannot but congratulate myself on the high honour conferred upon me by the ancient and renowned club of Auchterarder by being selected, at least thought worthy, to make the inquiries on their behalf referred to in your letter. As requested, I went to the Waterloo, and was rather surprised to learn that no apartment, either in what are properly called the Waterloo Rooms or in the Hotel, had been bespoke for the meeting advertised. Having thus failed in this quarter, I next went to the office of the *N. B. Advertiser*, when one of the clerks, after considerable search, &c., told me that the advertisement had been furnished by a Mr J. Allan, a bookseller and publisher in Haddington. Maclachlan & Stewart's shopman tells me that the pamphlet was sent to them by a Dr Arnott of Arlary in Kinross-shire, but whether he be the author is not known. The preceding, I am sorry to say, is all the information I have been able to obtain in reference to the meeting of the 20th.

"Your renowned club must of course judge whether they will send over one of their members to take a part in the proceedings of that day. I shall send the pamphlet by the carrier of next week. It cost 6d., which I can get first time I see you. I cannot but regret the scanty information I have been able to obtain for my initiated brethren of the far-famed Auchterarder Curling Club. I shall be glad can I be of any future service in making inquiries for the curlers, but would rather decline becoming their representative at the ensuing meeting, not so much from any disinclination to the duties as from an almost certainty that my office duties would not permit of my attending the meeting at all—11 o'clock being our busy hour.

Yours very faithfully,

WILL^{M.} MURRAY."

"Mr Jas. Murray, Auchterarder."

The information contained in this letter may be relied on as far as it goes. Mr Murray's inquiry had the advantage of that which was instituted five years later, for it was made a week before the advertised meeting was held. But in some respects it is like the Hielandman's character —we "would have peen as petter without it." If Du Chaillu offer us Vikings for ancestors instead of North German tribes, we may adopt them (if children may adopt parents) as a change for the better, but we may not always be so fortunate if we believe everybody who goes poking into the roots of our national pedigree. So with the National Curling Club: we would not have objected to Mr Murray's inquiry if he had given us the immortal Cairnie or some other ice-king for a father; but we cannot adopt Mr J. Allan, bookseller and publisher in Haddington, as the parent of the Royal Club. There is still a mystery about its origin, which this letter only throws further back. Mr Allan was a worthy man (and there was no excuse for the "Spartan men" of Auchterarder deciding as they did to have nothing to do with the meeting); but he was not a curler, and did not take the slightest interest in the game. His shop was a "howff," where the good folks of the burgh met to discuss the affairs of their neighbours and settle the affairs of the nation; but faithless Haddington had long forgotten her curling, and it was no interest of hers at that time to advance the game at a cost of 10s. 6d. by the hands of Mr Allan. We would have suggested that John Ramsay, who was now at Gladsmuir, might have got the bookseller to act as he did; but we find from the Gladsmuir minutes that Ramsay did not at first believe in the Grand Club, and advised the Gladsmuir curlers to have nothing to do with it. In a vision of the night the scroll may have been placed in Mr Allan's hands by the guardian angel of Scotia's ain game; but we are inclined to think that he inserted the advertisement by arrangement with some eminent curler or friend of curling who wished "to do good by stealth," or perhaps to conceal his identity in case the meeting should prove a failure. The Murray letter now published may yet lead to a settlement of the question. Meantime we may leave it under the shadow of the Lamp of Lothian, "until" (as our old session-books say of dubious births), "Providence shall see fit to cast further light upon the subject."

The advertisement was a success, but it narrowly escaped being a failure. About a dozen gentlemen—all keen curlers —met in the Waterloo Hotel, and after sitting for some time they were about to disperse, "the most part," like the Ephesian mob, "not knowing wherefore they had come," when a dapper little stranger entered the upper room where they sat, with some volumes under his only arm, and, throwing these on the table, presented his card—*John Cairnie of Curling Hall.* His air, manner, and address so impressed them all that he was with acclaim made chairman of the meeting. They then proceeded to business. No regular minute of their doings was taken, but in the *North British Advertiser* and other papers the following advertisement, drawn up by the company, soon thereafter appeared:—

"To CURLERS.—In consequence of an advertisement which appeared in the *North British Advertiser* of 26th May 1838, a MEETING of CURLERS was held in the Waterloo Hotel on the 20th inst., JOHN CAIRNIE, Esq., of Curling Hall, Largs, in the chair. Deputations from various Clubs appeared, who approved generally of adopting a uniform set of Regulations, applicable to the whole of Scotland, assimilating the technical terms, forming a court of reference, &c.

"But anxious for a fuller representation of the different Clubs throughout the country, in order to perpetuate and connect more closely the Brotherhood in this Ancient National Game, they adjourned to WEDNESDAY, 25th of JULY NEXT, at 12 o'clock, in the Waterloo Hotel, when they hope the different Clubs of Scotland will make a point of sending Deputations. JOHN CAIRNIE, *Chairman.*"

The meeting which took place in response to this advertisement was a thoroughly representative one, forty-four gentlemen being present, who represented thirty-six clubs, connected with the various districts of Scotland, from Dumfries to Perth.

Abdie.
  Jas. Ogilvie Dalgleish.
  John Pitcairn.
Avondale.
  Robert Armour.
  William Dalgleish.
Bathgate.
  Thos. Durham Weir.
  John Rankine.
Blairgowrie.
  Thomas Coupar.
Buchan.
  The Earl of Buchan.
  James Somerville.
  Dr Thomson.
Cairnie.
  Charles Robertson.
Currie.
  William Ramage.
Dalry.
  John Cairnie.

Denny.
  Andrew Hall.
Dolphinton.
  Rev. Dr Aiton.
Drum.
  John Laing.
Dunblane.
  James Boyd.
East Linton.
  Sir David Baird,
    Bart. of Newbyth.
Falkirk.
  James Aitken.
Kilmarnock Parish.
  ,,   *Junior.*
  ,,   *Townend.*
  ,,   *Morning Star.*
  H. Hutchison.
Kinnoughtry.
  Charles Robertson.

Kinross.
  J. W. Williamson.
  Robert Annan.
  J. Skelton.
Kirknewton.
  William Stark.
  John Gay.
  James Somerville.
Largs Gogoside.
  ,,   *Thistle.*
  John Cairnie.
Linlithgow Senior.
  Thomas Nimmo.
Linlithgow Junior.
  Andrew Mickel.
  John Hartly.
  William Greenfield.
Mauchline.
  Richard Gibson.
Merchiston.
  Archibald Thomson.
  John M'George.

Methven.
  Charles Robertson.
Millport.
  John Cairnie.
North Woodside.
  William M'Innes.
  George Dick.
Orwell.
  Robert Reid.
  John Black.
  Dr Walker Arnott.

Penicuick.
  Charles Cowan.
  John Renton.
  William Gilbert.
Scone and Perth.
  Charles Robertson.
Thornhill (Dumfriesshire).
  John Cairnie.

Whitburn.
  Sir William Baillie of
    Polkemmet, Bart.
  William Baillie.
  John Bishop.
  Alexander Waddell.
Willowbank.
  John Cairnie.

The resolution by which the Grand Club was formally instituted was proposed by Dr Renton, and agreed to with the utmost heartiness and enthusiasm :—

"That this meeting do form itself into a club, composed of the different initiated clubs of Scotland, under the name of the 'Grand Caledonian Curling Club.'"

Dr Cairnie was then, as a matter of course, elected first president of the club; Mr James Skelton, W.S., a "brother" of the Kinross Court, was chosen to be honorary secretary and treasurer; while John M'George and James Ogilvie Dalgleish were made vice-presidents.

From his throne of office the famous old curler of the West gave a short but comprehensive address, eulogising the ancient and national game. Cairnie also explained the system of artificial pond-making with which his name was connected, and the meeting had placed before them some specimens of improved curling-stones, alongside of which was exhibited a *luting-stone* which had been fished out of Lochleven. The day of its institution, 25th July 1838, was indeed a miniature of the history of the club. Even the social side of the club meetings was duly observed by a dinner, at which Mr Ogilvie Dalgleish presided, his admirable conduct in the chair contributing not a little to the hilarity of the evening. The Court was constituted in due form by a member of the Kinross deputation, according to the most ancient usage, and afforded to those who were not acquainted with that ceremony great interest and amusement. With due observance of all the best traditions of the game, and with a clear understanding of what was required to make it a national institution worthy of the support of future generations of curlers, the Grand Club was thus successfully started on its journey; and, as the first account of its origin (*Annual*, 1844, pp. 57, 58) has it—

> "There could not be a better instance of the attractive nature of curlers' sympathy than this day's history affords. The members met in the morning almost strangers to each other—they spent the evening like brothers, as if they had been all their lives acquainted, and separated rejoicing in the friendships they had formed, and in the expectation of often meeting again."

THE CONSTITUTION.

The Grand Club, thus happily instituted, could not do much without a constitution. Its founders did not forget this; but, as the constitution of such a club could not be framed in a day, they adjourned to 15th November 1838, leaving it to be drafted by a few of their trusted brethren. A glance at the list of those who attended the first meeting will shew how many there were among the number capable of doing this work. The author of the *Memorabilia* was not there, but he sent a communication which shewed that he was there in spirit. Dr Walker Arnott, who had this same year published the *Laws of Curling*, was at their service; so was the chairman himself, than whom there was no better authority, although the weight of years made it impossible for him to do much more active work in the cause. Then there were two amphibious heroes—Sir David Baird, Bart. of Newbyth, and Charles Robertson ("Golfing Charlie"). They both loved the *gutty* well, and had won high honours in the "Royal and Ancient," and both were splendid curlers, loving curling even more than golf, like *The Stranger* (*vide* p. 211), who sang over the toddy at Pitlessie:—

> "There's daily golf at Saint Andrewes,
>   And tea and turnout nightly;
> But I prefer the curling-stane
>   That skims the ice sae lightly.
> For oh! I like baith dear and weel
>   The curling-stane to handle!
> I wad na gi'e the blithe *bonspiel*
>   For a' their cards and scandal."

Any or all of these might have prepared a constitution for the Grand Club. It shews what a wealth of ability there was among the company when they were all left out.

To the following gentlemen as a committee the work was entrusted—viz., Dr Renton, Charles Cowan, and Mr Gilbert (Penicuick Club); John M'George (Merchiston); Thomas Durham Weir (Bathgate); J. Ogilvie Dalgleish (Abdie); J. W. Williamson (Kinross); and Messrs Simpson, Hill, and Scott. The three last-named were not present at the meeting. It is more than likely that they were Duddingston members, and that by their inclusion in the list, the founders of the Grand Club desired to gain the allegiance of the Duddingston Club, which, although it was the most important club in Scotland, had not sent a representative to the meeting at which the Grand Club was formed. In the selection of the committee Penicuick Club was specially honoured—its three delegates being all included. Of Mr Gilbert we have not heard much; but of Dr Renton we have heard a great deal, and all to his credit. He was a successful physician, a good curler, and an all-round man of the highest type. Dr Renton did a great amount of work in the cause of curling long before the days of the Grand Club, and of this club he was one of the best friends and brightest ornaments for many years. Charles Cowan, who was afterwards well known as member for the city of Edinburgh, and who of all the gallant band that formed the club was the only one destined to survive the first fifty years of its existence, was then in the prime of life, esteemed by all who knew him as a man of high moral principle, sterling worth, and excellent business capacity. His great aim in life was to promote everything which concerned the welfare and happiness of his fellow-men. He saw the beneficial moral effects of curling on the community, and became a keen curler, not so much because of any selfish delight to be had in it, but because it was social, manly, and healthy. John M'George was one of the most experienced of curlers, for he had played as far back as 1770, when he was only fourteen years of age. In his *Reminiscences*[*] (p. 115), Charles Cowan speaks of this old curler as "a perfect

---

[*] *Reminiscences*, by Charles Cowan of Logan House. Printed for private circulation, 1878.

gentleman," and tells in his praise how he absolutely refused to play his stone on one occasion when the game stood *peels*, and some one who had money on the match cried out, "Take care, M'George, there's a guinea on that shot." To the end of his life M'George was a most useful member of the Grand Club. For a good many years he was medalist to the club — an office which he also filled in the Duddingston Society. Of Mr Durham Weir and Mr Williamson we have spoken in our last chapter. They were both excellent men, and worthy to act on this committee. It was, however, to James Ogilvy Dalgleish, above all others, that the Grand Club was indebted for the framework of its first constitution. After a period of active service in the navy, Mr Dalgleish at a comparatively early age settled down in his native county of Fife, and devoted his attention to agricultural and county business. Residing at Lindores, he could not fail to be fired with the enthusiasm of the Abdie curlers, who met on the lovely loch there. As a member of the committee, he devoted his days and nights to the framing of the

FIG. 60.
CAPTAIN JAMES OGILVY DALGLEISH, R.N.,
OF WOODBURNE AND BALTILLY, FIFE.
(*From a photograph by P. Devine.*)

constitution, and his hand is visible in most of the earlier
legislation of the club, the plan for provincial spiels being,
like many other good things, due to him. For thirty years
he never missed an annual meeting. As he had witnessed
its birth and fostered its growth, he was with one voice
made president in the year 1851, when the club had
reached its maturity. In his home club (Abdie), and in the
Ceres Club, of which he was long president, Mr Dalgleish
was greatly beloved and respected. It is said that when he
was nearly seventy he entered the lists with twenty-one
competitors for the point medals. The storm was so violent
that they had to move from Lindores to a sheltered bit of
ice called the Dog Loch, and there the old man out-distanced
all competitors and won the first medal with twelve points.
He tied for the second, and amid great excitement the tie
was played off, when the veteran scored two beautiful
shots at "chip the winner," and beat his man. Another
incident, of a different kind, is no less characteristic of the
man. After a bonspiel between Abdie and Balyarrow, when
the two clubs had enjoyed their "beef and greens," Mr
Dalgleish, who was in the chair, rose up, and called on the
curlers to remember the poor. In response to his call a
handsome subscription was realised, which was at once forwarded to Newburgh soup-kitchen. Well might the Royal
Club Committee thus express their feelings when Mr Dalgleish died in 1875—

"Gentlemanly, genial and hearty in manner, a good curler and a
grand skip—we feel as curlers that we have all lost one of the best of
friends."

The essential features of the constitution of the club have
remained much the same as when it was presented by the
committee and unanimously adopted on 15th November
1838. In the course of fifty years, what with additions
and amendments, the constitution has, however, become
rather corpulent, and it would be improved by a course of
the Banting system. In recent years several proposals have
been made to revise it and make it clearer and more compact. We shall therefore give the constitution, as it now

Q

stands, at the end of our volume* (as it can there be amended without much difficulty), and in a series of paragraphs we shall try to bring out its essential features, while at the same time we trace the history of the club and of curling during the last half-century.

ROYAL PATRONAGE.

The flag of Royalty has waved over our National Curling Club during the greater part of its career. In 1842, when Her Majesty the Queen and the Prince Consort visited Scotland, they were entertained by the Earl of Mansfield at the palace of Scone. The Earl was at that time president of the Grand Club. While all classes were busy giving expression to their loyalty and attachment to the throne, the curlers requested Lord Mansfield to present Prince Albert with a pair of curling-stones, and at the same time to recommend the Grand Caledonian Curling Club to the favourable notice of His Royal Highness.

The stones transmitted to the palace of Scone were made of the finest Ailsa granite, the handles being of silver, and bearing an appropriate inscription. In presence of the Queen, Her Majesty's Ministers, and the guests assembled in the palace, the Earl of Mansfield duly presented them to Prince Albert, who was pleased to accept them, and to thank the curlers for "this mark of their respectful attention." The Prince at the same time, "in his own modest and winning manner," as Lord Mansfield afterwards wrote, "at once assented to the suggestion that he should be patron of the club." Her Majesty the Queen made particular inquiries of the Earl regarding the game of curling. To illustrate the explanations he gave in reply, Lord Mansfield had the polished oaken floor of the room converted into a rink, and initiated Her Majesty and His Royal Highness into all the mysteries of the game. The stones were sent "roaring" along the smooth surface, and Her Majesty "tried her hand" at throwing them, but they proved too heavy for her delicate arm. Both the Queen and the Prince expressed surprise when informed as to the usual length of

---

* Appendix A.

a rink, and appeared to imagine that it must require a very
great degree of strength to propel the stones to such a
distance. The Merchiston Club soon after had the honour
of enrolling Prince Albert in its list of regular members.
In the following year a petition was sent by the Grand Club
to Sir George Clerk, for presentation to the Queen, praying
Her Majesty to allow the use of the term *Royal*. The reply
received was afterwards lithographed as the club's royal
charter, and a copy transmitted to each affiliated club. It
was sent through Sir James Graham, Secretary of the Home
Department, to William Gibson-Craig, Esq., then president
of the club, and was as follows :—

"WHITEHALL, 12*th August* 1843.

"SIR,—I am directed by Secretary Sir James Graham to inform you
that he has laid before the Queen the petition of the 'Grand Caledonian
Curling Club,' praying that they may be permitted to assume the
designation of 'The Royal Grand Caledonian Curling Club.' And I
am to acquaint you that Her Majesty has been graciously pleased to
grant the prayer of the petition.—I have the honour to be, &c.,

"H. MANNERS SUTTON.

"The President of the
Royal Grand Caledonian Curling Club, &c."

The adjective *Grand* being deemed superfluous, permission
was given to drop it, and since that time the club has worn
its present title. Whether Prince Albert put the Ailsas to
any practical use we do not know, but both His Highness
and Her Majesty the Queen endeared themselves to the
curling brotherhood by their sympathy, and when on that
dark December morning in 1861 the word passed from
mouth to mouth "the Prince is dead," none grieved more
bitterly over his loss than the curlers of Scotland, and
none to this day cherish more tenderly the memory of
Albert the Good.

On the death of the Prince Consort, His Royal Highness
Albert Edward, Prince of Wales, through Lord Mansfield,
consented to become patron of the Royal Club (July 21,
1862). That their new patron might have facilities for
putting his patronage into practice, the club presented him
with a pair of stones, made of the green serpentine found
near Crieff, with silver-mounted handles chased with thistles,

oak leaves, and acorns, the wood being of oak from the palace of Linlithgow. The presentation was made by Lord Sefton, who was then president of the club. If His Royal Highness was fortunate in having such tutors as "Golfing Charlie" desired (*vide* p. 76), he must long before this have been initiated into "the incomparable game of curling," and the "Muthills" have, no doubt, enjoyed many an outing on the Royal ponds.

Under the patronage of the Prince of Wales we have continued in prosperity, the number of our clubs and our members having nearly doubled. We are grateful for his support. Our hope is that ere long we shall have our patron spending a curling season among us, now that he has family ties to bind him more closely to the North. He could have no better insight into the game than among the curlers of Braemar, with their popular president, the Duke of Fife, a keen, keen curler, at their head; and if His Royal Highness can find it possible to appear at our great national bonspiel at Carsebreck, we shall give him what for heartiness and enthusiasm surpasses every other expression of loyalty—a curlers' welcome.

REPRESENTATIVE GOVERNMENT.

The constitution of the Royal Caledonian Curling Club is thoroughly democratic. The power of Royalty lies mainly in the influence of its patronage, and the only review of our actions which is exercised by our Royal head is a perusal of the contents of the *Annual*.

The famous Duddingston Club for a long time laid down the law under the direction of wise and capable advisers, and in the transition period did much to advance the game; but it was impossible for that club to exercise authority over other clubs while these were not directly represented in its council. A new foundation had to be laid before order could be brought out of confusion. The founders of our Royal Club felt this, and so *representation* became the principle of that constitution which they brought forward for the adoption of their brethren. At first, individuals, apart from clubs, might be admitted members (with no voice in the management), by paying ten shillings entry-money and five shillings annually; but this was evidently regarded as a germ of disease, and it was speedily eliminated from the system. The credentials of each representative had to bear, as they still do, that he appeared in the name of "a club having at least eight members, a designation, a sheet of ice for their operations, and a set of office-bearers." The Grand Club thus brought all local clubs into connection, and proceeded to govern them by their own authority.

That this form of government has been thoroughly successful may be inferred from the way in which the curling parliament has for fifty years and more conducted the Royal Club's affairs. Any one who chooses to visit one of these annual gatherings must at once come to this conclusion. There he finds the duke, earl, or baronet in the chair, surrounded by intelligent curlers from every part of Scotland, all ready to give a reason for the faith that is in them, and able to do so when called upon. The secretary, with his "order of business," keeps the business in order. The conflict of opinion on some emerging point soon begins, steel strikes upon flint, and sparks of wit and wisdom fly about; each has his say and says it well, the stonemason being listened to as attentively by the chairman as his brother baronet or peer; the vote is taken and the decision accepted amicably by all; greetings from our brothers across the Atlantic are read and cheered, and sometimes an American steps forward to tell us how well curling fares in its adopted home, and to challenge us to a bonspiel at Toronto, Montreal, or New York. In two or three hours the work of a year is done, and the affairs of a community of 20,000 curlers are settled in a way that the greater conventions of Church or State might well envy. Prompt and practical as the representative meeting is, and always has been, yet in its legislation nothing has ever been done rashly. In the earlier days the members hesitated long before they made it compulsory to abandon the system of having eight players with one stone each on the rink. After prescribing foot-irons, when they heard the appeal of those brethren, who never felt that their "foot was on their native heath" unless it was in the *hack*, they gave way and allowed the hack to be used under certain conditions. In our constitution we also have a *Barrier Act*. No measure is passed which is not approved of by a majority of clubs. Even then it may still be rejected if two-thirds of the representatives do not support it at the July meeting. Beyond all this, our transactions are open to review by a general meeting of the club. It is very satisfactory to find that never once in the club's history has any act of its Representative Committee been objected to or overthrown.

As a national institution, it is right that the headquarters of the club should be in our Scottish capital, and that the representative gathering should be there convened. The club's office, with all documents and minutes, being in Edinburgh, it follows that a meeting elsewhere is attended with difficulties. These have not, however, deterred the Royal Club from holding the annual meetings out of Edinburgh, and seeking to awaken interest in the club and in curling by visiting various important centres. There seems to be a growing desire that this should be oftener done, and if the difficulties to which we have referred are not too great, there is no doubt that advantage would result to the club. In the constitution it is provided that an adjourned meeting be held in the winter, and, as will be seen from the following table of the club's various meetings, this was done in the earlier years of the club, the day chosen being that of the Grand Match. For a long time this adjourned meeting has not been held, the Committee of Management—that great beast of burden—being left to do the work that is required throughout the year.

REPRESENTATIVE MEETINGS.

1838	July 25, Edinburgh	1850	Jan. 19, Lochwinnoch	1869	July 27, Edinburgh
,,	Nov. 15, ,,	,,	July 25, Edinburgh	1870	,, 26, ,,
1839	July 25, ,,	1851	,, 25, ,,	1871	,, 25, Glasgow
1840	,, 24, ,,	1852	,, 27, ,,	1872	,, 25, Edinburgh
,,	Nov. 18, Glasgow	1853	Feb. 15, Carsebreck	1873	,, 25, ,,
1841	July 27, Edinburgh	,,	July 26, Edinburgh	1874	,, 24, Stirling
,,	Oct. 22, Kilmarnock	1854	,, 25, ,,	1875	,, 27, Edinburgh
1842	July 26, Edinburgh	1855	,, 25, ,,	1876	,, 25, ,,
1843	Jan. 12, Perth	1856	,, 25, Glasgow	1877	,, 25, ,,
,,	July 25, Edinburgh	1857	,, 24, Edinburgh	1878	,, 25, Dundee
1844	Jan. 23, ,,	1858	,, 27, ,,	1879	,, 25, Edinburgh
,,	July 25, ,,	1859	,, 26, Glasgow	1880	,, 27, ,,
1845	Jan. 23, Stirling	1860	,, 25, Edinburgh	1881	,, 26, ,,
,,	July 25, Edinburgh	1861	,, 25, ,,	1882	,, 25, ,,
1846	Jan. 30, ,,	1862	,, 25, Glasgow	1883	,, 20, Stirling
,,	July 24, ,,	1863	,, 24, Edinburgh	1884	,, 25, Edinburgh
1847	Jan. 15, ,,	1864	,, 26, Perth	1885	,, 24, Southport
,,	July 27, ,,	1865	,, 25, Edinburgh	1886	,, 27, Edinburgh
1848	Jan. 25, Linlithgow	1866	,, 25, Stirling	1887	,, 28, Perth
,,	July 25, Edinburgh	1867	,, 25, Edinburgh	1888	,, 25, Edinburgh
1849	,, 25, ,,	1868	,, 24, Liverpool	1889	,, 25, Glasgow

A dinner such as followed the first meeting of representatives was not provided for in the constitution of the club, but as it was found to supply a felt want in the constitutions of the representatives, and to be a capital way of cementing friendship, the custom thus happily inaugurated was kept up. Between the meeting at Kilmarnock in 1841 and that at Lochwinnoch in 1850 several dinners were held, which, if we may judge from the reports of them in the *Annuals*, were quite historical events. From 1850 to 1881 no report of the annual dinner is inserted, and since 1881 such reports as we have are meagre in the extreme. The enthusiasm of these gatherings seems to increase as we go backwards over the club's history. At Lochwinnoch, in 1850, we find the railway arrangements interfering with the attendance, as they have done ever since. Still, there were 130 at dinner in the "Black Bull" there. The genial Duke of Athole had 170 members round him in the "Star and Garter" at Linlithgow on the night of the Grand Match there, and a merry night it was. At the dinner held in the "Guildhall," Stirling, in 1845, the chairman was the Hon. Fox Maule, M.P., the number attending being 200. Two successive gatherings were held in Edinburgh, under the presidency of

William Gibson-Craig, M.P., the one in July 1843, when there were 80, and the other in January 1844, when there were no less than 200 curlers present. On each occasion it is interesting to find the ancient association of the Town Council of Edinburgh with the game of curling revived by the presence of the Lord Provost of the city. On each occasion a deputation from the Merchiston and Edinburgh Clubs appeared at a certain stage of the proceedings and conducted his lordship through "the dark passage," where he was initiated into the mysteries of the game, and made a regular "knight of the broom." The meeting at Perth in 1843 was a memorable one—worthy of the place where Ruthven, Gall, and Adamson had, more than two hundred years before, curled with their "loadstones of Lidnochian lakes." The clubs of Perthshire made a great bonspiel on Windyedge Loch in honour of the event, and so many curlers were prepared to dine that the County Hall had to be engaged, where 200 sat down under Lord Mansfield, with the celebrated Bugle Band of the Sixty-Eighth (Depôt) discoursing excellent music. The fact that Prince Albert had recently, through the noble chairman, become patron of the Grand Club, gave additional interest to the loyal toast, and the chairman himself, as the medium of this high favour, came in for special honour, while the many proofs he had given of his active devotion to the cause of curling added weight to what he had to say in its favour as

"A game of science, demanding an accurate eye and a steady hand, and a pastime in which men of every station and opinion might mingle freely and happily together, animated by no feeling of hostility beyond that of a generous emulation as to who shall get nearest the tee."

At this meeting Dr Renton delivered *the* speech *par excellence* of the many that have been spoken to the toast, "A' keen curlers," and as he finished the band struck up *The Royal Caledonian Curling Strathspey.**

It is at Kilmarnock that we find the enthusiasm of

---

* Specially composed for the occasion by H. Devlin, Music Master, Sixty-Eighth (Depôt). Can any one favour us with a copy?

the early "Caledonians" roused to its highest pitch. The business of the adjourned meeting being over, we look in at the Town Hall, where 150 curlers have met to dine, with the Earl of Eglinton and Winton in the chair.

"The dinner was laid out in a style of unusual splendour. The walls were beautifully festooned with wreaths of flowers, and tastefully decorated with paintings. Floral arches, and curling and sporting devices, surmounted the respective seats of the chairman and croupier. Above the former was the figure of a coronet, and on each side of the chair were two handsome arches, formed of flowers and evergreens. The Eglinton arms were displayed alongside of those of the town of Kilmarnock, and the words *Winter Sports, The Land o' Cakes, and her ain Game o' Curlin'*, all executed by Mr Robertson, painter, Kilmarnock. Over the chair of the croupier (J. W. Williamson) were suspended two fine transparencies, under the direction of Mr Tannock, artist—one of a curler with his foot on the trigger preparing to play his stone, and another of a fox-hunt. An artificial embowered orchestra was fitted up, whence the Kilmarnock Quadrille Band sent forth their inspiring national airs during the evening" (*Annual*, 1842, p. 23).

This was the devotion of many generations of Kilmarnock curlers expressing itself. The people there had never forgotten the example of William Guthrie: and the "neighbouring gentry," with whose ancestors the Covenanter curled two centuries before, still kept up their allegiance to the game. The worthiest of them all—that great patron of all manly sports and national pastimes, "Scotland's pride and Ayrshire's glory," as they loved to call him—the noble Earl in the chair, inspired by such memories and surroundings, could not fail to be eloquent, and with patriotism and spirit he carried the hearts of his hearers with him as he recounted the pleasures and advantages of the national game. When the great company cheered to the echo the toast of his health, Lord Eglinton's reply was (and it might be written up before every president of the Royal Club as a motto): "*I have the earnest wish to encourage the games and sports of my native country, and more especially such games and sports as by their nature are open alike to poor and rich. Among these I am sure there is none that can be compared to the game of curling.*"

Very touching it was to see the way in which that meeting did honour to the venerable John Cairnie of Curling

Hall, the first president of the Grand Club, and to hear his reply to the kind words spoken of him :—

"I am now an old curler, and very unable to speak as I should like; but I am a keen curler; the spirit is willing but the flesh is weak. I think I shall curl to the last."

It was the old hero's farewell; a year thereafter he played his last stone and quitted the rink of life, curling to the last, as he thought he should.

But with all this noisy fervour shall there be no *solemn silence* toast to chasten the mirth? One such there surely must be. What shall it be? "The Memory of Tam Pate?" No; "Tam" has been drunk already, not in solemn silence, but with all the honours, and there was no change in his habits, for in reply to the toast "Tam never uttered a single *cheep*." Why, what are you thinking about? This is Kilmarnock, and let skill depart from the right hand of Auld Killie's curlers if they forget their own Tam Samson. But no solemn silence about the toast. The "king o' a' the core" is dead, but "the image of himself," Tam the second, "who can draw a trigger or ride a shot with any man living," is at the table. And so it is "The living Tam Samson, gentlemen!" for which "Mr Thomas Samson returned thanks."

Representative government by day, and a representative social gathering at night—so it ought to be at each annual meeting of our National Club. But the founders had the advantage of us. They dined in winter, when a bonspiel could be added to the serious business of the day, and they met in the evening with bonspiel appetites. The flush of success in their new venture was upon them, the themes on which they spoke were fresh, and the times in which they lived were prosperous. *Now* the times are bad, the themes are stale, dinner is served on the afternoon of one of the dog-days, and the noble chairman is off with the train, leaving us in the hands of our senior *Vice*. We cannot come up to those old Caledonian nights, but we shall see what we can do.

THE VICTORIAN ERA.   251

OFFICE-BEARERS.

Since the institution of the Royal Club the various offices have been filled thus :—

PRESIDENTS.	VICE-PRESIDENTS.	PRESIDENTS.	VICE-PRESIDENTS.
1838-39, John Cairnie of Curling Hall	John M'George, Edin. / James Ogilvie Dalgleish, Lindores	1858-59, The Earl of Dalkeith	Sir Jas. Gardiner Baird, Bart. / Earl of Rothes
1839-40, Sir G. Clerk of Penicuick, Bart., M.P.	Dr Walker Arnott of Arlary / James Ogilvie Dalgleish, Lindores	1859-60, The Viscount Strathallan	J. A. Stewart Nicholson of Carnock / John Gordon of Aitkenhead
1840-41, Sir David Baird of Newbyth, Bart.	Wm. Bankier, Glasgow / Robert Palmer, Currie	1860-61, Sir Jas. Gardiner Baird of Saughtonhall, Bart.	Sir R. M. Shaw-Stewart, Bart. / Captain Kinloch, yr. of Gilmerton
1841-42, Earl of Eglinton and Winton	James Wright of Lawton / John W. Williamson, Kinross	1861-62, The Earl of Mansfield	W. Peddie of Black Ruthven / John Haig of Cameron Bridge
1842-43, Earl of Mansfield	Dr Renton, Penicuick / George Hogarth, Cupar	1862-63, The Earl of Sefton	Charles Macgibbon / Major Wedderburn
1843-44, Wm. Gibson-Craig of Riccarton	Alex. Cassels, W.S., Edin. / Thos. Durham Weir of Boghead	1863-64, The Duke of Athole	Provost Murrie, Stirling / Wm. Caldwell, Glasgow
1844-45, Hon. Fox Maule, M.P.	Hugh Fletcher Campbell of Boquhan / Colonel Dundas of Carronhall	1864-65, Lord Elcho	Dr J. A. Sidey, Edin. / Andrew Dempster, Liverpool
1845-46, Duke of Buccleuch & Queensberry	John Osborne, Carnock / John Fergusson, Leith	1865-66, Lord Stormont	A. V. Smith-Sligo of Inzievar / James Leishman of Broomrigg
1846-47, Duke of Buccleuch & Queensberry	John Osborne, Carnock / J. R. H. Craufurd, yr. of Craufurdland	1866-67, The Earl of Dunmore	Capt. Maitland-Dougall, R.N. / R. H. Gordon
1847-48, Marquis of Douglas and Clydesdale	Lieut.-Col. Low, Cupar / W. H. Dick Cunyngham, yr. of Prestonfield	1867-68, The Duke of Athole	Rev. A. J. Murray / James Lewis
1848-49, Duke of Athole	Charles Stein of Hattonburn / Major J. A. Henderson of Westerton	1868-69, The Earl of Minto	Andrew Dempster, Liverpool / James Hogg
1849-50, Earl of Glasgow	J. Murray Drummond of Megginch / C. E. M'Ritchie of Logie / Col. Macdowall of Garthland	1869-70, The Earl of Minto	J. B. Gallie / James Wood
1850-51, James Ogilvie Dalgleish of Woodburn	Sir W. H. Dick Cunyngham of Prestonfield, Bart.	1870-71, Lord Rollo	Sir C. M. Auchterlony, Bart. / James Wilson
1851-52, James Ogilvie Dalgleish of Woodburn	Col. Macdowall of Garthland / Sir John Ogilvy of Inverquharity, Bart.	1871-72, The Earl of Morton	C. W. Cowan, Penicuick / John Carswell, Paisley
1852-53, Earl of Morton	Sir P. M. Thriepland of Fingask, Bart. / R. B. Wardlaw Ramsay of Whitehill	1872-73, The Marquis of Lorne	Matthew M'Dougall, U.S. Consul, Dundee / Wm. Thomson, Dunblane
1853-54, Lord Kinnaird	Sir John Ogilvy of Inverquharity, Bart. / D. C. R. Carrick Buchanan of Drumpellier	1873-74, The Marquis of Lorne	Josiah Livingston, Edin. / Robert Knox, Alloa
1854-55, Lord Kinnaird	Sir John Ogilvy of Inverquharity, Bart. / Chas. Cowan, M.P.	1874-75, The Marquis of Lothian	James Beveridge, Dunfermline / Robt. Paterson of Brucehill
1855-56, Duke of Hamilton and Brandon	Sir James Gardiner Baird of Saughtonhall, Bart / A. Boyle	1875-76, The Marquis of Huntly	Admiral Maitland-Dougall of Scotscraig / John Carswell, Paisley
1856-57, Sir John Ogilvy of Inverquharity, Bart.	Robert Moubray of Cambus / George Kellie M'Callum of Braco Castle	1876-77, The Earl of Rosslyn	Sir Jas. Gardiner Baird, Bart. / W. A. Peterkin, Nairn
1857-58, Sir John Ogilvy of Inverquharity, Bart.	Robert Moubray of Cambus / E. A. Hunter, W.S.	1877-78, The Earl of Breadalbane	J.T. Oswald of Dunnikier / Gideon Pott of Dod
		1878-79, The Earl of Glasgow	R. Glass of Arlary / Col. Walker, Dundee
		1879-80, The Earl of Strathmore	Sir J. H. Gibson-Craig of Riccarton, Bart. / S. N. Morrison, Alloa
		1880-81, The Earl of Mar and Kellie	Robert Cathcart of Pitcairlie / James Myles, Renfrew

Presidents.	Vice-Presidents.	Presidents.	Vice-Presidents.
1881-82, The Duke of Roxburghe	Col. Colquhoun of Luss; J. C. Forrest of Auchenraith	1886-87, Sir Archibald Campbell of Blythswood, Bart., M.P.	Ebenezer Dawson, Dalkeith; J. T. Oswald of Dunnikier
1882-83, Lord Lovat	Thos. Usher, Edinburgh; J. T. S. Elliot, yr. of Wolfelee	1887-88, The Duke of Montrose	Col. Macdonald of St Martin's; T. S. Aitchison, Edin.
1883-84, Sir Michael R. Shaw-Stewart of Ardgowan, Bart.	Jas. Anderson, Glasgow; Sheriff Buntine, Stirling	1888-89, The Marquis of Breadalbane	J. Clark Forrest of Auchenraith; R. Burns Begg, Kinross
1884-85, Lord Melgund	Josiah Livingston, Edin.; J. S. Meggat, Manchester	1889-90, Lord Balfour of Burleigh	W. M'Inroy of Lude; Colonel Menzies, Glasgow
1885-86, Lord Aberdeen	Dr Pilkington, Mayor of Southport; J. Leadbetter		

Chaplains.	Secretaries and Treasurers.
1838-1840, The Very Rev. G. Husband Baird, Principal of the University of Edinburgh.	1838-1844, George Ritchie, W.S
1840-1862, The Rev. A. L. Simpson, D.D., Kirknewton	1844-1846, Alex. Cassels, W.S. (*Secretary*).
1862-1873, The Very Rev. Thos. Barclay, D.D., Principal of the University of Glasgow	1844-1846, Dr Renton (*Treasurer*).
1873- , The Rev. Cornelius Giffen, St Mary's, Edinburgh	1846-1876, Alex. Cassels, W.S.
	1876-1880, David Lindsay.
	1880- , Adam Davidson Smith, C.A.

From the above list it is apparent that the Royal Club has enlisted the support of the nobility of Scotland to a very large extent, nearly all our great historic families having furnished representatives able and willing to fill the president's chair. These presidents have not been mere aristocratic figureheads, but they have, most of them, taken a practical interest in the game of curling. When so many have rendered conspicuous service to the cause, and the influence of each has had so much to do with the encouragement of curling in his own particular district, it may be invidious to single out any name for distinction in the presidential list, but we may be permitted to make special acknowledgment of the work done by the late Duke of Athole during the term of his presidency, and through all the first half of this period. The Duke was a thorough enthusiast on the subject of curling, and was specially anxious to see the Grand Match a success, for he always looked upon the great battle between North and South as the chief attraction of the curling year; and he not only urged the men of Dunkeld to turn out in force, but with his own rink he never failed to take part in the match when it was possible. In the account of the Grand Match at Linlithgow the *Annual* of 1849 (p. 190) says:—

"The rink which had the greatest number of bystanders was that which included the Duke of Athole, the president-elect, and such is the genial influence of this manly game on the feelings of all engaged in it that it would have been impossible from his Grace's manner to have known that he stood '*a peer of the proudest title*' *among the honest and independent but humble sons of toil with whom he was united.*"

FIG. 61.   CHAS. CHRISTIE.   R. DOUGLAS.   GEORGE,   JOHN MILNE.
                                          DUKE OF ATHOLE.
           1st Player.   *2nd Player.*   *Skip.*   *3rd Player.*

The Duke did much to spread a knowledge of and a love for the game in the North, and was much beloved by the curlers there, for he always took the greatest interest in their welfare. When he died, at the comparatively early age of fifty, he was much missed and lamented.

> "The pibroch's shrill wailing was heard through the glen,
> And slow was the march of Blair Athole's brave men,
> As they bore from his home to his lone resting-place
> Their own beloved chieftain, the flower of his race."

Among the later names of our list of presidents that of the Marquis of Breadalbane is pre-eminent among many who have devoted their attention to the work of the Royal Club. He was selected to fill the chair when the club had completed fifty years of its existence, and every curler knows how successfully he discharged the special duties that devolved upon him on that important occasion.

Like his late father, whose good qualities he inherits, the Marquis of Breadalbane, with perhaps even greater success, has developed curling in the North, and mainly through his efforts there are now as many as *nine* local clubs bearing the *Breadalbane* name, and all ready, in obedience to their chieftain's family motto, *Follow Me*, to go forth under his banner to the icy wars. At the present time Lord Breadalbane is doing his utmost to secure a more central pond for the Grand Match. It is to be hoped that a successful settlement of a long-felt difficulty may soon be added to the numerous services his Lordship has been able to render to the Royal Club.

Of our vice-presidents it is enough to say that they are never chosen to fill the office without having first given practical proof of their interest in our representative meetings, for they can only be chosen from among the members present. A glance at the list will shew that in the various districts of Scotland the most influential among our proprietors, professional men, and men of business are sent up by the curlers to represent them in the management of the central club.

Of the various offices in our representative government that of secretary and treasurer is, of course, the most important, its holder being virtually both leader of the House and Chancellor of the Exchequer. Before the time of Mr Davidson Smith, three gentlemen had held the office as a double charge, Dr Renton having simply acted as temporary treasurer for two years. It is not difficult to single out, not only from the list of our paid officials, but from the whole list of the club's office-bearers, the foremost name in the ministry of service, in which there have been so many willing workers. It is that of Alexander Cassels, W.S., who was vice-president 1843-44, secretary 1844-46, and secretary and treasurer for the long period of thirty years, 1846-76. To the management of the Royal Club Mr Cassels gave his heart and soul, and the gift was a large one. He is described * by his friend Sheriff Campbell

---

* *Scotsman*, 11th March 1875.

Smith as "a tall, powerful, fine-looking man, and in his physical and mental gifts and proclivities he belonged to that class of which Professor Wilson was the highest type." One so richly endowed and so popular with all who could appreciate kindliness of heart, sincerity, and unselfishness, could not fail to advance the popularity of a society with which he so thoroughly identified himself, and there is no doubt that to this prince of secretaries the success of the Royal Club at the most trying period of its history was mainly due.

The work done for the club by Bailie Cassels could not be, and it was not, measured by pounds, shillings,

FIG. 62. BAILIE CASSELS.
(From a photograph by John Fergus, Largs.)

and pence, but the small salary he received as secretary and treasurer was always supplemented by a great amount of gratitude. When he could serve them no longer, and lay prostrate from an illness which had been aggravated by his attending the Grand Match, 24th December 1875, when he should have been in bed, the curlers did not forget how much they owed him, and, with the help of the brethren across the Atlantic, they raised 500 sovereigns, and had them enclosed in a silver kettle to be presented to him. It was too late, as good intentions often are. But Mr Cassels knew of the proposed gift, and it cheered his heart as he entered the valley of shadows to think that those whom he loved, and for whom he had lived, remembered him so kindly.

The Grand Club founders very gracefully recognised the interest which the clergy have always taken in the national game by appointing a chaplain as one of their office-bearers, the first to fill the honourable position being the Very Rev. Dr Husband Baird, Principal of Edinburgh University. The Principal's zeal in the cause, and his practical knowledge of curling, of which we have had so many proofs, made him pre-eminently worthy of the honour. He was succeeded by the Rev. Dr Simpson of Kirknewton, a keen curler, who in 1849 was Moderator of the General Assembly. Then came the Principal of Glasgow University, the Very Rev. Dr Barclay. The Principal was a native of Unst, our most northern isle, where curling was unknown; but he had been minister of several country parishes, Currie among others, and, like many of the country clergy, he had curled when frost permitted, and studied when curling permitted. His classical accomplishments were a credit to his curling. So thought the Royal Club, and they made him their chaplain. But the chaplaincy is like the fishwife's basket—*the last's best*. When minister of Dailly, that keen curling parish (of which Ailsa Craig is an appropriate part), the Rev. Mr Giffen was known and admired as a capital curling parish minister. The work of one of our largest Edinburgh congregations (St Mary's), and the city minister's multifarious duties, do not, as he told us in his eloquent speech at the Jubilee, leave much leisure for curling; but the old enthusiasm is there yet, and there is no keener hand in the *Drum* Club or in the *Edinburgh Northern* than the present worthy *custos morum* of the Royal Club. Our chaplain has a heart full of sympathy for all that is bright and manly in religion, amusement, and social life; and, in his own words, he "has learned some of the best lessons of how to deal with men by playing side by side with them upon the ice."

The chaplain's duties do not extend much beyond the

saying of grace at the annual dinner,* but by the respect paid to the office the curling brotherhood shew their appreciation of that support which the clergy very wisely give to the national game.
That the compliment is deserved may be inferred from the fact that of the 20,000 members of the Royal Club 500, or 1 in 40, are clergymen. Such a fact speaks more eloquently than any words can as to the high estimation in which the clerical profession generally hold the game.

Of the 461 curling clubs in Scotland affiliated with the Royal Caledonian, no less than 350 follow the example of the parent club and elect a chaplain as one of their office-bearers. Some appoint more than one. Of these chaplains, 290 are ministers of the Church of Scotland, 23 are F.C. ministers, 18 U.P., 13 Episcopal, 4 Roman Catholic, and the others nondescript. Principal Caird and the Moderator and ex-Moderator of Assembly head the Church of Scotland representatives, Dr Walter Smith the F.C.'s,

FIG. 63. REV. C. GIFFEN.
(From a photograph by John Moffat, Edinburgh.)

* In America the duties are heavier. In one report of the Convention of the Grand National Club (1886) we read that the chaplain (Rev. Dr Ormiston, New York) "opened the meeting with an eloquent and impressive prayer." On the first Sabbath of January 1888 the curlers in a body attended church, when the chaplain preached a special sermon (Mal. iii. 12), "a practice the officers of the National Curling Club hope to see carried out every year."

R

and Dr Brown of Paisley the U.P.'s; but no dignitary of the Episcopal or Roman Catholic persuasion is found among the few who, in these Churches, shew their sympathy with our national game. There is, therefore, some room still left for improving the connection between churches and curling.

LOCAL MEDALS—THE OLD POINT GAME.

The point competition in curling, originated at Duddingston in 1809 (*vide* p. 146), has not had a happy existence. It has done away with *Tam Pates*. No curler can now say that he *never missed a single shot*. But while the game may in some respects have benefited by this form of competition, point play has never been looked upon as curling in the true sense of the word. The *tout ensemble* is awanting, and the *lead* or *second stone*, who is accustomed to play to an empty *parish*, has a great advantage over others. We might as well try to decide skill at golf by a few strokes with play-club, spoon, iron, and putter, as to test curling by a competition at points. When the Currie worthies drew the diagrams for the eight point game, the Rev. Dr Somerville in triumph remarked, "We have now placed the point medal beyond the reach of *duffers*." At the very first competition, however, the medal was won by Willie Drum, who was admittedly the worst player in the club! For expressing a doubt, based perhaps on this Currie experience, a president of the Blairgowrie Club—Mr Anderson, banker—was once very severely punished. On the way to Marlee Loch, where he and the other members of the club were to compete for the point medal, 25th January 1841, Mr Anderson remarked that he should not be surprised to see the greatest duffer carry off the trophy. "After a keen and exciting contest," says the club minute of that date, "the medal was won by Mr Anderson, banker, by a majority of one shot." The Royal Club adopted the Currie points, as we have seen, and awarded what were called local medals for this kind of competition. For a time reports of these competitions were inserted in the *Annuals*, but the difficulty of making satisfactory comparisons, owing to the different conditions under which the medals were competed for, caused the club to give the practice up, and to cease encouraging point play by medals, though the diagrams and the rules remained. The great majority of our clubs continue to set apart a day in the ice season for point play, and most of them have trophies from private patrons to be competed for, but the point game has never really cleared itself of the dubiety of character which caused the Royal Club in its early years to give up supporting it. While this is said, and while it is undoubtedly true that the greatest duffer may sometimes carry off the point prize, yet when we find in some clubs the name of one particular member appearing year after year (as in the case of William Gordon, a famous Bathgate player, who won his club's medal twenty-one times), we may infer that the persistent winner is the best player in the club.

In 1888 the old system which only allowed *one* point for each shot was done away with, and the present system (see "Art of Curling") introduced, which allows some gradation of value in the shots. When this change took place, a curler who did not like it remarked to us, "*Ye shouldna get onything for rufflin' the feathers if ye dinna bring doon the bird.*" True, if in curling a miss were not often "as good as a mile." But in the case, *e.g.*, of *chip the winner*, the "chip" may not be taken, and yet in an ordinary game, if the winner is laid open, there is much advantage gained for the side of the player. It is, therefore, probable that the new system will prove a more satisfactory test of skill than the old. At any rate, it is entitled to have a fair trial.*

The adoption of the new system having made the old point game a matter of history, it was only fair that we should analyse the results of its fifty years of existence, however unreliable they might appear to us to be. The only way to do this was to call for returns of scores from local clubs, and as the most of them have favoured us with

---

* Many clubs have sent us communications testifying to their great satisfaction with the new point system and its advantage over the old.

replies, we may give the result of our analysis, and leave curlers to make what they choose of it. Out of the competitions of fifty years, the conditions being understood to be those laid down by the Royal Club—*i.e.*, four shots at each of eight points or thirty-two in all, with rink 42 yards, and diagrams as shewn under "Art of Curling"—we have the following as the highest scores:—

(21.) Angus, W., Breadalbane Locharnhead — 1887
Philip, James, Tillicoultry — 1887

(20.) Crichton, W. D., Bradford — 1880
Dickson, Archibald, Bradford — 1880

(19.) M'Aulay, George, Bonhill — 1887
Macdonald, Colonel, St Martin's — 1886
Mirk, George, Castlecarry Castle — 1885
Robertson, John, Rannagulzion — (?)

(18.) Fairley, Alex., Holyrood — 1880
Grant, Jas., Strathspey — 1886
Johnstone, Chas., Holyrood — (?)

(17.) Barbour, John, Newcastle-on-Tyne — 1888
Fleming, John, Tweedsmuir — 1872
Forbes, J., Kilgraston and Moncrieffe — 1879
Henderson, Alex., Orwell — 1857
Purteous, J., West Linton Junior — 1869
Rose, Martin, Innellan Wyndham — 1885
Veitch, Adam, West Linton Junior — 1869
Wilson, David, Oakley — (?)

(16.) Brodie, Peter, North Berwick — 1869
Brownlee, John, Whitburn — 1844
Cowan, Samuel, Bradford — 1876
Cowan, Neil, Innellan Wyndham — 1885
Dick, J. J., Hallingry — 1887
Dickson, James, Peebles — 1873
Elder, Thomas, Stevenson — 1885
Gordon, William, Bathgate — 1842
Greenhorn, James, Bridge of Allan — 1864
Maitland-Dougall, W. H., Scotscraig — 1853
" " " — 1876
Marshall, Robert, Ballankeir — 1881
M'Gregor, Duncan, Weem — 1863
M'Intosh, Wm., Blairgowrie — 1880
M'Kay, Peter, jun., Houston — 1878
M'Neil, Donald, Muthill — (?)
Marshall, Thos., Drummond Castle — 1876
Phillip, J., " " — 1876
Philp, Andrew, Inverness — 1867
Pullar, Thomas, St John's, Perth — 1864
Sharp, James, Aberuthven — 1886
Smith, Robert, Innellan Wyndham — 1885
Taylor, John, Carsebreck — 1872
Winchester, James, Strathspey — 1886

(15.) Aitken, John, Braemar — 1882
Black, John, Orwell — 1848
Cameron, Jas., Strathspey — 1886
Couper, John, Lochgelly — 1886
Crerar, Donald, Breadalbane Killin — (?)
Crerar, Alex., " " — (?)
Drummond, James, Muthill — (?)
Ewing, Michael C., Orwell — 1879
Gowans, William, Hamilton — 1873
Grant, Charles, Strathspey — 1886
Greig, James, Old Monkland — 1885
Hall, Robt., Ancrum and Rule Water — 1885
Hamilton, G., Breadalbane Strathfillau and Glenfalloch — 1879

(15.)—*continued.*
Hutchison, A., Douglas — 1875
Keanie, James, Lochwinnoch — 1888
King, Wm., sen., Drummond Castle — 1870
Liston, T., Meiklecur — 1878
M'Connell, W., Penninghame — 1882
M'Donald, Alex., Braemar — 1881
M'Kenzie, David, Clunie — 1853
M'Kenzie, Donald, Golspie — 1882
M'Laren, J., Meiklecur — 1881
Maitland-Dougall, W. H., Scotscraig — 1859
" " " — 1869
" " " — 1878
Miller, James, Tillicoultry — 1886
Mitchell, James, Bonnybridge — 1879
Morgan, John, Falkland — 1881
Murray, Joseph, Thornhill — 1887
Paton, R., Blairdrummond — 1887
Peddie, John, Logiealmond — 1873
Richardson, R., Stenhouse and Carron — 1880
Scott, John, Allander — 1859
Stewart, Peter, Breadalbane Killin — 1879
Taylor, James, Tillicoultry — 1871
Taylor, James, New Monkland — 1884
Thorburn, J. G., Ardgowan — 1857
Turner, John, Kirknewton — 1873
Walker, Robert, Tillicoultry — 1873
Wardrop, John, Sir Colin Campbell — 1880
Wentworth, Bruce C. V., Dall — 1888

(14.) Aitken, James, Carbeth — 1855
Aitken, James, Stenhouse and Carron — 1880
Blackwood, William, Peebles — 1886
Brown, A., Abdie — 1861
Bryce, Robert, Blairdrummond — 1882
Cameron, James, Strathspey — 1884
" " " — 1886
Cowan, Samuel, Bradford — 1876
Craig, Andrew, Crossmichael — 1884
Currie, Robt., Manchester Trafford — 1885
Dickson, Thos. W., Peebles — 1875
Dun, George, Abdie — 1848
Dun, George, jun., Abdie — 1871
Ewing, John, Orwell — 1848
Forgie, John, Merchiston — 1874
Gilmour, Andrew, Neilston — 1879
Gilmour, Hugh, Waverley — 1869
Gordon, R. R., Bathgate — 1887
Greig, Jas., Old Monkland — 1878
Hoggan, D., Ballankeir — 1881
Hoggin, James, Stow — 1886
Honey, James, Methven — 1862
Irving, Rev. A., Gartmore — 1873
Kirkwood, W., Ballankeir — 1881
Liston, T., Meiklecur — 1853
M'Arthur, A., Dyke — 1873
M'Bean, F., Strathspey — 1877
M'Beth, Arch., Auchleeks — 1887
M'Gill, John, Minniegaff — 1875
M'Gregor, Donald, Dall — 1886
M'Gregor, Peter, Ardgowan Barony — 1869

(14.)—continued.		(14.)—continued.	
M'Intyre, John, Strathspey	1878	Rollo, John, Balyarrow	1880
Martin, James, Lochwinnoch	1888	Sinclair, Alex., Caberfeidgh	1887
Maxtone, R., Strathallan Meath Moss	1882	Sinclair, Arch., Breadalbane Strath-	
Melrose, Wm., West Linton Junior	1871	lillan and Glenfalloch	1881
Morrison, Peter, Affleck	1886	Smith, Sam., Whitburn & Fauldhouse	1844
Oliphant, John, Rothes	1885	Stewart, Wm., Broughty-Ferry	1881
Pearson, John F., Methven	1862	Storrie, John, Whitburn & Fauldhouse	1856
Pitcairn, John, Abdie	1871	Telford, James, Newcastle-on-Tyne	1885
Preston, James, Thornhill	1882	Thorburn, J. G., Ardgowan	1886
Robertson, James, Delvine	1871	Whyte, William, Abernthven	1882
Robertson, D., Meiklecour	1878	Wilson, William, Abdie	1877

(13.) Alston, Robert	1863	Henderson, Æneas	1881	Ogilvy, Donald	1866
Archibald, James	1864	Henderson, John	1875	Oliver, George	(?)
Begg, Malcolm	1888	Honey, James	1864	Peach, George	1869
Bennie, J.	1887	Irving, Rev. A.	1873	Peat, Walter	1866
Black, G. B.	1880	Jack, Gavin	1886	Philp, James	1881
Blackwood, J. R.	1884	Jardine, Andrew	1879	Prest, Francis	1886
Brown, David	1867	Jardine, Robert	1865	Reid, J.	1888
Brown, James	1874	Keay, John	1860	Richardson, James	1887
Brown, John	1886	Kerr, James, jun.	1877	Ritchie, Rev. J.	1881
Bruce, John	1883	Kinloch, D. A.	(?)	Ritchie, James	1886
Buchanan, A.	1874	M'Allister, Arch.	1886	Robertson, Duncan	1886
Constable, G. W.	1879	M'Callum, Peter	1882	Robertson, Robert	1865
Craig, James	1886	M'Dougal, William	1887	Scott, D.	1889
Craig, Robert	1884	M'Dougal, Rev. W. L.	1884	Semple, Thomas	1888
Crawford, James	1861	M'Gregor, Duncan	1869	Seton, J.	1886
Cunningham, D., jun.	1886	M'Gregor, Peter	1867	Shanks, Henry	1849
Dawson, Ebenezer	1884	" "	1869	Sheach, John	1887
Dingwall, William	1873	M'Gregor, Walter	(?)	Sneaton, P. W.	1887
Dobie, John	1888	M'Gowan, George	1887	Smith, Alex.	1886
Dougal, L.	1883	M'Pherson, Wm.	1888	Spiers, George	1884
Douglas, J.	1881	M'Queen, L.	(?)	Stirling, John	1863
Dow, Andrew	1886	Mackenzie, Rev. J. B.	1880	Swan, John	1880
Elcock, Henry	1860	Mackieson, John	1881	Swan, W. A.	1887
Ferguson, George	1885	Maclaren, John	1882	Telford, Robert	1886
Ferguson, James	1869	Maitland-Dougall, W. H.	1857	Thallon, Henry	1855
Gibson, Thos.	1887	" "	1865	Todd, Robert	1888
Grierson, Thos.	(?)	Malloch, Peter	1885	Tweedie, James	1874
Hamilton, Andrew	1880	Martin, James	1873	Ure, James	1885
Hamilton, John	1879	Meikle, James	1880	Watson, George	1878
Hamilton, W. L.	1871	Mill, Andrew	1886	Weir, M.	1850
Hardie, David	1876	Nicol, George	1859	Williamson, J.	1853
Henderson, Capt.	1888	Nivison, William	1871	Wilson, William	1879
Henderson, William	1880				

When we consider how many players must in such a long period of time have struggled to get into it, the above list is surprisingly small. Below "13" we have, of course, a good proportion of victories won with double figures; but the great majority of point medal winners attained their position, and were proud of it, with only one figure, while the average scoring of all players did not exceed 5 shots.

A few *Willie Drums* must necessarily be shaken out of the above list, but the most of those who appear in it are entitled to be regarded as "good ingines" at the point game. On the principle of persistency which we have laid down as the test of a reliable point player, it is easily seen that the champion pointsman of the last fifty years is Admiral William Heriot Maitland-Dougall of Scotscraig, who, like many great curlers, is also a distinguished golfer. The gallant Admiral (in his case the adjective is not simply one of courtesy, for he served on the north coast of Spain in the Civil War of 1834-36, and in China, 1839-43, when he was severely wounded, and mentioned for gallantry in the despatches) twice scored "16," three times "15," twice "13," and once "12," besides making many other excellent scores, and won his club medal so often that it was presented to him by the members, when he gave them a handsome new one in its stead. He used to take a lively interest in the Royal Club, where his services were so much appreciated that when he retired from the Committee of Management (a committee which was originally suggested by him) they retained his name on the list as an ordinary member. The gallant Admiral, at the age of seventy, still shews great interest in the game.

A careful, practical comparison between the old and the new point game (the results of which were given in the *Annual* of 1888-89, p. 392) was made by the Rothes Club, and it was found that

"For every 2 hits made under the old rules, 5 were made under the new, so that if honours were gained formerly with 10 points—a fairly good score—they should not now be attained under 25."

If the line is to be drawn where we have it here drawn, and a list of *distingués* kept open for the ambitious players of the new game, the *minimum* entitling to distinction under the new, must be fully more than the *maximum* attainable under the old system (32). Let clubs, therefore, attest such scores as reach "32" and upwards, and transmit them to headquarters, for if we are to keep up the point game it should be kept up at its best, which can only be done by establishing a "record," and continuing to raise it. "Whatever is worth doing is worth doing well."

DISTRICT MEDALS—THE PARISH BONSPIEL.

The point medal may be won by a *fluke*, and the fortune of the draw for the provincial spiel or the Grand Match may allow a strong club to carry off the cup or the trophy "mair by luck than by guid guidin';" but in the competition for a district medal there is no mistake about it—the best club wins. Since the beginning of curling the parish bonspiel has always been the best of all curling matches, and so it will continue to be. No other comes near it in bringing out the best qualities of the game.

"In the whole range of rural sports," says John M'Diarmid,* "I know nothing more exhilarating than a *spiel* on the ice, where the players are numerous and well-matched, the stakes a dinner of beef and greens, and the forfeit the honour of rival parishes."

The founders of the Royal Club were wise. They did not meddle with the parish bonspiel, or if they did it was to make it a keener battle than ever. They introduced a little silver medal into the business, and the parish that lost a bonspiel not only lost the "stakes" and the "forfeit," but they also lost—the medal. The intrinsic value of that article was not great, but the loss of it was terrible. The beef and greens would be forgotten, and the honour of the parish might be recovered, but the blanks in the medal would be filled up— *Won by*............... *from*............... —and as a Royal trophy it would be hung up in the camp of the enemy, and be displayed at their feasts ever after as an irrevocable testimony against those who lost it. Not only so. The victorious club might keep no written record; or its records might be eaten by rats, or burnt, or stolen, as many records have been. But there was a recording angel in the office of the secretary of the Royal Club—a *statist*, to whom was transmitted by the umpire the result of every battle, and when his tabulated report had been published to the whole curling world, it would be locked away in the secretary's iron safe, where neither rats, flames, thieves, nor defeated clubs could destroy it. The tabulated records of the district medals for fifty years are before us. It is evident that some of our old clubs have kept up the reputation which made them famous before the Royal Club was formed,† and some of our newer clubs have speedily risen to distinction in playing for district medals. Shall we select

* *Sketches from Nature*, 1830, p. 70.
† Notably *Blairgowrie*, which won 22 district medals out of 24 played for.

the best hundred and single out the champion? The request has been made by many, but we would rather not. Before the throne of "Royalty" one club is really as good as another, "and better," as our Hibernian friend would add, for while we set the parishes to fight with our silver medals, our object is really to make them more friendly, and to bring good-fellowship out of rivalry. As the tables of fifty years are spread before us, we think more of the health, the brotherhood, the good-feeling which have been created by the contests than of the victories of one club and the defeats of another. Let us express the hope that these district medals are not taking the place of the meal or coals which used to make the poor folks take such an interest in the parish bonspiels. The tables would be all the more interesting to us if we knew that a boll of meal went with every medal. Why should it not?

PROVINCIAL SPIELS.

One of the most popular institutions—the most popular in the minds of many curlers—is the provincial spiel. Before the institution of the Grand Club, counties used to meet and measure their curling strength. We have referred to some of these contests—Midlothian against Tweeddale, and then against the Upper Ward of Lanark. Edinburgh also met Linlithgow at Midcalder in 1842, with forty rinks a side, and great interest was taken in this match. We must not confuse county bonspiels, which are meant to decide the claims of two rival counties, with provincial spiels, in which a certain number of local clubs associated together in a certain district, and constituting what is called a *province*, meet to determine which is the strongest club in the number. The arrangement of all the affiliated clubs into provinces was first suggested by Mr Ogilvie Dalgleish in 1846—

"To bring the clubs and curlers of the country into closer intercourse, to advance and perpetuate our valued national game, and instil increased life and spirit into our already gigantic Royal Club."

In 1848 a committee, to whom consideration of the subject had been entrusted, gave in an elaborate report, recommending—

"That the whole associated clubs, according to their locality, shall be formed into provinces, consisting of six or any greater number of clubs, according to their density in the neighbourhood, the advantage of a field of ice, and facilities for reaching it, &c."

Provinces were to elect their own office-bearers, and carry out their own arrangements. They were to meet as frequently as possible with the view of preparing for the Grand Match, between which and the district match their competitions were to rank in importance. In provincial competitions *the provinces were to be drawn against each other,* "according to the existing plan as to district medals, due consideration being had to proximity and facilities for meeting." Each club in the winning province was to get a prize—"a small silver star surmounted by the *crown*"— and this was afterwards to be worn by the president at club meetings, and by the representative member at the meetings of the Royal Club. In connection with the report an elaborate map was prepared by Mr Palmer, shewing the locality of the different clubs, the sheets of water of sufficient dimensions for provincial spiels, and the different lines of railway.

The scheme thus elaborately prepared hung fire for a considerable time, and in 1849 the same committee, while still approving of it, recommended that it be not pressed in the face of opposition from various clubs, its expense, and the great increase in the secretary's labours which it would entail, and which they had not taken into account. The committee, however, with the aid of their map, made a classification of the clubs into sixteen provinces, and left these to organise if they wished without the interference of the Royal Club, and to give their own prizes and appoint their own umpires—

"Taking care that any match which they might form should not interfere with the Grand National Match, which (so long as it is considered by the Royal Club advantageous to continue it) should have the cordial support of all 'keen, keen curlers.'"

The representative meeting of 25th July 1849 approved of the committee's report. Instead, however, of leaving it to provinces to provide their own prizes, district medals were promised to such provinces as proceeded to organise on the lines of the report, and whose plan of proceedings, list of office-bearers, &c., were approved of by a standing committee to be appointed that day. A copy of the report and of the curling map were transmitted to each local secretary, so that clubs might be able to take advantage of the resolution of the general meeting. The following were appointed "The Standing Committee on Provincial Spiels":—The office-bearers, Charles Cowan, M.P., Messrs Weir, Forrester, M'Gibbon, Renton, Piper, and J. W. Gray, with power to add to their number. The original proposal to pit province against province in a competition, and to award silver stars to each club in the winning province, was soon set aside, and it was decided that the object of the provincial spiel should simply be *to determine the best club in each district*. On what principle this was to be done fell to be arranged at the first meeting of the Standing Committee in November 1849. The rules of the Twelfth (Ayr and Renfrew) Province came up for approval, and were approved, with the exception of that which provided—

"That the club having the greatest majority of shots shall gain the medal, being according to the greatest principle of equity."

The committee were unanimously of opinion that this method "was not according to the greatest principle of equity,"* and after a month's deliberation they laid down these rules for provincial matches:—

"1. That all the rinks which are to play shall be balloted, to ascertain the rinks which they are to play against (no rink being allowed to play against another of the same club).

"2. That a correct account of the number of points marked by each *side* of *each rink* be kept throughout the game, and at the conclusion the numbers marked by the rinks of each club shall be added up and divided by the rinks which each club has playing, and the club which has marked the greatest number of points *per rink* shall be declared the winning club."

The Twelfth Province, from which this reference came up, obtempered the decision of the Standing Committee, but

---

* In this opinion they differed, as will be seen, from those who framed the rules for the trophy played for in the Grand Match; but the cases are in some respects different.

gave silver crosses to all the winning clubs in the provincial match. Their spiels on Lochwinnoch were, as they still are, very successful and popular. A good many disputes, however, came up, and were carried beyond the Standing Committee. As the number of provinces increased, the disputes became so numerous and took up so much time at the annual meeting that it was resolved, on the motion of Mr Dalgleish (24th July 1857), to give the provinces Home Rule. The resolution was to this effect :—

"That in provincial competitions all rules and regulations relating thereto shall be arranged within the province itself, umpires and ultimate and final referees appointed, and that all difficulties and disputes which may arise shall be settled within the province, and that no right of appeal to the Representative Committee of the Royal Caledonian Curling Club shall be competent."

After this the Standing Committee disappears. Although the results of the various provincial matches are each year chronicled in the club's *Annual*, the above resolution has been faithfully carried out, and all arrangements and regulations for provincial spiels have been made by the provinces themselves. The list of provinces as now organised is subject to alteration from time to time: it is therefore in the meantime relegated to the Appendix (B). The list shews the popularity of provincial spiels. The country has to a large extent been divided into curling districts, and a great impetus given to the game by the annual competitions. With their self-government the provinces are all faithful to the Central Club, and play the game under Caledonian rules, but there seems to be great variety in their methods of deciding their medals, and considerable confusion in other respects, several clubs being entered in more provinces than one, and many clubs having no province to enter. The increase of county competitions, with the great variety which is also found in the methods of deciding the medals or trophies awarded in these, has added to the confusion. At the representative meeting in Glasgow, 26th July 1859, Mr Peterkin brought forward a resolution to the following effect :—

"That the club shall offer special medals to be played for between the associated clubs of one county, or group of counties, and those of another county, or group of counties."

This resolution was adopted, it being understood that—

"These competitions shall not supersede provincial matches, and shall give way to the Grand Matches of the Royal Club."

It does not appear that it has been carried out, though it remains in our statute-book. But the liberality of private patrons has encouraged county match-playing by the presentation of valuable prizes. The county of Ayr has undoubtedly the finest curling trophy in the world—the Eglinton Cup, which is said to have cost £360, and which is much prized as a memorial of the famous Earl, as well as for its great value, and its possession is keenly contested each year by the Ayr clubs. Lanark has more than one trophy; Dumfries, the Waterlow Cup; Kirkcudbright, the Queenshill Cup; East Lothian, the Wemyss Cup; Berwick, a silver challenge kettle, presented by the Hon. E. Marjoribanks, M.P., and several other counties meet annually to decide in their various ways the possession of some handsome prize or prizes. The fostering of both *county* and *provincial* competitions is the duty of all patrons of curling. They come appropriately between the parish bonspiel and the Grand Match. They furnish a wider field than is called out for a district medal, and they can often be brought off in a season when frost does not permit of the Grand Match being played. It is a pity that there is so much confusion. The Royal Club, whose object is to advance the national game by bringing curlers and their contests under the reign of order and uniform methods and laws, might with advantage take up the whole subject, complete and confirm the provincial system, and place every county, which the liberality of a private patron has not blessed, on a level with its neighbours.

THE GRAND MATCH.

The desire of the late Duke of Athole to make the Grand Match a success was worthy of one who had the interests of curling and the prosperity of the Royal Club at heart. Every good president has been animated by the same desire, and every loyal member of the club will petition General Frost to allow North and South to have their annual Waterloo in his territory. It is surely right that the great national club should make the great national gathering its first and foremost care. The crown is not really put upon the season's curling, however many provinces, counties, or parishes have met together, if Scotland has not enjoyed the Grand Match at Carsebreck or Lochwinnoch. In this spirit the Royal Club's arrangements have been made. Everything must stand aside for the Grand Match. It is the nation's bonspiel, and all minor matches are to be held as preparatory to this, and as leading up to it. This great match was not at first provided for in the constitution of the club. It was as the club extended its domain that the propriety and advantage of such a meeting became apparent. When the Representative Committee met at Perth in 1843, a bonspiel of Perth County was arranged—Lord Mansfield and the North against the Master of Strathallan and the South of the Tay. A thousand persons were present as spectators, and they and the players (thirty-six rinks) were feasted to their hearts' content by the Lord-Lieutenant of the County—the Earl of Kinnoull. Next year a match was to be held at Penicuick, when several counties were to send rinks; but there was no frost. The first really national match was arranged, with the permission of Lord Abercromby, to come off on Airthrey Loch on the day of the Royal Club meeting at Stirling, January 23, 1845. This also was interdicted by General John; so that the Grand Match did not make a very promising start. It was on the beautiful loch embosomed among trees in the grounds of Sir George Clerk of Penicuick, "in the presence of Lady Clerk and family, and many spectators from the adjoining district who came to witness the bloodless conflict," * that the first Grand Match, North v. South of Scotland, was played.

---

* In the *Annual*, 1848, it is stated "that a fair artist, who was present as one of Lady Clerk's guests, sketched the scene, and that the painting was to be an heirloom in Penicuick House. The *Annual* editor was to try and get an engraving made of the picture, but as this never appeared, we may infer that he was unsuccessful. If a painting of the kind of any merit exists, it must be interesting to the members of the Royal Club as a memorial of the first gathering of North and South to measure strength on the ice, as they have since then so often done."

"The 15th of January 1847," says the *Annual* for that year, "will be marked with a white stone in the chronicles of curling. . . . The day throughout was one of unmingled pleasure, and, saving the absence of a barrel of exhilarating ale, which was unfortunately omitted among the items of preparation, there was nothing but universal satisfaction felt and expressed."

Only twelve rinks appeared from the North at this first match, the extra forty-four being arranged in a match, *Midlothian* v. *Dumbarton, Linlithgow, Stirling,* &c.—the former under Sir George Clerk, the latter under J. R. H. Craufurd, yr. of Craufurdland.

The second Grand Match, on Queen Mary's Loch, Linlithgow, January 25, 1848, was more successful. Thirty-five rinks appeared from the North, and when thirty-five were drawn out from the South to meet them, a hundred Southern rinks were left over for the odd match. Including spectators, about 6000 persons were present. In the Preface to the *Annual* for 1849, p. viii., it is said:—

"The ancient burgh of Linlithgow has its name emblazoned on many a stirring page of history, and has witnessed many gala-days in

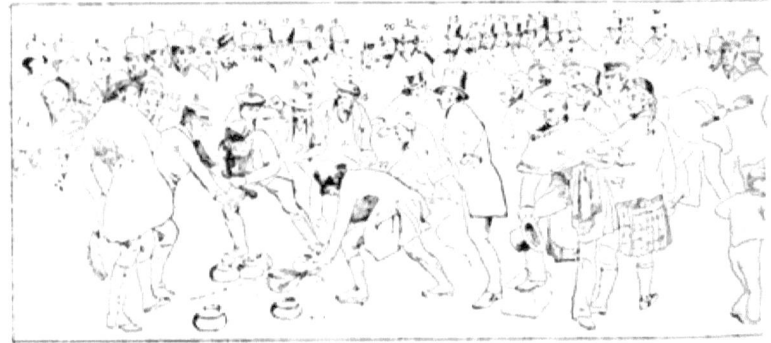

Key to Mr Lees' Picture of the
ROYAL CALEDONIAN CURLING CLUB GRAND MATCH AT LINLITHGOW.

1. Sir George Clerk, Bt., of Penicuick.
2. Rev. A. L. Simpson, D.D., Kirknewton.
3. Sir W. Gibson-Craig, Bt., of Riccarton.
4. Col. Dundas, of Carronhall.
5. Sir Patk. Murray Threipland.
6. The Right Hon. Lord Kinnaird.
7. C. Cowan, Esq., of Valleyfield, M.P.
8. Robert Palmer, Esq., Currie.
9. Allan Pollok, Esq., of Broom.
10. Arthur Pollok, Esq.
11. Major Henderson, of Westerton.
12. Col. M'Dowall of Garthland.
13. Mr Piper.
14. T. Durham Weir, Esq., of Boghead.
15. J. Moore, Esq., Solicitor, Edinburgh.
16. F. S. Wedderburn, Esq., of Wedderburn.
17. Capt. H. Maitland-Dougall, of Scotscraig.
18. Col. Low, Cairnie Lodge.
19. D. Gillespie, Esq., of Mountquhanie.
20. Wm. Horsburgh, Esq., Cupar-Fife.
21. Thomas Anderson, Esq., Newburgh.
22. Mr John M'George, late Medalist.
23. Archd. Thomson, Esq., Edinburgh.
24. Alex. Russel, Esq., Edinburgh.
25. W. Dumbreck, Esq., M.D., Edinr.
26. John Haig, Esq., Cameron Bridge.
27. J. W. Williamson, Esq., Kinross.
28. John Cunningham, Esq., Edinburgh.
29. W. Wilson, Esq., of Water Meetings.
30. Robert Moubray, Esq., of Cambus.
31. Andrew Gillon, Esq., of Wallhouse.
32. Robert K. Glen, Esq., Linlithgow.
33. Adam Dawson, Esq., of Bonnyton.
34. His Grace the Duke of Atholl.
35. J. Murray Drummond, Esq., Megginch.
36. David Wylie, Esq., Edinburgh.
37. Jas. Baird, Esq., of Gartsherrie.
38. R. B. W. Ramsay, Esq., of Whitehill.
39. Sir John Ogilvy, Bt., of Inverquharity.
40. Alex. Cassels, Esq., W.S., Secy. Royal Club.
41. J. Ogilvie Dalgleish, Esq., of W burne.
42. Provost Phillips, of Paisley.
43. George Gillespie, Esq., Glasgow.
44. John T. Renton, Esq., London.
45. Charles Elder M'Ritchie, Esq.
46. William l'Anson, Esq.
47. Robert Craig, Esq.

the 'merry times of old;' but we are much mistaken if, in time coming, the victory and defeat of 25th January 1848 be not treasured up in the recollection of the curlers of Scotland as the most memorable event associated with that interesting locality. Nor will it be any blot in the scutcheon of the noble representatives of the ducal house of Murray that he did not carry back to the Highlands his 'besom over his shoulder.' He proved that he deserved victory if he did not gain it."

In the painting by Lees of the "Grand Match at Linlithgow," the subject is treated with the licence allowed to the artist, his purpose being to give us portraits of the distinguished curlers of the period. These are understood to be faithfully depicted. The majority of those gentlemen whose names have been mentioned by us in connection with the curling of the first half of this century figure in the picture, the venerable M'George among the number acting then as a living link between the ancient and the modern game. Many others are introduced who are worthy of honour as prominent curlers in their day, such as Russel of the *Scotsman*, Pollok of Broom, Gillon of Wallhouse, Baird of Gartsherrie, Ramsay of Whitehill, William l'Anson "of *Blairathole* and *Blinkbonny* fame," and Robert Craig, one of the very few who now remain, and who, at the age of eighty-three, is bright, cheerful, and young in heart, his eye undimmed and his curling keenness unabated.*

The Clyde was made the boundary line between the contending forces, when the Grand Match of 1850 was arranged to come off at Lochwinnoch. Owing to some misunderstanding, the loch was refused by the proprietor of Castle Semple, but Colonel M'Dowall of Garthland, in a spirit worthy of his curling sires, flooded 200 acres of Barr Meadow, where the match was played on 11th January. This match was very successful, there being no less than 127 rinks on each side. Thousands of spectators crowded the scene, and the gathering was the largest of the kind that up to that time had ever been witnessed. Its

---

* The original painting was purchased by Mr Piper, whose portrait is one of those introduced into the scene. Artist's proofs, published at ten guineas, are scarce, but prints of the engraving of the picture by Forrester are plentiful and cheap.

picturesque surroundings, with the old castle of Barr in the foreground and sombre Mistilaw in the distance, might, with the scene itself, have inspired a greater artist than Lees; but no painting keeps alive the memory of the first Grand Match at Lochwinnoch. The match, however, has an excellent memorial in the following verses, written by one of our most esteemed Scottish poets, Principal Shairp of St Andrews :—

THE LOCHWINNOCH BONSPIEL.

"Cauld and snell is the weather, ye curlers, come gather!
   Scotland summons her best frae the Tweed to the Tay;
It's the North o' the Clyde 'gainst the Southern side,
   And Lochwinnoch the tryst for our bonspiel to-day.

"Ilk parish they've summoned, baith landward and borough,
   Far and near troop the lads wi' the stanes and the broom;
The ploughs o' the Loudons stand still in the furrow,
   And the weavers o' Beith for the loch leave the loom.

"The braw shepherd lads, they are there in their plaids,
   Their hirsels they've left on the Tweedside their lane;
Grey carles frae the moorlands wi' gleg e'e and sure hands,
   Braid bonnet o' blue, and the big channel-stane.

"And the Loudons three, they foregather in glee,
   Wi' tounsfolk frae Ayr, and wi' farmers on Doon;
Out over the Forth come the men of the North,
   Frae the far Athole braes, and the palace o' Scone.

"Auld Reekie's top sawyers, the lang-headed lawyers,
   And crouse Glasgow merchants are loud i' the play;
There are lairds frae the east, there are lords frae the west,
   For the peer and the ploughman are marrows to-day.

"See the rinks are a' marshalled, how cheery they mingle,
   Blithe callants, stout chiels, and auld grey-headed men,
And the roar o' their stanes gars the snowy heights tingle
   As they ne'er did before, and may never again.

"Some lie at hog-score, some owre a' ice roar,
   'Here's the tee,' 'There's the winner,' 'Chap and lift him twa yards,'
'Lay a guard,' 'Fill the port,' and now there's nocht for't
   But a canny inwick or a rub at the guards.

"Gloamin' comes ; we maun pairt ; but fair fa' ilk kind heart,
   Wi' the auld Scottish blood beating warm in his veins;
Curlers! aye we've been leal to our country's weal,
   Though our broadswords are besoms, our targes are stanes."*

The loch of Lindores was to be the scene of the Grand Match of 1851, but the match was not played for want of

---

* The two last verses of the poem will be found as prefatory stanzas at Part I., Chap. I. of our volume. The poem first appeared in the *Annual* for 1851, p. 234.

sufficient frost. Charles Cowan had, in 1847, contributed
to the *Annual* an article on "The Prospective Advantages
of Railways to Curlers," and had therein said—

"We should like the Royal Club to consider the propriety of sheets
of water being procured in juxtaposition with some one or more of our
leading lines of railway."

This suggestion met the attention of Sir John Ogilvy,
who had been impressed with the terrible consequences
that might follow such a match as that at Linlithgow if
the ice happened to give way, and at the July meeting in
1851 Sir John moved—

"That the Royal Club should have a piece of ground which could
be flooded for the purpose of affording a safe sheet of ice for the Grand
Matches."

A committee, with the honourable Baronet as convener, was
appointed to make inquiries. Several places (including a site
near Carstairs Junction) were examined by this committee,
who finally recommended Carsebreck, a piece of ground 63
acres in extent, lying near the Scottish Central Railway, about
midway between Greenloaning and Blackford Stations, and
about 280 feet above sea-level. The report was approved,
and the committee requested to proceed with the scheme,
the cost and expense to be raised by voluntary subscriptions
from clubs and members of clubs. The Laird of Buttergask
gave the necessary access from the railway; Mrs Home
Drummond Stirling Moray of Abercairney gave permission to
use her land, and for a rent of £15 per annum payable to the
tenant, the Royal Club was to have the full use of the
ground for four months—November-February—each year.
Plans and specifications, shewing soundings from 6 inches
to 5 feet 9 inches at the western extremity or sluice (where
rinks would not be drawn), were prepared by Alexander
Drummond, surveyor, Perth, and Mr Falshaw, Perth,
became contractor for the work. From the fact that a
considerable body of moss or peat lay above the retentive clay, the contractor met with considerable difficulty in constructing the pond; but he seems to have
lost no time, for when the committee met to inspect
the work on the 28th November 1852, they found it

s

completed and the pond covered with a sheet of beautiful
ice. Sir John Ogilvy, to whom the Royal Club was
indebted for the success of the scheme, presented a six-
pounder gun, captured by one of his ancestors at the
siege of Jean d'Acre, to be fixed on the Kilnknowe,
overlooking the pond on the south-west, and fired as a
signal when the match was to begin, and again when it
was to end. An office was constructed for the secretary
at the side of the pond, a bridge thrown over the Allan,
and a side station erected by the Railway Company, who
offered double tickets for single fare, and did all they
could for the curlers. All was now ready for the first
great national bonspiel at Carsebreck. This came off on
the 15th of February 1853. A stranger visiting the spot
on the morning of that eventful day would doubtless have
thought it cheerless and uninviting.

"The trees were a' bare, and the birds mute and dowie;
They shook the cauld drift frae their wings as they flew."

But as the morning wore on and the railway trains
poured in their contingents of curlers, brooms, crampits,
and channel-stanes from all parts of Scotland, and the
various skips, having drawn their cards at the secretary's
office, marshalled their men in the places appointed for
them—when more than 1400 curlers stood in battle array,
North v. *South*, waiting for the "cannon's opening roar"—
no one could look at Carsebreck without interest and
admiration. The long slopes of hilly ground in which the
pond quietly nestles, sprinkled as they were with snow;
the higher elevations of the Ochil range to the south-
east, and the sharp outline of Ben Voirlich far away to
the north-west, arrayed in a thicker garment of dazzling
white, were all enlivened by the presence of that intensely
earnest army in the foreground, with its regiments of strong,
stalwart heroes, and all combined made such a scene as had
never before been witnessed in Scotland, and of which Scotland might well be proud. It was the gathering of her
proudest clans, the mustering of her best and bravest sons,
not for mortal combat, as of old at Sheriffmuir, but for the

fellowship to be gained in the rivalry of the curling-rink.
As such it was an important event in the onward life of
the nation. It was not only a sign: it was also in itself
an influence never after to be despised by all who have the
prosperity of the country at heart, and who realise the value
of healthy amusements in improving the condition of the
people.

On that day the members of the Royal Club must have
been delighted to think that the Grand Match, which was
of such importance, could henceforth be played with no
"dread of ambush in the depths below." It has often been
played since then, although not so often as curlers would
have liked. On every occasion it has furnished a theme
for descriptive writers. The Grand Match lends itself to
eloquence. The muster from near and far; the meeting
of young and old, rich and poor, master and servant, peer
and peasant, on a common level, with curling skill the
only title to distinction; the hearty hand-shakings, the
impatient waiting for the battle to begin; the eager onset
of the combatants; the boom and the click of the stone
artillery; the variety of garb, and the diversity of appearance
and manner among the players; the nervous excitement of
one skip, the quiet reserve of another; the gesturing, and
shouting, and conjuring, and sweeping; the running, and
kneeling, and coaxing, and jumping; the groups of beautiful
women; the *skytchers* flying to and fro; the wailing of the
disappointed; the crowing of the successful; the inimitable
vocabulary of words and phrases; the *nips*, and *schnaps*, and
drams; the *deoch-an-doris* after the last shot; the summing
up; the grand result—have all been described so often and
so eloquently,* that we may soon have a book of "Days at
Carsebreck." Carsebreck also has its poets—none so good,
perhaps, as Principal Shairp, but many worthy of notice—
e.g., James Christie, who of the meeting on 15th January
1867 is thus inspired to sing:—

---

* Most of these descriptions of Grand Matches, and many other interesting papers which have appeared in the *Annuals*, will be found in *Curling*, by Dr James Taylor. Paterson, 1884.

"They come frae glens at John o'
    Groat's,
And south frae Gallowa',
And eastward frae the Neuk o' Fife,
    And west frae dark Loch Awe.

"Young Athole's Duke frae fair
    Dunkeld—
(His sire we miss him sairly),
Dalhousie frae the banks o' Esk,
    And Ogilvie frae Airly.

"Strathallan frae his lordly ha',
    Colquhoun frae Luss and Balloch,
M'Gregor frae Loch Lomond side,
    And Campbell frae Glenfalloch.

"The day has dawned, the tees are
    marked,
The crampits pointed fairly,
The cannon booms, the besoms wave,
    The combat opens rarely.
        .   .   .   .

"Hour after hour, alang the ice,
    The polished stanes are glancin',
While mirthful hope and ruddy
    health
On ilka face are dancin'.

"The wintry day draws near a close,
    The wintry sun's descended,
The cannon booms, the lists are still,
    A NATION'S BONSPIEL'S ENDED."

When so much has been said or sung about the Grand Match, we shall here content ourselves with the more prosaic part of furnishing our readers with the rules under which the match is played, and the results of the various battles which have been fought since it was first instituted.

RULES IN CONNECTION WITH GRAND MATCH.

"1. A Grand Curling Match shall be played (weather permitting) between the members on the North and South sides of the Forth, and that it shall take place on a day to be hereafter fixed, whereof notice shall be sent to each secretary.

"2. The fixing of the day of the match shall be regulated by an observance of the weather and the state of the ice; and the probable continuance thereof being such as to warrant a reasonable expectation of the match being played, the Committee shall thereupon give notice of the match; and, in order that members of local clubs may have the earliest notice of the match, local secretaries be requested to forward to the General Secretary a note of the *name, address,* and name of the *post office* of an individual to whom such notice shall be sent, and who will undertake to communicate the same, *immediately upon its receipt,* to those members of the clubs who agree to join in the match.

"3. In order to meet expenses, every secretary, in transmitting the names of skips, shall, *at same time,* remit 2s. 6d. for each skip, and failing thereof, the name of the skip shall not be entered on the list of the match.

"4. It being understood that all matches give place to the Grand Match, and much disappointment having been experienced on former occasions in consequence of rinks entered on the list not appearing, without intimation to their opponents that they could not appear, the General Meeting of the Royal Club, July 1853, resolved '*that in future, if any rink, which has been booked to play at the Grand Match, shall fail to appear at the match, they shall be liable for the expenses of the rink against whom they were balloted to play, unless the rink failing to appear shall give the Representative Committee a satisfactory excuse for their absence.'"*

To give curling clubs a greater interest in the Grand Match, the Royal Club, in the year 1886, provided, at a cost of £114, a silver trophy to be played for annually under the following rules:—

"1. The trophy shall be gained by the club on the winning side having the greatest net majority of shots.

"2. All disputes in connection with the trophy shall be referred to the Committee of Management for the time being, whose decision shall be final—the committee to have full power to make arrangements for the proper custody of the trophy."

FIG. 64.
GRAND MATCH TROPHY.

This trophy, which is in the form of a cup, rests on a shaped base of solid polished ebony, with the title "Royal Caledonian Curling Trophy" in raised silver letters in front. On either side of the stem of the cup stand two figures in silver representing the North and the South. In the centre of the body of the cup is a curling scene represented in raised figures, with the game in full swing. On either side of the two handles are four raised figures of players in various familiar attitudes. On the top of the cover stands the figure of a player on the ice, with broom in hand, in the act of playing the stone. The other parts of the cup are richly chased and relieved with raised stags' heads, thistles, laurel leaves, and broom, and other suitable and appropriate emblems, including the shield and arms of the club. All round the body are festoons enclosing spaces for engraving the names of the winning clubs and rinks. The height of the trophy is 27 inches. The cup, which is entirely of sterling silver, weighs about 150 ozs., and the whole of the modelling and workmanship was done by Messrs G. Edward & Sons, Glasgow, the present medalists of the Royal Club. Gold badges have also been secured, which are awarded to the members of the rink which scores the highest majority for the club which wins the trophy.

RESULTS OF GRAND MATCHES.

North v. South of Forth.

Date	Where Played	Rinks in Matches	Extra Rinks	North Score	South Score	Majority for North	Majority for South	Highest Club Score— Winning Side	Highest Club Score— Losing Side
1847 Jan. 15	Pencaitck	24	..	216	238	..	22	Currie II., 25	Bridge of Allan III., 1
1848 Jan. 25	Linlithgow	70	100	620	732	..	106	Buchan IV., 31	Dunblane IV., 27
1853 Feb. 15	Carsebreck	340	18	2488	2155	333	..	Dunblane VIII., 66	Currie III., 73
1855 Jan. 30	,,	352	..	3049	3501	..	452	Campsie Glen III., 61	{ Bridge of Allan IV., { Rattray II., 47
1860 Feb. 3	,,	230	..	1900	1742	142	..	Whitevale II., 45	Crieff II., 33
1861 Dec. 31	,,	272	46	1898	2255	..	357	Borestone VI., 65	{ Alloa Prince of Wal { III., 39
1867 Jan. 15	,,	266	10	1789	1885	..	96	Waverley IV., 59	{ Blackford V., 50 { Cairney II., 39
1871 Jan. 26	,,	112	6	913	894	19	..	Dunblane Thistle II., 44	Glasgow Lilybank V.,
1873 Feb. 12	,,	142	..	1161	1279	..	118	West Calder II., 39	Tullymet I., 17
1874 Dec. 24	,,	180	10	1196	1510	..	314	Glasgow Lilybank VIII., 44	Doune V., 46
1880 Jan. 23	,,	330	14	2830	2802	28	..	{ Strathallan Meath Mos { III., 45	{ Hamilton Douglas { Clydesdale II., 44
1880 Dec. 30	,,	386	34	3226	3456	..	230	Kirkintilloch III., 52	Thornhill IV., 46
1882 Dec. 15	,,	418	24	2392	2665	..	273	Merchiston V., 52	Pitlochry III., 37
1885 Jan. 12	,,	268	40	1670	2008	..	338	New Monkland III., 53	{ Breadalbane G { orchy I., 21
1886 Dec. 21	,,	270	8	2071	2496	..	425	,, ,, IV., 45	Auchterarder III., 45

North v. South of Clyde.

1850 Jan. 11	Lochwinnoch	254	22	2295	2062	233	..	New Monkland VIII., 37	{ Garnock of Kilbir { IX., 42
1864 Jan. 8	,,	236	..	1328	1680	352	352	Hamilton VII., 85	Partick IV., 41
1878 Dec. 13	,,	134	42	993	1098	..	105	Boreas IV., 32	Waverley IV., 31

* The Roman letters indicate the number of rinks.

There have thus been 18 Grand Matches, 3 of these having been North v. South of Clyde, and 15 North v. South of Forth. South of Clyde is 1 match and 224 shots in advance of North of Clyde—a state of matters which can easily be rectified during the present winter if frost and fortune permit. South of Forth has won 12 matches against the North, and lost 3, and is now 2493 shots ahead. It may be remarked that 6 of the Grand Matches were played in December, 9 in January, and 3 in February. Two matches were played in one year—1880—and the same occurred in 1886. The matches have all been arranged by the club secretary, upon whom they entail a great amount of labour and anxiety, and their orderly management has always been the subject of remark and congratulation. The services of the umpires, who are generally men of curling renown, and who parade the field of action with white flags, prepared to settle any disputes that arise among the rinks, have scarcely ever been required. On one or two occasions, notably in 1860 and in 1886, General Frost, after convening his army on the ice, ran off and left them in the hands of General Thaw, and many timid players beat a retreat to the banks, but the majority fought on till the firing of the signal-gun, some of them being nearly knee-deep in the water. London, out of sheer spite, sent down one of her fogs and tried to stop the match of December 13, 1878; but it was carried through successfully, although the curlers had to grope about without being able to distinguish friend from foe. As a result of that day's experience no curler ever goes to Carsebreck now without a flask in his inside pocket. When the regiments were crowding over the bridge after the close of the 1880 match the structure gave way, and a good many were precipitated into the river below. They were all safely brought to the bank, "including a young lady." One person (not a curler) had his leg hurt to the benefit of future Grand Matches, as three substantial bridges have since made the crossing of the Allan safe and speedy.

Barring these few incidents, which are not all of a melancholy sort, the conditions under which the various matches have been played have been most satisfactory, and no mishap has occurred to mar the confidence of the club in the perfect safety to life and limb, which they guarantee to all who take part in the national gathering at Carsebreck. Lochwinnoch has also an unbroken record of success as far as her three matches are concerned, and from soundings that have recently been taken it is evident that a match can be played there with as much assurance of safety as on the Royal Pond.

In our table we have brought out the "highest net majorities" in all the matches, and on both sides. From this it will be seen that on three occasions the "greatest net majority of shots" was scored by a club on the losing side in the match, and that Hamilton at Lochwinnoch in 1864 made the highest net majority which has yet been registered. The highest majority ever gained by an individual rink was 70 shots. The skip of this rink was Alexander Cunningham, Currie, who in 1853 made 71 to his opponent's 1,* and the combined score—72—is also the largest made by any two rinks playing together. In 1855 the rink of Donald Fisher, Dunkeld, although they were only able to score 1 shot, *soutered* their opponents, and in 1867 the same remarkable feat was accomplished by the rink of John Lawrie, Bute.

New Monkland, which scored the highest net majority on the winning side as far back as 1850, and which has won the trophy two years in succession, must, among clubs that have entered for the Grand Match, be accorded first place. Whatever we may have to discount from the method of awarding the honour, the principle of *persistency* which we laid down in the point game applies also in the Grand Match, and it is evident that the New Monkland players have well earned their title to distinction.

When we find, as we do, that they are the inheritors of skill and enthusiasm from far-back times, New Monkland curlers having been famous even in the last century, and that their achievements at Carsebreck are in keeping with their actions nearer home,† their success is not only well deserved, but it is a justification, if such were needed, of the institution of the Grand Trophy, and of the mode of deciding to what club it ought to be awarded.

The future of the Grand Match depends in great measure

---

* This is somewhat maliciously accounted for by saying that the Currieites, though privileged to be near the metropolis, are somewhat mountainous in their locality and habits, and have a pond hid among trees somewhere about the top of the Pentlands, where they practise every lawful day from Martinmas to Whitsunday.—ED. *Annual*, 1854.

† The New Monkland Club have played for ten district medals and won them all. They won the medal of the Glasgow Province in 1882, their 4 rinks being 35 shots up. In the two years in which they held the trophy they played 13 matches, of which 12 were won, their majority over the whole being 375 shots. Their keenness is evidenced by the following, for which their secretary is responsible:—" At the Grand Match of 12th January 1886, when New Monkland won the trophy and four gold badges, J. Scotland's rink would have won the badges had he not played his last stone, for in playing this he unfortunately knocked in a North stone. For a whole year he bitterly repented the playing of that stone, and earnestly prayed that he might yet win a badge, which he did that same year at the Grand Match of 21st December."

on the success of the efforts which are at present being made to secure another pond about Carstairs, or some place more convenient for Southern players. The match, to be truly *grand*, must be between the North and the South of Scotland. There is an indescribable charm about it when it is a battle between the Lowlands and the Highlands, and its national aspect is far more striking when the Saxon meets the Gael, than when East is set against West, or the Clyde drawn between the combatants. But North must meet South on equal terms, and in alternate years come to meet South in Southern territory. This is the remedy for the Northern defeats, which we believe are ascribed to the fact that Carsebreck is too accessible to the North, and that instead of select players only being sent to the field, all and sundry are in the habit of going. When the North descends to Southern territory it will be the other way — the tables will be turned, and the Highlanders will go home sounding the pibroch of victory. Southerners will not be sorry, for we can assure our Northern friends that, while we shall fight to win, we shall always have more pleasure in meeting them than in beating them. There is, however, a sinister star in the horoscope of our Grand Match if our Western and more Southerly regiments are debarred from joining us, as they now are, by the inconvenient situation of Carsebreck, and we look to the North to support the Royal Club in any new arrangement that has to be made to remedy the just complaints of the South.

THE ANNUAL.

To the original constitution of the Grand Club an Appendix was attached by the framers with recommendations, suggestions, &c. The first of these refers to the publication of the *Annual*, and is as follows :—

"When the revenue of the club will warrant such a measure, after carrying into effect the proposals under 2nd General Head, the Committee would strongly urge the interest which would be added to the Club's proceedings by the yearly publication of an *Annual*, under the title of the *Annual of the Grand Caledonian Curling Club*, containing, 1st, Correct lists of the office-bearers and general representative committee ; 2nd, Of the local clubs composing the Grand Caledonian

Curling Club, with their office-bearers and members ; 3rd, Individual members of the Grand Caledonian Curling Club unattached to any local club ; 4th, Rules and regulations as altered or amended at last general meeting ; 5th, Proceedings of the club during the past year ; 6th, Accounts of prize competitions during the past winter ; 7th, Curling anecdotes, songs, and anything of general interest, and possibly embellished by a portrait of some eminent curler, or illustration of the most improved artificial rink, &c. And with the view of carrying this into effect, recommend an estimate being obtained from some bookseller of the probable expense, and a list through the different local secretaries of persons who would subscribe for it."

With the omission of the list of *individual* members, and the adoption of a compulsory system of sale instead of the voluntary subscription—each club being now bound to take a certain number of copies in proportion to its membership—the *Annual* has adhered to its original *Table of Contents* throughout the fifty years of its publication. With the progress of the club the *Annual* has kept step, its first number (1839) being a "tiny bookling" of 48 pages, of which 300 copies were printed ; its last (1889), a formidable volume of 442 pages, of which 4000 copies were printed and supplied to the affiliated clubs. From the works on curling to which we have referred in our last chapter, the *Annual* Committee made ample quotations in the earlier numbers, and Dr Walker Arnott, Charles Cowan, and others contributed original articles of interest and value ; but they had considerable difficulty in mitigating the dulness of dry lists and regulations by lighter and more literary reading. In 1845 we find the committee appealing to the brethren for materials in words which might be stereotyped, and read every year with advantage.

"The topics are numerous, and do not require to be specified ; anything is interesting to a curler which has reference to his favourite game. To the *antiquary* they would recommend an inspection of any burgh records to which he may have access, for the purpose of obtaining facts to establish the antiquity of the game ; from the *mineralogist* they would gladly receive an account of the different kinds of stone which are best adapted for moving easily on the ice, and possess at the same time the requisite toughness ; from the *humorist* they would expect interesting anecdotes of curlers ; and from the *meteorologist*, the result of his observations on the weather, or hints respecting the laws by which our insular climate is regulated.* These are inter-

---

* With the progress of the science of *meteorology* our Royal Club might have had more to do if this appeal had been regarded by local clubs. It is worthy of special attention.

esting subjects, and there are many members of the Royal Club who are capable of doing them justice."

Curling poets are not included in the appeal. It would have been derogatory to their dignity to have classified songs among *materials*. The songs and poems that have been sent to the *Annual* Committee have, however, been welcomed as heartily as any other offerings, for the popularity of curling owes much to the curling muse. No fewer than 215 different songs and poetical pieces have appeared in the *Annual* since its first three numbers (in which there were no songs) were published. Many are too *locally* tinged, and too weak to be transplanted from the numbers of the *Annual* in which they are found, but an interesting memorial of this Victorian era—the most important in the annals of curling—might be made by collecting the best songs of its best singers, and thus preserving from oblivion the sentiments of those who have illuminated the path of the club's progress by the sunlight of their song.*

The most useful contributors to the earlier *Annuals* were Charles Cowan, Dr Walker Arnott, and Professor Fergusson of Aberdeen. Messrs Palmer, Ogilvie Dalgleish, and Forrester were also on the committee, and for the first half of the Royal Club's existence some or all of these names are identified with the *Annual*. One or two continue their work into the other moiety, when we find the names of Dr Sidey, Messrs Peterkin, Murrie, Carswell, Caldwell, and Admiral Maitland-Dougall succeeding theirs, and in the last decade we have the names of Sir James Gibson-Craig, Bart., Messrs Cathcart, Usher, Shaw, Wylie, Forrest, Ure, Breingan, Gilmour, and Rev. J. Scott. In the preparation of the *Annual* the principal burden falls on the secretary. From the list of those who have given their services in assisting him, and who have in the latter half of the Royal Club's history brightened the literary department of the

---

* It is impossible to do this in a volume of this kind devoted mainly to the history of curling. At some future time, if opportunity can be found, we hope to devote a volume to the poetry of the game, and shall be glad to have suggestions or contributions from curlers to help us in carrying out the proposal. *The Curler's Garland* should be a companion volume to *The History of Curling*.

Annual, we must single out Dr Sidey, who, in this and in other respects, proved himself one of the most active and useful friends of the Royal Club. Dr Sidey was in his day one of the busiest and most hard-working medical men in Edinburgh, a "beloved physician," on whose skill his numerous patients relied with confidence, and whose merry heart often did them more good than a medicine. Dr Sidey's sympathies, however, went beyond his professional duties. He was a friend of artists and a lover of art; a well-informed antiquary,

FIG. 65. DR SIDEY AS "FATHER CRUCELLI," ONE OF THE "MONKS OF ST GILES."

and a poet of considerable power, as all know who are familiar with the riant humour, blended with most delicate pathos, that is to be found in *Mistura Curiosa* * and *Alter Ejusdem*,† the now rare volumes which contain the songs and verses composed by him as he travelled about visiting his patients. In social gifts Dr Sidey had few to equal and none to excel him. These made his presence always welcome at the Pen and Pencil Club, and among the "Monks of St Giles," that old society of "merry men a'" who demand of their "Prior" a song of his own making, and that he shall sing it, if possible, when the "gude kaill" has been discussed and the bowl is going round, there

* Edinburgh: Maclachlan & Stewart, 1869.   † *Ib.*, 1877.

was none merrier than Dr Sidey, and none who could give a better account of himself in the Prior's chair than "Father Crucelli." As we might expect of such a social, brotherly soul, the doctor was a curler and the friend of curlers and curling.

> "They're canty chaps the curlers, O,
> They're cheerie chiels the curlers, O,
> There never met a rarer set
> Than Scotland's keen, keen curlers, O."

This was what he thought of the brotherhood; but his devotion was more than poetical, for while he gave to the *Annual* some of the best and most delightful songs of the period, he worked with all his might to get the Royal Club out of financial difficulties, and to make its various undertakings successful. He worked and sung, and sung and worked for the club, just as he did when he followed his special calling. The sense of the loss sustained by his death was well expressed by Mr Josiah Livingston, at the first representative meeting thereafter, when he said—

"There was no one to whom they were more indebted than to Dr Sidey. Their meetings were really no meetings unless he were present. There was not a keener curler anywhere, nor one who took a deeper interest in the affairs of the Royal Caledonian Curling Club."

FINANCE.

For some years we hear nothing about the finances of the Grand Club. The subject seems to have been ignored at the earlier annual meetings, as if it were of the earth earthy, and unworthy the attention of men wrestling with a higher problem. Like Antaeos of old, they had to touch down that they might recover strength. Their first secretary, Mr Skelton, served the club gratuitously for two years, and left it in a sound condition. Their second, Mr Ritchie, served two years for a small salary, and left the club in financial difficulties. Clubs were then called upon for contributions ranging from 12s. 6d. to £2, according to the number of members, towards clearing the debt, and nearly £200 was raised. It is from this date that we have a statement of accounts produced at the

annual meeting, audited by a committee and inserted in
the *Annual*. Dr Renton then became treasurer, and
Mr Cassels secretary, the former acting without salary,
and the latter at a salary of £25 per annum. Two years
afterwards the two offices were combined, and their duties,
as we have seen, ably discharged by Mr Cassels for thirty
years. The cost of the provincial map to which we have
referred was about £100, the engraver (Mr Forrester) receiving £70, and Mr Palmer, " for condensing, methodizing,
and copying the lists," £26. The map was sold at 5s. per
copy, and the sale was highly successful. In 1850 it
was resolved that Mr Cassels, who had as secretary been
receiving £25 per annum, should as treasurer " be
allowed 7½ per cent. on all sums received by him, and
5 per cent. on all disbursements on account of the Royal
Caledonian Curling Club." The effect of this was to more
than double the salary Mr Cassels had previously received.
In constructing the Grand Pond at Carsebreck the committee of the club seem to have " outrun the constable "
to a serious extent. The cost was much larger than its
promoters expected, and for a good many years the club
lay under the burden of a heavy debt which could not be
cleared off. The estimates for the work and the engineer's
fee did not exceed £500, but what with claims for damages,
additional embankments, bridges, repairs, &c., more than
double that sum was incurred. The account was kept
separate from the ordinary account of the Royal Club,
and subscriptions were received towards the cost from clubs
and individuals to the amount of £780. This left a large
balance, which went on increasing with interest, litigation
about damages, and additional repairs. In 1861, when a
committee, with Dr Sidey as convener, took up the affair
to see how things stood and what had to be done, it was
found " that £600 would be required to meet past and
contingent liabilities in connection with the Grand Pond."
Of this amount fully £300 was due to Mr Falshaw.
Dr Sidey and his committee set themselves to work to
raise the sum, but after seven years' exertion they had

only succeeded in raising about half the amount, and were about giving up in despair. While in this state Mr (then Bailie) Falshaw invited the whole committee to dinner, and when the cloth had been removed and the loyal and patriotic toasts had been duly proposed and honoured, the Bailie laid upon the table the three-hundred pound bond. The committee were in consternation—they were in the hands of Shylock. But the Bailie speedily put an end to their suspense by committing the bond to the fire and proposing "Success to the Royal Caledonian Curling Club."

At the July meeting in 1869 Dr Sidey and his committee were able to report that all the Grand Pond accounts were now cleared, and a balance left of thirteen guineas. Out of this, in recognition of his unwearied efforts, a "pair of the handsomest curling-stones" was presented to Dr Sidey; and in their jubilation over the extinction of the debt, the Royal Club did not forget to place on record its gratitude to Bailie Falshaw for such a fine *bonfire*. The first published balance-sheet of the club (1844-45) shewed an income from the three sources of revenue amounting to £110. For the closing year of Bailie Cassels' secretaryship the income was £625. The handsome collection of £500 for presentation to the secretary, when he was struck down by his fatal illness, shews how much the members of the Royal Club felt their indebtedness to Bailie Cassels, and their appreciation of his management of the club's affairs during the long period in which he held office. Dr Sidey discharged the duties of secretary and treasurer for nearly a year after Bailie Cassels' death, Messrs Livingston, Usher, Rowatt, Aitchison, and Don assisting him as a committee. In October 1875, Mr David Lindsay, who had acted as clerk to Bailie Cassels, was appointed to the double office. When this gentleman died in 1880, Mr Adam Davidson Smith, C.A., was elected secretary and treasurer in 1880, his salary being £100 per annum. This was increased to £120 in 1884, and, after the Club Jubilee, a silver cup and a cheque for a handsome sum were presented to Mr Smith, in testimony of the successful way in which he had carried through the celebrations. During the present secretary's term of office the finances have increased more rapidly than in any former period of the club's history, the income from the three sources formerly mentioned being now fully £750, while the balance in favour of the club, as in last balance-sheet (year ending June 30, 1888), was no less than £530. A grand snow-man to set up in honour of the approaching Jubilee. Come, genial rejoicings, and thaw him down!

THE JUBILEE.

Fifty years of the Royal Club were completed July 25, 1888, just a year after the whole country had united in celebrating, with unequalled splendour, joy, and enthusiasm, the Jubilee of Her Majesty's reign. There was still a jubilee atmosphere everywhere, and the Royal Club was fortunate in having its Jubilee to celebrate when everything was in a condition to make the event a success. It was after some consideration decided—

"(1.) That a Jubilee Dinner be held in Edinburgh in November 1888.

"(2.) That a Literary Committee be appointed, with powers, for the purpose of preparing a sketch of the club's history during the last fifty years.

"(3.) That a bronze medal be issued to each affiliated club, to be preserved or played for as each may determine."

The bronze medal (a representation of which is seen in the heading of this chapter) was duly issued, and received a hearty welcome from the clubs as a suitable memorial of the event. The following, in terms of the resolution, were appointed a Literary Committee:—Thomas S. Aitchison, Richard Brown, C.A.; R. Burns Begg, F.S.A.S.; Dr Carruthers, J. Clark Forrest, Rev. John Kerr, Dirleton (*Convener*); Captain Macnair, Rev. A. J. Murray, W. A. Peterkin, George Seton, M.A.; and A. Davidson Smith, C.A., Secretary. The Revs. Dr Taylor, W. L. M'Dougall, and G. Murray, Colonel Menzies, and John Smart, R.S.A., were afterwards added to the number.

The Jubilee Dinner was held in the Waterloo Hotel, in the upper room of which the club had, fifty years before, been instituted. The attendance numbered 360, there being representatives from no fewer than 130 affiliated clubs, every district of Scotland being represented. The gathering was certainly worthy of the occasion, and when the great company met in the banqueting-hall of the hotel, the Most Noble the Marquis of Breadalbane in the chair, the sight was a most impressive one. It had taken forty or more years to do it, but we had beaten the old days at last, and quite eclipsed the gaiety of the early gatherings, shewing to the world that the curling enthusiasm of Scotland had not lessened with the lapse of years, but was fresh and strong as ever. Everything had been arranged in orderly manner by the secretary and a special committee, and each member on taking his numbered place at the table found before him a massive four-page *menu*. On the front was a drawing by John Smart, R.S.A., with the inevitable lean crow perched on a twig and perusing a signboard stuck upon an old tree-stump, which read as follows:—"*Tak' Notice.— Jubilee Dinner, Royal Caledonian Curling Club, Waterloo Hotel, Nov. 28th*, 1888." On the outer page was a "*Programme of Music by the Edinburgh Reel and Strathspey Society—Mr W. Simpson, Conductor.*" The inner pages contained the *Bill of Fare* and the *Toast List*, which the secretary had allowed us to garnish with sundry curling phrases to help the digestion, and two verses from the curling poets, Henry Shanks of Bathgate, and Rev. J. Muir of Beith. We give them as they stood, although one or two alterations had to be made in the toast and song list.

"*A' here, men?*"   "*Aye, a' here and fit.*"

Bill of Fare.
"*Tak' your wull o't.*"

SOUPS.
"*Soop, lads, soop!*"

Hare.	Cockie-Leekie.
"*Gie him heels.*"	"*A vera patlid.*"

FISH.
"In the way o' promotion."

COD AND OYSTER SAUCE.   TURBOT AND LOBSTER SAUCE.
"Rest on him."   *"Clap on a guard."*

HAGGIS.
"The king o' a' the core."

JOINTS.
"Oh! be cannie!"

CORNED BEEF AND GREENS.   ROAST SIRLOIN OF BEEF.
"Ne'er a kowe!"   *"About the board we gather
Wi' mirth and glee, sirloin the tee."*

ROAST TURKEY.   BOILED HAM.
"Curl in to your grannie's wing."   *"It's a hog."*

SWEETS.
"Big on."

PLUM PUDDING.
"Tak' what ye see o't."   *"It's jist perfection."*

LIQUEUR JELLIES.   COMPOTES OF FRUIT.
"Kiggle-kaggle."   *"Stones and besoms an' a'."*

ASSORTED PASTRY.
"Dinna let them see that again."

CHEESE AND CELERY.
"Draw the port."

DESSERT.
"Check by jowl within the brough."

"BESOMS UP."

Toast List.

Come, fill the glass, and send it round, | Aye may we meet wi' social glee,
Sae jovial and sae hearty; | Devoid of strife and snarling—
Let mirth, unmixed with care, abound | Sae send it round, wi' three times three,
Amang ilk curling party. | To freedom, love, and curling.

CHAIRMAN—
The Most Noble the Marquis of Breadalbane,
President of the Royal Caledonian Curling Club.

THE QUEEN, ... Chairman.
"God save the Queen."

THE PRINCE OF WALES, PATRON OF THE CLUB, . Chairman.
"God bless the Prince of Wales."

THE ROYAL CALEDONIAN CURLING CLUB, . . Chairman.
Song—*"The Channel-stane."*—Mr GLENCORSE.

SCOTLAND'S AIN GAME, . . . Lord Balfour of Burleigh.
Song—*"Curlin' yet!"*—Mr MONRO.

CLUBS FORTH OF SCOTLAND, . . Sir James Gibson-Craig.
Song—*"To every land the world o'er."*—Mr SOMERVILLE SHAW.
Reply—Mr Meggat Manchester.

| CURLERS' WIVES AND SWEETHEARTS, | . | . | Marquis of Huntly. |

Song—"My ain kind dearie."—Mr MONRO.
Reply—Colonel Stirling of Kippendavie.

| THE COMMITTEE AND OFFICE-BEARERS, | . | . | Rev. Arthur Gordon. |

Song—"When snell o'er our snaw-tappit mountains."—Mr GLENCORSE.
Reply—The Secretary.

| THE CHAIRMAN, | . | . | . | . | . | Mr J. Clark Forrest. |

In canty cracks, and sangs, and jokes,	Wi' heavy heart, we're laith to part,
The night drives on wi' daffin',	But promise to forgather
And mony a kittle shot is ta'en	Around the tee, neist morn wi' glee,
While we're the toddy quaffin'.	If cauld, cauld, frosty weather.

Before proceeding to the toasts, the curlers on that memorable occasion did a graceful act in remembering the one only survivor of the fifty who had founded the club in that hotel half a century before—Charles Cowan of Logan House. From the assembled gathering the following telegram was despatched to the venerable curler who had done so much for curling and for the Royal Club :—*

"Three hundred and sixty members of the Royal Caledonian Curling Club, met in joyous jubilee, send you heartiest greetings and good wishes.
"BREADALBANE."

To this the following reply was in a short time received:

"WESTER LEA,
MURRAYFIELD,
EDINBURGH, 28th Nov. 1888.

"DEAR SIR,—I am much gratified by your kind message this evening, and thank you for your kind remembrance of me. Please assure the assembled company of my continued interest in the 'roaring game,' and of my regret that I am unable to be with them this evening.—I am, yours very truly,
"CHARLES COWAN, per MARGARET M. COWAN."

FIG. 66. CHARLES COWAN.
(From a photograph by W. Crooke, Edinburgh.)

---

* Mr Cowan died 29th March 1889, aged 87.

A full report of the Jubilee Dinner will be found in the *Annual* for 1889, but no report can worthily describe the scene or convey an adequate idea of the good humour and enthusiasm that characterised the gathering. The various speeches were eloquently delivered and heartily received, the applause being led by that enthusiastic brother, Charles Morrison, and some of the Waverley men, with their besoms high in air. From first to last it was a splendid meeting, one, indeed, that can never be forgotten by those who attended it, and worthy in every way of the event that occasioned it. To us the most notable feature was the singing of the chorus to *The Channel-stane* by the large assembly, led by Mr Glencorse, who sung the old song with great power. The curlers threw their soul into that chorus.* They seemed with one voice, deep, strong, and unmistakable, to utter the joy with which they crowned the work of the most successful half-century of curling, and commemorated the deeds of the departed heroes of the Royal Club. It was also the expression of their own devotion to the grand old game, and sounded like the undivided testimony of the three hundred that, come what might, their love of curling would, like the Scottish prejudice of Burns, ever " boil along the veins till the floodgates of life shut in eternal rest."

OUR PATRONESSES.

Ladies do not curl—on the ice.† The Rational Dress Association has not yet secured for them the freedom that is

---

* The tune was not that given on a former page of our volume, but *Green grow the rashes, O.*

† There are exceptions to every rule. About fifty years ago a ladies' bonspiel was played on Loch Ged in the parish of Keir, two rinks of the maidens of Capenoch against two rinks of the maidens of Waterside, with skips of acknowledged skill presiding over them. An enormous concourse of spectators assembled, and the sun in honour of the occasion shone out brightly upon the scene. The ice was bad, and, according to our informer, the maidens had to play the match "fetlock-deep in water;" but great skill was displayed on both sides, the curling-broom being handled as dexterously as the domestic one, and channel-stanes, which female arms are supposed to be unable to cope with, being whirled with all the ease of the distaff. After a keen contest the maidens of Capenoch were victorious by a single shot. In his *History of Sanquhar Club* (p. 46), Mr Brown records a match between the wives of Sanquhar and Crawick Mill.

On 10th February 1841 the married ladies of Buittle challenged the unmarried, and the match came off at Loch-hill, twenty ladies a side, and necessary to fling the channel-stane, and like Her Majesty at Scone, the majority find the curling-stones too heavy for their delicate arms. But ladies are the patronesses and friends of curling. With that fine instinct which enables them readily to detect what is good for their country, they have been led to give it their hearty support. They, in some measure, did this before the days of the Royal Club, but it is since, and owing to the institution of that club, that the interest of the fair sex in our national game has been thoroughly secured. Nothing, indeed, is more remarkable in the history of the club than the way in which the patronage and support of the first ladies in the land has been enlisted in the curling cause. Out of 461 Scottish clubs, no less than 278 have ladies of rank and position as patronesses. The list is headed by H.R.H. the Princess Louise, Marchioness of Lorne, who is patroness of Inveraray Club. Then we have the Duchesses of Athole, Buccleuch, Hamilton, and Sutherland; the Marchionesses of Bute, Breadalbane, Huntly, Lansdowne, and Tweeddale; the Countesses of Aberdeen, Airlie, Camperdown, Dunmore, Elgin, Glasgow, Home, Kinnoull, Kintore, Lindsay, (Dowager) Mar and Kellie, Morton, Rosebery, Rosslyn, and Strathmore, the majority of the others being influential ladies of quality in

---

a gentleman skipping each team. So novel a scene attracted such a crowd that the players were compelled to shift the rink several times. The game was carried out with the determination peculiar to the sex, and resulted in the defeat of the married party, who declared that there had been treachery in their camp. That they had some ground for their suspicion was proved by the fact that soon afterwards the skip of the married ladies was united to a young widow who had played on the unmarried side, and had cast sheep's eyes over the hog-score all the time of the match.

In a description of the opening of Pitfour Curling Pond, 31st January 1884, it is stated that "the Hon. Mrs Fergusson took her place on the crampit, with a stone of 36 lbs. weight, and delivered the same in true curling style, sending it the full length of the rink with such a true and unerring aim that it drove a stone which was placed on the *tee* to the bank and lay itself *a perfect pattlid*. The lady's excellent *chap-and-lie* shot, it is needless to say, was awarded a vociferous cheer." We had, on one occasion, to raise a hue-and-cry for two ladies who went amissing from our manse on a Saturday afternoon, and found them curling by torchlight with the enthusiastic secretary of our local club, quite oblivious to the near approach of the Sabbath. There are doubtless many other cases which shew that gentlemen have not a monopoly of the national game. We may add that among the accounts of curling clubs sent to us that regarding Dunkeld is furnished by a lady.

their different districts, so that we may safely say we have
enlisted in the ranks of our lady friends the wealth, wit,
and beauty of Scotland. But it is not simply their
patronage that we are proud of, though that is something
to be thankful for. We have looked into the returns of
fully 300 clubs which possess prizes for annual rink or
point competition, in addition to medals purchased by these
clubs or conferred by the Royal Club, and we find among
them 440 silver or gold medals, and 300 trophies of
various kinds, such as cups, jugs, kettles, quaichs, snuff-
mulls, curling-stones,* &c., and of these 740 prizes as many
as 125, or fully one-sixth of the whole number, are direct
gifts to these clubs from lady patrons and friends. While
our gratitude toward the majority of our fair patronesses is
"a lively sense of favours to come," nearly one-half of the
number have thus made us grateful for favours already
received in silver and gold. This is most satisfactory, and
fortunate indeed are those clubs which have been so favoured.
Their competitions are all the keener when the prize is given
by some Queen of Beauty. More so when it is not simply one
fair donor but many from whom the gift of honour comes.
Scotscraig Club has a ladies' challenge medal, subscribed for by
the wives of the members. *Aberuthven, Alyth, Blackburn, Darlington, Dunalastair, Eskdaill, Middlesborough, Orwell*, and
Rohallion and Birnam Clubs have all trophies, subscribed for
by the *ladies of the district*. The ladies of Saline and Carnock
gifted a silver snuff-box to the *Oakley* Club. Most fortunate

---

* Besides the snuff-box of the Gladsmuir Club, to which we have already
referred (p. 205), there are several remarkable curiosities in the list of
curling trophies. Coates Club holds the gold medal of the old Duddingston
Club, but does not endanger its safety by putting it up for competition.
Braemar Club plays for the annual possession of one of the membership medals
of the Duddingston Club, dated 1795, and presented to Braemar in 1886 by
R. G. Foggo. For a rink trophy the Partick Club has the old "Partick
Village Bell," dated 1725, and used in the last century by the town-crier
for intimating sales, &c. It was found in a marine store in Paisley, and
presented to the club by John Ross in 1859. It is very highly valued by
the club. The Waverley Club play annually for a Morrison Jug, which is
made of silver got at the taking of Lucknow; Coupar-Angus and Kettins
for a "silver medal, with miniature curling-stones of granite taken from
the fortifications of Sebastopol," presented to the club in 1857 by Mrs E.
Collins Wood of Keithock. The Menzies Cricket Club shew their goodwill
to the Weem curlers by presenting them with a silver medal.

of all, the curling clubs of *Alva* and *Delvine* have medals presented by *the young ladies of the district*. If this book should ever reach the hands of wives, ladies in general, or young ladies in particular, we would say to them all, "Go and do likewise." They certainly could not do better than combine in this way to shew their sympathy with the manliest and best of our national games. In recognition of the interest the ladies had then shewn in the Royal Club, it was proposed by Major Henderson of Westerton, in 1853, to have a grand ball in connection with the Royal Club. The subject was remitted to a special committee, but we do not hear whether the ball ever took place. A good many local clubs * follow the examples of Ayr and Penninghame, and organise annual or occasional dances.

There is, however, a more popular way of shewing appreciation of the interest taken by ladies in curling; and it is followed by nearly all our curling clubs—not that they love dancing less, but that they love curling more. They have an annual match, *The Married* v. *The Unmarried*, the purpose of which is the same as that of our young patronesses—viz., to exterminate the race of bachelors and send them over to "the great majority." In this match the married are generally successful, and the poor bachelors who chance to escape with their lives very soon put the chain of Hymen round their necks in despair, and commit "the happy despatch."

At the close of its first fifty years we would here, in the name of the Royal Caledonian Curling Club, offer our hearty thanks to all the patronesses and lady friends for the kindly interest they have taken in the curling clubs of their different districts. Some, we are glad to think, who did much in the earlier period of our history are still here to receive

---

* The curlers of *Ballingry*, in arranging a ball, wisely deprecated the excessive expenditure on gew-gaws common on such occasions, as appears from this club minute of 27th December 1839:—"In the course of the evening it was proposed to have a ball in connection with the club. The following gentlemen were appointed a committee for the management of the same:—Messrs Briggs, Dowie, Mitchell, R. Henderson, Robertson, Wilson, Russel, J. Reddie, and Dr Neil. It was agreed that the ladies invited be requested to appear in their usual dresses, and not put themselves to unnecessary expense, as *curlers like everything plain and substantial*."

honour from us; notably the Dowager Duchess of Athole, who seconded her noble husband's endeavours in every way she could, and by many prizes encouraged the men of Dunkeld to prepare for the Grand Match as the great event of the year. Of many whose gifts were cheerfully bestowed on the curlers these gifts are now their memorials. The Countess of Breadalbane, the Countess of Home, Lady Jane Hamilton, Lady Mary Nisbet-Hamilton, Lady Murray Thriepland, the Hon. Mrs Stewart Mackenzie, Mrs Dundas of Arniston, Mrs Aytoun of Inchdairnie, and many others did virtuously by endowing clubs with silver and gold, and their deeds are remembered with gratitude. And surely Rosslyn and all the curling brotherhood will ever cherish with affection the memory of that dear old Lady Wedderburn who excelled all the many daughters of curling by knitting with her own hands worsted vests for five rinks of the Rosslyn curlers. It was a beautiful act. In the annals of curling we know of nothing more beautiful, and if the spirit of devotion and enthusiasm of which it was the expression only lives on among our ladies, what we owe to them, and what we here thank them for, will be only the shadow of the good that curling is yet to receive from their patronage.

PROGRESS.

Endowed by its founders with a sound constitution, the health of the Royal Club through the fifty years of its existence has never given its friends any cause for anxiety. The club has never "lookit ahint it." It was thought by some that its founders were visionaries, and the author of the first advertisement regarding it was evidently doubtful about anything good coming out of it. The success of the club has, however, exceeded the most sanguine expectation, and no institution of the kind, we may safely say, ever prospered in a more remarkable manner. The steady growth of its popularity in the various counties may be seen at a glance by the following table, shewing the affiliated clubs in each county and the number of members at the

institution of the Grand Club and at the close of each
decade of its history :—

PROGRESS OF THE ROYAL CLUB.

Counties.	1838.		1848.		1858.		1868.		1878.		1888.		Population at last Census.	Percentage per 1000.
	No. of Clubs.	No. of Members.	No. of Clubs.	No. of Members.	No. of Clubs.	No. of Members.	No. of Clubs.	No. of Members.	No. of Clubs.	No. of Members.	No. of Clubs.	No. of Members.		
Aberdeen	..	..	..	..	1	57	1	43	3	91	14	526	267,990	1·96
Argyll	..	..	..	..	2	71	4	141	6	209	8	270	76,468	3·53
Ayr	7	142	26	1069	30	868	26	816	20	582	14	423	217,519	1·97
Banff	..	..	..	..	..	..	..	..	..	..	1	49	62,736	·78
Berwick	..	..	..	..	4	185	..	223	7	275	13	520	35,392	14·60
Bute	..	..	..	..	..	..	1	54	1	55	1	68	17,657	3·85
Caithness	..	..	..	..	..	..	..	..	..	..	1	35	38,865	·90
Clackmannan	..	..	5	211	7	268	5	297	5	247	5	308	25,680	11·99
Dumbarton	..	..	4	76	13	371	17	416	16	573	18	670	75,333	8·80
Dumfries	..	..	..	..	7	208	6	268	7	251	8	369	76,140	4·84
Edinburgh	4	159	15	610	23	957	25	1111	24	1609	27	1588	389,164	3·56
Elgin	..	..	..	..	1	38	2	56	7	206	8	263	43,788	6·69
Fife	3	104	18	740	32	1226	40	1537	42	1632	45	1887	171,931	10·97
Forfar	..	..	4	164	10	430	10	499	20	761	27	911	266,360	3·53
Haddington	1	21	2	96	6	254	10	368	12	409	13	445	38,502	11·55
Inverness	..	..	1	30	1	65	3	110	7	196	10	323	90,454	3·57
Kincardine	..	..	..	..	1	36	1	34	2	68	3	112	31,464	3·24
Kinross	2	142	2	146	2	148	2	107	5	183	5	190	6,697	28·37
Kirkcudbright	..	..	2	79	5	138	5	182	4	160	3	111	42,127	2·63
Lanark	3	162	10	494	34	1495	25	1122	23	1047	36	1627	904,412	1·79
Linlithgow	3	86	8	314	11	420	13	420	9	234	6	240	43,510	5·51
Nairn	..	..	..	..	..	..	..	..	..	..	1	32	10,455	3·06
Orkney	..	..	..	..	..	..	..	..	..	..	..	..	32,044	0·00
Peebles	..	..	1	42	6	152	6	198	11	353	8	299	13,822	21·63
Perth	5	77	37	1289	53	1815	63	2243	73	2568	93	3568	129,007	27·65
Renfrew	..	..	10	380	25	906	28	1085	29	1125	27	1060	263,374	4·02
Ross (and Cromarty)	..	..	..	..	1	11	3	77	4	112	5	209	78,547	2·66
Roxburgh	..	..	1	24	6	283	10	417	9	390	11	600	53,442	11·22
Selkirk	..	..	1	41	3	87	2	87	3	111	4	188	25,564	7·35
Shetland	..	..	..	..	..	..	..	..	..	..	1	27	29,705	·90
Stirling	..	..	15	543	27	904	37	1184	39	1285	43	1556	112,443	13·83
Sutherland	..	..	..	..	..	..	..	..	..	..	2	59	23,370	6·12
Wigton	..	..	..	..	1	42	2	117	6	325	4	248	38,611	6·42
Total	28	893	162	6348	310	11,413	354	13,050	393	14,418	465	18,647	3,735,573	7·15

It must be kept in mind that our table simply represents
the curling connection of the Royal Club. If we deduct
women and children and those who by youth, age, or
infirmity are unable to "owrehog a channel-stane," and if we
remember that there are many who enjoy curling without
being connected with any clubs, and many clubs which are
not connected with the Royal, we may confidently say that
of those who are possible curlers 10 per cent. or thereabouts
do curl, and that of the curlers of Scotland 80 per cent. are
connected with the Royal Club. It is apparent from the

table that there has been a steady growth of the curling cult throughout the country, due in great measure to the Royal Club. Some of the older curling counties, by reason of their inconvenient situation, have never been properly got hold of. The same reason accounts for a falling membership in Wigton and Kirkcudbright. Difficulties about the Grand Match to which we have referred may, but ought not, to account for a diminution of clubs and members in Ayr and Renfrew. The decline noticeable in Peebles and Linlithgow is to us quite unaccountable. We are certain that curling is not going back in any of these counties. It is satisfactory to find that in twenty-six of the thirty-three Scottish counties the Royal Club has made steady progress. Kinross, as we might expect, stands first on our list. Nearly every one who can curl does curl in that happy little county. Then comes Perth, worthy of its old traditions. The small proportion in such counties as Lanark, Edinburgh, Forfar, Renfrew, and Aberdeen is due to the existence of their large towns, where the facilities for curling are few, and the landward curling of these counties must be understood to be much larger than the table brings out. What the Royal Club ought to be most thankful for is the extent to which it has been permitted to break new ground and to introduce the game where it was before unknown, or to revive it where it had for long been forgotten. In ARGYLL, which is new ground, we have ten clubs,* the oldest and the strongest being at *Oban*—" the Brighton of the West Highlands." Specially in the north of Scotland has the Royal Club's influence been felt. At the close of the last period we found the game struggling onward without much success in Forfar. There are now no less than twenty-seven clubs in that county. In ABERDEEN, where there were none, we have now fifteen clubs, with the Duke of Fife, the Earl of Aberdeen, the Marquis of Huntly, Sir W. Cunliffe Brooks, A. H. Farquharson of Invercauld, Lord Sempill, the Earl of

---

* As Lochawe is not supposed to have been frozen over more than once in a century, it is interesting to note that in 1879 the *Lochaweside* Club curled for several successive days in mid-channel, between Taycreggan and Portsonachan Hotels. The previous time Lochawe was frozen was in 1815.

March, the Earl of Kintore, Colonel Ferguson of Pitfour, and many other gentlemen (not to speak of ladies) who are devoting their attention to the progress of the game. The towns of *Aberdeen* and *Peterhead* are too near the sea to allow of as much curling as is needed to satisfy the curlers there; but in the more inland districts they have it in abundance, and share their enjoyment with the shoreward curlers. We may infer this from the delightful sketch of a curling scene at *Pitfour* by the secretary of the *Pitfour* Club—William Ainslie, who carried North with him the curling enthusiasm and ability for which the Ainslie family were noted in the Rosslyn Club, originating the Pitfour Club in 1883, and in many other ways doing much to popularise curling "Aberdeen awa'."

"On Hogmanay night, the last night of 1886, a great gathering took place on Pitfour Lake. Hundreds of torches lighted with petroleum, and oil lamps, used during the herring-fishing season for gutting herrings at night, were hung all over the lake, and one at each end of every rink. Curling began at eight o'clock and finished at twelve, after which a procession of torch-bearers was formed, headed by a piper, curling and patriotic songs were sung, healths proposed, then a bonfire was made and all unburned torches thrown on it. The lake during the night was covered with hundreds of skaters. The scene was at the same time weird, grand, and thoroughly enjoyable. A special train in early morning took off the Peterhead portion of the skaters and curlers. Such a scene was never known to have taken place in Aberdeenshire before."

In BANFF county there is one club, and it is not surprising that the liberal donor of our National Portrait Gallery —J. R. Findlay of Aberlour—is here a liberal supporter of our national game.

A member of the Doune Club, writing to Dr Cairnie in 1833, says (*Essay*, p. 87):—"The game is, I believe, not known about *Fochabers*, in ELGINSHIRE, and perhaps has not yet been practised so far to the northward." Now there is a capital club at *Fochabers*, with the Earl of March as patron, and J. P. Gordon of Cairnfield president. The town of *Elgin* has a large club, with the Duke of Fife at its head. *Strathspey* has given us some of our best point players, and has the Dowager-Countess of Seafield as patroness. Besides these, there are five other clubs able to give a good account of themselves, and in alliance with the noble families in their districts. We have in the county of INVERNESS ten clubs, where there were none at the time the Royal was instituted. These have mostly owed their origin to sheep-farmers from the South, as in the case of *Laggan*, to which we have referred, and *Glengarry*, where George Malcolm, about twenty-five years ago, got some of his South countrymen who had settled in the district brought together, and, under the patronage of the late Edward Ellice, M.P., started a club. Lord Lovat is patron of the *Fort-Augustus* Club, and *Lochaber* has Lochiel for its head, with a curling-pond on the western slope of Ben Nevis nearly 2000 feet above sea-level. Curling in the county town, Inverness, was set a-going about the time the Royal Club was instituted, and the *Inverness* Club dates back to 1841. On February 22, 1843, the curlers met on a small pond near Tomnahurich, and as the first stone went booming along the ice, a loud cheer burst from the spectators assembled to witness the new sport, startling the echoes of the Hill of Fairies with sounds never heard before in that picturesque and secluded spot. We next hear of the curlers playing their first bonspiel for beef and greens on Loch-na-shannis, or the Whispering Loch. Then we find them at Culcabock; but where to find them now it would be difficult to say, although their records have been in our hands for perusal. Instead of requiring a surgical operation to get a joke into the skull of the Inverness Club, it would require one to get anything serious out of it. That club has, however, lifted a burden off our mind. When we left the ancient minute-books and entered the Caledonian period, we found a painful sameness about the club records—they had all lost individuality, like the curling-stones; but when we took up the minute-book of the *Inverness* Club, we felt that it was still possible, under the iron reign of uniformity, to have freshness, originality, and variety. This volume is full of "quips, and cranks, and jollities." Everything that is seriously worth recording is studiously left out, and *Ye Palladium of ye Curling Club of Inverness*, lettered in gold and bound in green morocco, contains

"Poetic effusions of no mean order, learned dissertations on abstruse subjects, free-hand sketches of prominent members, and gems of thought sparkling among the dust."

Secretary P., like other secretaries, threatens to resign, but is prevailed on to continue in office another year, whereupon Brother B., while the secretary is engaged in "assisting the president to mix another tumbler," enters in the minute a reflection on office-bearers in general, and their ingratitude, as shewn in not presenting their clubs with prizes, in return for the honour done to them. The hint has a good effect, a medal is presented, and won with the excellent score of "six." The record then says :—

"Few more extraordinary matches have ever been witnessed. During the play the wind blew so strongly from the south that no one but a native could keep his feet, and, from another cause, few even of the natives could do that. The thanks of the club are due to the doctor of a neighbouring asylum, who kindly allowed the inmates to fraternise with and assist the members of the club in the above match. The inmates, it was gratifying to observe, had a most intelligent appreciation of the proceedings of the curlers."

In the evening, when the business is over, the poet-laureate sings a song "of his own making," entitled *The Manly Curler*, of which these are some stanzas :—

"Behold him poised on the crampit serenely,
With one leg before and the other behind;
He envies not Victoria her sceptre so queenly,
His sceptre's a boulder, made fit to his mind.

"With impetuous velocity he hurls the huge granite;
Its roarings, resounding, make nature alarmed,
Till reaching the tee it reposes upon it,
As if its own music its fury had charmed.

"A pipe of dimensions appropriate he smoketh,
Its aromatic vapour incenses the view,
While to revive his vitals he openly evoketh
The powerful assistance of pure mountain dew.

. . . .

"Behold him returning in a homeward direction,
A delicate contentment pervading his breast,
To his couch he retireth with the proud reflection
That at Scotia's great game he has—done his best."

In vain we listen for the usual applause. The criticism which followed this Gaelic Tupper's effort simply resulted in breaking up the meeting. These extracts shew how much humour there is at Inverness, and how pleasantly *Ye Pat-*

ladium of ye Curling Club there breaks up the monotony of the minute-books of this period. In the counties north of Inverness—ROSS, SUTHERLAND, and CAITHNESS—we have not many clubs, but we have broken ground in them all, and seen John Frost give *John o' Groat's* a hearty curler's grip. The oldest club beyond Inverness is the *Golspie* Club, instituted by Robert Hill in 1850. Its first contest for a Royal medal was with Inverness in 1855, when the two clubs met at Logie, in Ross-shire. Southerners may form an idea of the difficulties with which the men of the North have to contend when they are told that the Golspie curlers on that occasion started at 4 A.M. in the midst of a heavy snowstorm, crossed the Meikle Ferry in an open boat at great risk, the ferry being covered with loose masses of ice, won their match, recrossed the same dangerous ferry, "stanes an' besoms an' a'," and reached home about midnight, when Ben Bhraggie was made to echo back the sound of their victory. The *Caberfeidh*, from which Dingwall and other clubs have branched off, was founded in 1855 by Frank Harper, a native of Tweedside, who long remained the leading spirit of the club, and skipped his rink or sung his song—*The Bold Caberfeidh*, with equal success. Harper and his brethren had an unhappy experience in the early years of their curling. One day they left their stones on the "Old River" pool, where they used to play, and when they returned from refreshing themselves they found that the old pool had been doing the same, and that the stones had gone to the bottom, from which it was impossible to recover them. Their patroness, Sir Walter Scott's "Heiress of Kintail," the late Hon. Mrs Stewart Mackenzie of Seaforth, saved the curlers from further mishap by giving them a pond in the Seaforth policies at Brahan, and to this good lady the club were indebted for many favours. The Duke of Sutherland, Viscount Tarbert, Sir Kenneth Mackenzie of Gairloch, Colonel Davidson of Tulloch, Major Randle Jackson of Swordale, Sutherland of Skibo, M'Kenzie of Allangrange, and many other gentlemen of influence are among the patrons of curling in these further northern counties.

The game has now taken a firm hold in them all and
become popular. We have noticed its progress in the
North more fully because it is the special triumph of the
Royal Club to have secured for the game a Highland
welcome, and in this way completed its claim to nationality.
Now that the enthusiasm of the Gael has been evoked we
may be sure that curling has a future before it in this
country that will throw the past into the shade, and as
the Royal Club has done so much for the North the club
may depend upon the North to do great things in the future
development and progress of the national game.

We do not forget that in the North we have one county
where the sound of curling is unheard. The Orcadian or
the Shetlander views Scotland like the Millport minister,
who was in the habit of praying for " the Great Cumbrae
and the Little Cumbrae, and the adjacent islands of Great
Britain and Ireland." ORKNEY is really more *furth of
Scotland* than some of the places to be included under that
description. Still, it is not creditable that there should
be such a sad blank where Copinsha in early times furnished " in great plentie excellent stones for the game called
curling " (*vide* p. 88). Is Orkney to be our man-in-the-
moon because Bishop Grahame was accused of curling on
the Lord's day? Or is it that John Frost fears the *mal-de-
mer* of the Pentland Firth? That cannot be, for he has
crossed Sumburgh-roost, which we know to be more
formidable, and *Ultima Thule* has its club as a memorial
of his visit—a *peerie* club, but a plucky one, for it sent no
less a person than Sheriff Thoms to represent it at our
Jubilee Dinner. The Orcadians, we guess, are afraid for the
staple trade of the islands, for they know that the curler's
delight is to *crack an egg*, and that to gain his end he never
scruples to remove a *clockin' hen*. Alas, poor Orkney!
Who shall first pity her solitary plight, waken up the old
man of Hoy with the channel-stane's roar, and establish the
St *Magnus* Curling Club in the shadow of the old cathedral
pile?

THE OUTLOOK.

With such a record to look back upon, we may surely look hopefully forward, certain that the Royal Club, whose history we have traced as the history of the past fifty years of curling, will continue to be identified with the development and progress of the game. It has more than fulfilled the purpose of its founders, which was to bring order out of prevailing confusion, and to establish a system of uniform laws and regulations which would command the respect and obedience of the whole curling brotherhood. It has advanced the game in other countries, as we shall presently see, and in our own Scotland has made it more truly national, attracting to it the patronage of Royalty, the support of the nobility, and the influence of the ladies in a most remarkable degree. But there is much yet to be done; for with the development of curling new points emerge which require careful attention and wise settlement, while the bond of such a central institution as the Royal Club is needed and appreciated all the more as the game is taken up in countries far apart from each other. Curling cannot get on without the Royal Club. Like many good things, we should only understand its value by the loss of it. It shall never be lost if those who have it in their

FIG. 67. A. DAVIDSON SMITH, C.A.
(From a photograph by John Moffat, Edinburgh.)

keeping in time to come are loyal to the founders and supporters of the club, and if the same spirit animates them which is found among those who are the club's office-bearers and workers at the present time. We could not have a better secretary than the present holder of the office, Adam Davidson Smith, C.A. A man of sterling principle and excellent business habits, it is no wonder that every member of the "Royal" has implicit confidence in his administration, and that under his management the club has made extraordinary progress. Every curler who has visited our secretary at his office, where he sits surrounded by the gabions of ancient curling and the portraits of distinguished curlers, ancient and modern, can testify how ready he is to give counsel in difficulty and to listen to all who have any suggestions to make which concerns the welfare of the club. His bright, genial manner and his curling enthusiasm always make such a visit a pleasure either to the home curler or to the brother from across the Atlantic, who always receives a specially hearty welcome at 29 St Andrew Square.

Our present president, Lord Balfour of Burleigh, is a tower of strength. Ever animated by the spirit of his family motto—*Omne solum forti patria*—he knows what it is to "scorn delights and live laborious days," that he may advance the welfare of his country. As his patriotism has led him to set the highest value on the national game, he will not spare himself in the service of the Royal Club. For vice-presidents in our jubilee year we had one of the best and most esteemed curlers of the west of Scotland—J. Clark Forrest; and a grand-nephew of our national bard, Robert Burns Begg, who has not only made Lochleven tell us all it knew about ancient curling, but has lately given to Lochleven fresh interest for curlers and others by telling them all that is known about the old loch and its connection with the beautiful but ill-fated Mary Queen of Scots.* Suc-

---

* *History of Lochleven Castle, with Details of Imprisonment and Escape of Mary Queen of Scots.* By Robert Burns Begg, F.S.A. Scot. Kinross: George Barnet. 1887.

U

ceeding these we have W. M'Inroy of Lude, who has done much in England for the curling cause, and Colonel Menzies, the worthy and enthusiastic president of Glasgow North Woodside; while on our committee we have Sir James Gibson-Craig, who has always taken an active interest in the work of the Royal Club; T. S. Aitchison, whose good humour and good sense make him ever welcome at our meetings, and who as "Maltini" of the "Monks" contributes some good songs to our *Annual*; the Rev. A. J. Murray of Eddleston, a typical clerical curler; Josiah Livingston, who has long and faithfully served the club; and Robert Knox, one of the famous Alloa players (all of whom have at one time or other been vice-presidents); Dr White, and Messrs Breingan, Gilmour, Kerr (Cumbernauld), and Ure. It was not to any trifling cause that the founders of the Royal Club gave their nights and days, and that so many good men and true devoted so much attention during the past fifty years of the club's career. Those who serve the club now—many of them hard-wrought business and professional men—are not thoughtlessly spending their time to no purpose. All have been working, as all are working now, in the firm conviction that by doing what they can for the prosperity of curling they are doing what they can to advance the welfare of their own and of other nations, and to hasten the triumph of the brotherhood of man. Fifty years have now come and gone since the twig was planted which was to become the shelter and support of our ain game. How it was planted and watered and pruned, and how by faithful tending the sapling developed into a tree, sending its roots deep down into Scottish soil, and extending its branches to far-off lands, this chapter has been written to shew. It remains for those who follow us, and we trust them without misgiving, by earnest attention and watchful care to foster the growth and further the usefulness of the Royal Caledonian Curling Club, that it may continue to be the life-tree of curling, uniting, as root, stem, and branches, Scotland and all curling countries furth of Scotland in one unbroken brotherhood.

CHAPTER III.

CURLING FURTH OF SCOTLAND.

THE introduction of curling into countries furth of Scotland has always been the work of Scotsmen. While other nationalities have readily taken up the game, its progress has also chiefly depended on Scotsmen. At one place in Switzerland, 6000 feet above sea-level, curling, we believe, has been introduced. But we hear of no club having been formed in that country; and where no club is formed, curling never seems to succeed. It is only by tracing the various clubs which have been formed that we can give the history of the game furth of Scotland. This chapter will therefore be found to be mainly an account of foreign clubs. Without any expectation of permanent results, the channel-stane has been abroad on one or two holiday expeditions. In the Paris International Exhibition of 1867 a pair of curling-stones, made of fine porphyry, appeared in the department set apart for games of sport and amusement. They were sent there by William Chambers of Glenormiston, who was then Lord Provost of Edinburgh, and were set in a glass case with this explanation :—

"Pierres à Jouer sur la Glace
("Curling-stones.")
"Faites de porphyre de Glenormiston, dans le comté de Peebles en Ecosse, la propriété de l'honorable William Chambers, Lord Provost d'Edimbourg.
"On emploie ces pierres au jeu Ecossais national qu'on appelle curling, ou on les fait glisser sur la glace vers un but, en cherchant à les faire arriver le plus près de ce but qu'il est possible."

The stones were presented to the Emperor Napoleon III. at the close of the Exhibition, but where they are now we cannot say. Who knows but that Prince Bismarck may have annexed them along with Alsace and Lorraine, and that they may yet turn up somewhere in the Low Country, to prove that curling not only originated there, but was played with the most advanced style of implements? This fanciful appearance certainly did not have any practical result in France, and when the Comtesse de la Gasparin, in translating one of "John Strathesk's" stories, rendered *curling club* into *club des barbiers*, she no doubt did full justice to the French idea of the game.

The following table indicates as nearly as possible the present distribution and membership of curling clubs beyond Scotland:—*

				Brought forward,	63	2986
1. England,		53	1607	7. Ontario Province,	99	3051
2. Ireland,		3	64	8. Manitoba,	14	700
3. Norway,		1	15	9. Nova Scotia,	7	287
4. Russia,		1	26	10. Newfoundland,	3	89
5. New Zealand,		6	193	11. New Brunswick,	3	155
6. Canadian Branch, or Quebec Province,		19	1081	12. United States (Grand National Club),	40	800
Carry forward,		63	2986	Total,	229	8068

ENGLAND.—No one has ever suggested that curling had its origin in England, or that it was known there previous

---

* Clubs under Nos. 1, 2, 3, 4, 5, 6, 9, 10, and two (*Yonkers* and *St Andrew's*) under No. 12 are in full association with the Royal Caledonian Club—in all, 75 clubs, with a membership of 3414, which, added to the Scottish list, make the total number of clubs now affiliated with the Royal 540, and the total number of members 22,061. Nos. 7 and 8, Associated Provinces. Nos. 9, 10, and 11, with a few more clubs, have lately been united in what is called the Maritime Province, which is also in association with the Royal Club, and of which E. P. Whitaker, St John's, New Brunswick, is secretary and treasurer. No. 12, the Grand National Club, is an independent association, but a very friendly correspondence is kept up between it and the mother club—the Royal.

to its introduction from Scotland. Neither Rastell,* who is the oldest authority, nor Strutt,† who is the fullest and the best, in describing the rural amusements and recreations of the English people, ever refers to curling. We have never heard of a curling-stone of the oldest type having been found across the border. The only discovery of any stone of the second type of which we are aware is that made by Canon Wannop of Haddington, who informs us that when he was a boy he was accustomed to bathe in the river *Line*, in the north of Cumberland, and that one day he came upon a number of old boulders, oblong in shape, with iron handles battered into them. He was informed, on inquiring about their use, that they were called *curling-stones*, and that the rector, when he came to the parish, had introduced the game, the stones having been taken from the river and played with in their natural state. The rector was then (1836) alive at the age of ninety, and as he was quite a young man when he was appointed, the introduction of the game there carries us back to about the year 1776. Pennant, it will be remembered, made his famous tour a few years previous to this, and found curling a favourite sport in the Border, while (*vide* p. 56) it was "unknown in England." It is not difficult, therefore, to trace a connection between this earliest English report of the game and the curling of the Scottish borderers. That curling was at that time practised in the north of England may also be inferred from an Ossianic description of a celebrated bonspiel between England and Scotland, played at Kirtlebridge in the year 1795, in which the Cumberland rector may probably have taken a part.‡

From the northern counties curling seems to have taken a hop-step-and-leap journey to London, for Ramsay in 1811 says:

---

* *The Pastyme of the People. The Chronycles of dyverse Realms, and specyally of the Realm of England.* By John Rastell. 1529.

† *The Sports and Pastimes of the People of England, including the Rural and Domestic Recreations, May Games, Mummeries, Shows, Processions, Pageants, and Pompous Spectacles, from the earliest to the present time.* 1801.

‡ Sir R. Broun, in whose *Memorabilia* (pp. 68-69) the poem is quoted, ascribes it to Dr Clapperton, the Lochmaben antiquary, and says it was found among the MSS. of the late W. D. W. H. Somerville of Whitecroft.

"Within these few years *curling* has even found its way to the capital of the British Empire. There, the first essay was made upon the New River; but the crowd of spectators, attracted by such a novel spectacle, becoming very great, the ice threatened to give way, and the curlers were with reluctance compelled to desist."

The wonder is that curling in a city where so many Scotsmen were collected was then such a novel spectacle. Both before and after that time we hear of visitations of King Frost,* which prove that London of old time was even better off for ice than Edinburgh. The neglect of Scotsmen to cultivate the game in the Metropolis was discreditable. It is not the way of their countrymen to abandon a cause for such a reason; but those who made this first essay seem to have taken fright, and we hear no more of curling in London till the winter of 1846-47 or 1847-48, when the "novel spectacle" was again witnessed. On this occasion, as we have been told by Sir James Gibson-Craig of Riccarton, his father—the late Sir William Gibson-Craig, then M.P. for Edinburgh, and the Hon. Fox Maule, M.P. (afterwards Lord Dalhousie), both keen curlers, with a few other Scotsmen, started a game on the Serpentine, but the curious Londoners again crowded in upon the curlers to such an extent that they had to relinquish play. At the great Exhibition held in the Crystal Palace in 1851, a pair of Ailsa Craig curling-stones made an appearance more practical in its results than that of the Peebles *porphyry* at Paris, if we may judge by the fact that a *Crystal Palace* curling club now exists. Each of these stones weighed 40 lb., and measured $10\frac{3}{4} \times 5\frac{1}{2}$

---

* In 1684 (January to February) the Thames was so frozen that coaches plied from Westminster to the Temple and elsewhere to and fro as in the streets, and for some time there was a carnival of sleighing, skating, bull-baiting, horse-racing, &c., with shops furnished with all kinds of commodities on the ice.
"When maids grow modest, the Dissenting crew
Become all loyal, the false-hearted true,
Then you may probably, and not till then,
Expect in England such a frost again."
Spite of *Errapater's* prophecy, a similar frost occurred in 1739-40, and again in 1788-89, when there was a regular Bartholomew Fair on the Thames from Putney Bridge to Rediff for seven weeks. Another great frost occurred December 27, 1813, to February 5, 1814, when a grand street on the ice, lined on either side with booths of all descriptions, extended from Blackfriars Bridge to London Bridge.

inches. One sole was hollow, the other level. They were made by John Guthrie, mason, Dalmellington, and cost, with handles, £3. They were meant to represent the ordinary shape, weight, and price of a curling-stone of the period. Mr Cassels, the Royal Club secretary, was asked to shew cause why such articles should find a place in the "Exhibition of the Industry of all Nations."

"This he did" (according to the *Annual* 1852, p. 207) "by setting forth the number of curlers connected with the Royal Club, and those unconnected with it. The former he stated at 12,000, and the latter on a moderate estimate at other 12,000—together, 24,000 curlers, who took an active part in the game. Each curler required to be provided with at least one pair of curling-stones, which, upon an average, were worth £2, 10s.—in all, a capital of £60,000, invested in curling-stones alone. The manufacture of these stones was, in a great measure, confined to tradesmen throughout Scotland, and to a great extent they were made by masons and others during that part of the year when there was little employment."

John M'Diarmid, in one of his articles in the *Dumfries Courier*,* tells how an Englishman, Mr Hill, Inspector of Prisons, when he made his official visit to Dumfriesshire in the winter of 1836, found both the Convener of the County (Mr Leny of Dalswinton) and the Sheriff (Sir Thomas Kirkpatrick, Bart. of Capenoch) engaged in curling with their tenants, friends, and neighbours. Mr Hill greatly enjoyed the sight, and was so impressed with the moral influence of the game that, when he returned to England, he embodied a glowing *éloge* on curling in his official report.

The *Sussex Express* a year or two after this announced that Sir Charles Lamb had introduced the "manly but novel game" into the district, and had played a match with Lord Antrim, six men a side. Mr I'Anson, when he settled at Malton, took a few pairs of stones with him, and had a game now and then with his stud-grooms, who had seen curling in Scotland. In the *Annual* for 1855 a touching reference is made to the *Cameron* Club at Portsmouth, which had lost many of its members in the Crimea, and the secretary of which was at that time absent with his regi-

---

* Reprinted in *Chambers's Journal*, April 28, 1838.

ment at Sebastopol. In a few places, especially where a Scotch family or two may happen to be found, the sound of the channel-stane is occasionally heard; but the progress and extent of curling in England, as well as the location of the Scotch element in the country, may best be inferred from the following list of curling clubs now affiliated with the Royal Club, and the dates of their institution:—

CLUBS IN ENGLAND.

Club	Year	Club	Year	Club	Year
Barrow-in-Furness Caledonian,	1878	Derwentwater,	1874	Newcastle-on-Tyne,	1843
Belle Vue,	1879	Durham,	1880	Newcastle Tyneside,	1879
Birkenhead Mersey,	1879	Harrington,	1871	North Staffordshire,	1872
Birmingham Caledonian,	1881	Harrogate,	1871	Preston,	1871
Blackburn Rose & Thistle,	1879	Hepburn and Jarrow,	1885	Sheffield,	1861
Bolton,	1884	Leeds,	1820	Southport,	1879
Bradford,	1810	Leeds Rose and Thistle,	1886	Spennymoor & Tudhoe,	1887
Cleator Moor,	1879	Liverpool,	1859	Sunderland Caledonian,	1885
Crystal Palace,	1870	Manchester Caledonian,	1856	Whitehaven,	1884
Darlington Caledonian,	1860	Manchester Trafford,	1884	Wigan and Haigh,	1861
		Middlesbrough Caledonian,	1879	Workington,	1875

The oldest of these is the *Leeds* Club, but as no records were kept till it was joined to the Royal in 1866, we cannot say much about it. The late Adam Brown was for twenty-five years president. The *Wigan* Club had, in 1866, as many as 168 members on its roll, much of its early success being due to its first president, James Wood of *Haigh*, factor to the patron of the club, the Earl of Crawford and Balcarres. The first English club to affiliate with the Royal was the *Liverpool* Club, which is perhaps the largest and most successful in England. In their early days the Liverpool curlers used to meet at the sign of the "Green Man Still," then in the outskirts of the town, and proceed to curl on St Domingo Pit. The pit is now filled up and built upon, and the "Green Man" has become the "Prince of Wales," in the heart of the city. The club was called *Liverpool and Everton* until Everton was merged in Liverpool. The curlers, on their return, used to repair to *Everton Coffee-House*, where mine host, who bore the curling cognomen of Halliday, regaled them with a beverage more potent and more national than coffee. The Liverpool Club had a famous match with *Manchester* at Haydock Lodge, Newton, in 1853, which was honoured by being made the subject of a sketch in the *Illustrated London News*. The Earl of Sefton, the constant friend and patron of the club, about 1850 gave the curlers the use of an ornamental pond in Croxteth Park, and frequently entertained them at their spiels with victuals and old baronial ale. His successor, the present Earl, did the same. In 1862 he was elected president of the Royal Caledonian Club, the first English nobleman who filled the chair. The Royal Club honoured Liverpool by holding their annual meeting there in 1868, when they were most hospitably received. This meeting gave an impetus to the game, and when the corporation granted them permission to curl in Shiel Park the curlers were in high spirits at their prospects. At their first outing on the pond, however, the skaters in a body besieged the rink, and disputed the right of the curlers to appropriate any part of the ice to themselves. The parks being public property, an appeal to the corporation was in vain, and the curlers had to retire discomfited. Colonel Bourne of Rainhill, having kindly granted them ground, they then constructed a pond within easy access by rail; their membership increased; they were able to invite their neighbours to a friendly match, and in their own house, by the aid of a nice little stove, to enjoy a glass of the curler's auxiliary. That their experience had not taught them the beauty of the golden rule is, however, evident from this minute:—

"July 14, 1872.—The secretary was instructed to write to Mr Roby, Rainhill, respectfully to request him to keep his duck off the curling-pond."

The members of the Liverpool Club occasionally give a ball, and their annual dinner, under their excellent president, J. Shankland, brings together as many jolly curlers as you can hope to meet furth of Scotland.

THE GLACIARIUM.—The most important contribution which our English friends have made to the development of curling is the construction of the *Glaciarium*. The *North British Advertiser* of December 31, 1842, contains a notice of a "miniature Alpine lake," 70 feet long × 50 wide, the composition of which had been laid down in London by a Mr Kirke, who claimed to be the inventor of it. The 'Glaciarium,' as it was called, had been tried by Sir W. Newton and some members of the Skating Club, and pronounced satisfactory, "the ice having a cracking sound as the skaters glided over it or performed their 'spread-eagles' and 'back-strokes.'" How long the skaters used this "lake" we are not in a position to say, and we do not hear of curlers having tried it. In the *Graphic* of 24th March 1877 we have a sketch of a curling match played on the Rusholme Ice Rink, Manchester. This rink was manufactured by a process which was patented at that time by Professor Gamgee as his invention. The Real Ice Co., Manchester, paid the Professor £8000 for the use of the same within a radius of ten miles of Manchester, and including building and plant—£12,000, the cost of the Rusholme Ice Rink was £20,000. Mr Hyde, secretary to Professor Gamgee, seems to have proceeded on a mission to Scotland with many testimonies from curlers in favour of the new summer-ice, and to have tried in Edinburgh and Glasgow to get up artificial rinks. He appeared at the annual meeting of the Royal Club in 1877 and laid the subject before the representatives. A letter was also read to the meeting from Professor Gamgee. The Committee of Management were entrusted with further consideration of the matter, but we hear no more of it in the Royal Club, nor of the success or failure of the Manchester Company. At *Southport*, however, a rink was laid down on Gamgee's principle, which has been the scene of many a gallant curling contest. This rink was opened on January 10, 1879, the total cost having been over £30,000. On February 5, half-a-dozen English curling clubs had a spirited competition for a cup, which was won by Liverpool. Since then the great event at the Glaciarium has always been the tournament for the Holden Challenge Shield, value 50 guineas, presented by Edward Holden, Esq., for competition every half-year. We give the last ties in each of the competitions:—

	Winner.	Runner-up.	Majority.	No. of rinks entered.
Sept. 1879,	Manchester Caledonian	v. Glasgow Lilybank,	8	13
April 1880,	Liverpool	v. Alloa Prince of Wales,	1	7
Oct. 1880,	Alloa Prince of Wales	v. Liverpool,	6	17
April 1881,	Newcastle	v. Belle Vue,	3	17
Oct. 1881,	Glasgow Lilybank	v. Belle Vue,	15	21
April 1882,	Sheffield	v. Glasgow Lilybank,	1	22
Oct. 1882,	Belle Vue	v. Manchester Caledonian,	3	24
Oct. 1883,	Hamilton Douglas and Clydesdale	v. Cameion,*	3	24
April 1884,	Alloa Prince of Wales	v. Southport,	1	21
Oct. 1884,	Manchester Caledonian	v. Southport,	13	19
July 1885,	Bolton	v. Drummond Castle,	2	24
Mar. 1886,	Bolton	v. Manchester,	2	24
Nov. 1886,	Southport	v. Manchester Caledonian,	7	23
Mar. 1887,	Hamilton	v. Dall,	4	25
Nov. 1887,	Alloa Prince of Wales	v. Liverpool,	12	25
April 1888,	Dall	v. Dunkeld,	20	18
Nov. 1888,	Belle Vue	v. Alloa Prince of Wales,†	3	29
April 1889,	Bolton	v. Belle Vue,	3	19

In ten of the eighteen Southport competitions English clubs have won first place, and of the thirty-six in the final ties fifteen are Scottish clubs. The *Alloa Prince of Wales* Club has done honour to the name of our Royal patron, by three times carrying off the shield from this curling Wimbledon, while on two occasions this club was second, and on another third. *Bolton* has also three times won the shield, thanks mainly to the redoubtable skip M'Nabb, whose rink was on each occasion composed of the same players.

In recognition of the great benefit conferred on curling by the Glaciarium, the Royal Caledonian Club decided to hold its annual meeting at Southport in July 1885. The competition for the Holden Shield was fixed to come off at the same time, and several other valuable prizes were offered. Mr Nightingale, the excellent manager of the Glaciarium, and the English curlers made every preparation to give the Scotsmen a hearty reception, and as a result the Southport meeting was one of the most successful ever held by the

* In the course of playing this tie the Hamilton men (J. Clark Forrest, skip) scored 8 shots at one end.
† "The best contested and most brilliant exposition of the popular Scottish pastime ever witnessed at the Glaciarium."—*Southport Guardian*, November 10, 1888.

Royal Club. The excellence of the ice and of the English play more than astonished our Northern representatives, and the hospitality shewn to them by the Southern curlers was unbounded. To crown all, a complimentary dinner, "essentially a Scotch one," was given to the Scottish delegates by the Southport Club in the Prince of Wales Hotel, at which over 200 were present. The Mayor of Southport extended to the Royal Club a cordial welcome, and Mr Josiah Livingston, who presided at the Southport meeting, made an eloquent reply, the whole proceedings being characterised by the utmost enthusiasm and good-feeling.

John Frost, it seems, is to have his revenge on the English curlers for wresting his patent out of his hands. As we write, we are informed that, after a loss of £25,000, the burden of which has mainly to be borne by Mr Holden, the Glaciarium is being dismantled, the company being in process of liquidation. Many will join with regret in the lament of Mr M'Inroy, who has always taken a great interest in the scheme:—

> "Alas! on Southport ice no more
> Shall sound again the curlers' roar;
> The song of 'Nightingale' is hushed,
> And Holden's hopes for ever crushed."

Where there is sufficient frost such an institution is not required. As the Wigan secretary expresses it, "the Glaciarium slackens the interest in outdoor curling, while its expense has a tendency to bring the game within certain social limits." There is a *natural* want about it of which the curler is conscious, even when the air is bracing and the ice is good. On the other hand, where there is little frost and little facility for outdoor curling when frost comes, the Glaciarium is an undoubted boon; and we hope to hear of the Southport machinery being transferred to Manchester or some larger city, so that the benefit of the remarkable invention may not be entirely lost.

IRELAND.—Curling is said to have been carried into Ireland by the Scottish colonies who were planted there so early as the reign of James I. of England. The game was, however, quite unknown in Ireland at the beginning of this century. Indeed, it cannot be said to be known much beyond the neighbourhood of Belfast at the present day. The excellent secretary of the Belfast Club, Alexander Gibb, to whom any curling enthusiasm that does exist in Ireland is very much due, gives us one good reason for the absence of the game:—

"The winters in Ireland," he says, "being so very mild, good curling ice is, and has always been, very rare; and from personal observation over a period of thirty years I may state that ice in Ireland is always six to eight days behind ice in Scotland, should frost last there so long at one time; but when thaw sets in over that country, it is certain to thaw here also at the very same time, or at all events within a few hours either way."

Not only the climate, but also the condition of the country, has been unfavourable to curling; for there never has been in that country the sympathy and cordial understanding between

"The tenant and his jolly laird,
The pastor and his flock,"

which in Scotland make curling so enjoyable. To John Cairnie belongs the credit of reviving curling in Ireland, he having prevailed on his friend, James Boomer of Seaview, *Belfast*, to make a pond in his grounds and establish a club there in 1839. Boomer, like Cairnie, kept a yacht, and often crossed, with his rink on board, to have a game at Curling Hall when there was no ice at home. On his death (1846) the club became extinct, but it was revived by Thomas Callender, a curler well known in Mauchline and the west of Scotland; Robert M'Kenzie, formerly of St John's Club, Perth; David Dunlop, who had been a Tarbolton player; and Alexander Gibb, who served his apprenticeship as a curler on Queen Mary's Loch. For some time after this the Belfast curlers had no pond, and used to meet at the "Thistle" when frost came, and drive off in an Irish car, "wi' stanes, cramps, and kowes," in search of suitable ice. They fared better the farther they went, for on one occasion, when curling not far from Belfast, the "roughs" invaded the scene, and were about to make off with everything, when a detachment of the Royal Irish fortunately hove in sight. At another time,

when, through the liberality of Messrs Callender and
M'Kenzie, they had secured a pond of their own, and
had made preparations for a good day's play, the curlers
found that a "hummle cow" had been driven through
the pond, and the ice destroyed. Mrs Boomer having
renewed the privileges of Seaview Pond, they had peace
for a time. John Hill, the gardener, was, like a true
Scot, glad to see them back, and, as Mr Gibb relates,

"John got hold of a real live Highland piper, and made him march
round and round the pond during the game, playing Scotch airs, with
now and then a touch of *The Protestant Boys, Boyne Water*, &c., so that
between the boom of the channel-stane, the shouting of the players,
and the skirl of the bagpipes, the Irish welkin rang and rang again,
and the glories of the early days of Seaview were revived."

Toward the Belfast Club all Scotsmen who knew the game,
and were within hearing, were naturally drawn, and in the
history of the club we come across some interesting characters. Here is a sketch of one whom all curlers will
recognise as a worthy—Edward Skinner, who died in 1877,
aged seventy-eight.

"He was a fine and very intelligent old man, and quite an authority on every outdoor sport. For some winters he played more by
hearing than by sight, his eyes having become dim, but his curling
keenness and vigour remained unabated. He was well known in his
younger days with the Penicuick and Currie curlers, and assisted at
the drawing of the rink diagrams in the *Annual*. Having heard there
was curling in Belfast, he left his home, Ivy Lodge, Ballyronan,
County Derry, one snell frosty morning in the winter of 1859, travelling by gig and rail some fifty miles, 'stanes an' kowe an' a',' and
reached us in the middle of a game, all ready for play. We were very
glad to see him, and we gave him a 'striking' hearty curler's welcome.
He wore a *Piper* curling coat, with the very button, Glengarry cap
with ribbon, vest, hand-embroidered in silk with curling-stones and
besoms, and had a walking-stick with 'kowe' combined—the latter
made of esparto grass and carried in his pocket. His Ailsas were
single soled, with handles of peculiar make—his own idea. He was a
good-living man, most enthusiastic and strict in carrying out the rules
of curling, and resembled the late Dr Cairnie very much in his dress
and physique."

In the winter 1878-79 there was a good deal of curling
in Ireland, and at *Clandeboye* a club was then formed, with
Lord Dufferin as president, his lordship taking the lead in
its formation. Irish curlers who have been privileged to
enjoy the hospitalities of the Castle, and to have a day's

curling on the beautiful and romantic Clandeboye Lake,
know how keen an interest the Prince of British Ambas-
sadors takes in the "roaring game." As truly can the
curlers on the St Lawrence or the Neva testify to Lord
Dufferin's personal devotion to this favourite winter sport.
No one has ever achieved greater distinction in the "bloodless art of diplomacy."

> "His rule has made the people love
> Their ruler. His viceregal days
> Have added fulness to the phrase
> Of 'gauntlet in the velvet glove.'"

Among curlers it is a matter of congratulation that one
so distinguished has done so much to advance curling both
at home and abroad,
and a special place of
honour is allotted to
Lord Dufferin among
the noble patrons of
the rink. Through
the praiseworthy ex-
ertions of William
Sibbald Johnston,
J.P., a club was
formed at Kiltonga,
Newtonards, in 1879.
These three Irish
clubs have had vari-
ous interesting con-
tests for Caledonian
medals, and they all
pay some attention
to the point game,
though no high scor-
ing is recorded. Bel-
fast has several times
been drawn against

FIG. 68. THE MARQUIS OF DUFFERIN AND AVA.
(From a photograph.)

clubs in Scotland, and its meetings with the *Ardrossan*
Club are always spoken of with great pleasure as hav-

ing been productive of genuine amusement and good-feeling.

NORWAY.—A curling club appears to have been formed in Norway in the year 1881, which, under the title of the *Elverhae* Club, was enrolled in the *Annual* of the following year, the Hon. Mrs Arbuthnott being patroness, and Amtmand Arveschang, president. From the fact that the members of the *Evenie Water* Club (Forfarshire) are enrolled as honorary members of this Norwegian club, and that the members of the Elverhae Club are enrolled as honorary members of Evenie Water, we infer that there is a strong bond of connection between the two clubs, due, perhaps, to members of the Carnegie family, who appear in the lists of both clubs.

RUSSIA.—In 1870 Charles Cowan introduced to the secretary of the Royal Club William Hopper, "a genuine son of Caledonia, who had raised himself to eminence in *Moscow*," and who was anxious to establish a curling club there. The "roaring game" had been previously known and practised by Scotsmen resident in the city, but it received more attention when Mr Hopper was successful in carrying out his intention, and organising a club in 1873. In 1876 this gentleman writes that there is a prospect of a club being started at *St Petersburg*. In 1879 we find Lord Dufferin, who was then British Ambassador at the Russian Court, taking up the proposal and writing to the "Royal" secretary that he is endeavouring "to establish a curling rink at St Petersburg on the Canadian principle." His Lordship promises to let the secretary know later on about the fortunes of the projected club. As no more is heard of the subject in our *Annuals*, and no St Petersburg club is as yet affiliated with the Royal, the project evidently did not succeed. It is a pity; for Lord Dufferin's idea of having covered rinks on the Canadian principle is the best way to meet the difficulties in the way of curlers in Russia. One might imagine that they were better off for ice there than we could possibly be, but the secretary of the Moscow Club (J. R. Hopper) informs us that—

"They very rarely get a true rink to play upon. The intense frost (occasionally 40° Fahrenheit) warps and cracks the ice out of all shape, and it is impossible to flood it as the hose-pipe freezes solid. It has therefore to be patched somewhat indifferently with a watering-pot and scraper."

The difficulties which we have mentioned account for the fact that no particularly high point scores are recorded at Moscow, the Rev. H. M. Bernard occupying premier position with a score of 12, made in 1885. Curlers in Russia have a "specialty" in the way of felt boots, called *valinki*, which afford an excellent foothold on their keen ice, and keep the feet warm and comfortable in the lowest temperature. Notwithstanding the excessive frost, they have not been driven, like the Canadians, to play with iron, but find the Ailsas and other kinds of stones imported from Scotland quite suitable. It need scarcely be added that in the territory of the Czar the low temperature gives a special zest to "beef and greens, and their warm surroundings."

NEW ZEALAND.—In this colony the most active promoter of curling has been Thomas Callender, whose name has already been mentioned in connection with the game in Ireland. He was the means of founding a club at *Dunedin* in 1873. In that same year a club was formed at *Mount Ida*, where, at an altitude of 2000 feet, the curlers could generally enjoy the game for about six weeks in the year, while the Dunedin players could not count upon more than a week. The *Haldon* Club was next instituted. Its secretary, writing in March 1878, while grateful for a fortnight's continuous play in the previous winter, says:—

"We are placed at a great disadvantage compared with most of the other clubs in your list; our pond is distant 100 miles from the nearest town, Timaru, and the members of the club are squatters, shepherds, and labourers, scattered about the various stations, distant from six to sixty miles from the pond. Under these circumstances it shews what a strong love for the roaring game possesses them, when they assemble round the rink for several days' continuous play."

The first bonspiel in New Zealand was played between *Naseby* and *Palmerston* in 1879, the latter club driving fifty miles to meet their opponents. The first provincial medal competition south of the Equator came off on August 7,

x

1884, when four clubs from the interior of Otago met at Naseby to contend for the coveted silver. The clubs were *Kyeburn, Upper Manuherikia, Mount Ida,* and *Otago Central,* the last-named proving victorious. Remarking on this memorable gathering, the Naseby secretary, J. T. Ferguson (*Annual,* 1885, p. 328), wrote :—

> "Newman's dam presented a busy scene from early morn till late at night, the visiting teams remaining over the greater portion of the week. It is no uncommon thing to see representatives of almost every nation under the sun 'around the tee.' We venture to say curling here does much to sink caste and make all men equals, for when met around the tee as keen, keen curlers, creed and colour are forgotten in the brotherhood of man."

While this wider result is manifest, it is evident that at the Antipodes the old curling traditions are not forgotten. The *Otago Times* of July 28, 1881, in an account of the annual dinner of the Dunedin Club in Wane's Hotel, says :—

> "The curlers partook of the time-honoured repast of beef and greens, washed down by copious draughts of the white wine of Scotland."

In the year 1886 the seven New Zealand clubs were formally organised into a province, when a trophy was given by Mr Callender, who was elected president. This will doubtless cause keen competition, and increase the popularity of the game. The stones used by the New Zealand curlers are mostly Ailsas, and average about 38 lb. Not much attention has as yet been given to point play, but 12 and 13 have often been reached, and in 1879 W. Guffie won the Mount Ida Club medal with the fine score of 15 points, while W. M'Hutcheson made scores of 16 and 17 in the year 1882.

TRANSATLANTIC CLUBS.

CANADIAN BRANCH, QUEBEC PROVINCE.—" Westward the star of *curling* takes its way." It is when we cross the Atlantic that we meet with the most remarkable development of curling furth of Scotland. In some parts of North America it is not too much to say that in keenness and enthusiasm they surpass even the curlers of Scotland. Introduced by Scotsmen, the game has now been taken up by Young America, and made the most popular winter sport in Canada and the States. That Scotsmen started it there cannot be denied. It followed the footsteps of the early fur-traders of the North-West, and the march of Fraser's Highlanders. The eagerness of the Scotch to enlist for active service in Canada during

FIG. 69. THE MARQUIS OF LORNE, K.T., PRESIDENT R.C.C.C., 1872-1874.
PATRON OF QUEBEC AND ONTARIO CURLING PROVINCES, 1878-1883.

the old contest between England and France is said to have been due to the opportunities there afforded for curling. This may also explain the popularity of Canada as a field for Scottish emigrants. Our curling countrymen were fortunate in having a fair field and plenty of ice. The Red Indian had vanished and left no trace of his amusements behind, so that curling, which suited the national predilections, might at once take the field, and hold it as the winter sport. Quebec seems to have been the point from whence the game, after coming from Scotland, started on its successful career. We hear of curling there about the close of the last and the beginning of the present century; but the first transatlantic curling club was formed at *Montreal* in January 1807, by "some natives of North Britain, who wished to introduce their favourite national game on the St Lawrence." In that same year a game was actually played on the river a little below the Port so late as the 11th April. The membership of this club was limited to twenty, and among the original rules were these:—

"The club shall meet at Gillis's, on Wednesday, every fortnight, at 4 o'clock, to dine on salt beef and greens. The club dinner and wine shall not exceed seven shillings and sixpence a head, and any member infringing on this rule, under any pretext whatever, shall be liable to a fine of four clubs. No member shall ask a friend to dinner, except the president and vice-president, who may ask two each. . . . The losing party of the day shall pay for a bowl of whisky toddy, to be placed in the middle of the table, for those who may chuse it."

In recording a resolution passed in February 1820, that the club should "dine at the beginning and at the end of winter," the secretary adds:—

"N.B.—This was adopted when the club had not met to dine for more than six years, partly occasioned by the war in which we were engaged with the United States."

At first the Montreal Club, for want of proper stones, had but a feeble existence, but *irons* of a rude description, in shape something like huge tea-kettles, were adopted, and were found to suit better. These weighed from 46 to 65 lb. each, and were the common property of the club. A regular club was formed at *Quebec* in 1821. We find the two Canadian clubs engaged in their first tussle at Three Rivers in 1835, when Montreal had to pay the dinner. In regard to the use of wine on the occasion the Montreal secretary wisely enters in the minute-book:—

"The secretary has never *seen* such a thing, and as this is the first, so he hopes it will be the last time that ever he shall *hear* of *champagn* being exhibited at a bonspiel dinner."

Colonel Dyde, a famous Canadian curler, in describing these early days, says that the cause of this unusual proceeding was that "there was no good, not even tolerable whisky to be had in Three Rivers," and he adds:—

"There were twenty-six guests at the dinner, which was good and substantial, and though we had no haggis the deficiency was in some degree supplied in roast turkeys, of which it is said no less than nine graced the board. Owing to 'the slender means of the club,' the eight Montrealers had to pay £3, 2s. 6d. each as the cost of the meal, and about the same sum for going and returning. An amusing scene took place when the company separated, just before starting at daylight. The wine bill being rather high, some of the Montrealers objected, and, as a convincing proof that the host had charged too much, one of them produced from his pocket the cork of every bottle that had been emptied, and the number of corks and bottles did not correspond. But a little investigation shewed that several bottles had been consumed by some of the guests out of sight of the cork-keeper, and the bill was paid without further parleying."

When the Grand Club was formed in 1838, our Canadian brethren, finding that in a few particulars their rules of play differed from those adopted here, at once threw all differences to the wind, and in a truly patriotic spirit gave in their allegiance to the mother club. The *Montreal Thistle* Club was formed in 1842. For a good many years these three were the only clubs on the Caledonian list, but we hear of military clubs at Quebec, the officers of the Dragoon Guards at Chambly, and the officers of the 71st Regiment, having their respective clubs in 1841, when they proposed to challenge Montreal. A third club—the *Caledonia*—was formed at Montreal in 1850. *Kingston* comes on the scene in 1859, *Ottawa* in 1862, *Belleville* in 1867, and *Arnprior* in 1868. Within the last twenty years ten other clubs have been added, so that we have now nineteen clubs in the province, all affiliated with the Royal Club. From the first, district medals have been awarded there as they are at home. The distance between the competing clubs is often, of course, very great, but it is no obstacle to the bonspiel. Montreal goes 200 miles to play Quebec, and thinks nothing about it. "Some of the medals," says the secretary of the branch in 1860, "cost the winners £50, and a journey of four or five hundred miles, but they are all highly prized." They have the usual "beef and greens" after their matches, and the "haggis and Athole brose" are not forgotten. They toast the Queen, the Governor-General, and then "oor auld respectit mither—the Royal Caledonian Club." Never, through all their history, do we find the Canadians, as they follow the old game, forgetting its old home, and the home of their own fathers. At the same time, in the spirit of true brotherhood, they are ever found anxious to enlist the interest of those who belong to other countries and nations in the health-giving and manly sport. Here is a cutting from a Canadian paper, which illustrates vividly the progress of curling among the non-Scottish, and its unchanged attraction for the Scottish citizens of Quebec as far back as 1854:—

"The great event of the past week was the monster curling match. Scotchmen had challenged all who came not from the north of the Tweed to beat them at their national game. The challenge was instantly responded to by the curlers of Quebec, or *Barbarians*, as they facetiously styled themselves, and immense excitement ensued. Sir James Alexander, A.D.C., acted as umpire. The game commenced at one o'clock, and continued with great zeal until half-past four. The scene on the river was novel and interesting; hosts of ladies and gentlemen and many gay equipages surrounded the rinks; bursts of merriment, snatches of broad Scotch, cries of 'Soop him, soop him,' resounded on all sides; curling-stones with red or blue ribbons came gliding towards the tee, now quietly, anon with thundering force, as the skips directed; the curlers, besom in hand, seemed all absorbed in the game, occasionally coaxing on some favourite stone with honied expressions, as though their very lives depended on the issue, and not infrequently a *great* player would lose his footing in the excitement of the moment, to the infinite amusement of the bystanders. In the background arose the fortress of old Stadacona, whose cannon were manned by a company of artillery at target practice, and firing, as it were, a royal salute to the curlers. The playing was keen, aye, as keen as the N.-W. wind which forced many of the fair admirers unwillingly from the spot, and the result of the game has clearly proved that the *Barbarians* are but little behind their civilised brethren in this manly sport. *Scotchmen*, 94; *Barbarians*, 83."

One of the most interesting bonspiels in our Canadian Branch is the "Scottish parish game," instituted in the year 1864, when four *callants* from the parish of Coulter, Lanarkshire, challenged "ony four frae ony ither parish in a' braid Scotland, or the world, to play a friendly game o' curlin'." Four lads from the parish of Ayr accepted the challenge, and were beaten by two shots. Next year, however, Ayr, under the Hon. John Young as skip, with Davie Mair and his big Kilmarnock bonnet, big Sandy Fleck, and Davie M'Kay, all "frae the auld toun," challenged Coulter, skipped by Geordie Denholm, president of the Montreal Club, who had few equals on the ice, with Jamie and Tam Brown and Wee Tam, all well-known Coulter curlers, and beat them, Ayr being victorious by eight shots. The Montreal Club has had a share of Royal patronage, Prince Arthur being elected an honorary member in 1869. The Canadians have been particularly fortunate in the support curling has always received from the Governors-General of the Dominion. One of the first *Annuals* (1841) refers to the interest taken in curling at that time by His Excellency Sir George Arthur, and in one of the last (1888-89), the departure of the Marquis of Lansdowne from Canada is referred to with regret, as he had "not only conferred on the game the prestige of his name and promoted it by prizes, but had during his residence there learned the game, and become a *keen, keen curler*." Between these two distinguished Governors several others have endeared themselves to the fraternity by their support and their sympathy. Lord Dufferin during his term of office gave a decided impetus to curling by the personal part he took in the game, and his disinterested endeavours to increase its popularity throughout the whole Dominion. A vice-regal club was instituted by His Excellency, of which he was patron, president, and a regular member (as all patrons and presidents ought to be), while the Countess of Dufferin was patroness. The members of the club were chiefly members of his Lordship's suite. The most notable among Lord Dufferin's measures for the advancement of curling was the institution of the Governor-General's prize. This was open to all the clubs in the Dominion. They first competed—eight chosen men of each—on their own ice, the game being one of points. The two clubs with the highest average scores for their eight players then met on the Governor-General's rink to play for the prize, and the winning club was held to be the champion club for the year. When Lord Dufferin was about to leave Canada, the clubs of the Quebec Province, through their president, Colonel Dyde, presented him with an address expressive of their gratitude and esteem, accompanied with a picture of

"A Canadian curling match, portraying a thoroughly outdoor winter scene, with all the characteristics and surroundings of an exciting curling contest, and comprising also faithful portraits of many of Canada's keenest curlers, and some of His Excellency's most attached friends."

The Marquis of Lorne, who had twice been president of the Royal Caledonian Club, very naturally and very enthusiastically took up the cause for which Lord Dufferin, his predecessor, had done so much. The very first year after Lord Lorne's arrival we find the Vice-Regal Club winning a Royal medal from the *Carilion* Club, "his Lordship," according to the report of the match, "playing a fine lead." H.R.H. the Princess Louise, Marchioness of Lorne, also shewed her interest in the game, as Lady Dufferin had done, by becoming patroness of the Vice-Regal Club. The prize of the Governor-General was continued in the form of a cup, and in that form successive Governors have continued it, its possession being still the great ambition of the Canadian clubs.

The competition for this cup brought about an important change in the mode of playing the game of points in Canada. This game from the first received a good deal of attention, and the scoring rose very high. In 1846 the Montreal Thistle play averaged $8\frac{1}{2}$ to each competitor, two members tieing with 12 points. For the Montreal gold medal in 1856, 13 players averaged 12 points each, Charles Sumner scoring 21, Captain Gallwey 18, James Tyre, John Dyde, and Walter Macfarlane, 15 points each. In 1875, W. F. Fenwick won the silver medal of the Thistle with a score of 21 points. For the final tie in the Governor's cup competition of 1879, two clubs appeared with averages for their eight players which threw all others into the shade— Ottawa with $20\frac{1}{2}$ points to each man, and Quebec with an average of $19\frac{7}{8}$. This *tall scoring* must have alarmed the Canadian curlers themselves, for immediately thereafter we find the secretary of the Canadian Branch, Mr A. Murray, writing the secretary of the Royal Club (December 9, 1880), that they had adopted a new series of positions in point play to regulate the competitions for the Canadian Branch tankard and the Governor-General's prizes. "The emulation excited by the latter has," says the secretary,

"Been wonderfully keen, until experience has proved that, either by constant practice or by manipulation, a *lead* has been established on the ice to the several positions, resulting in some wonderfully large scores being made at points, thus placing at a great disadvantage such clubs as endeavoured honestly to carry out the competition."

According to the new diagrams which were sent to Mr Davidson Smith at the same time,

"No two stones are played on the same lines, so that any manipulation of the ice for one point will effectually spoil the ice for any other, and the positions given are also more closely assimilated to the actual play of an ordinary rink match than the old positions."

The Quebec system of points is, we believe, generally followed in Canada, but whether it has fully met the difficulties which led to its adoption we are not informed. The crown of the Canadian winter sports is the great carnival held annually at Montreal, when people flock from every district to enjoy the toboganning, sleighing, snow-shoeing, &c., and to witness the wonders of the ice-palace, or attend at the Burns supper. To a great many, however, the one attraction of the carnival is the curling, which is always the principal item in the programme. The international trophy, the gift of Robert Gordon of New York, is then played for, and there is a keen contest for the Quebec Province tankard, with gold medal, for the winning club, this competition being conducted on the same lines as those laid down for the Governor-General's cup.

The clubs of the Canadian or Quebec Province are iron-playing clubs, the irons being much improved since they were first used, and having hollow bottoms like ordinary stones, but at the carnival the wooden blocks and granites are allowed to take part in the show, as the following account, by Mr Murray, of the winter gathering of 1883-84 shews:—

"The most novel feature of the whole scene was the competitions, at one and the same time, of clubs playing wooden blocks, granite stones, and iron 'stones;' and many a joke was cracked on the respective merits of the different 'stanes:' one of the best—of course being made by an 'iron'-playing curler—to the effect that even in curling the evolution theory held true; and here it was exemplified—first the primitive wooden blocks, like overgrown cheeses; next these developed into granite stones, a vast improvement; until finally we get perfection in the 'iron,' where the fun and frolic of genuine curling were just as good and the play infinitely better than in either of its predecessors. It is needless to say the 'granites' did not see the joke."

The rinks at this festival (as is usually the case) were all formed under cover, in long sheds. The covered rink is an advantage in such intense frost. The ice is, of course, a

FIG. 70. CANADIAN IRON-PLAYERS.
(From a photograph by Mossman & Son, Montreal.)

solid block, and is thickened by each new watering, so that the old "hack" can safely be used, as it is, by the Canadian players. The Fenwick twist is carried out to perfection on the rinks, and, from all accounts, they have with their irons reduced the game to a perfect science. The utmost good humour prevails among them, and seldom has any dispute ever come up from their district matches for settlement. All who have visited Canada can testify to the hearty hospitality extended to curlers from the mother country, and to the excellent way in which they uphold the ancient traditions of the game.

They have their bad winters on rare occasions, as in 1885-86, when an epidemic of smallpox put a stop to their carnival and their curling, and weakened many of the clubs; but, compared with us, they are the privileged classes in the dominion of frost. An *old-fashioned winter* with them begins in the middle of November and ends about the middle of April! Truly the ice may well be accounted a great emigration agent in the eyes of Scotsmen tired of the old country.

In the history of curling in this province, perhaps the most notable figure is Colonel Dyde, who was for a long time president of the branch. The colonel died in 1886, full of years and honours, having been up to his latest hour an enthusiast in "the roarin' game." In his day he was one of the most expert exponents of the art, and he used to ascribe his long-continued vigour and health to his curling. A few years before his death the colonel, along with three other curlers of the Montreal Club—Sir Hugh Allan, the Hon. John Young, and James Tyre, whose united ages as a rink amounted to 287 years—challenged any other four to a friendly game. In the course of two or three years the challenge was accepted nine times, and the veterans won in every instance. The colonel was one of the sixteen Quebecers, all about six feet tall, who played in the match against Montreal, at Three Rivers, as far back as 1835, so that for over half-a-century his commanding influence and good example popularised the game in the Dominion. Two distinguished divines—Dr Cook of Quebec and Dr Barclay of Toronto—identified themselves with the curlers and their sport, the latter taking a prominent part in its advancement. And now the Canadian Branch has for its chaplain one who is honourably remembered by us all for his excellence in curling and other manly sports, as well as for his abilities as a preacher—the Rev. James Barclay, formerly of St Cuthbert's, Edinburgh.

ONTARIO PROVINCE.—In the year 1874 the curling clubs in the Province of ONTARIO were formed into a branch, separate from and independent of the Canadian or Quebec Branch of the Royal Club. The headquarters of this branch was Toronto. It was to be self-governing, with office-bearers of its own, and an *Annual*; but its proceedings were to be reported for approval to the Royal Club, to which the branch was to be subject "in all curling matters." In 1882 the Royal Club resolved, "in the interests of curling in the Ontario District, to allow the Ontario Branch to be a *corresponding* association, no longer subordinate or contributory to the Royal Club, which, however, retained the right to continue on the roll such clubs as wished to remain in affiliation with the Royal. Since that time the best of feelings have always existed between our Ontario brethren and the mother club; they have our list of office-bearers in their *Annuals*, and a list of their clubs is given in ours; they distribute our medals, and send us annual reports of their doings. In our Jubilee they took the warmest interest; and the secretary of the branch—J. S. Russel, who is the best authority on the subject of Canadian curling at the present day—drew up for our use a history of the game in the Ontario Province, which we had better give as it stands, for it seems to us to indicate fairly and fully the various streams which have contributed to the full flood of curling as it now rolls along in Ontario:—

CURLING IN ONTARIO, CANADA.

"The history of curling in the Province of Ontario leads us back only to about A.D. 1830, and indicates the date of the first considerable immigration of Scottish families into the Province.

"Previous to 1783, when the British Government located about 10,000 United Empire loyalist refugees from the United States of America in the eastern part of the Province, then called Western Canada, it had been known 'only as a region of intense cold in winter, a dense wilderness of forest and swamp, tenanted by venomous reptiles and beasts of prey, and the hunting-grounds of numerous savage Indian tribes, whose hatred of white men made its exploration perilous, and with no redeeming feature except abundance of fish and game.'

"This original colony was considerably increased in subsequent years by the removal into the Province of a large number of the same class who had been settled in Nova Scotia, but, growing dissatisfied with their condition and prospects in that Province, sought to better themselves by seeking a home in what was then considered the Far West.

"At the close of the French wars in 1815, the British Government directed a large emigration from the United Kingdom into the Province, and the population increased from 80,000 in 1815 to 120,000 in 1822. The Canada Land Company was formed in 1824, 'with the design of acquiring lands in the Province, and promoting their colonisation,' and, being mainly a Scotch company, its efforts were very naturally and most successfully employed in planting Scotch families in the lands it had acquired in the Province of Upper Canada; and, accordingly, we find characteristic evidence of the presence of Scotchmen in the Province, in the erection of St Andrew's Church in Toronto, 1830, and the introduction of 'ye glorious game of curling' about the same time.*

"At first the curlers of each settlement played amongst themselves, and occasionally the curlers of two contiguous settlements would have a 'spiel,' and by-and-by clubs were organised, *Fergus* leading the van in 1834, *Flamborough* following in 1835, *Toronto* and *Milton* in 1837, *Galt*, *Guelph*, and *Scarborough* in 1838, *Paris* in 1843, and *Elora* in 1847; and in the next decade *Ancaster*, *Bowmanville*, *Woodbridge*, *Hamilton Thistle*, and *Dundas* Clubs were formed. These may justly be called the pioneer clubs of the Province; they are to this day, every one of them, in vigorous activity. The sons and grandsons have all the enthusiasm and the skill of their sires, and they still occupy a first place among the curling clubs of the Province.

"A goodly number of these clubs used from the very first granite curling-stones, made by the curlers themselves from ice-borne boulders, which are found plentifully scattered all over the Province; the metal is very hard, and is susceptible of a good polish, but with rare exceptions it is very 'dull' and 'sticky' when the ice is soft. They are now given up, being superseded by the Ailsa Craig, and blue and red Hones, and Tinkernhills, which also find considerable favour.

"In later years several clubs made a beginning with iron curling-

---

* By way of illustrating the process of the formation of curling clubs in Ontario, the following may be cited, viz.:— 1st. *Of the olden time:* Galt Curling Club. In the words of Robert Wallace, one of the players, still surviving: "Our family came to the township of Beverley in 1834, and I moved in April 1836 to the town of Galt, which then consisted of a few straggling log huts; in the winter following my father came to pay me a visit, and we drove out to see the family of Hugh Wallace, living about two-and-a-half miles west of the town. Among other topics of conversation the subject of curling was raised, and we resolved to get up a game at once; so we went to work, cut blocks out of a beech tree, to which Hugh Wallace, being a blacksmith, quickly fitted rough but serviceable handles, and, adjourning to a pond on a field belonging to John Angus, we had a jolly good game, and a club was formed in Galt in 1838."

2nd. *Of the more modern time:* Waubaushene Curling Club.—"In the fall of 1879 a few of the residents of Waubaushene happened to meet in the village store, and the conversation drifted to skating, and then to curling. Few of those present knew anything about the game, so an illustration of the manner of playing it was given by means of coppers on the counter, and quite an interest in the game was raised. A committee was appointed to canvass the village, and ascertain what the chances were of raising money enough to build a rink to be used both for skating and curling, and in a few days the necessary funds were raised, and soon afterwards the rink, a spacious structure 200 feet by 24, was erected. The cost of granite curling-stones to people who had never seen the game was a formidable difficulty, but it was happily surmounted by the opportune visit to the village of an old Port Hope curler, who suggested wooden blocks of the proper shape and size, which were at once turned out of green beech, and strengthened with an iron band two inches wide and three-quarters inch thick, shrunk on hot, and with these the game was played until 1882, when the club procured a full supply of Ailsa Craigs."

stones, cast hollow, with a 'skin' about one inch in thickness, and having one sole turned, with a slight concave, and chilled and polished; these, being of a good shape, size, and weight, were found very suitable in cold and cloudy weather, or under cover; but where the temperature got above the 32 degrees, or the sun's rays fell upon them when at 'rest,' they melted hollows in the ice, and left the 'tee-head' pitted with circular marks, as if the ice had 'come through' a severe attack of monstrous smallpox.

"Others, and by far the largest number, made their first essays in the game with wooden blocks, cut from the solid bowl of a beech or maple tree, or turned on a lathe, and girt about with a massive iron band to add weight and prevent splitting, and fitted with handles of bent iron made in the village blacksmith's shop. In the Province of Quebec, and in a few places in Ontario adjoining Quebec, solid iron blocks, weighing from 60 to 75 lb., are still used, but everywhere else, all over the Continent of America, the time-honoured granite or 'whinstane' is considered the only proper material for making curling-stones.

"The pattern of stone which is now universally used in all parts of Canada and the United States has the dull sole (that usually played with) made concave, with a well-raised bearing from one-eighth to three-eighths of an inch in width, and having a diameter of from five to five and a half inches; this style of sole gives the best results in playing the game, and as in the points game scores of from 18 to 21 are not uncommon, and 25 has been made, there is substantial proof of the excellence of the pattern and the wisdom of its adoption in Ontario. The 'keen' sole is also made concave, but is not so much 'cupped' as the 'dull,' the diameter of the 'cup' is less, and the width of the bearing is more than that of the 'dull' sole; and this sole is used when the ice is rough or damp, and on such ice it is 'just the thing.'

"In the early days of curling in Ontario, and before the introduction of railways, curling intercourse was limited, and could only exist between clubs situated near to each other; horses were not very numerous, and oxen were very slow; and as a shovel was as necessary a part of a curler's outfit as his stanes and his besom, and 'shovel exercise' in removing snow from the ice often occupied as much of his time as playing the game did, an early house-leaving and a late return did not admit of a good game and long travel. Stories are told of curlers setting out the night before, travelling all night on shanks' pony, playing the game during the day, and making for home thereafter. But such feats are not generally practicable; it took three days for the Toronto and Hamilton Thistle Clubs to play a match—one day travelling to, one day travelling from, and one day playing—although the cities are only about forty miles apart. And an 'annual' match and the 'return' was as much as could be reasonably expected between these clubs; while the Toronto and Scarborough Clubs played an annual match with each other every few weeks while the frost lasted.

"In 1859 the first 'big Canadian bonspiel' was played on Toronto Bay, the Province being divided into East and West, with 21 rinks a side, Fergus, Guelph, Scarborough, and Toronto Clubs contributing 5 rinks each, Bowmanville and Hamilton Thistle 4 each, Ancaster and Flamborough 3 each, Burlington, Dundas, and Newcastle 2 each, and

London and Montreal 1 each. The next large bonspiel took place in 1865, and was played at Black Rock, near Buffalo, between Ontario and the United States, with 23 rinks a side, Ontario having 4 rinks over—in all 27 rinks, the representative curlers of 19 Canadian clubs. On this occasion a rink from the Toronto Club, called 'Her Majesty's Rink,' and wearing cardigan jackets of the royal scarlet, played against a rink of the Buffalo Club, called 'The President's Rink,' and wearing small U.S. flags (stars and stripes). The Americans dubbed the Canadian rink with the name of 'Red Jackets,' and in a few years, and somewhat changed in its members, it became famous as the 'Red Jacket Rink' of the Toronto Club, which played against picked rinks of the best clubs in the Province with wonderful success, and also carried the name and fame of Canadian curlers throughout the United States from New York to Chicago, and greatly extended the interest taken in the game.

"Since that time several large bonspiels have been played, at Burlington Bay near Hamilton, and at Toronto on the bay, or divided among the rinks belonging to the city clubs; and to these have been attracted from 100 to 110 rinks of players from all parts of the Province. But for many reasons they have been discontinued; one of the main reasons being the difficulty of finding a large enough field of good ice and suitable weather, a Canadian snowstorm making curling out of doors impossible; and another being the frequent 'misfits' of opposing rinks. There is no pleasure to either party when the scoring is all made by the one side, and in promiscuous matches, such as these large bonspiels are, such unfortunate competitions are bound to occur.

"Of late years a very interesting annual match has been played by the combined clubs of the city of Toronto, against one rink from each of the other clubs of the Province, and they have been most successful. The playing has been good, and the competitors well matched; and as there is a well-marked dividing line between the two sides, the interest often rises to anxiety and excitement before the final issue is ascertained.

"The competitions, 'primary' and 'final,' for the Ontario tankard are the great events of each curling season. For the 'primary,' the clubs in connection with the branch club are arranged into sixteen groups, with about six clubs in each, and these engage in a playing-off contest, club v. club, until only one club in each group remains undefeated; the champion clubs of the sixteen groups then meet in Toronto to play off the 'final' in the same manner; this contest occupies two full days, two sets of matches being played each day; and as the players are all experts, tried and true, the ice as level as a billiard table, and the result the highest honour attainable in curling in Ontario, it may be justly considered to afford the finest possible illustration of the game.

"The Ontario Branch Club makes an annual allocation of Royal Caledonian district medals, to be played for between each two clubs in the association which did not win one the preceding year; and these medals are competed for with the greatest enthusiasm.

"Besides these more public competitions, all of the clubs have numerous contests to be played by and between their own members, such as the points game, at which the winning scores run from 16 to 21, and sometimes higher, 25 points out of the 32 possible having been made; single hand matches with three pairs of stones; and an inter-rink match between all the rinks of the club, each against every other; and thus during our curling season, extending from the middle of December until about the end of March, our curlers are busily engaged in their most exciting pastime.

"In January 1887, twenty-nine rinks of curlers from the United States paid a friendly visit to Ontario by way of a return to the international match played at Black Rock in 1865. A much larger company had arranged to visit Toronto on the occasion, but a series of heavy snow-falls occurring immediately before the date named for the 'gathering' rendered railway travelling almost impossible, and thus prevented many from 'keeping the tryst.' Those who did come were greatly impressed by the number and extent of our rinks, by the resources and skill of the caretakers of the various rinks, and by the wonderful facilities available for the practice of the game; and most of them remained the whole week, curling forenoon, afternoon, and evening on such ice as they had never seen before.

"At the formation of the Ontario Branch of the R.C.C.C. in 1884 His Excellency Lord Dufferin, Governor-General of the Dominion, graciously accepted the office of patron of the club, and, taking to the game, became a good and keen curler. His successor, the Marquis of Lorne, a former president of the Royal Caledonian Club, was, before his arrival in Canada, an adept at the game; and the Marquis of Lansdowne, who followed him in the vice-regal dignity, became, during the term of his high office, an enthusiastic curler; and thus, by their official patronage, by their annual donations of curling prizes, by many eloquent speeches in praise of the game, but most of all by taking an active part in the practice of it, these noblemen, occupying the highest position in the Dominion, greatly promoted the game of curling, and gave it a 'standing' in public estimation it had not previously held.

"The A. M. Stewart Scottish Counties medal, presented as a challenge trophy, to be played for between natives of Scottish counties now residing in any part of the American Continent, although it has perhaps not done much to promote the game of curling directly, has been the occasion of a great many interesting matches. The medal was brought into Ontario by natives of Lanarkshire, and has been held by that county very successfully, although it has been won by Roxburghshire, and is at present held by Stirlingshire, whose 'braw lads,' after several unsuccessful attempts, did at the 'lang last' manage to run up the better score against the Lanarkshire callants.

"This medal deserves notice, because the competition for it is open to Scotsmen living anywhere on the Continent of America, and because it brings together in friendly rivalry men now 'sindered far and wide,' who as schoolboys sat on the same forms, were taught to dread the same 'tawse,' engaged in the same frolics, and maybe courted the same lass; and because it revives and promotes friendships among 'one's ain,' which is one of the principal ends sought to be obtained by 'the grand old game.' There is little doubt that Mr Stewart would gladly extend the right to contend for this medal to any eight natives of any county in Scotland who would cross the Atlantic to make an effort to win it, and 'tak' it hame;' the three counties already named are sufficiently well represented in Canada, but there is a fine opening for the other counties, or shires, to win immortal renown by sending out eight curlers to contest for this

trophy, and especially if they succeed in winning it, and carrying it
'over the sea' to auld Scotland.

"The early curlers of Ontario were not inappreciative of the honour
and benefit of being connected with the Royal Caledonian Curling
Club, although the first club to join the Royal was that of Toronto,
and not until 1845, and was followed by the Paris Club only, after a
long interval, in 1857; and when the Ontario Branch of the Royal
Caledonian Curling Club was established in 1874, only twenty out of
forty-two clubs then in active existence were connected with the
parent club.

"Two reasons sufficiently account for this seeming apathy, the
first being that a Canadian Branch of the Royal had been established
with its headquarters in Montreal, in the Province of Quebec, and the
distance was too great to admit of regular attendance at the meetings
held there of any deputies from the clubs in Ontario; and the second
was that the curlers of the Province of Quebec then, as now, used solid
iron blocks, weighing from 60 to 80 lb., in the practice of the game,
while those of Ontario used the time-honoured granite stones, con-
form in weight and size to the rule of the parent club.

FIG. 71. CANADIAN STONE-PLAYERS. (From the Ontario Branch *Annual* for 1878.)

"In 1861 a Royal Caledonian medal was played for at Montreal
between the Toronto Club and the Stadacona Club of Quebec city, the
former travelling 700 miles, and the latter about 350, in going to and
returning from the match; one rink of the Stadaconas played 'stone,'
and one Toronto rink played 'iron,' and the result was what might
have been anticipated—each rink playing its accustomed 'metal' was
winner, and those playing with the unfamiliar were losers. Such an
arrangement, while probably 'fair,' was not satisfactory, and this difference in the stones used in the game presented an insuperable barrier
to curling intercourse between the curlers of the Provinces, and led to
the establishment, in 1874, of a branch of the Royal Caledonian Curling
Club for the Province of Ontario, with its headquarters in Toronto.

"From this date, and under the auspices of the Ontario Branch,

Y

curling has developed marvellously throughout the whole of the Dominion of Canada. A branch of the parent club similar to that for Ontario has been established for the Maritime Provinces, and steps are now being taken to establish another for Manitoba and the North-West; and a Grand Canadian Curling Association, to be formed by a confederation of these various provincial clubs, and maintaining an intimate connection with the Royal Caledonian, 'the mither of us all,' seems to be looming in the not far distant future.

"With the Ontario Branch ninety-nine clubs are now affiliated, having a membership of over 3000. Since the formation of the Ontario Branch, and more particularly since, in the wise liberality of the parent club, the branch was granted a measure of 'Home Rule,' including the privilege of making its own regulations, and of using its funds to promote curling in Ontario, the game has been taken up largely by Canadians generally, without respect to original nationality, and the game, which a few years ago was looked upon as slow and devoid of interest, good enough, perhaps, for a lot of 'old fogey Scotchmen,' is now followed with the keenest enthusiasm by 'young and middle-aged Canada,' who have found it to be of most engrossing interest, and a grand relief to the worry of business and the weariness of prolonged mental application.

"The erection of covered rinks in almost every city, town, and village in Ontario is, in some measure, both the cause and effect of this state of things in regard to curling; every club has a covered rink, where, by day or by night, 'whatever storms may blow,' the voice of the skip and the 'curring' of the curling-stone may be heard as long as frost continues. Some of these are built of slabs, many of rough boards, while in the larger towns and cities brick and stone are the materials most commonly used. In the city of Toronto alone there are five rinks, affording under cover ample space for twenty-eight curling rinks, and thirty-seven in the open air—the covered rinks being preferred for play only when snow is falling or darkness comes on. The property is valued at over $250,000, and affords a means of delightful and healthful recreation to about 600 curlers belonging to the city clubs, while it is found indispensable to the curlers of the country in playing off the more important matches of the Ontario Branch.

"In fine, the warmest admirers of the game are completely satisfied with the progress it is making in Ontario, and with the healthful influence it is exercising on the physical and moral condition of those who engage in it; excesses of every kind are fatal to the clearness of eye and steadiness of arm required to attain and retain a good position in the game.

"One most desirable object still remains to be accomplished, and that is the initiation of curling intercourse between the curlers of old Scotland and Canada: it can be carried on only in 'this Canada of ours.' Our Scottish brithers of the 'stanes and besom' who first make the venture to spend a month or two with us in curling weather will receive a welcome which they will never cease to remember with joy and pride—joy in the remembrance of the pleasure they received and conferred by their visit to Canada, and an honest pride in being pioneers in the establishment of another link of friendly intercourse between the mother country and her colony. It rests with the keen, keen curlers of old Caledonia to say when this desirable consummation shall be attained."

MANITOBA BRANCH.—The secretary of Ontario Branch (Mr Russel), in his report of the year 1882, says:—

"The large emigration from our Province to the new Province of Manitoba and the North-West Territories has thinned the ranks of many of our curling clubs; but the emigrants are everywhere carrying with them the love of the game, and already about half-a-dozen clubs have been organised in that land, so eminently adapted for curling; and we who remain in Ontario are calmly awaiting our fate, when these curlers, perfected by six or seven months' daily practice every year, will come down and 'scoop us out,' not giving us a shot; *soutering* is, I believe, the proper term."

Since these words were written emigration to Manitoba has doubled the number of curlers and clubs there, and at a convention held at Winnipeg in 1888 it was agreed to form a branch of the Royal Caledonian Club for Manitoba and the adjoining territories. This branch has now 14 clubs, with an active membership of 737 curlers, Mr J. B. Mather being president, and Mr J. P. Robertson secretary and treasurer of the branch. The first great bonspiel of the branch was held at Winnipeg in March 1889, and was looked upon as one of the most successful events in connection with curling that has ever come off in America. A sum of $1127.70 was raised as a bonspiel fund, from which a grand challenge medal, an international trophy, and several gold medals were secured. Other handsome prizes being offered by private parties, the association was able to institute at once a series of very interesting and exciting competitions, and to attract curlers from other associations in Canada and the United States. A bright and prosperous future is doubtless in store for this young branch, and its progress will be marked with attention by curlers in the old country.

NEWFOUNDLAND.—About the year 1843 a few Scotchmen formed a curling club at *St John's, Newfoundland*, which used to meet on Guidi Vidi and other lakes near the town. Year by year this club increased in numbers. There was always plenty of ice to be had, but the snowstorms in some winters made curling impossible, and several attempts were accordingly made to secure a covered rink, where the game could be enjoyed without hindrance. It was only in 1869 that Mr R. Grieve and a few other leading gentlemen by a determined effort succeeded in raising a sufficient sum for the purpose. A handsome covered rink was constructed at a cost of £2000. It measured 160 feet by 90 feet, and as the skaters of the city had assisted in raising the money, a part in the centre, 60 feet wide, was reserved for them, and a curling rink, 150 feet by 15 feet, was left available on each side, where with every comfort the curlers were able to have their matches. This *Avalon* Club (as it was called) received a Caledonian medal to play for in 1874, and this created such a *furore* for curling in St John's that another club, the *Arctic*, had to be started. The *Heart's Content* Club followed in 1878, and the competitions between the clubs put new life into the curlers in Newfoundland. A district medal was awarded between the Avalon and the Arctic, but owing to the many obstacles in the way, it was some years before it could be played. Neither club could find it convenient to reach the other's ice. At last the people of Harbor Grace, twenty miles from Heart's Content and eighty-five miles from St John's, erected a rink, and placed it at the disposal of the clubs; and having made all preliminary arrangements, a team of the Heart's Content proceeded there, and a team of the Arctic Club left St John's to meet them on the ice.

"After a very tedious journey by rail," says the skip of the winning Arctic, C. Duder, "being snowed up in the train for some hours, and having to cut several snow-drifts of from 7 to 10 feet deep, we arrived at Harbor Grace at 6.30 P.M., and the opposing team having had the ice prepared, we played the match that evening, and returned to St John's next day. . . . The undertaking of a journey in the middle of a Newfoundland winter of twenty miles across our open barrens by the Heart's Content Club, and a rail journey of eighty-five from St John's by the Arctic, will shew you that the dear old 'roarin' game' is as keenly enjoyed in the 'oldest colony' as it is on any of the bonny lochs of auld Scotia ; and the pleasant meeting of total strangers on the ice told the onlookers that 'curlers are brithers' all the world over."

A few point scores from their returns shew what these Newfoundland curlers can do in that department of the game :—

"16 points—C. Duder, H. W. De Messurier, J. Jackson, E. C. Watson.
15   „   G. M. Archibald, A. Rankin, W. Thorburn.
14   „   C. F. Harvey, F. Berteau.
13   „   J. Strang, J. Syme, and J. Skeoch."

NOVA SCOTIA.—In the early part of this century curling was practised by Scotsmen in Nova Scotia, and Captain Houston Stewart (whose name occurs in our account of the Penninghame Club) had, prior to 1843, organised a club at *Halifax*, where Dr Grigor, a fiddler "second only to Neil Gow," Colonel Gray, and others, were keen supporters of the game. The *Halifax Thistle*, *Dartmouth*, and *Pictou* Clubs joined the Royal in 1852, the *New Caledonian* and *New Glasgow* in 1854. Clubs were also instituted at *Stellarton*, *Sydney*, *Truro*, and *Cape Breton*. Among the earliest Nova Scotian matches we have one in 1854 between the president and vice-president of the branch for the benefit of the poor, £5 a side, "to which were added sundry bets among the members, making the sum £12, 5s., which was handed over to the Mayor of Halifax." Another match for "firewood to the poor" took place that same year. In 1862 a great match came off between the Halifax and Pictou Clubs, on a mill-dam about two miles from Truro, three rinks a side, with five players in each rink. Of this match the secretary of the New Caledonian Club, Pictou, W. N. Rudolph, writes:—

"The play excited deep interest, and was witnessed by 2000 people. A sleigh accommodating about fifty persons, and drawn by six horses, conveyed passengers to and from the pond throughout the day. Numbers of the fair sex were on the spot, and added in no small degree to the beauty of the scene. The day was very fine. The utmost good-feeling prevailed during the whole play, and on the termination of the game the opposing forces adjourned to the 'Prince of Wales' Hotel for dinner. Here speeches and songs passed the time merrily until a late hour, when the company separated with expressions of mutual esteem to return to their homes."

The New Glasgow Club, which subsequently adopted the sneering designation of the *Blue-Nose* Club, has acquired high distinction for excellence of play, having for three years in succession won the Governor-General's prize, open to all stone-playing clubs in the Dominion of Canada. In the lists of the club we find a good many *M'Gregors* and other Highland names, which may account for the club's success. To play the final tie for the cup in 1881 the Blue-Nose curlers travelled 1100 miles each way—a striking proof of the keenness of our transatlantic brothers. The curling-stones in general use in Nova Scotia average about 43 lb. each, and are usually flat-bottomed, not cupped. They are mostly Ailsas. Some of the scores at points reported from the province are very high, the medal of the Halifax Club having been won in 1887 by Sydenham Howe with 22 points, while seventeen competitors averaged 13 points each.

NEW BRUNSWICK.—Previous to the year 1869 there must have been a good deal of curling here, for in that year we hear of a match between native curlers and Scotsmen, in which the former were victorious. Then we have a match between those hailing from north of the Forth and those from the south. The earliest clubs we meet with are the *Frederickton* and the *St Andrew's*. The secretary of the latter, writing from St John in 1862, says:—

"A great accession to the interest of our proceedings arose from several of the officers of the regiments at that time in St John's honouring us with their countenance, and heartily entering into our sports, most of them being first-rate curlers, and qualified to honour Scotland in any part of the world."

In 1875 the same gentleman, in his report to the Royal Club, remarks:—

"I sometimes think that the curlers on this side of the water are even more enthusiastic than you are, for we do not hesitate to go some 300 miles for a bonspiel with the thermometer below zero."

The highest point scores reported from New Brunswick are 15, made by S. F. Matthews in 1874, and 16 by H. F. Messurier in 1885.

UNITED STATES.—In the year 1867 the great majority of the curling clubs in the United States were formed into a Grand National Curling Club, the object of which was to do for the States what had been done for Scotland by the Royal Club. Alongside of its own list of office-bearers the Grand National published in its *Annual* a list of the office-bearers of the parent club, and at their annual dinner the States curlers do not forget to toast the Royal as "oor auld respectit mither," ever, like their Canadian brethren, paying the old lady the highest respect. A report of their proceedings is also transmitted annually to the Royal, Mr David Foulis having for many years, as secretary of the Grand National, drawn up these reports, which never fail to interest curlers in Scotland. Mr Foulis has not, however, like the Ontario secretary, sent any special statement for our volume, and in the absence of such we must do our best to give an account of curling in the United States. The oldest club is the *Orchard Lake* Club, organised about the year 1830 by eight hardy Scotsmen away in the wilds of Michigan, on the banks of the lake from which the club took its name. The curlers there used hickory blocks for want of their native whinstone.

FIG. 72. THE HON. ALEX. MITCHELL.
(*From photograph in "Annual" of G. N. Club.*)

Alexander Mitchell, who, in the year 1887, was elected to the high office of patron of the Grand National Club in succession to Robert Gordon of New York, along with other pioneer Scotsmen, introduced curling at Milwaukee, Wisconsin, so far back as the year 1847. No better instance could be given to illustrate the Scotsman's undying attachment to Scotland's ain game and the connection between curling and the highest development of character than Alexander Mitchell's career. When they settled there he and his companions were poor emigrants, but they stuck to their work, their channel-stanes, and their good principles, and when the Grand Club makes Alexander Mitchell their patron it is because "his name is a household word in the Far West, and is synonymous with progress and business integrity." He is then the owner of a palatial residence in the Grand Avenue, Milwaukee, but his delight is to meet the curlers, and, "with his braid blue Kilmarnock bonnet," to mingle among them as one of themselves, and take a personal interest in all their proceedings. "His heart," says their *Annual* for 1888, in announcing his death. "was as large and kindly as his influence, and his name will go down to posterity as a striking example of what can be accomplished by integrity and business capacity."

It was by such Scotsmen that here and there throughout the States clubs were formed in the first half of this century. *Portage* Club followed Milwaukee in 1850, and then the game spread through Columbia. *Boston* Club, which was entirely composed of Scotsmen, was formed in 1854. *Boston New England* Club was formed in 1856, *Philadelphia*, *New York Thistle*, and *Caledonian* in 1857, *St Andrew's* in 1858, *Paterson* and *New Jersey* in 1860, *Yonkers* in 1864, and *Detroit* in 1865. Those were the pioneer clubs of the States previous to the formation of the Grand National Club, which, since it was instituted, has added fully thirty to the five who were originally affiliated with it, so that it now contains about forty clubs, with a membership of over 800. Curling has not made such progress in the United States as it has in Canada. But it must be kept in mind, in estimating its progress in the States, that the facilities there are not so great, the Scotch element is not so large, and, besides, the progress of the game was considerably interrupted by the American War. Thus we find the secretary to the New York Thistle writing Mr Cassels in 1862 :—

"On the whole, the roaring game is on the increase in this section, although our ranks have been much weakened by some of our members joining the army. Nevertheless, there is a curling spirit of the right kind manifesting itself, and no doubt it will increase with better times and peace from war."

The war did not stop the play, for we find the New England Club repairing on February 24, 1862, to Spot Pond, Kelvingrove, the residence of their patron, John Leishman, who was a good curler and a strong supporter of his club, to play for two medals. The "yill caup," with something to put in it, was planted, for the comfort of the day, under the shadow of a granite bluff which projected into the pond, and in the evening the players had a substantial dinner at their patron's residence, when

"The sentiment and song, embellished with stirring narratives of bygone days in the land of the heather and blue mountains, closing with the singing of 'Auld Lang Syne,' made the occasion one of happy remembrance."

Still there was a skeleton at the feast, for after such a happy picture by Samuel Gibson, the secretary, there follows this P.S.:—

"I am sorry to see our friends at home having so strange views of the unhappy rebellion in our country. For the sake of *suffering humanity*, for the sake of civil and religious liberty and good and free institutions, let the cause in which we are engaged go on, and the world will bless us for the heavenly efforts we are making."

The headquarters of United States curling and of the National Club is New York, where the annual meetings are usually held; but the club follows the example of the Royal, and has visited various centres of influence in the States, such as Buffalo, Chicago, Albany, Yonkers, Coney Island, Utica, and Milwaukee. These summer gatherings are made the occasion of a great annual quoiting competition, the principal prize in which is the Bell gold medal, presented by David Bell, a Dumfriesian gentleman, who was first president of the Grand National Curling Club, and who has himself won the medal three times out of the four occasions on which he played for it. This revival of the custom of the old Duddingston Club (*vide* footnote, p. 36), and of the still older connection between curling and *quoiting*, is very interesting. It certainly makes the summer gathering more of an event to the representatives who attend. The occasion is further improved by the curlers, with their wives and daughters, taking excursions into the surrounding country after the business is over.

The New York Corporation has set a noble example to public bodies by the liberality shewn to the curling clubs in giving them ice to play upon in the Central Park, and fitting up for them a movable house, with eight club-rooms, shelved to hold stones, brooms, &c. The National Club, to develop the game, gives district medals, as we do at home, and these are keenly contested. Private patrons have endowed the club with many valuable national trophies. They have two champion rink medals, presented by their two patrons, Robert Gordon and Alexander Mitchell; an interstate medal, the gift of John L. Hamilton, a president. Several States have medals of their own of great value, while a grand match between North v. South of Scotland is fought annually for the Dalrymple medal, and the M'Lintock medal pits the Scotch v. All other Nationalities. The most important prize of all is the Gordon medal, to be played for between the United States and Canada.

This match was first played in 1865, at Buffalo Rock Harbour. Over fifty of the players are said each to have travelled 850 miles to take part in it. It was, of course, "a Montreal bank to a shaving shop" in favour of Canada, the States players being mostly beginners at the time, and Canada won easily. The last account of this match which is before us tells a similar tale: Canadians, 789; United States, 501. This was at Toronto in 1887. The "reasons annexed" by the Grand National secretary are interesting as throwing light on the points in which the States and Canada diverge in play. Omitting *superabundant hospitality*, which all curlers know to be fatal previous to a big match, we have *covered rinks* and *hack playing* assigned as causes of defeat. From this it may be inferred that curling in the United States bears a closer resemblance to curling in Scotland than the Canadian style. How closely they are bound to us, these curling Americans, is shewn by many an incident in the history of their curling, by the names they bear and the language they use. Everything is redolent of the Land o' Cakes, and curling, Americanised as it happily is, wears the old countenance and follows the old ways. One of the oldest of the New York clubs took the name of the *Thistle*. In the days when there were no medals, and the *Thistle* wanted a bonspiel with the *Caledonian*, Andrew Barr, a member of the *Thistle*, gave his *Glengarry bannet* to be played for! Andrew had to go home bannetless, having lost the match; and for twenty years did he address the *Thistle* men in vain, "Bring back my bannet,' for the *Caledonians* sternly held on to it. When, in 1879, the *bannet* was regained at last, every "brug" of the *Thistle* was assembled together at William Meikle's, and the curlers' wives and children were there, and there was great rejoicing. Poor Andrew died happy very soon thereafter. To the curlers of the States the monuments to Burns and Scott in New York were in great measure due. In the foundation-stone of each, along with the usual newspapers, there was deposited a copy of the curling *Annual*. Dumfriesshire, as we have seen, gave them their first president. John Johnstone, who held the office more than once, belonged to the county of Aberdeen; and in 1878 he writes them from Inverurie, where he has been scampering among the heather hills, "near where Gaudie rins, at the back o' Benachie." John Patterson, another president, was from Minnigaff. Their worthy secretary, if we mistake not, is from Inverkeithing, in the kingdom of Fife. The slogan of the beloved William Ritchie, which will not soon be forgotten, was "Kilbarchan for ever!" James M'Laren, who wins the gold quoit medal, is announced as from Clackmannan, "a Scottish county justly famed for its small size, good soldiers, and good quoiters!" Then who in all the States has not heard of Willie Kellock, the renowned skip of the renowned rink of the renowned *Yonkers* Club, who carried off the blue ribbon of American curling, the Gordon championship medal, no less than five times between 1869 and 1886? Willie was "a native of one of the bonniest villages in Scotland—viz., Thornhill, Dumfriesshire." And so on. We cannot but feel at home among these American curlers, for their names are our own. When under their star-spangled banner they form their Grand National Curling Club, they are not content with the States' motto, "*E pluribus* wmm," they add a motto still more suggestive, "*We're brithers a'!*" They seldom burst into song over their curling as their brethren do at home; but if on rare occasions they do, it is in guid braid Scotch:—

> "Hae ye trouble? Hae ye sorrow?
> Are ye pinched wi' warldly care?
> Redd the roaring rink to-morrow,
> Pench! they'll fash ye never main."

The songs at their social gatherings are mostly "the auld Scotch sangs," the dinners are like ours, if that to the Wisconsin rinks given by Milwaukee may be taken as a specimen:—

> "From half-past seven till nearly twelve the crowd of jolly curlers ate, drank, sang songs, proposed toasts and healths, and testified to their good opinion of each other's skill in the roaring game, and their love for the grand game itself."

When the convention met at Milwaukee in 1885, it is said in an account of the dinner that

> "During the evening a corps of bagpipers paraded round the dining-hall, blawing wi' micht and main, and thrilling the pulse of every Scotchman within hearing with their wild, weird strains."

In recognition of the kindly relationship in which it stood to the Grand National Club of America, the Royal Club, in 1872, elected Mr M'Dougall of the St Andrew's (New York) Club, who was then American Consul at Dundee, to be one of their vice-presidents. Deputies have sometimes been sent to Scotland by the two clubs which keep up the old alliance with us—St Andrew's and Yonkers, and at the fiftieth anniversary meeting of the Royal Club in July 1888, Mr J. B. Gillie appeared as the first accredited delegate of the Grand National Club who had attended our annual meeting. It is surely matter of regret that we have not more "comings and goings" with each other, united as we are by the ties of kinship and curling. A proposal has more than once been made to have a match between Scotland and the United States. In 1870 Sir William Elliot sent a challenge across the Atlantic to play any rink for a sum of £500. This was discussed at the Grand National Convention of 1871, but set aside, because of the objection urged by Mr Hoogland, that a match for money, even though the sum should be devoted to a charity, would drag down curling to the level of baseball. John Johnston, president of the Grand National Club, brought a challenge with him to the Royal Club in the year 1878, but only three curlers were found to volunteer their services. As far back as 1858 our Canadian Branch, through David Mair, their secretary, sent us a challenge, which has been several times renewed. The Ontario Branch, when the Marquis of Lorne was Governor-General of Canada, thought that would be a suitable time for a match between the Canadians and the curlers of the old country, and sent, by the Rev. Dr Barclay of Toronto, a message, which was "not a challenge, but a kindly invitation to a friendly match." Still nothing was done. The Marquis of Lorne and H.R.H. the Princess Louise, on leaving Canada, both promised their assistance in the matter. Lord Melgund did his best to bring off the match during his presidency. Since then several invitations have been sent from our brethren in Ontario, but up till this time the difficulties in the way have evidently been too great. If it is merely a *friendly match* that is proposed, there are surely too many formalities being observed. Home curlers with time and money may any winter visit America, and be sure of a hearty welcome on the rink, and transatlantic curlers may rely on the same in the old country. Why not let us have an international match, which would at once be a test of curling skill, and a *friendly match* with no dubiety about it, the Beaver and the Eagle combining, if they choose, to attack the Lion Rampant? Or, since our Scottish clubs outnumber all the others put together, why should it not be *Furth of Scotland v. Scotland?* Such a Grand Match would indeed be an epoch in the history of the game. It is due to Scotland that it should first be played there, and the contest would be all the keener if "oor auld respectit mither"—the Royal Club, whose position in the matter ought to be neutral—held in her hand a trophy, subscribed for by the whole curling brotherhood, to be awarded to the side of the house which asserted the right to hold it till another match should be played.

THE CURLER'S GRIP.

Air—*Auld Lang Syne.*

Losh man ! I'm glad to see yoursel',
　I'm glad to meet a freen' ;
But, man, the pleasure's greater still
　When he's a curler keen.
　　　　Sae gie's the curler's grip, my freen',
　　　　　Sae gie's the curler's grip.
　　　　Losh man ! I'm glad to see yoursel',
　　　　　Sae gie's the curler's grip.

We've played thegither mony a time
　Around the curlin' tee ;
I've sooped ye aften up the ice,
　You've dune the same to me.
　　　　Sae gie's the curler's grip, my freen',
　　　　　Sae gie's the curler's grip.
　　　　Losh man ! I'm glad to see yoursel',
　　　　　Sae gie's the curler's grip.

Man ! when I feel a grip like that,
　I'm unca sweir'd to part ;
The blood rins din'lin' up my arm
　An' warms my very heart.
　　　　Sae gie's the curler's grip, my freen',
　　　　　Sae gie's the curler's grip.
　　　　Losh man ! I'm glad to see yoursel',
　　　　　Sae gie's the curler's grip.

But as the nicht is gye weel thro',
　Let's hae anither "nip,"
An' drink success to ilka ane
　That kens the curler's grip.
　　　　Sae gie's the curler's grip, my freen',
　　　　　Sae gie's the curler's grip.
　　　　Losh man ! I'm glad to see yoursel',
　　　　　Sae gie's the curler's grip.

　　　　　　　　　　　　Dr Sidey.

CHAPTER IV.

"THE MYSTERIES."

EGEL must have been "uninitiated" when he laid down the dictum that "the things which cannot be uttered are the things which are not worth uttering." The "mysteries" which from time immemorial have been associated with curling are of great practical value, and they shed considerable light on the origin and antiquity of the game. We might, therefore, with less doubtful motives, act the part of a Clodius, and reveal the *arcana* of the craft. The temptation is strong, but we resist. We shall, however, sail as near the wind as we can, and permit the profane to hear a few sounds from "the dark passage."

INITIATION.

The *Word* and the *Grip*.—Even before the formation of curling societies curlers appear to have bound themselves together by the use of a certain *password* and *grip*. Johnny Gude in his young days used to hear old curlers mentioning the Rev. Mr John Witherspoon of Paisley as having been a keen curler, and as the first person that gave what is called the *Heigh Linn* curling word, which was about the year 1757 or 1758.*

---

* Cairnie's *Essay*, p. 81.

From the account of the formation of the Sanquhar Society in 1774 (p. 126) it is apparent that a *word* and *grip* had been in use before the society was formed. Two years later we have some indication of the nature of these in the following minute:—

"SANQUHAR, 16*th January* 1776.
"In order to prevent all disputes concerning the curler word and grip, the master, who always is preses during his office, and the rest of the society, have agreed that the following shall be held and reputed the curler word and grip of this society for the future:—

The curler word:—

"If you'd be a curler keen
Stand right, look even,
Sole well, shoot straight, and sweep clean."

The curler grip, with the explanation:—

"Griping hands in the common manner of shaking hands is the griping the hand of the curling-stone. The thumb of the person examined or instructed thrust in betwixt the thumb and forefinger of the examinator or instructor signifies running a port. The little finger of the person examined or instructed linked with the little finger of the examinator or instructor means an in-ring."

Mr Brown, the historian of the Sanquhar Club, is evidently right in supposing that these are only fragments of the old forms—"all that was left upon which there was any general agreement." In a footnote to page 14 of the Kilmarnock Treatise on Curling (1828) we have a much simpler form of initiation, given as "a curious old custom in many parishes of Perthshire":—

"The curler is initiated by receiving the *grip*, which consists in catching him by the thumb in the manner that the curling-stone is held, and in making him repeat the *curling* word: 'I promise never to go to the ice without a broom; I will fit fair, sweep well, take all the brittle (angled) shots I can, and cangle (dispute) to a hairbreadth.'"

In the *Annual* for 1842 (p. 60) we have this account of the origin of the Blairgowrie Club:—

"In the course of 1782 an inhabitant of Coupar-Angus, 'whiteheaded Jamie Cammell,' having occasion to be in Edinburgh in the prosecution of his trade of cattle-dealer, went out to Duddingston Loch to see the play of the south country brethren. During the game a very difficult shot occurred, on which all the curlers present tried their skill and failed; and Mr Campbell having remarked that he thought he could take the shot, was invited to try it, which he did, and was successful. He afterwards continued to play during the remainder of the day with the Duddingston curlers, who were so well pleased with his skill in the game that they invited him to dine with them, and initiated him a member of the club by communicating to him the *word* and *grip*. On his return to Coupar-Angus he initiated the members of his own club, from whom the Blairgowrie Club received the sign and secret in the following year."

The Duddingston Club of that date was the successor of the old Canonmills Club, from which it no doubt received the initiation which it is said to have thus transmitted to Blairgowrie. From Blairgowrie many other clubs received the "mystery." If the above statement be correct, it furnishes us with an interesting link of connection between the curling of Edinburgh and that of the north of Scotland. Like their brethren at Sanquhar, the members of the old Douglas St Bride Society reduced to writing the traditional mysteries, and on 14th February 1794 the following was brought up by the office-bearers and adopted as "the correct form":—

Question.	Answer.
1. Are you a curler?	Keen.
2. What is the duty of a curler?	To behave peaceably, and play to direction.
3. What is the greatest pleasure of a curler?	With a good stone on hard ice to beat his adversary.

Nix......Gelu......Glacies.

Foot firm and fair,
Play to a hair;
  Your stone, if well directed,
Will hit your aim,
And win the game;
  If not, be not dejected.

(*The sign, grip, &c., will be communicated by the office-bearers.*)

An improved version of the Douglas word was adopted by the oldest Canadian club—that formed at Montreal in 1807. It is prefixed to the minute-book, and reads thus:—

"Foot fair: draw to a hair:
  Your stone being well directed,
You'll hit your aim, and win the game;
  If you miss, be not dejected."

When we remember that the secrecy of the "mysteries" was carefully protected, we are not surprised that we hear so little about them in the old records, but in the majority of ancient societies we can infer from the records that they were observed. No one was *brothered* or *entered* till he had got the word: the entry-money was generally spoken of as payment therefor; and once in possession of the precious *sesame*, all the privileges of his own and other clubs were open to him; he was a fully-equipped K.B., or knight of the broom, and one of the noble brotherhood of *keen, keen, keen curlers*. It was the custom to inflict a severe fine on any one who betrayed the secrets. Thus, in the Douglas Society, while the word itself could be had for 6d., a fine of 1s. was imposed on any one who divulged it. The purity of the word was of the greatest importance. It was a smaller offence in the eyes of the Sanquhar curlers to be ignorant of it altogether than to pretend to have it and be found defective. In the one case they gave instruction, in the other they inflicted a fine. An entry in the Hamilton record, of date 19th December 1796, shews how the offender was treated there :—

"A complaint was made by Robert Pender against Robert Purdie, who gave a new grip to Mr Sands, one of the new members, never known before to the society; he was accordingly fined of 2s. 6d. to the society and 6d. to the officer, which he refused to pay, and appealed to a general meeting."

To preserve the knowledge and purity of the word, it was usual at the annual meetings of ancient clubs to examine all who had been initiated. *Rusts* or *rustys* were condemned and fined. In the early days these fines were invariably devoted to the *bowl*. Drouthy members were tempted to take advantage of this custom to "wet their whistle" at the expense of their rusty brethren, and the following from the Hamilton minutes shews how such abuse was dealt with :—

"HAMILTON, 10*th March* 1789.
"The meeting having taken into their serious consideration the many irregularities that occur from meetings and members of the society trying and examining individuals respecting the word, and bringing them in for *rusty pints:* they, therefore, to prevent any such irregular behaviour for the future, hereby agree to enact it as a regulation that no member who has got the word and entered in the book as a member shall ever be tried for the word afterwards."

The later and more famous Duddingston Society did not follow its predecessor in having a *word* and *grip*. Its initiation ceremony was simply the payment of entry-money, and its only "mystery" was a silver medal "to distinguish the members from any other gentlemen." Curling ceremonies, thus ignored by the Duddingston Society, suffered even more than the laws of curling in the confusion which prevailed in the transition period. If they had a common origin, they had in the course of transmission from club to club been so altered as to prove a cause of division rather than a bond of union among clubs. The Lasswade and Roslin Clubs, after a match on December 28, 1829, met in the evening, and when it was decided to increase the supply of liquor by trying the *rusts*,* it was found that the words were slightly different in the clubs, and the *rusts* escaped. At an after meeting,

"The difference was found to be so small that it was referred to the toss of a penny, when fortune favoured the Lasswade Club, and it was agreed that instead of the word *stand*, it should now for both clubs be *stan'*."

This was a small difference and easily adjusted. But in other districts the difference was so great and the variety in the form of the word of initiation so confusing that Dr Arnott suggested a "convention of the principal initiated clubs in Scotland" to deal with the subject. His suggestion, as we have seen, led to the formation of the Grand Club. The scope of this club was very soon widened. Its founders included therein the whole subject of curling. This was a wise afterthought, for which the curling world may be thankful. There is, however, no doubt that the primary purpose of those who first moved in the matter did not extend beyond the institution of a kind of Grand Lodge to govern the Freemasonry of the ancient game. In the constitution of the Grand Club, *initiation* had an important place. It was decided that there should be—

"(1.) A *fixed word of initiation* which no one, as an individual, is to commit to writing without special permission from the G.C.C.C. or the Representative Committee. Each club was to be furnished

* In 1865 the Roslin Club had to alter their custom, and resolve, "That *rusts* should be tried in the morning before competing for the medal, instead of being tried in the evening, as this appeared to have a tendency to interfere with the harmony of the evening."

with *cyphers*, to be inserted in the minute-book, by which the word would be understood by the brethren.

"(2.) A *grip*.
"(3.) A *pass* and *counter-word*."

Without committing the same to writing, we may permit the uninitiated to enjoy as much of the forbidden fruit as he can taste without the "cypher key."* Here is

The Fixed Word of Initiation.

Drink	little	get	up	early	be	no	long	and	clean	the	rink
ply	well	your	besom	to	guide	that	stone	up	to	the	tee
try	not to	be a	hog	not	Keen	never	promise	to	take	a shot	you are
not	able for	to	no	besom	play	well	I am	the	skipper	I	Keen
to	refuse	and	to	side	keep	to	a	Keen	stone	curler	appear
port	intending	of	to	from	nay	curler	ever	on	to	without	that
and	I am	the	rink	play	it	the	stone	not	if	my	the
ice	the	by	past	draw	foot	tied	to	rink	straw	neighbours	score
with	adversary's	straight	to	take	can	and	suck	to	sweep	I am	direction
to	I am	all	I	to	and	the	to	and	my	for	I am
tee	if	and	can	the	I will	to	giggle	not	well	I am	the
direct	I	word	breath	nor	them	to	write	sticks	hog	kiggle	fr-
be a	hair	reveal	cause	I	curler	or	written	and	shots	neither	or
brittle	nor	promise	Keen	stone	curler	that	this	any	a	to be	than
to	a	good	Keen	soled	pair	of	stones	to	secrets	all	co-
the	Keen	side	ought	to	be	any	like	the	not	glass	every
person	curling	ought	to	keep	good	faith	and to	form	a	good	court
of	justice	gleg	ice	and	Keen	curlers	fair	play	oil	auction	the
ice	may	curlers	on	life's	slippery	rink	frae	cruel	tube	be	free

The founders of the Grand Club appear to have arrived at this long word by comparing the various forms submitted to them, and then framing a form of word which should comprehend them all. According to the report of the Kinross deputation inserted in that club's minutes, 20th August 1838,

"The various clubs gave a general detail of their regulations, and also their 'words,' which, though in many very imperfect, yet the general resemblance and similarity of the whole was gratifying to all present as shewing that the institution of curling in Scotland proceeded from one common root or origin."

* Dr Arnott invented a set of "magic rods" for reading the *word*. This, which is simply an ingenious adjustment of the twelve columns, is in the possession of the Orwell Club, and is enclosed in a neat case made by Alexander Forfar in 1849.

At a later meeting, November 16, 1838, the same deputation reports:—

"That the word of the Kinross Court might be said to form the basis of the one now adopted by the Grand Club, some small additions from those of certain other clubs being made to it; a *grip* also was agreed on, identical with that used at Kinross, with one slight addition."

It appears that the "ancient mysteries" had from time immemorial been carefully observed at the old county town of Kinross. Other clubs were in the habit of repairing thither to receive in their "pristine purity" the *word* and the *grip*. When the Grand Club was formed the Kinross brethren gladly communicated these to the committee to assist them in drafting the constitution. At the formation of the club J. W. Williamson of Kinross, to whose good work as a curler we have already referred, is said to

FIG. 73. J. W. WILLIAMSON,
The Arch-Initiator.
(*From an old photograph.*)

have initiated upwards of thirty-six individuals from different clubs. Mr Williamson was for a long time the high priest of the temple of curling mysteries, presiding over the solemn ceremonies of "the dark passage" in such pomp and pride as became his office. No traveller returned from the mysterious bourne to tell his experience—the lips of the initiated were sealed. *Cave canem* was all that was said to trembling candidates. From which, and from certain shrieks that now and then reached the uninitiated outer world, it was generally supposed that the master only gave the *word* when Cerberus immediately gave the *grip*, which transformed the calf of a common mortal into that of a *keen, keen, keen curler*. The committee which prepared the constitution of the Grand Club gave a laudable reason for adopting a *word* and *grip*. The club was "intended to unite the whole kingdom into one brotherhood of the rink," and a form of initiation was accordingly designed—

> "To enable members to recognise each other as such, although personally unknown, and thereby to ensure them, when visiting distant clubs, a participation in their game, which, owing to the numbers who resort to the ice (particularly near large towns), it would be impossible to extend to strangers indiscriminately."

This the committee distinctly stated was "the only purpose" they had in view. They seem to have felt that their action required some apology. They disowned the spirit of exclusiveness, and did not commit themselves to the approval of many uses to which "initiation" had been or might be put. In so far as the representative meeting of the Royal Club has been concerned, the law as at first laid down has been faithfully obeyed. New clubs on their affiliation have had the "mysteries" communicated to them. It is otherwise with the majority of our affiliated clubs. The law is virtually set aside. Many members object altogether to the shibboleth of initiation, and the tendency seems to be to neglect "the mysteries" altogether. Indications of this tendency are distinctly visible in the history of the Royal Club. In the year 1850 an additional "mystery" was invented. This was a curling uniform, in which the bodies of the "initiated" were to be enswathed and distinguished from the vulgar crowd. It was to consist of "coat, vest, and trousers of one pattern and quality, the groundwork of the cloth to be as nearly as possible of a *granite* colour, checked with blue and green bars, the *blue* being the royal colour, and the *green* emblematic of the broom." For this "mystery" curlers were to pay Mr John Piper—who was appointed clothier to the Royal Club—4s. 6d. a yard, and for making up—coat, 14s.; vest, 6s. 6d.; trousers, 4s. 6d.: while "the very buttons" were to be paid for at 5s. 6d. per set for the coat, and 1s. 6d. for the vest. But it would not do. Mr John Piper and the club uniform very soon had to disappear from the scene.

By the original rule "none but *initiated* curlers were allowed to be present at the business or the convivial meetings of the Royal Club." This was found to interfere with the development of sociality, and a relaxation of the rule had to be made by the addition of the words *while curling ceremonies or mysteries are being practised*. To enforce a stricter observance of the law of initiation, a representative member at the annual meeting in 1883 moved:—

"That no names be printed in the *Annual* but those of *initiated* curlers."

Only three were found to support this motion, Mr Rouet (representative of Frederickton, New Brunswick) remarking that "in Canada not one in twenty was initiated, and if the motion was carried, it would sweep the whole of the Canadian names out of the *Annual*."

These are sufficient indications of the tendency to which we have referred, and which is not unlikely in the long run to lead to the total abolition of the ceremony.

THE CURLING COURT.

In addition to the ceremony of initiation, some of the ancient curling societies, after the usual dinner of beef and greens, were accustomed to hold what was called a curling court. Sir Richard Broun, in his *Memorabilia* (p. 67), gives a brief account of this court, which he describes as "a sort of game of high jinks, or mock heroic tribunal," but we are not aware that it was customary to hold it in the south of Scotland. The author of the Kilmarnock Treatise speaks of the court as "a curious old custom in Perthshire," from which we infer that it was not common in the west of Scotland.* It is to Kinross that we

---

* Cairnie, in his *Essay* (p. 35), has an account of the nature of the *word* in the Largs Club, and says that "curling courts are generally held where clubs are formed," but no court seems to have been held under his auspices.

are again indebted for the preservation of this "mystery" in its most complete form. In view of the formation of the Grand Club, the curlers of Kinross drew up a description of the court as it had been handed down orally from generation to generation, and transmitted this by the hands of their delegates to the meeting. With the ceremony of initiation the Grand Club did not associate the more elaborate ceremony of the court, as was the custom at Kinross, but left it to clubs to "communicate the mysteries" in their own way. The Grand Club, however, awarded the custom a certificate of antiquity. It "had been held for upwards of 200 years." Clubs might wish to revive it. The Kinross Court, with a few slight alterations, was therefore entered in the club minute-book, and copies printed for the use of such clubs as applied for them. At the dinner after the first meeting of the Grand Club a court was held, which was fenced "in auld style" by J. W. Williamson, "to the great satisfaction of all present."

CURLING COURT.

"The first requisite is to elect a President, termed 'My Lord;' he is usually the Præses of the club for the time, but any other brother may be chosen. 'My Lord,' on taking the chair, immediately appoints one of the brethren present to be his officer, whom he directs to fence the court. This is done as follows :—

"A pewter stoup, varying from a mutchkin to a pint (Scottish measure) is procured, which the officer presents to 'My Lord;' and he, in order to make a noise, drops therein some silver, or a few pence, according to his pleasure. The officer, after rattling the money in the stoup three times, and repeating alternately with each shake, 'Oyez,' 'oyez,' 'oyez,' fences the court thus :—

"'I defend and I forbid, in Her (or His) Majesty's name and authority of 'My Lord' presently in the chair—(1) that there shall be no legs oer'em; (2) no hands a-bosy, or across; (3) no supports on your neighbour's chair, or on the table; (4) no private committees; (5) no rising up, or sitting down, or going to the door, without leave asked and granted by 'My Lord;' (6) no touching the cup or glass but with the curler's right hand, which is understood to be every ordinary man's left; (7) every man his name and surname; (8) every breach of these articles a halfpenny, and every oath a penny.'

"The officer then *points* out and gives in an audible voice the name and surname of every *brother* present, commencing on 'My Lord's' *left* hand, and going regularly round the whole company, thus: 'A. B. is A. B.; C. D. is C. D.; E. F. is E. F.; G. H. is G. H.; (and on coming to 'My Lord'), 'My Lord's' 'My Lord,' and I am his officer—*both absolute*. God save the Queen (or King).' The officer usually stands opposite to the person named, at the other side of the table, when this can be conveniently done.

"*If any individuals are present not yet brethren, as is the case with those to be initiated that evening, the officer passes them over, and these are not subject to the fines and regulations of the court till after initiation.*

"The proceedings of the court then go on; and it is the special duty of the officer, who remains on his feet rattling the stoup occasionally, to observe and detect all breaches of the regulations, and to collect the fines in the stoup, rattling it at the ear of the offender till the fine is paid.

"The decision of 'My Lord,' and, through him, of his officer in fining, is perfectly *absolute*, and *must* be obeyed. Any one member has a right to report the breaches of another to 'My Lord,' or his officer; but if the person complained against conceives himself aggrieved by the report he may *protest* and *appeal*, which is done by depositing a penny on the table, to be forfeited to the *stoup* in case of being decided against, *which generally happens* when an appeal is made. 'My Lord' very shortly hears the *protester*, and gives an absolute decision.

"When candidates for the brotherhood are present, 'My Lord' (after the court has sat a reasonable time) directs the business of initiation to proceed.

"The candidate thereupon respectfully approaches 'My Lord,' with a curler's besom in his hand, holding it over his right shoulder, and craves to be admitted a member of the honourable court and club. 'My Lord' now appoints *one* of the brethren to give him the 'word' and 'grip,' and *two* others (one or both of whom must be masters of the whole secrets), to be *reporters* as to whether these have been given correctly. The three then conduct the candidate to an adjoining room, which has been previously prepared for the purpose, and after a careful examination that no intruders are present, and shutting the door, the initiation commences by the person appointed by 'My Lord' first giving the 'word' and then the 'grip.' If the reporters find that he is unable to give these correctly, they return with him to the court, and report him to 'My Lord' as deficient, who immediately appoints some other to the office. The same proceeding is repeated, and appointments made, till a brother is found sufficiently qualified.

"'My Lord' often fixes *at first* on some one to give the secrets whom he suspects to be deficient; and all who fail in this duty are fined, before the close of the court, at the option of the company—a penny, or twopence, or threepence. When a brother is so appointed, he may decline, and come under the mercy of the court, by saying, 'I submit;' but he is generally fined in a larger sum than those who make the attempt, but fail.

"The reporters, after the candidate receives the secrets, introduce him to 'My Lord' in court, as 'brother of the broom, and a keen, keen, keen curler.' He then goes forward to 'My Lord,' and holding his hand under the table, out of view, *gives* 'My Lord' the grip; after which he goes to the brother on 'My Lord's' *left*, and holding his hand also below the table, requests that member to *give him* the 'grip.' The newly admitted member must on no account give the grip to any one except 'My Lord,' but himself receive it; and if the brother, through inattention or otherwise, does not give it to him correctly, he notes the circumstance, and when he has gone round the company in this way (or until 'My Lord' says he may stop), he reports to 'My

Lord' all those who were deficient, and they are fined at the discretion of 'My Lord.'

"*When there are more candidates than one, the same proceedings take place with each separately.* The court is then fenced anew by the officer, the names of the new brothers being of course included.

"During the sitting of the court 'My Lord' says, '*I give a toast not to be repeated;*' and he immediately proposes one, of which he and the other officer keep note, and generally write down for accuracy. Any member who repeats the toast before being specially requested to do so is immediately fined a halfpenny to the stoup. Sometime afterwards, and when the toast may be supposed to be forgotten by many, 'My Lord' directs the officer to go round the company and ask each individually what it was: each must whisper it to the officer, so that the person next him cannot hear: if he fail to mention the toast *to the very letter*, the officer rattles the stoup at his ear, as an intimation that he has failed, and proceeds to the next person, and so on. When he has gone round the whole, he reports to 'My Lord' those who failed, and his lordship directs a fine to be levied from each—generally one penny. Any person conceiving himself aggrieved may protest and appeal in the manner already mentioned.

"When 'My Lord' thinks that the court has continued a sufficient length of time (usually from half-an-hour to an hour), he directs the officer to 'roup the stoup,' which is done by him in the character of an *auctioneer*, descanting all the time on the great weight and value of the stoup: offers are made for the contents in the way of an ordinary auction or roup; and after it is knocked down to the highest bidder, trifling bets are sometimes taken as to whether the purchaser has gained or lost, two reporters being appointed to count the proceeds in another room. While the reporters are absent for this purpose, the court goes on, another stoup being used; and any fines collected during that time, and also during the roup of the stoup, are added to the original amount, and belong to the purchaser. 'My Lord' then declares the court closed.

"*The purchase money is either applied towards defraying the expense of the social glass, or added to the club funds, according to the general regulations of the club.*

"*It is obvious that, as one brother is required for 'My Lord,' another for the officer, and three to perform the ceremony of initiation, the court cannot well proceed unless seven be present, and this only provides for two sitting in court during the absence of the initiators; but there is little amusement if there be not from fifteen to twenty in company.*"

Another set of rules for the curling court, as practised throughout Strathallan, from Auchterarder to Stirling and Doune, is said to have been in writing as far back as 1711. Dr Walker Arnott had a copy inserted in the minutes of Orwell Club, where it is stated that

"These rules had been introduced into the district by Lord Strathallan previous to the first rebellion, but it is not known whether he obtained them from among his ancestors' papers or introduced them from other districts; the current belief is that he received the copy from some of the Scotch then in Paris."

The Strathallan rules are also inserted in the old minute-book of Dunblane, by which club they were used in the beginning of this century. They differ a little from the Kinross set, but the latter is simpler and more comprehensive.

The high jinks of the curling court have been carried on by the older clubs in which they have been handed down. A few younger clubs have also revived the proceedings of the court in other districts, adding some "jinkses" of their own. Inverness, of course, carries *Ye Palladium* in solemn state and places it, like the mace, before "My Lord." "Ye stoup" is an old tin kettle, which a rink of the club, "by the assistance of a drunken porter from Perth," won at the Grand Match and brought as a trophy to the capital of the Highlands. The kettle is silvered o'er (in the inside) with shilling fines: the chairman makes the highest bid at the "roupin'" and loses a crown: while Paul (the bagpiper) is presented with a sovereign. Where courts were held the old practice was to apply the *stoup* to the payment of the bill. This, according to Dr Arnott, "occasionally induced a sederunt too long for modern customs," and some clubs began to apply the contents to the funds of the club, so that "all practical *curlers* were benefited by those who loved *bowls*." The Abdie Club, under the licence of the court, actually made up the most of its funds by court fines of the most *hanky-panky* description, inflicted on all and sundry without rhyme or reason. We give a few specimens:—

"February 1, 1841.—Dr L. was fined 1s. for shooting at a hare in her seat, the offence being aggravated by the fact that the hare had been dead for some days previous.

"January 31, 1844.—Mr Russel, without consent of the club, having purchased an estate, was fined 2s. 6d.

"February 1859.—A. W. R., 'for having, to the great danger of the digestion and bodily health of the members present, supplied hard, tough beef for this day's dinner, was fined 1s.'

"Mr Pitcairn was fined 'for being the first member of the club who had condescended to the use of chloroform in having a tooth extracted.'"

The Belfast Club at their annual meetings had much "exhilarating and side-splitting mirth" under the court. On one occasion (January 9, 1880) a live donkey, which had, unknown to most of the members, been placed in a large press in the banqueting-hall, gave a loud bray in the middle of an eloquent speech by the chaplain (Rev. W. C. M'Cullagh), and "brought down the house." The "noble steed" was afterwards trotted out, and each candidate for initiation had to approach "My Lord" on the donkey's back, with his face to the tail and a broom kowe over his right shoulder. *Dulce est desipere in loco.* "Weel-timed daffin'" is very enjoyable, and the quaint custom of the curling court may have a place among the diversions that help

> "To cheer us through the weary widdle
> O' war'ly cares."

Any practical value it may have must, however, be lessened by the neglect of those initiation ceremonies with which in the Kinross form it is so closely connected. The "Royal" rules and regulations under which curlers now play have made the old court quite unnecessary as a forum for deciding disputes, or a tribunal "before which it is competent to try, fine, and punish curlers for all trifling offences and misdemeanours committed upon the ice." Fining is one of the lost arts among curling clubs, and few of them carry on the practice. A club which depended on the precarious revenue of the "stoup" would in these days soon come to grief; and in the permit-me-to-prevent-you-period on which we are entering we must make a virtue out of a necessity, and cease to replenish the bowl. It is still left to those who would uphold this ancient ceremony to plead with curlers to continue it on the ground that

> "It was chiefly intended to diffuse around the festive board the same free, unconstrained, and jovial familiarity and feeling of rough equality and brotherhood which curling never fails to create on the ice."

There is something in this plea. If by this means we can break down the dividing walls, let us invoke "My Lord" and "his officer" and honour their "court" to the end. But have they not in their very foolishness been preparing the way for a recognition—wider, freer, and less constrained—of the truth expressed in the American mottoes, "*E pluribus unum,*" and "*We're brithers a'*"?

PART III.

MISCELLANEA.

MY BONNY BROOMY KOWE.

TUNE—*The Nameless Lassie.*

In summers past I've seen thee bloom
   On mossy bank and knowe;
I've revell'd mid thy sweet perfume,
   My bonny broomy kowe.
I've garlanded thy yellow flowers,
   I've lain beneath thy bough;
I'll ne'er forget thy youthful prime,
   My bonny broomy kowe.

You've been my friend at ilka spiel,
   You've polish'd up the *howe*,
You've mony a stane brocht owre the *hog*,
   My bonny broomy kowe.
As mem'ry noo recalls the past,
   My heart is set alowe,
Wi' moistened e'en I gaze on thee,
   My bonny broomy kowe.

Time tells on a'; your pith has gane,
   And wrinkled is my brow;
We're no sae fresh as we ha'e been,
   My bonny broomy kowe.
Your wizzen'd sair, and maist as thin
   As hairs upon my pow,
I doubt our days are nearly dune,
   My bonny broomy kowe.

When death comes o'er me, let my grave
   Be sacred frae the plough;
For cypress plant a golden broom,
   That yet may be a kowe.
Nor rest nor peace shall e'er be yours—
   A' curlers hear my vow—
Unless there grow abune my head
   A bonny broomy kowe.

                    W. A. PETERKIN.

CHAPTER I.

CURLING EQUIPMENTS.

Hearken, thou craggy ocean pyramid!
Give answer from thy voice—the sea-fowls' screams!
When were thy shoulders mantled in huge streams?
When, from the sun, was thy broad forehead hid?
How long is't since the mighty power bid
Thee heave to airy sleep from fathom dreams?
Sleep in the lap of thunder or sunbeams,
Or when grey clouds are thy cold coverlid?
Thou answer'st not, for thou art dead asleep!
Thy life is but two dead eternities—
The last in air, the former in the deep;
First with the whales, last in the eagle-skies—
Drown'd wast thou till an earthquake made thee
   steep,
Another cannot wake thy giant size.

(FIRST.)

UT from the entrance to the Frith of Clyde stands "the craggy ocean pyramid" which John Keats, in that fine sonnet, apostrophised as he halted at the King's Arms Inn, Girvan, in the summer of 1818. But Ailsa Craig, still as deaf as when Burns told the tale of Meg and Duncan Gray, neither heard nor heeded the questioner. About the very time that Keats wrote his sonnet Ailsa Craig was becoming known as "a place of arms" for curlers. As such it has become more and more popular. We are within the mark when we say that one-half of the curling-stones used in Scotland, and three-fourths of those furth of Scotland, have been taken from Ailsa. The chief equipment

of the curler is his *curling-stone*. While the frost lasts, that
stone is the *dimidium animæ* of its owner—aye, and more.
It cannot but be interesting to a curler to know something as to how his chief equipment is itself equipped. In
this belief we ask him to accompany us to the Craig, and
follow the career of the stone. The origin of the rock itself
we had better regard as a mystery, like the origin of the
game of curling and of the Royal Club. Any answer to the
poet's questions seems to open up awkward points. We are
safe enough to believe that Hew Barclay of Ladyland tried to
make Ailsa a fortified place, to help the cause of Spain and
that for his treason he shared the fate of the Armada, or that
the solan geese were its "inhabitants" as far back as 1549,
when Dean Munro of the Isles wrote the first account of
the rock. Beyond that the ground is dangerous. One
tradition is that about the year 1000 A.D. the island belonged
to the Irish king, Brian Boru. If so, pity the Marquis of
Ailsa, the tenant, and the stone-makers! According to the
Irish song—

> "Bad luck to the gosoon spalpeen,
>   Or Saxon idle drone,
> Who would make filthy lucre
>   Out of Brian's blessed stone."

If, as another tradition reports, the witches dropped *Paddy's
milestone* in the North Channel on their way over to Ireland,
then there are more curlers than those at Monzie* under a
debt which they may find it troublesome to pay. Another
common tradition is that Ailsa Craig owes its origin to the
Prince of Darkness. That potentate has never taken to
curling:† it has generally been supposed that he does not

---

* Called *Maggie Cadzan's Band*, after a witch who is said to be their
patroness.

† A Kilmarnock collier on his way to the pit one morning got so alarmed
at what he saw on a curling-pond near the town that he rushed home and
informed his wife that "he had seen a *sicht* that would keep him from
going farther that day; he had seen Bryan o' the Sun Inn and the deil
quitin (curling) on the auld water." In the light of Ailsa traditions the
juxtaposition of the two names is suggestive. The collier's vision was
satisfactorily explained. John Bryan, landlord of the Sun Inn, a tall
portly man and a keen curler, had got a blacksmith to go and have a spiel
with him at a very early hour. The contrast between Boniface and Buru-
the-wind, who was "a wee, black, towsy, ill-washed body," led the collier
too readily to a wrong conclusion.

allow ice to be formed in his dominion, and that he hates the channel-stane as his worst enemy. No respectable curler mentions his name, nor is he an initiated member of any affiliated club. What if, after all, the game be under his royal patronage, and he be actually furnishing the world with curling-stones to work out his wicked purposes! Let us away from these traditions, and breathe the fresh air of geologic facts. But it is "out of the frying-pan into the fire." "Ailsa Craig is the plug of the throat of a volcano," says our petrologist in the next chapter. Can the roar of the Ailsa channel-stane ever again then be "music dear to a curler's ear?" The ten thousand voices which have carried the sound of the Craig to the ends of the earth have been proclaiming Scotland's doom. This is the simple question :—

"Ailsa Craig is 370 yards high, 1300 yards long, 860 yards broad, and 2¼ miles in circumference—area, 220 acres. At the rate of 1000 pairs of curling-stone blocks per annum (twelve blocks to a ton), how long will it take to remove the Craig, clear the throat of the volcano of which it is the plug, and overwhelm the country?"

Enough of petrology and tradition. Let us begin with May 16, 1889, when, with Messrs Douglas and Thorburn, we visited Ailsa, and heard the rock tell its own story. The Craig is rented from the Marquis of Ailsa by Andrew Girvan, who, for £30 a year, has the pasturage of the island, and a monopoly of the supply of stone. Under the charge of Andrew we left the town of Girvan, which is 9½ miles distant, and our boat drew up at the neat little jetty erected by the Northern Lighthouse Commissioners, in connection with the lighthouse which stands on a spit of level ground on the east side of the island. We found James Millar waiting there to receive us. James, whose profile is accurately given in the frontispiece of this chapter, is a man of great intelligence and physical power. He is the blocker-general in the curling-stone world, visiting Ailsa Craig for two or three months in the year, and then returning to Ochiltree, of which place he is a native, to prepare the Burnocks. The majority of our curling-stones have come through the hands of James Millar. There is a knack in blocking the stones, as there

2 A

is in most other things, and James has it. "You must have a good straight run in the boulder," says he; and from what we saw it is not easy to get. Once James gets it he soon divides up his subject into squares, leaving to one or two subordinates to chip the squares into such roundness as they are seen to possess in our drawings. Match-making among the Ailsa blocks is most difficult. Nature has joined them together, but not in "happy pairs." It is under the hands of James Millar that like is drawn to like. James is Mormon in his match-making. When he gets a block with some sweetness and regularity in its disposition, he numbers it, say "38" or "39," as the case may be, and then selects five, ten, or twenty companions for it, giving them all the same number, to shew their similarity, and leaving the pairing process to the manufacturer. There are, as all curlers are aware, three kinds of Ailsas—the Blue Hone, the Red Hone, and what is called the Common Ailsa. The last, as its name implies, is most plentiful. The Red is scarce, and getting scarcer every year. At the time of our visit workmen were busy blasting a seam of this variety on the north side of the island, about 200 feet above the sea. One of the men, bound by a rope, descended the precipice, inserted a blast, and was then pulled up. When the blast came off the dislodged stone was dashed down on the shore and broken into fragments. It is the difficulty of getting it that makes the Red Hone so dear. James Millar unhesitatingly places the other varieties before it, and gives the Blue Hone the highest place among the Ailsas. The prices of these blocks put on the rail at Girvan run from 3s. 6d. to 9s. per pair, the highest price, of course, being paid for the Red Hone. At a cost of about 10s. per ton, or about 2s. per pair, the blocks are carried by railway to the principal manufactories in the west country. In the workshop the block is first of all *cheesed*, *i.e.*, chiselled into the shape of a gouda cheese. The stone is thereafter bored. When it has been properly swung and balanced, it passes into the hands of a workman with a teethed hammer, who gives it a rough finish all round, and then rolls it off with a mould, and prepares it for the grinding machine. The cost of this machine is about £20. It is in two parts. The curling-stone, in a cup at the base of a vertical, is whirled round at great speed by the upper belt operating on two meeter-screws, and held firmly on a Nitshill grindstone driven in an opposite direction by the lower belt, as shewn in our drawing. The stone is reduced and roughly polished by this process. In making the concave sole, the stone, instead of being allowed to run in a hollow, is run upon a raised ridge—A, in the grindstone

FIG. 74. STEAM GRINDSTONE.

In ordinary grinding, the stone, by means of a lever which raises the cup, can be taken out, and another inserted without stopping the machine. In grinding the concave sole both parts of the machine are, however, slowed in case any injury should be done to the running ridge of the stone—a matter of the greatest importance, for no stone can run correctly when this delicate ridge is in any way impaired. On its removal from the grinding machine the curling-stone, which is now quite respectable in appearance, is fixed in another cup set in a frame, as shewn in Fig. 75, and is then driven round at tremendous speed by a belting which operates underneath. The honing

FIG. 75. POLISHING MACHINE.

process is now begun; rough freestone, then Crakesland stone, and finally Water of Ayr hone being successively applied by the hand to both sides. To the one side or sole no more is now done. This is the *dull* side. To the other side *polishing putty* is applied on flannel held firmly on the heated stone by a wooden lever. This is the *keen* side. Don't be impatient. The stone is not yet finished. A rough ridge runs round the circumference, which must be reduced. With a diamond two zones are drawn, and this ridge is chiselled into a neat *belt*. Neither under nor above but upon this belt the channel-stane is destined to receive all its "plaguey knocks." Now let us have an iron *bolt*, with a round or a square head, and a screw on the other end to meet the screw of the handle, a *washer*, and finally a *handle*—none of your gew-gaws of ivory and silver, but one of plain brass; not too much of a swan-neck, but rather square, with neck and grip about the same thickness. We screw the handle firmly on the bolt, having previously numbered them that the one may know the other and give us no further trouble. With his chief equipment fully equipped, at a cost of from 30s. to 50s., according to the material used, the curler may now take his place on the ice. Not, however, without a broom, and that "neatly tied." Let him respect that old Dunblane rule. When the majority of our curlers have provided themselves with housemaids' besoms, we may bring these articles down upon us by condemning them. But duty compels us to do so, and to urge young curlers to reform the present state of affairs by universally adopting Scotland's ain *broom kowe* as their sweeping equipment. There is character in a kowe; there is nationality about it. Let the curler swear by the kowe. As to Russian *valinki*, roon shoes, rubber overshoes, *et hoc genus omne*, we condemn them all as elephantine. No proper curler requires them. Let him take care of his head, and his feet will take care of themselves. We have always admired the hill lads of Largs,* who could curl in their stocking-soles and never feel cold, and "when at a

---

* Cairnie's *Essay*, p. 52.

push could mend the pace of a coming stone very dexterously by plying before it with their *Kilmarnock bonnets.*" These bonnets are the orthodox head-gear of curlers. An indispensable equipment, according to the majority of curlers, is a *flask.* Our counsel regarding it is given like that of the dealer who exhorted his son to follow honesty as " the best policy," quietly adding, " I ha'e tried baith." A flask is useful, but not indispensable. It is certainly dangerous to the feet if it affects the head. It is possible to have too much even of " the auld kirk ; " and whatever latitude may be allowed to common players, every skip must take special care to keep this equipment in its proper place. The best rink in the world must lose the match when it comes to this :—

    Skip—What d'ye see o' this ane [*hic*], Donald ?
    Donald—I see naethin o' 'er, whatever.
    Skip—Aye, weel, then, Donald, my man, shist [*hic*] tak' what ye see o't.

FIG. 76. SHIPPING STONES FROM AILSA.

(SECOND.)

Such equipments as we have been describing are the property of the curler as an individual. Of those which fall to be provided by the club the most important is, of course, the *curling-pond.* Where there is a subsoil of clay the formation of a pond is a very simple matter. Where the subsoil is gravelly, a layer of clay at least six inches thick must be prepared. Clubs will not expect us to give them advice on this subject. They will get specifications from a practical authority, and accept the estimate of a reliable contractor. Inverness, in its funny *Palladium*, records some experiences which may be useful. Year after year a committee was "appointed to look out for a curling-pond." At one meeting it was agreed "to provide an omnibus so that the committee might enjoy a drive in the suburbs of the town for the ostensible purpose of looking out for a suitable spot." Still nothing was done. One inventive brother now came forward with "a scheme whereby ice of any thickness would be had all the year round without puddling or asphalting." After sundry discussions (not *dry*) it was found that the scheme "would not hold water," but the brother "was graciously permitted to continue his experiments at his own expense." At last, by the determined effort of a fresh committee, a pond was constructed, and opened with an imposing ceremonial.

"It may be remarked, in passing," says *Ye Palladium*, "that the total expense of the completed pond did not exceed by more than *three times* the original estimate. Another committee had therefore to be appointed, with full powers, to devote all their time, attention, and energies to waiting on all the members of the club, and any other person or persons they think proper or improper, without prejudice, for subscriptions to any amount."

If we had frost enough we would condemn all kinds of cement or artificial ponds. They raise the price of curling, and destroy the glorious *roar* of the channel-stane. With our little frost they must, however, be accounted an enormous boon. Since Cairnie's time great improvements have been made on these ponds. Every club that can afford it has one, and with a silvering of ice a game can be had on the cement with the thermometer at 33°. Recently one or two clubs have had the artificial pond so constructed as to be available for lawn tennis when there is no frost. As in the case of the natural pond, the club with a cement pond in view, will employ a good contractor, and see that the expense does not overrun the estimates. Special care should be taken that the pond is laid down east and west, and in a situation sheltered from the rays of the sun. The making of the pond is not the difficulty; it is the upholding of it. These ponds are all liable to crack, and the filling up of their cracks is troublesome. The Edinburgh Northern Club has improved the usefulness of the artificial pond by fitting up the electric light, thus enabling many who could not otherwise do so to enjoy the game. The Coates Club has done the same, and others are likely soon to follow suit.

In the arrangement of the *curling-house*, which ought to adjoin the pond, the club must chiefly consider the comfort of the stones. Everything here should be kept neat and clean. Order in the curling-house is a proof that the club is well managed, and it conduces to order on the ice. Without a little stove, and a good press to store away a few needful and valuable articles (the nature of which we do not require to indicate), no well-regulated curling club should look upon its curling-house as complete. The house and the pond ought to be under the charge of a *keeper* or *officer* who has some force of character, and who can take a turn at the game when required. Where a competent officer is responsible, no club will have to suffer, as the Spott Club once had, by malicious persons destroying the ice. The plan adopted by that club was rather original. They advertised as follows:—

"SPOTT CURLING CLUB.—*Wanted immediately*, a man accustomed to the use of firearms to watch the curling-pond during frost. He will be provided with good accommodation, including use of stove, &c., in the pond-house. For further particulars, apply by letter, stating wages expected, to the Hon. Sec.—Dunbar, Feb. 27, 1873."

Among applications from gamekeepers and other "great guns" there was the following:—

"Deer Sur, i Am a man who wil wach yer pound at ane shiling the nite fur frost. A can shut an furearms in the house write tae John Grubb at Mrs Firds at Linton."

Without John's services, the evil-doers were paralysed with terror, and the Spott Club got their pond cheaply protected for the rest of the season.

One of the most useful ice-implements is the *Tee-ringer*, invented by Mr Palmer of Currie. By means of it, broughs, hog score, and sweeping score can all be drawn with accuracy in a very short time. The *Foothold* of the Canadian curler is the *Hack* in the ice, and in Lanarkshire and some

FIG. 77. TEE-RINGER.

other districts of Scotland this is still used. The majority of our clubs, however, are now supplied with an improved form of Cairnie's *Foot-iron* (*vide* p. 159), a fillet of hard wood being fitted at the back end, bevelled so as to keep the player's centre of gravity within the outline of the crampit. A folding form of crampit has recently been patented by Duncan Cameron, Aberfeldy. This gentleman has also invented a *snow-cleaner*, which receives high commendation from the Marquis of Breadalbane, who says that one man can with it do as much work as six can do in cleaning a pond by the ordinary methods. Its cost is £3, 15s. If some machine of a light description could only be invented to clear away snow when the ice is too weak to allow of any person working upon it, this, we have often thought, would be of great benefit to clubs. The Kilwinning Curling Club, when they met to play Dalry on the water of Garnock, in the year 1801, found that no form of spade or *snaw-shool* could be got without

much delay. "Look here," said one of their number—
J. C.—"I tell you what to do. Here is my grey plaid.
I'll roll myself in it; I am six feet. Two of you will
take the one end and two the other, and draw me broad-
side the length of the rink up and down, and you will
soon clear the ice." This was done; the rink was effectively cleared, and J. C. was none the worse.* It would
not be safe for any club to depend on such chivalry in
our days, so they had better mind their snaw-shools. The
Rev. Dr Somerville of Currie invented an instrument, which
he called *The Justice*, for measuring disputed shots. It
is simply a big pair of iron-shod compasses, one leg to be
fixed in the toe-see (*vide* p. 155), and the other to be adjusted
so as to determine the nearest stone. It is a good thing of
its kind. The same gentleman invented *The Counter*, for
indicating the state of the game on a pillar before the eyes
of the players. A better way of recording matches is for
a club to have a supply of such scoring-books as can be
had from Carswell, Paisley, or Fairgrieve, Edinburgh.†

One word as to the *rinks*-equipments, on which the enjoyment of curling so much depends. In the little matches
made up on the ice from day to day—*scrub games*, as the
Canadians call them—each curler may look after himself;
but on medal days the members of a club should see what
their secretary can do in providing for them. A bonspiel
between rival parishes is a good occasion for the chief
nobleman of the district to renew his patent of nobility.
Many take advantage of it, and shew hospitality to the
curlers. When no baronial mansion smiles upon the scene,
the club on whose ice the match is played must entertain
the other, and that right well, as becometh curlers. On
neutral ice for a "Royal" medal, if the two clubs have no
common *rinks* forward, for any sake let them remember

---

* J. C. died in 1841, aet. 84. *Vide Annual* 1843, p. 134.
† Curlers should keep their scores and records of their matches—if they are worth keeping. A well-known skip, Peter Shaw, has shewn us his rink record—1870-1886. Matches played with other clubs, 68; won, 53; drawn, 3; lost, 12; shots up, 593; shots down, 54; net majority, 539. This is what we call "worth keeping."

the umpire. It would be cruel to give names, but the worst account of a curling match on record is this—found in one of our *Annuals*:—

"The umpire got neither meat nor drink during the match, and a very cold day it was."

That must never occur again. A plate of *Irish stew* will satisfy an umpire or any other man. There is no "equipment" to match it among curling-*cieres*. Sure and a "black strap" of *Dublin* will do your honour no harm. If this is too much of "Ould Ireland," a bottle of *Old Edinburgh* for the Scot, or one of *Trinity Audit* for the Sassenach, will safeguard his nationality. "*Beef and greens*," as from time immemorial, must be the feast of brotherhood when the day is over, and every innovation must be resisted to the death which interferes with "curlers' fare." In "beaded *Usquba* with sugar dash'd," let them also, as long as curling lasts, pledge their loyalty to each other and to "auld lang syne."

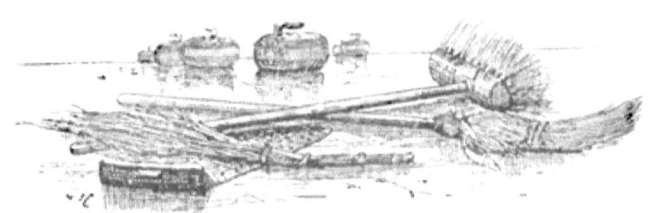

CHAPTER II.

THE SCIENCE OF CURLING.

WHAT is the Science of Curling? The question was put to us by a practical curler when he saw the heading of this chapter, and we were not surprised when he added that he had never heard of such a thing before. We are not responsible for the title. "The Science of Curling-stones" might perhaps be a better one. But we are quite prepared to defend it as it stands, and our readers, we are sure, will see the propriety of keeping the subject separate from the "Art of Curling," which falls to be treated in our next chapter. In former times curlers generally took the material that lay nearest them, and nearly every district of Scotland has at some time or other furnished curling-stones. Now, when machinery has been introduced for their manufacture, and the facilities of railway carriage are so great, it is important to know where suitable material for curling-stones can be found. In order to decide among the varieties of stone found in different districts, it is necessary to have some fixed standard or test by which to try the different varieties. This is difficult to get. In Canada, where the ice is keen, the prime requisite is a stone that is not liable to break under the excessive frost. This makes Ailsa popular there. At home we have very often to play on dull ice, and this makes Ailsa popular here. But Ailsa is too big for its weight when a Canadian wants to do the port shot in his point game, and in keen ice at home it is too keen. Burnocks, Crawfordjohns, and Blantyres are neither too keen on keen ice nor too dull on dull ice, and for these reasons they rank before Ailsas as *true* stones. Now, whatever our test may be, when we come to decide among varieties of stone, it is apparent that the science or exact knowledge of their composition and nature must be useful. This is why we have made a "new departure," and called in the assistance of an expert to throw light on the subject. In the coloured plate which accompanies this chapter we have given illustrations of the six kinds of stone most popular at the present day. These six varieties will be found, we believe, to cover two-thirds of the curling-stones now in use, the other third embracing such stones as are found at Carsphairn, Tinkernhill, Blantyre, &c. They have all been submitted to Professor Forster Heddle, who, as one specially fitted to do so, has been asked to explain their composition and to pronounce on their respective merits. The learned Professor's statement we now give *in extenso*:—

THE SCIENCE OF CURLING.

The writer, as a physicist and a petrologist, has been requested to say something upon curling, the request being formulated as follows:—

"Give a description of the varieties of stone used—such as curlers of intelligence would appreciate.
"What is the best kind of stone for the purpose?
"Supply, if possible, some information which may be made practical and useful."

This is, in a word, to speak to the *science* of curling—if it has any—in contradistinction to the *art* and to skill; to act as the guide to the inexperienced; to explain the causes of successful experience; to deal with the *pabulum*, and not with the performance.

The writer is not a curler. He occupies, therefore, the "coigne of vantage" of the elevated onlooker who perceives every failure, and many of their causes; though he may never be able fully to appreciate that wondrous copartnery of eye and brain and muscle, in rapidly sequential unison, guaging, decreeing, and executing that marvellous shot which elicits an applause which frequently is nothing short of *ferocious*.

The earliest historian of curling states that the stones employed are made from blocks of whinstone, or *granite*.

If this last were so, then there is no *science* connected with it.

But it is not so. Of ten stones in the writer's hands, and some five others named to him as in use, not one is granite. That granite could not hold its own is shewn in the following extract from a letter of an old curler :—

"I spent a winter in Aberdeen in 1846-47, got a club started, and about twenty pairs of stones from the Ayrshire quarter; but some of the club did not like the idea, and supplied themselves with Aberdeen granite ones, at a much greater cost ; but they were found useless, as they could not be sent up the length of the rink. I have often wondered what could be the cause of this. I don't think it could be porosity; but, possibly from interstitial matter between the crystals, the polished bottom might not be so compact but that the edges of the crystals might act as scrapers sufficiently to retard the stone. Whether that be the reason or not, the fact was that they were a failure at that time."

The shewing how stones of granite are contra-indicated, and for reasons apart from those shrewdly speculated upon by my correspondent, will form the text of my remarks upon the science of curling.

In two ways can the stones be made to shoot round a corner, to *circumvent* a guard.

First, by an out-elbow or in-elbow screw. *Second*, by inwicking. Without these it may be said there would be no game. In no way can a side bias be given to a sliding object which is left at any moment free to change its sides.

By the screw or spin one side of the stone—the inner—is ever to some extent receding from and diminishing the *medial* amount of friction upon the ice ; while the other—the outer—is ever, to a corresponding extent, increasing that amount. The stone yields to this doubled difference, and curves away from the side of greatest resistance. Again, when the narrow sole is used, there must be some amount of *lift* away from the side of greatest resistance, and so will the lean to the inner side bring direct gravitation into play.

In wicking the *elasticity* of both stones is depended upon ; and no amount of experience and skill could compensate for an ever-varying quantity, if that variation exceeded certain limits. Still less could it do so if the amount of elasticity varied at different sides of the same stone, for here experience of one side would entail error as regards the other.

As different kinds of stone have different elasticities, theoretically, and to perfect the game, a single kind should be adopted ; but, as different weights of stone are permitted, and as the force of the impact is divided between striking and struck stone (in amount, of course, always depending upon the angle of striking), and as a stone will recoil further off a heavy stone than off a lighter one, there can be no hope of this theoretical perfection until men become of one strength as well as of a single mind in the matter.

By far the greater number of the rocks used as "stones" are melanges of minute crystals of different substances, interlocked in more or less confused arrangement with one another.

If this arrangement is absolutely confused and promiscuous, that may be called perfection of structure in a stone. Any diversity in this respect—any evident special structure in any part of a stone—anything that makes it "bonny," unless it is equally bonny all over, is a step in the direction of the *imperfection of inequality*.

It is a prettier thing to see a stone with an ugly face sitting right over the tee, than a stone lately handed round a railway carriage as "a new one, and a beauty," lying an inglorious outsider.

The point is that stones are built up of myriads of crystals, which should lie, as regards their position to each other, *in all directions*—and why?

A crystal is a structure which is made up of little bricks, as it were, which are termed molecules. These, in being arranged in a crystal, are not allowed to go indiscriminately in any position, or in equal numbers to this side or to that. They are as much subject to positional law as are the bricks or integers in a regiment, which are not allowed to take position indiscriminately, but have appointed positions: major here, captain there, sergeant in this place, corporal in that.*

This arrangement is one of design—to resist impact, and throw back the impacter. If assaulted upon flank, the regiment cannot do this well; if upon rear, it has to face about.

So is it with a crystal. Its power of resisting impact, of repelling the impacter—its elasticity, in fact—is much greater when it presents its forefront than at the sides—nearly as 4 to 3.

Granite is made up in largest amount of a crystal substance called felspar or orthoclase. This name expresses that it splits in two directions, which lie at right angles to one another; and in most granites, although there is a general appearance of confused arrangement of ingredients, there is a dominant polar arrangement of this main ingredient. This exists to so marked an extent that not only is the quarry foreman guided by his knowledge thereof in the disposal of his blasts, but every causeway block-dresser *cleaves* the stone by blow and cross blow, leaving only one direction in the shaping to be *chipped* into the necessary form.

From this dominant polar position of a material which possesses an elasticity greater in one direction than in all others, it results that curling-stones made of granite, while they would only travel 6 feet after an inwick on one side, would travel 8 feet if they were hit upon another; while if *both* stones were of granite the 8 might become 10. Uncertainty is introduced all round; and it is just in delicate play that the difference would make all the difference.

Aside altogether of sluggishness of the stone, as noticed in the above letter, granite is clearly unfitted as a material to be used in curling, as are all stones which, by any very distinct uniformity in the directions in which they split, indicate a uniformity in the position of the crystals which go to build them up.

This is *one* of the reasons why *boulders* are superior to the rock mass from which they apparently were derived. Many of these had existed as kernels or concretionary segregations in the mass of the parent rock, and, from having somewhat of a concentric arrangement of parts, they have not the tendency to definite lines of fracture which many of these rocks exhibit (though none to the extent seen in granite).

Next to uniformity in elasticity in stones, stands their being "true" in all states of the ice.

Without assuming to have arrived at *all* the causes of sluggishness of stones on "drug" ice, the writer would say that he is not prepared to assign it to plates of mica, or of any ingredient projecting above the

---

* Except the general, who, it is generally believed, is allowed to go to the rear; but this may be a civilian error. Perhaps, however, it proves that he is not "a brick" at all!

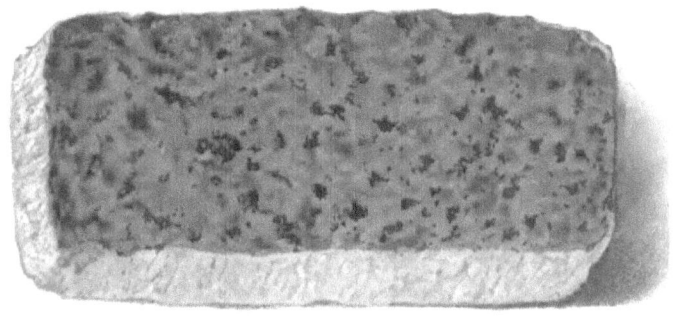

COMMON AILSA.

RED HONE AILSA.

surface of the stone, and so acting as scrapers; but to certain of the ingredients crumbling away and leaving depressions, each of which becomes a lodgment for water or slush.

It is well known that friction between surfaces differing in nature is much less than between two surfaces of the same metal or nature. In the last case cohesion is always attempting to establish a reunion, and frequently succeeds.

The natural state of matters, is the friction between the dry stone and dry ice; in the "drug" it is between the wet stone and wet ice; in other words, between water and water. The little particles of water, lodging in the minute depressions or roughnesses in the sole of the stone, unite with the water on the surface of the ice, and the drop or drops so formed are being constantly torn through, only to reform immediately and be again ruptured. As the cohesion of water is considerable, the travelling energy of the stone is soon exhausted.

It may appear that in a highly polished stone there are no depressions for such lodgment; but there are linear pores, and where such exist there is in damp weather an instantaneous absorption of water. I find notes of this on six rocks, in some old experiments of my own. I give as extremes:—

The dolerite rock from—
  Marchburn, Ayrshire, absorbs $\tfrac{1}{435}$ of its weight of water.
  Knockdow,   ,,   ,, $\tfrac{1}{414}$,,   ,,
  Ratho, Edinburgh, ,,   ,, $\tfrac{1}{32}$,,   ,,

Considering that this is little more than a surface action, the difference is very great. Moreover, the Ratho rock accomplishes the absorption in one-fiftieth part of the time taken by the others. As well curl with a sponge as with Ratho. (*N.B.*—Granites are very bad in this respect.)

The various stones which I have examined in thin section in the microscope, to be able to speak to their composition and structure as bearing upon their suitability for curling purposes, and their relative value therefor, are:—

Ailsa, Grey.	Crawfordjohn.	Crieff, Common.
Ailsa, Mottled.	Burnock Water.	Crieff, Serpentine.
Ailsa, Red.	Tinkernhill.	Crieff, Hornblendic.
Carsphairn.		

Excepting the first three, which are varieties of the same, all are rocks differing in components, and more or less in properties from one another.

The mineral substances which go to form them are: *quartz*—which confers (relative to the others) hardness, brittleness, and lightness; *common felspar*—somewhat brittle, light, and with a tendency to rot; *plagioclase felspar*—less brittle, more weight; *augite*—heavy, sometimes brittle; *olivine*—hard, heavy, tough; *hornblende*—heavy, when fibrous very tough; *magnetic iron*—very heavy, hard, brittle; *micas* (rarely)—soft, brittle.

The excellence of any one rock depends upon the relative amount of the *hard, heavy,* and *tough* ingredients; upon their relative firm adhesion one to the other, through a promiscuous interlocking of the component crystals; and to uniformity in structure throughout. *Ceteris paribus*, the smaller the grain the better.

It is upon the above lines, and especially upon the structure as disclosed by the microscope, that relative values are assigned below.

AILSAS.—Of the above stones, the first three are varieties of a rock which is the plug to the throat of a volcano of geologically recent times—a volcano which apparently had done no more than form a throat and then plug it. The rock would at present bear the general term of *granophyre*. From its containing a blue-green mineral, not yet found in the usual varieties, it has been termed *Ailsite* distinctively. It contains much quartz, much felspar—both, structurally and chemically, in a bad condition; the green mineral is not uniformly distributed, but is in patches; there are not infrequent small holes in the rock, and its whole structure is confused and "messy." The *Red Ailsa* is in a state of incipient rotting, its felspar is kaolinised and greasy, and stained with iron oxide.

On account of the large amount of quartz, the stone must be light and hard; from its general uniformity not liable to flaws, but it is a uniformity in a poor, if not in a bad direction.

From most of the above defects the *Blue Hone* is, however, free. It is a stone of remarkable uniformity of structure and fineness and closeness of grain. No cavities are to be seen, and although there is much the same superabundance of quartz, and want of precision in the development of its crystals, it is a stone of marked excellence.

CARSPHAIRN.—This is a stone the first inspection of which is not in its favour, but which increases in apparent excellence the more it is examined. The rock is a quartz porphyry, and that which is unpromising is the large amount of quartz, bringing in lightness and brittleness; and, secondly, that it is a *porphyry*, which, in a certain sense, implies absence of uniformity.

A porphyry has a structure in which crystals are embedded in a paste, in the same manner as raisins are embedded in a dumpling. Here is absence of uniformity. As the raisins may be picked out of the dumpling, so might the crystals be knocked out of the paste; and though it might be held that the raisins were the best part of the dumpling, yet it is not so if the "raisins" bring in lightness and brittleness, and if their removal left a number of holes.

An examination of sections of the rock, however, shews that the surfaces of the quartz crystals are rough, enabling the paste firmly to grip them; and as that paste is itself of remarkable uniformity—as is the general structure of the stone, there being an absolute freedom from holes—this stone, apart from its lightness, probably is one of great excellence. Never having seen it in mass, I cannot speak to freedom from flaws.

CRAWFORDJOHN.—Another porphyry, but here a porphyritic dolerite. Dolerite is our present name for what used to be called "greenstone." They consist of *augite, plagioclase, felspar, magnetite;* and sometimes, and all the better for curling-stones, of *olivine*. In a paste or magma of the former of these, pea-sized crystals of augite are impacted—fortunately in every position.

For reasons above given, the *structure* of this rock would not be in its favour, were it not that here also the surfaces of the embedded crystals are rough. Did the crystals lie all in one direction, the rock would split somewhat easily in a certain direction. From the general compactness of this rock, and its freedom from vacuities, it should be an excellent one; while its components confer upon it surpassing weight.

BURNOCK WATER.—Another dolerite, but contains no embedded crystals. It has much olivine, and finely-sprinkled magnetite, with an

BURNOCK WATER

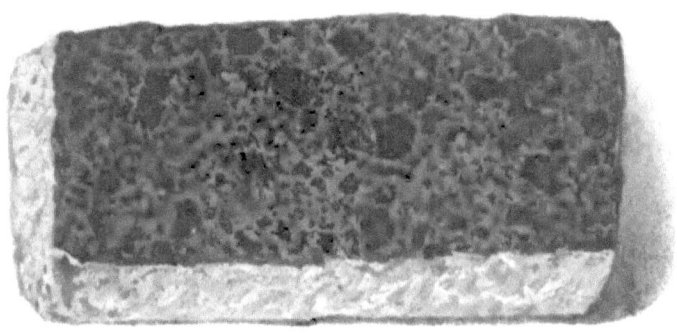

CRAWFORDJOHN

exceedingly fine, sharply interlocked, and well-developed crystalline structure of marvellous uniformity. The olivine gives increased weight, hardness, and toughness; and this, taken along with its structure, places it *markedly the best of all the stones*.

TINKERNHILL.—This consists of a rock of much the same structure as dolerite, but it contains hornblende and not augite, and is termed *diorite*. This special diorite has the hornblende passing into epidote. It is a good rock, but not so good as dolerite. It seems porous.

CRIEFF, *common*.—A very strange rock. Being got solely from boulders scattered over a considerable range of country, it varies a good deal in character, though all may be called hornblende rock. The large size of the crystals of hornblende which it contains, and their flakey nature, are far from promising. Still, when polished, they "come up" wonderfully close and compact in appearance. Epidote, which is seen in yellow patches, and a massive granular felspar, are the chief other ingredients. From the distinct foliacious appearance of the hornblende, I should be suspicious of this rock with water on the ice.

CRIEFF, *black*.—This, found on the south, instead of the north side of the Earn, is a hornblende schist, formed of minute sparkling scales of hornblende, with small kernels of quartz.

It is very uniform and fine grained, excessively tough, and hard to break; will be almost black when polished. It also stands with a slight mark of doubt as regards water; but otherwise excellent.

CRIEFF SERPENTINE.—At first sight a strange rock to make use of in a game of "dunts," for most serpentine is soft. Some varieties, however, approach in hardness to the diorites; and for closeness none of the others can approach them; their oily polish, also, should make them impervious to water.

In adjudicating relative total merits, I would put them—

Burnock Water,	10	Carsphairn,	6
Crawfordjohn,	8½	Crieff Serpentine,	} 5½
Ailsa Hone,	7½	Tinkernhill,	
Crieff Black,	6½		

That is, supposing thoroughly good examples are got of each, and not quarried, and, still less, *blasted* stones.

Gunpowder expands in being fired in every direction; and though the block may have *rent* in only two or three, it may have been *strained*, though invisibly, in others; and after a succession of whacks, upon the point opposite to the entrance line of such strain, the strain becomes a fracture.

Boulders have, when well rounded, come through a long experience of grinding against each other, and against mother earth, under the pressure of enormous masses of ice; or, if angular, of rolling down cliffs, to lie upon the surface of the ice, and to be air-wasted, so that every rent would be found out and delineated on the surface.

This brings the writer to useful hints.

1st. Give twice the price for a *boulder* of any of the first five rocks in above list that you would for the finest-looking pair of stones of any not *known* to be boulders.

2nd. If you cannot get a boulder, search the foundations of the dykes. Whole boulders, or portions large enough, are there stored away.

3rd. In purchasing stones, reflect the light from the polished soles; and if you see any small holes, roughnesses, or lines of any kind, have nothing to do with them.

4th. *Suggestion.*—Get the stones gently heated up, for, say, a day (if previously "dry"), above the temperature of warm water (not before the fire), and then soak them for twenty-four hours in "finish" (a solution of 3 oz. of shellac to the gallon of methylated spirit). Rub them dry after dripping them, and set them in a warm place for other twenty-four hours. This will prevent water soaking into them.

5th. *For the collective advantage of curlers.*—Have "stones," 3 inches in diameter, made of all stones used, or proposed to be used—shape and polish to be perfect. Have a billiard-table, or dead-flat table, cloth-covered. Have a circle, size of width of the table, graduated in angles, printed upon the cloth, with central tee, and also with a number of gradually diminishing circles. Have one test stone, of same size as others, suspended by cord or wire, of 8 or 10 feet in length, fair above the tee, and so as barely to touch the cloth. Draw back the test-stone in straight line one or more feet from the tee, and tie it back by thread. Place the various stones, successively, upon the tee, and set fire to the retaining thread. The relative amount of recoil or elasticity of the various kinds of stone will so be ascertained. Accurately replace the tee-stone, and draw back the test-stone, in succession to the different angles marked upon the home-half of the circles, allowing it to strike successively at different angles. So may be ascertained—

   1. How far the angle of impact departs from the angle of take-off.
   2. If the angle of recoil of the struck ball, as in inwicking, is the same as the angle of deflection of the striking ball.
   3. What is the relative amount of travel of the striking and struck balls—relatively to the angle at which they are struck?

The player who carries such knowledge in his head will have a great advantage over the man who plays by hand and eye alone.

6th. Let pieces of each kind of stone, about a cubic inch in size, be well dried, weighed, soaked in water for an hour, and then dried with blotting-paper and re-weighed. The porous absorption of the stone, and its liability to "shut up" on drug ice, may so be known.

The writer is of opinion that the black rock which occurs north of the railway station at Huntly would make better curling-stones even than Burnock Water. It contains olivine, enstatile, magnetite, serpentine; it is tough, heavy, dense, and very compact.

A still better stone used to lie as boulders, sprinkled over the fields in the vicinity of Portsoy. The rock is so tough that these boulders were locally termed *heathens*. A Free Church minister took the most of these, not into his fold, but he built his fold of them! Sufficient have escaped, however, to be experimented on.

CHAPTER III.

THE ART OF CURLING.

"What numbers can describe
The various game? . . .
Or couldst thou follow the experienc'd play'r
Through all the myst'ries of his art? or teach
The undisciplin'd how to *wick*, to *guard*,
Or *ride full out* the stone that blocks the pass?"—GRAEME.

"AN ye no curl, man?" said a brawny Dumfriesian herd to an artist whom he found sitting on the hill-side, trying to transfer to canvas the sparkling snow-clad scene. It was a fine clear curling morning, and that shepherd could not for the life of him understand how a sane, able-bodied person could employ himself in such a contemptible way when the ice was bearing on the loch in the valley below, and the curlers, with their brooms over their shoulders, were gathering from all directions to join in the manly sport. He glanced at the "bit picter," then carefully surveyed the artist from head to foot, and seeing no physical defect to account for such strange conduct, the shepherd, with a look of pity and scorn, blurted out his blunt question, and wended onward to the bonspiel, muttering something about the "puir, feckless body, that couldna belang hereaboots." The painter, in return, pitied the curling keeper of sheep, and worked his honest countryman and his brother-curlers as "objects" into the landscape. The curler and the artist did not see eye to eye. Anybody could paint, thought the one; and a sensible man would not waste his time in such a silly way on a fine frosty morning. Any rustic could curl, thought the painter. There was certainly no *art* in the game; and as for any enjoyment in it, his idea was like that of the Oriental who, on being informed that many of the players in a cricket match which he had been looking at were rich men, expressed his surprise that they did not employ some poor people to do it for them. A person who does not know anything about a game generally sees little in it. In the case of curling the uninitiated onlooker sees even less than

FIG. 78.

usual, and what he does see appears absurd. A Canadian farmer at Quebec, after witnessing the game for the first time, gave this description of it:—

"J'ai vu aujourd'hui une bande d'Ecossais qui jetaient des grandes boules de fer, faites comme des bombes, sur la glace, après quoi ils criaient soupe, soupe; ensuite ils riaient comme des fous; je crois bien qu'ils sont vraiement fous."

An Englishman, who is now a keen curler, tells us that when he first saw a game of curling, one of the players— a very lean, hungry-looking individual—was gesticulating wildly, and yelling at the pitch of his voice, "Soop! ye deevils; soop!" The Englishman thought the poor fellow was starving, and crying out in despair for some "soup" to put warmth into his benumbed frame. In a match between the Bradford and the Blackburn clubs, several doctors happened to be in the rinks. One native, who, in his own opinion, knew all about it, was overheard informing another, who did not disguise his ignorance, that the players were lunatics from a neighbouring asylum going through their exercises, and that what they were now and then drinking was medicine to keep them right. The curler's equipments do not help the outsider to understand the hidden art. When the members of the Darlington club first appeared in the streets of the town flourishing their besoms, some municipal changes had just taken place, and the people took the curlers to be a special force of scavengers sent forth to perform the proverbial clean sweep. In the winter of 1876-77, the pond of the Wigan and Haigh

CURLERS AT PLAY.

club having been rendered useless by a heavy snowstorm, the members sallied forth to play on Martin Mere, a large tract of water lying between Wigan and Southport. The day was densely foggy, with intense frost; and as the curlers had all long beards, their Father Christmas appearance and the queer weapons they carried frightened the villagers of Martin so much that the landlord of the inn actually refused to supply them with refreshments.*

Now, whatever aspect the game of curling may assume in the eyes of the uninitiated, there is really no game

---

* The stationmaster, who had a better idea of them, took pity on the curlers, and presented them with a small barrel of beer. But this did not end their day's troubles. The barrel was conveyed in a cart to the field of battle, placed in position, duly tapped, and left ready for use. In the keen play the barrel was left unnoticed for three hours, but at last "the weary

which, to be played with any degree of perfection, requires so much skilful resource on the part of the player. Precision of eye, clearness of head, steadiness of aim, accuracy of judgment, dexterity of hand, force tempered by discretion, decision of character, coolness, confidence, and enthusiasm are all necessary. No two "ends" are exactly alike. There is infinite variety in the game—

"New efforts, new schemes every movement demands."

In a moment the whole situation of affairs may be changed, and the best-laid schemes of the skip be sent agley. New tactics must then be adopted, and fresh resources must ever be available to overcome new difficulties and cope with new emergencies.

"I doubt," says an excellent authority,* "if any one who has participated in a curling bonspiel between two neighbouring parishes, where skill and enthusiasm were nearly matched, could be found to admit that there is anything in sport that can compare with the earnest enthusiasm, the skilful manipulation, the combination of strength and science, with just sufficient of chance to lend a charm to the uncertainty that is experienced in a well-fought game of curling."

It is in the bonspiel that the true art of curling is exemplified. The renown which certain curling clubs have gained for excellence in the art is based on the matches they have gained against other clubs. The heroes whose names are remembered with honour in their different districts won their spurs in the bonspiel.

Point play is not the most difficult part of the curling art. The art must always be held to include a great deal more than "points." The low average scoring in the point game to which we have referred may, however, shew how difficult it is to attain to anything like perfection in curling. Perhaps it is as well that perfection is unattainable. Tam Pate appears to have been the only perfect curler that ever lived, and they dubbed him *warlock*. We must be content with a qualified measure of proficiency. To be human, we must err. If a curler never missed a single shot, he might

---

drouth cam' up their throats." A truce was called, and with one accord they invoked the favour of the kindly barrel. Judge of their horror when the curlers found that beer and barrel were frozen into a solid lump! They left for home.

* Thomas Brown, the "Maida" of *Bell's Life* and other papers.

get an ill name and be hanged. On the other hand, a
right-minded curler would rather be hanged than be a
duffer; he would rather be "awa' to the caff-neuk" than
be a senseless "hog." In our treatment of the art of
curling we shall bear this in mind; and, without entering
too minutely into technical and mathematical niceties, or
attempting to explain the miraculous feats by which the
highest fame has been achieved, we shall try to bring all
curlers into the "parish" or "the way of promotion,"
leaving them to become "perfect patlids" by dint of their
own genius and ambition. There are no curling *professionals;*
the game does not admit of them; it is better without
them. Nor in curling is there any code of hard and fast
rules by which a knowledge of the art is to be attained.
The art is too fine for that. It is only by practice that any
degree of perfection can be reached. An ounce of experience
is worth more than a pound of instruction. But there
are certain general rules and principles which the collective
experience of curlers has laid down to regulate the curling
art. The general rules we shall here give as they are found
in the Royal Club *Annual.*[*] The general principles we shall
keep before us in discussing thereafter the various features
of the game and giving counsel to players. At the close of
our chapter we shall give the rules for point play recently
adopted by the Royal Club, which will be found useful to
the curler in giving him such practice and experience as
shall fit him for the higher stage of the bonspiel.

GENERAL RULES OF THE GAME.

1. The length of the rink for play, viz., from the back end of the crampit
to the tee, shall be 42 yards, and in no case less than 32 yards. Alterations
are provided for in Section 17.

The tees to be set down 38 yards apart. Around each tee as a centre a
circle of 7 feet radius shall be drawn. (In order to facilitate measurements,
2 feet and 4 feet circles may be laid down.) In exact alignment with both
tees, a line, called the "central line," shall be drawn, extending to a point
4 yards behind each tee. At this point a line 18 inches in length, at right

[*] With these may also be read the Rules for District Medal Competitions (Appendix A, chap. vi.).

angles to the central line shall be drawn, on which, and 6 inches from the central line, the heel of crampit shall be placed. The hack in this position shall be 3 inches from the central line, and shall not be more than 12 inches in length.

Lines shall be drawn across the rink at right angles to central line, as indicated in diagram, and called "hog scores," "sweeping scores," "back scores," and "middle score."

The hog score shall be placed at one-sixth part of the entire length for play.

The sweeping score shall be placed across the tees, for the use of the skips, and the middle score midway between them, for the use of the players. (For regulation of sweeping see sections 9 and 12.)

The back score shall be placed just outside and behind the seven foot circle.

N.B.—Every stone shall be eligible to count which is not clearly outside of the seven foot circle. Every stone shall be a hog which does not clear the score, and must be removed from the ice, but no stone to be considered as such which has struck another stone lying in position. Stones passing the back line, and lying clear of it, must be removed from the ice, as also any stone which in its progress shall touch the swept snow on either side of the rink.

Note.—Reference in forming rinks is made to the diagram or plan, called "The Rink."

2. All matches to be of a certain number of heads, to be agreed on by the clubs, or fixed by the umpire, before commencement; or otherwise, by time, or shots, if mutually agreed on. In the event of parties being equal at the conclusion of the match, play shall be continued by all the rinks engaged for another head; or, if necessary to decide the match, for such additional heads as the umpire shall direct.

3. Every rink to be composed of four players a side, each using two stones. The rotation of play observed during the first head of match shall not be changed.

4. The skips opposing each other shall settle by lot, or in any other way they may agree upon, which party shall lead at the first head, after which the winning party shall do so.

5. All curling-stones shall be of a circular shape. No stone, including handle, shall be of a greater weight than 50 lb. imperial, or of greater circumference than 36 inches, or of less height than one-eighth part of its greatest circumference.

6. No stone shall be changed after a match has been begun, but the side of a stone may be changed at any time during a match, provided sect. 10, chap. v., is adhered to.

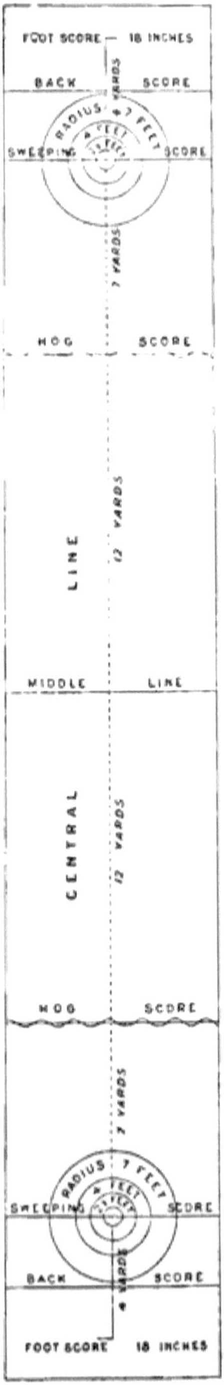

FIG. 79.

7. Should a stone happen to be broken, the largest fragment shall be considered in the game for that end—the player being entitled to use another stone, or another pair, during the remainder of the game.

8. If a played stone rolls over, or stops, on its side or top, it shall be put off the ice. Should the handle quit the stone in delivery, the player must keep hold of it, otherwise he shall not be entitled to replay the shot.

9. Players, during the course of each end, to be arranged along the sides, but well off the rink, as the skips may direct; and no party, except when sweeping according to rule, shall go upon the middle of the rink, or cross it, under any pretence whatever. Skips alone to stand within the seven feet circle—the skip of the playing party to have the choice of place, and not to be obstructed by the other, in front of the tee, while behind it the privileges of both, in regard to sweeping, shall be equal.

10. Every player to be ready to play when his turn comes, and not to take more than a reasonable time to play. Should he play a wrong stone, any of the players may stop it while running; but if not stopped till at rest, the stone which ought to have been played shall be placed in its stead, to the satisfaction of the opposing skip.

11. If a player should play out of turn, the stone so played may be stopped in its progress, and returned to the player. Should the mistake not be discovered till the stone be at rest, or has struck another stone, the opposite skip shall have the option of adding one to his score, allowing the game to proceed, or of declaring the end null and void. But if a stone be played before the mistake has been discovered, the head must be finished as if it had been properly played from the beginning.

12. The sweeping shall be under the direction and control of the skips. The player's party may sweep the ice from the middle line to the tee, and any of their own stones when set in motion,—the adverse party having liberty only to sweep in front of any of their own stones which have been set in motion by a stone played by the opposite party. Both skips have equal right to clean and sweep the ice behind the tee at any time, except when a player is being directed by his skip. At the end of any head, either of the skips may call upon the whole players to clean and sweep the entire rink, but being subject in this, if objected to, to the control of the acting umpire. The sweeping shall always be to a side; and no sweeping shall be either moved forward or left in front of a running stone. When snow is falling, the player's party may sweep the stones of their own side from tee to tee.

13. If, in sweeping or otherwise, a *running* stone be marred by any of the party to which it belongs, it may, in the option of the opposite skip, be put off the ice: but if by any of the adverse party, it may be placed where the skip of the party to which it belongs shall direct. If marred by any other means, the player shall replay the stone. Should any *played* stone be displaced before the head is reckoned, it shall be placed as near as possible where it lay, to the satisfaction of, or by, the skip opposed to the party displacing. If displaced by any neutral party, both skips to agree upon the position to which it is to be returned; but should they not agree, the umpire to decide.

14. No measuring of shots allowable previous to the termination of the end. Disputed shots to be determined by the skips: or, if they disagree, by the umpire: or when there is no umpire, by some neutral person chosen by the skips. All measurements to be taken from the centre of the tee, to that part of the stone which is nearest it.

15. Skips shall have the exclusive regulation and direction of the game for their respective parties, and may play last stone, or in any part of the game they please, but are not entitled to change their position when once fixed. When their turn to play comes, they may name one of their party to act as skip for them, and must take the position of an ordinary player, and shall not have any choice or direction in the game till they return to the tee head as skips.

2 B*

16. If any player engaged or belonging to either of the competing clubs, shall speak to, taunt, or interrupt another, not being of his own party, while in the act of delivering his stone, one shot may be added to the score of the party so interrupted, for each interruption, and the play proceed.

17. If from any change of weather after a match has been begun, or from any other reasonable cause, one party shall desire to shorten the rink, or to change to another; and if the two skips cannot agree, the umpire shall, after seeing one end played, determine whether the rink shall be shortened, and how much, or whether it shall be changed, and his decision shall be final. Should there be no acting umpire, or should he be otherwise engaged, the two skips may call in any neutral curler to decide, whose powers shall be equally extensive with those of the umpire. The umpire, moreover, shall, in the event of the ice being in his opinion dangerous, stop the match. He shall postpone it, even if begun, when, in his opinion, the state of the ice is not fitted for testing the curling skill of the players; and except in very special circumstances, of which the umpire shall be judge, a match shall not proceed, or be continued, when a thaw has fairly set in, or when snow is falling, and likely to continue during the match. Nor shall it be continued when such darkness comes on as prevents (in the opinion of the umpire) the played stones being well seen by players at the other end of the rink. In every case the match, when renewed, must be begun *de novo*.

The Rink.—The general rules of the game, it will be noticed, give very particular directions as to the proper construction of the *rink* or *board*. It is of great consequence that these rules should be attended to, and that the rink should be correctly drawn. There is no excuse for the club which plays on a board laid out in a slovenly and imperfect way. The formation of the double rink, as shewn in the diagram, is the result of the experience of many generations of curlers, and it is a visible sign of the unity of the brotherhood—it has been adopted and is used in every country where the game is played. An imperfect form of rink leads to an incorrect style of play. *Fitting the ice* is the first duty of the player, and it is evident that this cannot be properly done if the *crampit* or *hack* is not related to the central line as the diagram requires. We have seen many matches played where the measurements of the rink were left entirely to the eye, and some clubs never trouble to draw a central line. Such neglect implies disregard for scientific play, and no club which wishes to attain distinction will be guilty of it, but will strictly observe the rules which are so distinctly laid down. The shortening of the rink allowed under the rules is rendered necessary by the arrogance of the climate, which claims a right to interfere with a match without the consent of the players, and to prohibit them from "making up" in a rink of forty-two yards. It is a question whether too much has not been conceded to the weather. A match should certainly not be played when the condition of the ice makes the game one of brute force and not of skill.

The Choice of Stones.—To one who wishes to excel in the art of curling the choice of a pair of curling-stones is almost as important as the choice of a wife. It must not be done "lightly or unadvisedly." To those who are about to choose their channel-stanes before they begin their curling, we certainly give the advice of *Punch* to those about to marry—"Don't." The channel-stanes are made for the curler, not the curler for the channel-stanes. It is only after he has tried stones of different material, weight, and build, and has made himself acquainted with the *soles* of stones, even more than with their bodies, that the young curler is in a position to choose a pair for himself. For a season or two his best plan will be to test the capabilities of the various stones alongside of his own powers, to study the points of the game, and discern with what kind of *sole* these can best be taken, and to find out in what position in the rink he is most likely to be of use. He will then know that *truth* in curling-stones, as in other companions, is of greater value than *beauty*, which is only skin deep, that fitness is a better guide than fancy, and he will choose accordingly. If the beginner carefully reads the learned Professor's statements in our last chapter, he will know as much about the *matériel* of curling-stones as is good for him. As to *weight*. The maximum allowed in the "Royal" rules is 50 lb. (including handles). There are very few stones of this weight in use on modern ice, and more than once a petition to reduce this maximum has come before the representative meeting. The average weight of curling-stones is now from 35 to 40 lb. There are more below 35 lb. than there are above 40 lb., and between the two weights we may safely say that three-fourths of the stones now in use are to be found. In the famous rink of Lord

Eglinton, John Napier, stud groom, led with a pair of 50 lb. stones; Robert Brown of Lileston came next with a pair at 48 lb.; Hugh Conn, auctioneer, played 46 lb. or 44 lb., as the day might require; while his lordship skipped with a pair of 42 lb. This rink in *weight* was above the average of its own period, and it is much above the average of ours; but in playing up to the maximum the Eglinton rink gives us a capital idea of the relative *weights* suitable to the four players of a rink. When so much can be done by *polish* to improve the running of stones, we do not see the necessity for such a reduction of weight as some desire. A "parish" of pigmies is no proof that skill has superseded force. We would therefore prefer to see young curlers trying to climb up to the maximum rather than to climb down to the minimum weight. At the same time a light *dour* stone is a better stone to lead the ice than a heavy keen one. The beginner must avoid choosing stones which are beyond his control, for he cannot master the art if he is overbalanced by a too heavy implement. The stone will no doubt lessen with years of play, but the years of the player will tell even more upon his constitution, and he will therefore be wise to select such stones as he can command and play with ease through a match of three or four hours' duration. In regard to the *build* of a stone, a 50-pounder is generally about 36 inches in circumference. This is also the maximum allowed in the rules, while the height is not to be less than "one-eighth part of its greatest circumference." The orthodox height of a stone of maximum weight and circumference is generally about 6 inches. For a 40 lb. stone a circumference of $35\frac{1}{4}$ inches, and a height of about $5\frac{3}{4}$ inches, gives a good build, and this proportion holds for other weights. Extremes of height or breadth are bad, as both render the delivery of the stone difficult and uncertain, and the curler must bear in mind that the diameter of the stone will continually be diminishing under the blows it receives upon its belt, so that in his choice he had better err on the broad side. The most important part of the curling-stone is its *sole* or *bottom*. Whatever conclusion may be come to in regard to breadth and shape of bottom, one thing must be guarded against, and that is a sharp *cridge* between the sole and the upper part of the stone. A flat-edged stone throws the water up over itself, and sits down under the shower: it collects the snow before it, and any refuse that may be on the ice. On the other hand, the stone that is gradually chaffered off or rounded wins its way through water like a duck, and casts aside snow and refuse like the plough fixed in front of the wheels of a locomotive. A favourite subject of discussion among the curling authorities of the transition period was this: "*Whether is a broad or a narrow sole the best?*" The broad sole was championed by Dr Somerville of Currie, whose statement we may here quote:—

"Stones should all run on a broad surface 7 inches in diameter at least. We committed great blunders here at one time making our stones run on a small centre, some of them as narrow as 3 or 4 inches; the consequence of which was that, running on so small a centre, they quickly found every bias of the ice, and, however fairly set on, often thus missed the object. This is cured by broadening to 7 inches, for, running on so wide a centre, their motion is much more steady; they do not so quickly feel the bias of the ice, and of course are much surer in their aim and more certain in their effects. I need not add that the stones running in this wide centre must be of the keenest metal and of the finest polish, otherwise it will require too much power to play them home to the object intended. We don't, however, gain in power as we narrow in bottom, for two sufficient reasons—first, because the narrower the surface the deeper the pressure, just as a narrow wheel sinks deeper into the sludge than one that is broad; and secondly, because when playing upon a narrow centre you are obliged to use your force more cautiously, for fear of overturning your stone altogether. This fact is further proved by my own experience. I can play my present stone, 7½ inches in sole, better and further than my former one of three."

With Dr Somerville Sir Richard Broun cordially agreed, and recommended broad soles to all curlers. Dr Cairnie differed from these authorities, and recommended for keen ice a running bottom of 4 or 5 inches; for dull ice, one of from 2 to 2½ inches, which latter, he says, was generally adopted at Largs. Cairnie's correspondent on the subject of "curling at Kilmarnock" says that experiments there had proved that a sole of 6 inches, with a level of 1½ or 2 inches for running on, the rest of the sole being *very gently* rounded to its edge, is best adapted for ice, in whatever state it may be; and in reply to Dr Somerville, this gentleman goes on to add:—

"The advantage of a narrow bottom is principally perceived on keen ice, when the stone does not sink at all. On damp ice, the broad, flat sole runs almost as well as the gently convex one, which we are advocating. Dr Somerville's other objection of the great danger of overturning stones running on a narrow level is proven, from experience, to have no foundation. A curler may play for a whole season with a stone of 6 inches of sole, running on even 1½ inch of level, without once overturning it, and that with only ordinary care in delivery, provided it be made of the approved slightly convex shape."*

The question so keenly discussed was not unlike that propounded by King Charles—"*Which is heaviest*, a dead or a live fish?" Coulomb in France, and Rennie in this country, proved that the friction of one body passing along another is not influenced by the extent of surface, but depends on the weight of the body. With stones of equal weight, the retardation of friction is therefore the same. The distance each will travel depends on the initial velocity, and not on the size of the stone. With stones of different weight, the heavier stone has the advantage: it presents, comparatively, less surface to air, or snow, or water. If a player has command of his stone, so as to give it the requisite velocity, the heavier it is the better on ice covered with slush or water; while on keen ice, if its weight is not required to remove obstacles, it keeps it from being too easily sent spinning when once it has settled down.

While we keep in mind that friction is a uniformly retarding force, there is this, however, to be said on the question of broad or narrow bottom. On keen and clear ice the broad bottom certainly gives the stone more stability, and prevents it from too readily taking biases; while on spongy ice, or where there is snow or slush on the rink, the narrow bottom cuts more easily down to the hard ice below, thereby diminishing the friction, which is, of course, less on a hard than on a soft surface. The fact that there were two sides to the question led to the conclusion that there should be two sides to the curling-stone. Nearly all the stones are now made with reversible soles—the one for keen, the other for haugh ice. In

* Cairnie's *Essay*, p. 71.

the transition period there was great variety of bottom among curling-stones, as may be inferred from some drawings here given from Cairnie (Fig. 80). The white portion of each disc is meant to indicate the running portion of the sole of the stone; the dark disc representing the upper side of a one-soled stone, while the two upper pairs of discs shew the opposite sides of double-soled stones. The stone with the uppermost pair of soles was a favourite at Wishaw. It was the stone which "ran on feet" in the match of Cam'nethan against Bathgate (*vide* p.182). There can be nothing new in curling-stone soles. Steel, brass, and lead have all been tried, and iron stones like those now used in Canada were, in the transition period, manufactured by the Shotts Iron Co., tried and discarded as unsuitable on our ice. Among stone-players in Canada the stone now in general use has a concave or hollow on both sides.

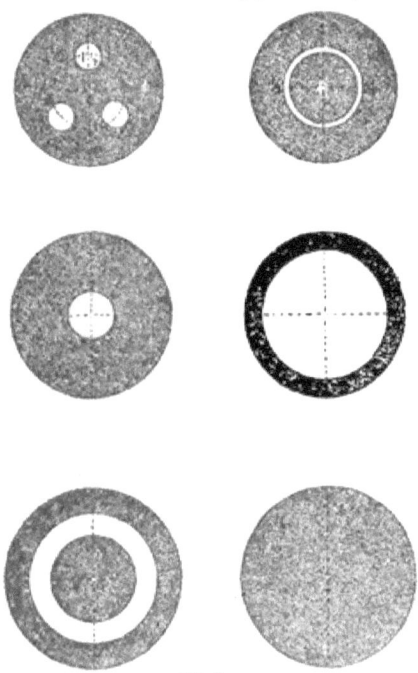

FIG. 80.

The hollow of the dull side is generally about 5 inches in diameter, with a depth at the centre of ¼ inch, and the running ridge or ring is narrow and sharp, so as to grip the hard ice. The hollow of the keen side is neither so wide nor so deep. The diameter is generally about 2½ inches, and the running ridge is not sharp, but rounded and smooth. In the home country a good many stones of the Canadian pattern are in use, but the keen side of the stone is very often convex, gently rounding to a pivot centre of 1½ or

2 inches, on which the stone runs, while the dull side has a concave of about 4 inches diameter, and the running ridge not so sharp as in the Canadian. We can commend this doubly-modified form. On keen days the concave keeps the ice well; and on dull ones the convex lends itself readily to "kiggle-caggle"—or the oscillating motion which skilful players who want to reduce friction communicate to their stone on very haugh ice. A good many flat-bottomed stones are still in use. Our countrymen have not come to any common understanding as to the best form of sole. It is not quite a case of *tot homines quot sententiæ*; but there is much difference of opinion. The beginner in the art must therefore examine and judge for himself, and choose a pair of stones when he has made up his mind as to the best material and outline. It will greatly increase his enjoyment of curling if he is careful to attend to the *polish* of the stones. His calculations may all be upset if this is neglected. He will have more delight in their companionship if he now and then send his curling-stones to the manufacturer to have their appearance and manners polished and improved.

Position.—Our curler having chosen a pair of suitable stones, must now prepare to play them. In curling, *position* is not quite "everything," but it is of primary importance. *Fit fair* is the first command of the old curler's *word*. There are "divers manners" of doing this, as may be seen by looking at Figs. 81 and 82, where the players are caught in the act; but whatever position the curler may assume, there must be no dubiety about his *fitting the tee*. This is the absolute imperative of the

FIG. 81. FITTING THE TEE.

curling position. To obey it, the player must see that the crampit or hack is placed as directed in No. 1 of the general rules. Looking toward the farther tee, he must then place his right foot in the hack, the sole of his boot pressing against the perpendicular back, and the ball of the great toe resting about the centre of the sloping part: the left foot, as indicated at p. 161, he will place at a right angle about 18 inches forward. In playing from a crampit, the right foot must, of course, rest against the back or fillet of the crampit. A good many players place the left foot farther forward than we have indicated, and fit their tee with the legs firmly poised like the sides of an equilateral triangle, as in Fig. 82. We prefer the *couchant* position of the player in Fig. 81, as one in which there is greater purchase over the stone. The curler must, however, poise himself in such a way as to secure ease and accuracy in his play, and not be hampered by any fixed rule as to position. The *sine qua non*

FIG. 82. "SHEW ME THE WINNER."

is that he *fit fair*, and that no flank movement be possible, as in the old days of movable triggers and crunching crampits. The player must also decide for himself in what way he shall grip the handle of the stone as he prepares to swing it. Some do this in a gingerly style, as if they were ashamed to touch the handle with the tips of their fingers; others grip it as if they meant to squeeze the life out of it: some grip from above, others from below. Some deliver with a side hand, the thumb pressing on the back of the handle's neck; others, with the handle at right angles to the central line, and pointing across their body (*vide* Fig. 81), send it away to its destination in a free, open-handed manner. The last method is the one we prefer when a straight shot has to be played. In playing the "twist," of which more anon, the right-angle position, however, puts rather a heavy strain on the wrist; and to relieve this, it is better to modify the position of hand and handle as indicated in Fig. 82, where (the player looking north) the thumb points north-east, and the twist to left or right is played without any undue straining of the wrist in either case. For a particular player that method is undoubtedly the best which enables him to perform most effectually the next function of the curling art which falls to be considered, viz. :—

The Swing.—The curler must exercise a wise economy by refusing to his stone of 35 or 40 lb. weight the luxury of any "preliminary waggles" to prepare it for the swing. Such things please the light-headed clubs of the golfer, and put them in good humour, but the "stone of might" does not need to be coaxed in that way to do its work. *Near and sure* is the motto of the rink, as *Far and sure* is that of the links. For *Keep your eye on the ball*, the curler substitutes *Look at the mark with all your een*. There must be no looking down at the feet, or at the stone, or at some guiding point half-way up the rink, when the swing is in course. The player must fix "a basilisk glance" on the mark. The swing is to convey the life to the stone, and the eye must communicate the information by which the mind of the player through the swing determines what kind of life is needed. The hand is worked by the head, and the head by the eye.

> "Low o'er the weighty stone
> He bends incumbent, and with nicest eye
> Surveys the farthest goal, and in his mind
> Measures the distance, careful to bestow
> Just force enough."

The golfing motto *Slow back* (or, as Sir Walter Simpson would have it, *Taut back*) is a good one for the curling swing. "A cannie draw to the besom." "Jist tee-high weight." "Cannilie doun howe ice." To such direction the stone is drawn slowly backward and upward, the body of the player rising gently in unison with the swing till his weight rests on the right foot. It is poised a moment, while more intently than ever the player's eye is fixed on the mark. Then quietly the stone is brought back by the way it came, the body of the player bending down, and his weight gradually coming upon the left foot. The force of the body is thus thrown into the arm; and when the stone meets the ice at the spot where it was lifted, it is instinct with life, and moves away, "wi' a whirr and a curr,"

FIG. 83. "THE CANNY SWING."

to carry out its master's purpose. It was "bonnilie laid doun," the kowe smoothed its path: it went snoovin' up the howe and toddled ben to the tee— "a gran' shot, man; jist like yoursel'." The canny swing for a drawing shot is that which is oftenest required in the art of curling. When more than drawing weight is

FIG. 84. "A HAIR O' PITH."

needed, the height and force of the swing must be increased. "There's a truck o' Benhar blockin' the line, laird; ye maun remove 't in your ain quiet way." Such is the direction we have heard given when a fifty-pounder of the enemy had settled down in front of the tee. The player in that case had to put on a little steam, and he knew how to do it. This was the laird's quiet way (Fig. 84). Curlers in olden times did not worship the "canny swing." They believed more in the *swing maximum*, which is *uncanny*. He was the greatest hero who, when occasion required, could best display

"The might that slumbers in the yeoman's arm."

To *rebut* or drive a thunderbolt up among double and treble guards when the game was hopeless or desperate, and to *cannon*, or make a guard butt off the winner and follow in so as to lie shot, were two favourite points by which the ancient curlers were wont to win distinction. "Often," says Sir R. Broun, "from the opposite end of the rink have we seen the sole of our president's stone over his head when he had to *lift* up double guards." William Gourlay and Aleck Cook must have excelled at these shots. They are not much played in our cultured and skilful age, but occasions do occur when the player must rise to the highest height of endeavour. "A' the pouther i' the horn." "Come doun like a vera judgment and clear the hoose." "Rattle up the guards." Such directions have at times to be issued, and then the player must give "a thunnerin' cast."

FIG. 85. "A THUNNERIN' CAST."

THE ART OF CURLING.

> "Long swings the stone,
> Then with full force, careering furious on,
> Rattling it strikes aside both friend and foe,
> Maintains its course and takes the victor's place."

Such flights of the art we cannot follow, nor can we shew how they may be taken. When a curler has to raise his stone above his shoulder, his moral responsibility is at an end, and his brethren must take care of him.

Soling and Delivering the Stone.—When the curler does not swing back his stone properly, but lifts it straight up, he will in delivering *clink* it on the ice and break its back. Again, he may swing the stone quite correctly, but if he do not sole it properly, the force and effect of the swing will be destroyed. The proper *soling* of the stone is of great importance. A stalwart player who cannot sole his stone is nowhere against a man of half his power who has the secret of "a guid delivery." The *chaffering* of the stone to which we have referred is of great consequence for correct soling. Sharp-edged stones

FIG. 86. "SHARP-EDGED SOLING."

FIG. 87. "WELL LAID DOWN."

must be put down with great nicety and caution if the player would avoid mangling the ice and spending the stone. By letting go the stone too soon he will dump its forehead on the ice, and by holding on to it too long he will do the same with the back edge, and either way the stone will be made to *wobble*. The curler must guard against this by letting the stone gently off his hand as soon as it meets the ice. It is right that every curler should watch with interest the career of the stone after it has left his hand. Nor is there any law to prevent him shewing his mental anxiety by various bodily contortions. We rather admire than condemn the eager gamester who, after the act of delivery,

> "Bends
> His waist, and winds his hand, as if it still
> Retained the power to guide the devious stone."

But this kind of thing may easily be overdone. In the *jeu d'esprit*, *Closeburn* v. *Lochmaben*, Professor Gillespie introduces "a fat, round, oily bailie, with his beetle legs and bald head, who lay flat upon the ice eyeing up his stone, and writhing from side to side, as if in the act of determining its direction." It is said that James Millar, advocate, who was such a popular player in the Duddingston Club, used regularly to squat on his belly on the middle of the rink after the stone went off, and kick, roar, sputter, and gesticulate wildly after it, to the infinite amusement of the numerous onlookers, some of whom were shocked to see a learned member of the Faculty of Advocates so conducting himself. We have seen some who came pretty near to this, and many make a practice of following the stone halfway up the rink. The reason why some players run forward so absurdly is to recover their balance after the stone is delivered. This would not be necessary if, according to the custom of the best players, the left foot were lifted and slightly advanced as the stone is sent away. In the delivery the centre of gravity of the player is advanced, and by moving forward the left foot his base line (so to speak) is also advanced, and his stable equilibrium preserved. While we would not have curlers to be too self-conscious, or to refrain from manifestations of enthusiasm in case they may be laughed at, we would remind them of the rules which say that they must not take more than "a reasonable time" to play their stone, and that "no party, except when sweeping according to rule, shall go upon the middle of the rink, or cross it, under any pretence whatever." If they *must* step off the crampit in their eagerness to see their stone ushered in to victory, let them do so as gracefully as the veteran curler in Fig. 88, and we shall forgive them.

FIG. 88. "AT THE CURL."

Sweeping.—According to Shakespeare, "to smoothe the ice" is as much a work of supererogation as "to gild refined gold" or "to paint the lily." *Ne sutor ultra crepidam.* We do not expect a dramatist to know the advantage of "soopin'." In the art of curling no man can ever excel who does not learn "to smoothe the ice." It is the broom that wins the battle. Every good curler knows that. Neither age nor dignity exempts a player from the duty of sweeping. As far as our experience goes, neither the old nor the noble require to be reminded of it. The Nestor of a club is generally the member who believes most in the virtue of *elbow-grease*, for he has oftenest been witness of its good effects. We have seen the present Lord High Commissioner to the General Assembly (the Marquis of Tweeddale) plying his broom on the frozen Tyne as nimbly as his humblest retainer, and thus helping the Yester men to win the county cup. It is the young man of the period who requires to be taught his duty in this respect. He curls—because it is fashionable; he has a broom, but he might as well be without it, for when he steps off the crampit he puts it under his arm, and with his pipe in his teeth and his hands in his pockets he sludges about the edge of the rink till his turn to play again comes round. One fellow of that kind in a rink will ruin its chance of winning the match. He ought simply to be put off the ice and expelled from all respectable curling society. After he has taken his place on the crampit every curler should give the soles of his stones a rub to see that no dirt or snow adheres to them; he should then give the ice in front of him "a bit soop." When his stone has been played he ought to take his place among the sweepers, and with his besom ready for action, await the skip's direction. In olden times, when there were eight players on each side, the orderly arrangement of the sweepers was no easy matter. The following account of the Wanlockhead curlers shews how effective such arrangement was, and how much attention was given by ancient curlers to this department of their work:—

"Almost without exception, tall, strapping young men, strong and hardy, they possessed every quality necessary to make good curlers. Their discipline, too, was absolutely perfect. At the time when there were eight men in a rink this was most apparent. Arranged three and three on each side of the rink, they waited with the greatest attention till the stone was delivered, following it quietly but eagerly in its course, till, at the call of the skip, 'Soop her up,' down came the besoms like lightning, hands were clasped, the feet kept time to the rapid strokes of the besom, and no exertion was spared until the stone was landed at the desired spot, when a good long breath being drawn, the player was rewarded with a universal shout, 'Weel played, mon.' Dispute as we may as to the relative merits of the different parishes as to curling in the general, we believe that all who have seen Wanlockhead curlers play will admit that in the matter of sweeping they 'bear the gree.'" *

In the modern rink of four players the skip must look after the *boardhead*, and two only are left to sweep between the middle line and the boundary of the *parish*, when the fourth is on the crampit. Elaborate arrangement of the sweeping department is therefore unnecessary. For a long

---

* Brown's *History of the Sanquhar Curling Society*, p. 29.

time the law was that "parties, before beginning to play, must take different sides of the rink, which they must keep throughout the game." This, however, was rescinded, and the practice is now to sweep from either side; but it is still important that order and discipline should be maintained, and that strict attention be paid to the duties of the besom. The rule that "all sweeping must be to the side" still holds, and the kowe must never be used to put obstacles in the way of the stone. The earlier law of the Royal Club prohibited sweeping until the stone had reached the hog. In Sir George Harvey's *Curling Match* the players are seen sweeping from tee to tee. The painter on being challenged defended his picture as a faithful representation of the old custom. And so it is. Lord Eglinton and the Ayrshire curlers stuck out for this old system, and in 1852 a compromise was arrived at by which sweeping was allowed from the "middle line" and from tee to tee if snow should be falling during the play. It is the duty of the sweeper to abide by the order of the skip, who only can determine whether or not sweeping is necessary; and when "Ne'er a kowe" or "Brooms up" is sounded he must be as ready to stop as he is to begin when the cry of "Soop, lads, soop," is heard. It is in the power of either skip to call upon all the players at the close of an end to clean the rink. This should never be taken advantage of simply to delay a match, but it is right that the game should always be conducted on a clean board, and every club ought to avoid the necessity for any such delay by keeping the rink in good condition, and acting up to the old motto—

"QUHAIR EUER THEY GO IT MAY BE SENE
HOW RINK AND TEE THEY BOTH SOOP CLENE."

The Twist.—To be able by a turn of the wrist to give the stone a rotatory motion which shall make it run against the bias of the ice, or to transform an object of offence into one of defence by making the stone curve round the right or the left side of a guard by an *elbow out* or *elbow in* delivery, is one of the highest accomplishments in the art of curling, and greatly increases the interest and skill of the player. This secret is said to have been discovered at Fenwick in the first year of the century,* and it is therefore generally called the *Fenwick Twist.*

Now, there may be no harm in connecting the twist with *Fenwick*, that famous centre of keen curling since the days of Covenanter Guthrie. But we are not sure that the origin of the twist is any clearer than the origin of the Royal Club or of curling itself. The name of *Kilmarnock* is sometimes attached to it, but this may simply be on the principle that the greater includes the less. The Cambusnethan curlers hold that the secret of the "turn of the hand" was known there about the end of last century, and that it was the discovery of William Bell, grandfather of the present patron of the Buchan Club, Robert Bell of Cliftonhall. In a match played against Lesmahagow at Garionhaugh, near Dalserf, 24th January 1809, the Cam'nethan curlers are said to have distinguished themselves by this scientific style of play, and Lesmahagow and other parishes are said to have acquired the secret from Cam'nethan.† Now, we are quite convinced that the secret of the twist was discovered long before the end of the last century, and that some of the remarkable feats of curlers in ancient times were accomplished by the aid of what is now called the *Fenwick Twist.* Among the songs at the end of Cairnie's *Essay* (p. 133), there is one said to have been composed *extempore*, in 1784, at the match between the Duke of Hamilton and M'Dowall of Castlesemple. In this song there occurs the following stanza:—

> "Six stones within the circle stand,
> And every port is blocked,
> But Tam Pate he did *turn the hand*,
> And soon the port unlocked." ‡

---

* *Vide* Taylor's *Curling*, p. 69.
† Captain Paterson, in the *Douglas Bonspiel*, p. 9 (1806), refers to some curlers
"Who can, with subtle wrist,
Give to their stane the true 'Kilmarnock twist.'"
This reference, if it does not settle the question, bears strongly against the Cam'nethan theory.
‡ In the *Sketch of Curling*, published at Kilmarnock in 1828, the song, considerably altered and enlarged, appears above the signature of "J. Bicket, Fenwick." The reference to Tam Pate is there omitted. Cairnie's version is certainly the best.

Who is so foolish as to suppose that *warlock* Tam had not the twist among his secrets? Some would go a long way farther back and find in the word *curl* itself a proof that the ancients could turn the hand and bend the course of the stone even without a handle. This much having been said for the antiquity of the twist, we must acknowledge that the old curling *word* did not notice this style of play. Its command was—*Shoot straight*. With obedience to this command the practice of the twist does not, however, interfere. Paradox though it may appear, a curler who cannot shoot straight cannot put on the proper *curl*. To be able to shoot straight is to be able to deliver the stone without any rotatory motion. Before we can deliver the stone with such a rotatory motion as we wish to give it, we must first be able to protect it from taking a rotatory motion which we do *not* wish to give it. The young curler should therefore obey the old word, and he should never play the twist until he is able to shoot straight. A good straight player is a good curler. On some kinds of ice he will hold his own against the most efficient practitioner of the Fenwick twist. No curler is, however, entitled to be reckoned a graduate of arts in curling until he has mastered the knowledge of the *in-turn* and the *out-turn*. When he begins to try these his play will very likely deteriorate. He will go off his game in trying to get on with it. This is a common occurrence. Experience of the kind has discouraged many a player, and made him condemn the *twort* altogether. If the young curler has the pluck to persevere; if he lose no opportunity of having a quiet practice and studying the curve made by each kind of sole; if he carefully guard himself against losing his power to play the straight game, while he is trying to master the other style of play, he will find his patience amply rewarded. Occasions will arise when the power thus gained will stand him in good stead. He will triumphantly sail up the howe when his neighbour is driven helplessly aside by the bias, and the straight player will be completely dumfoundered at seeing his wily opponent remove the winner which he had thought impregnable, for

> "By the turning of the hand
> All guarding's but a mock."

In the twist, as in other departments of the art, practice is the only way to perfection. While the direction given by the skip is *elbow in* or *elbow out*, the player must remember that it is the *wrist* that communicates the *twirl* to the stone. This should be given just at the moment when the stone in its downward swing makes a tangent with the ice. The old order *Shoot straight* is, as we have said, quite consistent with putting on curl. The player must not swing his stone toward the right or the left when he wants it to turn to the one or the other, but it must be sent off straight toward the mark. The twist will direct it in the desired curve, and its effect will be felt most in the *dying moments* of the stone's career.

Skipping a Rink.—The goal of a curler's ambition is to become a skip. For this high office not only masterly play but the best qualities of head and heart are required. The man who can skip a rink well may rule a kingdom. With the club it lies to determine upon whom the honour is to be conferred, and this is usually done at the annual meeting. In choosing their skips clubs cannot be too careful, for upon this choice their reputation very much depends. There should be no flunkeyism, and no hole-and-corner work. All should be fair and square, and the skip should be chosen on his merits, not because he is patron, president, or chaplain of his club. The best curler in the club often plays in homespun. Clubs should appoint skips *ad vitam aut culpam*, and not change them every year, unless they are found guilty of intemperance, ill-nature, or the *driving* game. The choice of players should be left to the skips, and these again should not be annually disarranged, but vacancies should be filled up as they occur, and the continuity of the rink preserved. The skip will place his men according to their powers—the lead, one who can draw with a stone of weight; the second, one who can guard well; the third, a player who can take brittle shots and put on the curl when it is needed. *Esprit de corps* is a grand thing in a rink. The quartet must work well together, and be attached to each other and to their head. In America they have a *Four-brother* club, which is made up of *family rinks*, to illustrate the advantage of keeping together. We have seen on the Dalkeith pond a display of fine curling by a rink of *four brothers*, who knew each other's play to a tee, and worked as if they had discussed every situation together the night before, and settled how to act.

We may talk of equality on the ice, but not in presence of the skip. The Autocrat of all the Russias is not more absolute in his sway than the doupar or director of a rink of curlers.

"The skipper's advice is imperative law."

To this very end he is elected, that he may dictate what is to be done, and it is his duty to brook no interference with his rule. When he gives orders, he must see that they are obeyed. But while a skip must rule with a rod of iron, and allow no one to question his direction, he must deal gently with the erring, and must not flyte when a player misses a shot. " That's no like you ; " " It's no vera often ye dae that ; " " As guid as a better ; " or " Ye'll get it next time," are remarks more likely to improve the form of the player than a volley of abuse. The skip should believe that his men are always doing their best ; and even when the battle is going against him, he must not sulk, or sputter and foam at friends and enemies alike, as the manner of some is. Curling is a slippery game, and many a match has been saved at the eleventh hour by the splendid courage of the skip who never played better than when he was playing a losing game. And oh, the victories which have been gained by dint of praise! How it puts mettle into the men and fires their enthusiasm, and cheers them on to victory, when the skip sings out his salutations in such phrases as these, which have gladdened the hearts of keen curlers in every age: " You for a curler ; " " Come up an' look at it ; " " You're the king o' players ; " " Gie's a shake o' your hand ; " " I'll gie ye a snuff for that."

There is no end to the resources which a skip may call

into play. He must never allow the attention of the players to flag, for a quick rate of game is generally most effectual. To carry on the game with proper speed, the skip must take in the situation at once, and not dawdle about the "parish" till the "thow" comes. He must at the outset of a match "tak' up the ice"—*i.e.*, judge of any bias there may be, and how best to counteract it; and he must be prompt and decided in his orders, never giving two or three directions at one time, and so confusing the player. We must not suppose that a rattling game requires a raging style of play. For all ordinary purposes *tee-high weight* is enough for a stone. Curling cannot be played on bare rink-heads. A good skip will therefore avoid the *driving* or *striking* game. Shakespeare must have been a curler after all, for we find him[*] warning skips in these words—

> "We may outrun
> By violent swiftness that which we run at,
> And lose by over-running."

But skips must not quote Shakespeare. If they must have a motto for quiet play, let it be that of Boswell's *Damback*,

> "A gude calm shot is aye the best."

Or, better still, that fine old saying, *Oh, be cannie!* It is to our skips that we must look to preserve pure the auld Scotch phrases and words which connect the game with bygone times, and to make the rink a sanctuary of refuge for the mither tongue when every other comes to be shut against it. To our skips we also look to preserve the venerable and time-honoured traditions of the noble game: to maintain its high tone, and never to permit anything that is vile, or low, or ungentlemanly to disfigure the beauty of it.

RULES FOR LOCAL MEDAL COMPETITION.
POINT GAME. ADOPTED 1888.

1st. Competitors shall draw lots for the rotation of play, and shall use two stones.

2nd. The length of the rink shall not exceed 42 yards; any lesser distance shall be determined by the umpire.

3rd. Circles of 7 feet and 4 feet radius shall be drawn round the tee, and a central line through the centre of the 4 foot circle to the hog score.

---

[*] *Henry VIII.*, i. 1.

THE ART OF CURLING. 415

4th. Every competitor shall play four shots at each of the eight following points of the game, viz. :—Striking, inwicking, drawing, guarding, chap and lie, wick and curl in, raising, and chipping the winner, according to the following definitions. (See below.)

5th. In Nos. 2, 6, 8, and 9, two chances on the left and two on the right.

6th. No stone shall be considered *without* a circle unless it is entirely clear of that circle. In every case a square is to be placed on the ice to ascertain when a stone is without a circle, or entirely clear of a line.

NOTE.—The above rules and definitions are applicable only to medals given by the Royal Club, and are not intended to supersede any regulations made by local clubs in competing for their own private medals.

NOTE 2.—It will save much time if, in playing for local medals, two rinks be prepared lying parallel to each other, the tee of the one being at the reverse end of the other rink ; every competitor plays both stones up the one rink, and immediately afterwards both down the other, finishing thus at each round all his chances at that point.

It will also save time if a code of signals be arranged between the marker and the players, such as the marker to raise one hand when one is scored, and both hands when two are scored. In the case of a miss hands to be kept down.

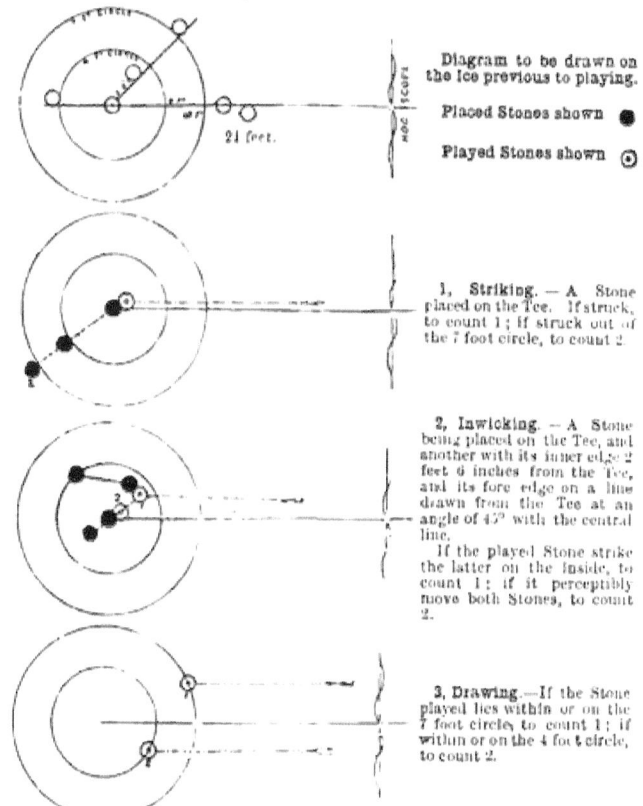

Diagram to be drawn on the ice previous to playing.

Placed Stones shown ●
Played Stones shown ◉

1, **Striking**. — A Stone placed on the Tee. If struck, to count 1; if struck out of the 7 foot circle, to count 2.

2, **Inwicking**. — A Stone being placed on the Tee, and another with its inner edge 2 feet 6 inches from the Tee, and its fore edge on a line drawn from the Tee at an angle of 45° with the central line.

If the played Stone strike the latter on the inside, to count 1; if it perceptibly move both Stones, to count 2.

3, **Drawing**.—If the Stone played lies within or on the 7 foot circle, to count 1; if within or on the 4 foot circle, to count 2.

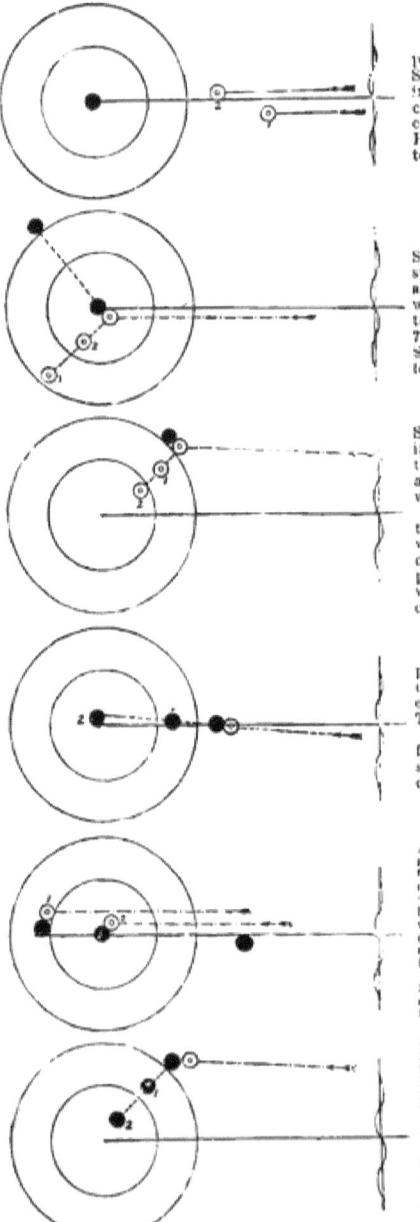

4, **Guarding.** — A Stone placed on the Tee. If the Stone played rests within 6 inches of the central line, to count 1; if on the line, to count 2. It shall be over the Hog, but not touch the Stone to be guarded.

5, **Chap and Lie.** — If a Stone placed on the Tee be struck out of the 7 foot circle, and the played Stone lie within or on the same circle, to count 1; if struck out of 7 foot circle, and the played Stone lie within or on the 4 foot circle, to count 2.

6, **Wick and Curl in.** — A Stone being placed with its inner edge 7 feet distant from the Tee, and its fore edge on a line making an angle of 45° with the central line.

If the Stone is struck, and the played Stone curls on or within the 7 foot circle, to count 1; if struck, and the played Stone curls on or within the 4 foot circle, to count 2.

7, **Raising.** — A Stone placed with its centre on the central line and its inner edge 8 feet distant from the Tee.

If struck into or on the 7 foot circle, to count 1; if struck into or on the 4 foot circle, to count 2.

8, **Chipping the Winner.** — A Stone being placed on the Tee, and another with its inner edge 10 feet distant, just touching the central line, and half guarding the one on the Tee, and a third Stone being placed 4 feet behind the Tee, with its inner edge touching the central line, but on the opposite side from that on which the guard is placed.

If the played Stone strikes the Stone placed behind the Tee, to count 1; if it strikes the Stone on the Tee, to count 2.

9, **Outwicking.** — In the event of two or more competitors gaining the same number of shots, they shall play four shots at Outwicking, that is, a Stone being placed with its inner edge 7 feet distant from the Tee, and its centre on a line making an angle of 45° with the central line.

If struck within or on the 7 foot circle, to count 1; if struck within or on the 4 foot circle, to count 2.

If the competition cannot be decided by these shots, the Umpire shall order one or more of the preceding points to be played again by the Competitors who are equal.

FIG. 89. POINT GAME

Of the point game as a test of skill we have given our opinion in a former chapter. It is the skeleton of the curling system. The living figure of curling can only be studied in the bonspiel. For practice it is, however, invaluable; and by point play curlers may prepare themselves for the higher art. They may by such practice test the various rules which we have laid down in this chapter, and thereby correct us if they find we have made any mistakes. There are many other *points* which might be added. The Canadians have one more in their list, viz., *drawing through a port*, as represented in Fig. 90. The diagram shews how the Canadians run each point of the game on fresh ice, the first stone being played to the left, the second to the right of the central line. This, the Marquis of Lorne informs us, is a favourite point in Canada, and the small size of the *irons* in use in Montreal, Quebec, &c., gives them greater facility in threading the port. For irons, 18 inches is the width of port allowed; for stones, 2 feet. The variety of size in our stones is no doubt the reason why we do not play the porting shot. Its omission is to be regretted. If drawing

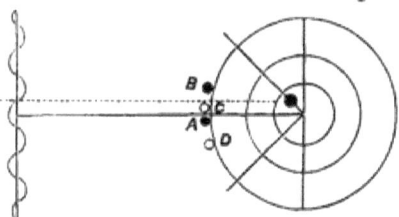

FIG. 90. DRAWING THROUGH A PORT.

itself is so fine a point, how much finer is it to draw *inter Scyllam et Charybdim*, and through a narrow port find the winner that lies on the tee. In ancient times many a reputation was made by porting. Not to mention the power of the immortal Pate, this was Bailie Hamilton's great shot, as recorded by Captain Paterson (*vide* p. 138). It was in passing through the port that Deacon Jardine *birsed the needle* (*vide* p. 152). "Lord, I kent I wad tak' it out—ay, like a bullet," shouted Doupar John Robertson,[*] and as his *wee stane* came gliding through the narrows, took the winner and lay game shot, the Lochwinnoch curlers were so overjoyed that they lifted the doupar and carried him off shoulder-high to the inn.

---

[*] Cairnie's *Essay*, p. 96.

On Lochmaben ice a feat of "the Tutor" is handed down by tradition. The winner was only reachable through a port so narrow that the Tutor's players objected to him trying it. With the skip's permission the port was tried and the winner taken, the bystanders actually declaring that they heard the stone grazing upon the others, as it passed through. Provost Henderson said to Dickson, "I'll give you my curling-stone if you do the same again." The Provost had to pay, and the Tutor offered to "repeat the dose" as often as was wanted! One of the finest incidents in the history of bonspiels (shewing how good curlers always admire good play even in their opponents) is that recorded in an account of the match *Cam'nethan* v. *Bathgate*. When Henry Shanks for Bathgate, amid breathless excitement, had played a most difficult and unlikely shot, and thereby completely turned the game, Mr Storry of Bed-Allan, the Cam'nethan skip, forgetting the discomfiture to his own side, rushed forward, and grasping the burly farmer by the hand, said, "Oh, man, Harry, just lie down and dee on the spot, for you will never play sic anither shot again." It was a port shot, in which a slight rub was needed from a back-lying stone to let Henry go straight through, and after this was safely done, the Cam'nethan stones, which lay first and second, were displaced by a double cannon, and Bathgate lay winner in their place. Life was certainly not worth living after such a shot. We could multiply instances to shew how in olden times distinction was won in this way. We have *eight:* why should we not have the proverbial "*nine* points of the law," and thus be brought into closer union with our Canadian brethren and with the days of old?

CHAPTER IV.

BIBLIOTHECA CURLIANA.

IN the course of our history of the game we have given an account of the various works which have been written on the subject of curling. We should like to see curling literature further enriched by the histories of local clubs. Sanquhar and North Woodside have led the way, and the history of Rattray Club is now in the hands of the Rev. Mr Davies, the club's chaplain. Such local records furnish us with interesting information; and it is to these that we must look for such fresh intelligence about the past as may at some future time help to improve this volume, or create the necessity for a fuller account of the history of the national game. The curler who is anxious to have a complete library of curling literature as one of his "equipments," will find such a worthy ambition no easy task, and if he is of Grangerite tastes he may have his time fully occupied in hunting up all the publications connected in one way or another with curling; but for those who wish to limit their attention to works devoted in whole or in part to the game, we shall here furnish such lists as shall enable them to make a pretty exhaustive collection of curling literature.

I. CHRONOLOGICAL LIST OF BOOKS AND BOOKLETS ON CURLING.*

1. *Songs for the Curling-Club held at Canon-mills.* By a Member. Edinburgh: Printed by J. Robertson, No. 39 South Bridge-Street. 8vo, sewed, pp. 16. 1792. *Vide* pp. 118-122.

2. *An Account of the Game of Curling.* By a Member of the Duddingston Curling Society. Edinburgh: Printed at the *Correspondent* Office. 8vo, sewed, pp. 46. 1811.
   > This work was written by Rev. John Ramsay, Gladsmuir, and is the earliest history of the game. *Vide* p. 141 and p. 195.

3. *A Descriptive and Historical Sketch of Curling:* also Rules, Practical Directions, Songs, Toasts, and a Glossary. Published by H. Crawford, Kilmarnock. 12mo, sewed, pp. 48. 1828. *Vide* p. 176.

4. *Memorabilia Curliana Mabenensia.*
   > "May curlers on life's slippery rink
   > Frae cruel rubs be free."

   Dumfries: Published by John Sinclair. Cloth, 8vo. Frontispiece, and plate at p. 99. Pp. 111. 1830.
   > The work of Sir Richard Broun, Bart. of Coalstoun. *Vide* p. 187.

5. Correspondence between the Kilmarnock and Maybole Curlers, regarding the challenge of the former which appeared in the *Ayr Advertiser*, of 4th February last [1830], to play Sixty Players of any parish in Ayrshire, within fifteen miles, for twenty sovereigns. Ayr: Printed by W. Wilson. Pp. 28, 8vo, sewed, 1830.

6. *Essay on Curling, and Artificial Pond Making.* By J. Cairnie, Largs. Cloth, 8vo. Frontispiece and three plates, pp. viii and 144. Glasgow, 1833. *Vide* p. 178.

7. *The Crune of the Warlock of the Peil.* Pryce A Bawbee. 8vo, sewed, pp. 4. Prentit be W. C. Logan. 1838. *Vide* p. 180.

---

* For this list we are mainly indebted to Captain Macnair, to whose *Channel-stane*—Fourth Series, pp. 97-106—the reader is referred for fuller information regarding the various works.

8. *Laws in Curling;* with Notes by Petrostes. Printed for J. Whitehead, Kinross, and Maclachlan and Stewart, Edinburgh. Sm. quarto, sewed, pp. 25. 1838. *Vide* p. 214.

9. *The Douglas Bonspiel:* A Poem. Inscribed to Lieut. George Black, Fifty-second Regiment of Foot. 8th January 1806. Lanark: Printed by D. C. Budge. Post 8vo, sewed, pp. 23. 1842. *Vide* p. 138.

> The work of Lieut. John Paterson, 1st Batt. 1st Regiment Bengal Native Infantry. The whole of the poem, with copious notes, is published in the Appendix to the *Annals of Lesmahagow*, by J. B. Greenshields.

10. *The Curler's Magazine;* or, Curliana Memorabilia of the several Parishes and Clubs in Dumfriesshire, Galloway, Ayrshire, Lanarkshire, Renfrewshire, and generally throughout Scotland. Printed and Published for the Proprietor and Editor at the Printing Office of the *Dumfries Times* Newspaper. 8vo, sewed, pp. 16. Dumfries, 1842. *Vide* p. 187.

11. Report of Dinner and Presentation to Alexander Shedden, Esq. of Morrishill, 17th February 1846. Beith: Printed by John Smith & Son. Quarto, sewed, pp. 24, two plates. 1846.

12. *Four New Curling Songs:* With a Dissertation on the Game of Curling. By an Old and Keen Curler, Author of "Allan M'Gregor" and "Autumnal Rambles." 12mo, sewed, pp. 16. Published by James Hogg, Edinburgh. Price 3d. N.D. *Circa* 1853. Written by Rev. Thomas Grierson. *Vide* p. 189.

13. *Curliana.* Dumfries *v.* Lochmaben and C., 17th February 1855. Lockerbie: Printed by D. Halliday, Stationer. 12mo, sewed, pp. 8. 1855. Price Twopence. Poet Tam.

14. *In Memoriam*, Bathgate Curlers' Annual Dinner, 1862. Edinburgh: R. & R. Clark. 12mo, cloth, pp. 63. 1863. *Vide* p. 201, n.

15. *History of the Sanquhar Curling Society.* Published on the occasion of the Centenary of the Society, 21st January 1874. 12mo, cloth, pp. 61. Printed at the Office of the *Dumfries and Galloway Courier*, 1874. Vide p. 125.
16. *The Curler's Guide.* 12mo, sewed, pp. 16. Toronto, 1880. By J. S. Russel.
17. Smith, J. Guthrie, President of the Carbeth Curling Club, His Havers. 20th January 1881.
    > Verses spoken by Sheriff Guthrie Smith at the annual dinner of the C.C.C. at Strathblane. Privately printed at the request of the club. 12mo, sewed, pp. 8. 1881.
18. *Curling, Ye Glorious Pastime.* Reprint of Nos. 1 and 2 of this list, with Preface by Captain Macnair. Vignette. 250 copies privately printed. Pp. 80, sm. 4to, parchment. 1882.
19. Reprint of No. 3, under the title of *The Kilmarnock Treatise on Curling.* Preface by Captain Macnair. Vignette, sm. quarto, parchment, pp. 81. Edinburgh, 1883. Impression limited to 250 copies.
20. Reprint of No. 3, to p. 48 of volume. From thence to p. 58 we have an account of "The Scottish Game of Curling" by "Maida" (T. Brown), and "The Curler's Song," by the late Francis Love of Stevenston. 12mo, sewed, pp. 60. J. M'Kie, Kilmarnock, 1883.
21. *Curling.* By the Rev. John Kerr, A.M., Dirleton. Vignette. Post 8vo, pp. 16, sewed. Edinburgh, 1884. 50 copies printed for private circulation.
22. *The Channel-stane;* or, Sweepings frae the Rinks. Series I.–IV., 4 vols., post 8vo, sewed. Edinburgh, 1884.
    > Of a parchment edition only 125 copies were printed. A collection of papers and notes on curling, carefully edited by Captain Macnair, and finely printed.
23. *Curling:* The Ancient Scottish Game. With Illustrations by C. A. Doyle. By James Taylor, M.A., D.D., F.S.A.Scot. Edinburgh: W. Paterson. Cr. 8vo, cloth, pp. 404. Plate to face p. 13. 1884.

24. *Sixty-six Years of Curling:* Being Records of North Woodside Curling Club, 1820-1886. Compiled by Captain Crawford, at the instance of Colonel Menzies, President N.W.C.C.
25. *Curling Phrases and Tactics.* (Reprinted from the *Scotsman* of August 27, 1888.) Alloa: Buchan Brothers.
    <small>By the Rev. G. Murray, B.D., Sauchie. Printed for private circulation. Pp. 12.</small>

II. LIST OF BOOKS, PARTS OF WHICH ARE DEVOTED TO THE SUBJECT OF CURLING.

1. Cassell's Book of Sports and Pastimes.
2. Chambers's (W. & R.) Useful Handbooks. Gymnastics, Golf, Curling. 1877. Curling, pp. 49 to 66.
3. Chambers's Out-of-Door Recreations. Curling.
4.   „   Encyclopædia.
5.   „   Book of Days.
6. Encyclopædia Britannica (W. M‘Dowall).
7.   „   Metropolitana, Vol. XVII. *Vide* p. 7, n.
8. Greenshields' Annals of Lesmahagow. 1864.
9. Jamieson's Scottish Dictionary.
10. M‘Diarmid (J.) Sketches from Nature. 1830.
11. Macgregor (Robt.) Pastimes and Players. 1881.
12. M‘Kay (A.) History of Kilmarnock. P. 14, *et seq.*
13. Mactaggart (John). Scottish Gallovidian Encyclopædia. 1824. 1876.
14. Out-of-Door Sports in Scotland: Their Economy and Surroundings, &c. (Curling, pp. 365 to 378.) By "Ellangowan." London: W. H. Allen & Co. 1889.
15. Rockwood (T. Dykes). Stories from Scottish Sports. 1881.
16. Sportsman's Dictionary.

III. LIST OF CURLING *ANNUALS*.

1. Royal Caledonian Curling Club. 1839 to 1889.
2. Grand National Club (United States.) 1868 to 1889.
3. Ontario Branch of the R.C.C.C. 1875 to 1889.
4. South-West of Scotland Grand Curling Club. 1886 to 1889.

IV. LIST OF MAGAZINE ARTICLES, ETC.

Annals of Sporting, VI. 74. 1824.
Ardrossan and Saltcoats Herald, December 14, 1867; November 28, 1884.
Ayr Observer, January 15, 1850 (Counsels to Curlers, by "Timothy Twist"); December 27, 1850 (Sweeping).
Baily's Monthly Magazine. March 1875.
Belgravia. *34*: 99.
Bell's Life in London, January 5, 1884 ("Rockwood").
Blackwood. Vols. 6, 28, 29, and 30.
Cassell's Sportsman's Year-Book for 1880.
Chambers's Journal. Nos. 732, 748, 942, 992.
Courant, January 2, 1885.
Daily Review, February 13, 1873.
Dublin University Magazine. *87*: 206.
Edinburgh Evening Dispatch, Jan. 13, 1886; Nov. 28, 1888.
Fraser's Magazine. *49*: 269.
Glasgow Herald (Curling Sermon,"Rockwood"), Jan. 14, 1882.
Glasgow Weekly Citizen, January 24, 1885.
Haddingtonshire Advertiser, January 5, 1883.
Hamilton Advertiser, January 24, 1885.
Johnston's Edinburgh Magazine, Vol. I. 1834.
Kilmarnock Standard, January 5, 1884.
Largs Mirror, January 1, 1879.   Leisure Hour. *21*: 38.
Littell's Living Age.   148, 639.   London Society. *41*: 99.
Montreal Daily Witness, Carnival No., February 1884.
North British Daily Mail, July 1888.
„   „   Advertiser and Ladies' Journal, Jan. 5, 1889.
Pall Mall Gazette, December 1869; February 20, 1873.
Penny Magazine.   *7*: 478.   People's Friend, p. 20, 1883.
Saint Paul's Magazine.   *4*: 185.   May 1869.
Saturday Review.   *57*: 669.   January 29, 1881.
Scotsman, July 23, 1888; August 27, 1888.
Scottish American Journal, December 27, 1883.
Standard, October 3, 1883.   Temple Bar. *4*: 492.
The Field, 644, &c.

APPENDICES.

A.—CONSTITUTION OF THE ROYAL CALEDONIAN CURLING CLUB.
(1888.)

CHAPTER I.—GENERAL REGULATIONS.

1. Any local curling club consisting of not less than eight members shall be admissible into the Royal Caledonian Curling Club, and must have a designation and sheet of ice for its operations, and be governed by office-bearers elected in accordance with the rules of this club.

2. The designations of clubs desirous of joining the Royal Club, together with a list of their office-bearers and members, and also the names of their proposer and seconder, must be lodged with the secretary a week previous to the general meeting in July, or with the assistant secretary a week previous to the adjourned meeting of the Representative Committee, at any of which meetings they will be balloted for. (*Vide* Chap. II., Section 11.)

3. Clubs asking admission ought to have, at least, one of their number at hand to be initiated in case of admission, who will be empowered and instructed how to initiate the brethren of his club; but if no one can attend, it shall be lawful for any member of the Representative Committee, along with any two initiated ordinary regular members of the Royal Club, to initiate the club afterwards.

4. Two kinds of admission tickets or diplomas shall be issued, both signed by the secretary, the one to be given to each club on initiation, the other to be furnished to the initiated members of the local clubs by their secretaries, who shall countersign and date them.

5. No new law, except with regard to prizes, shall be enacted, nor any existing law altered or repealed, until approved of by at least two-thirds of the members present at the Annual General Meeting of the Club. (*Vide* Chap. II., Section 7.)

6. Every ordinary member of an associated club shall be a member of the Royal Club, and entitled to vote at general meetings.

7. A general meeting of the Royal Club shall be held annually, in Edinburgh, or such other place as may be appointed at the previous general meeting, for the transaction of business immediately after the meeting of the Representative Committee has been concluded. These meetings shall take place on the 25th of July annually, or in case the 25th of July happening to be a Saturday, the meeting shall be held on the previous Friday. If the 25th fall on a Sunday or a Monday, it shall take place on the Tuesday following, seven to be a quorum. Provided that the Committee of Management shall have power to alter the day of the general meeting if circumstances should render it expedient to do so, within the month of July; and in case of alteration of date fourteen days' intimation of the meeting shall be given.

8. None but initiated ordinary members of associated clubs shall be present at business meetings of the Royal Club, or at any of its convivial meetings, while curling ceremonies or mysteries are being practised.

CHAPTER II.—REPRESENTATIVE COMMITTEE.

1. Each local club shall, under a penalty of not being allowed to draw for prizes, elect annually two of its ordinary members to be its representative members for the ensuing year, it being understood that the second elected member shall act only in absence of the first, and that both shall be held as coming into office on 1st October in the year of their election. The first representative must be a resident and ordinary regular member, in whose practical knowledge the local club can confide.

> When a club finds that, from its distance from Edinburgh, or other causes, none of its members can be present at the meetings of the Representative Committee, it ought to admit as an *ordinary occasional* member some member of another club, who can conveniently attend, and elect him their second representative member; the first or principal one, however, ought to be a resident and regular member, in whose practical knowledge the local club can confide, as he will be occasionally called on to be umpire in matches. The same individual can represent two clubs.

2. It shall be competent for a representative member of any club, in the event of his not being able to attend the Annual Meeting, to grant a mandate in favour of any member of the same club to attend and vote for the club, said mandate to be signed by the president or secretary of the club.

3. The representatives of local clubs shall constitute the committee above referred to as the Representative Committee; and this committee shall have the entire management of the affairs of the club, which management must be strictly in accordance with the rules and regulations in force at the time.

4. An Annual General Meeting of the Representative Committee shall be held for the transaction of business, at eleven o'clock A. M., or such hour as to the Committee of Management may seem most suitable, on the same day as the General Meeting of the Club; seven to be a quorum. This meeting shall appoint a president, a president-elect (who, if present, shall preside in the absence of the president), two vice-presidents, a chaplain, a secretary, and a treasurer of the Royal Club for the ensuing year. These shall also be the office-bearers of the Representative Committee, and their duties shall begin immediately on their appointment, and continue until next Annual Meeting, at which the president-elect shall become president for the ensuing year. The vice-presidents must be elected from the representatives present. Every office-bearer of the Royal Club must be an ordinary member of some one of the associated clubs. A general meeting of the club shall take place immediately after the meeting of the Representative Committee. (*Vide* Chap. I., Section 7.)

5. Clubs shall only be admitted at the Annual General or Adjourned Meeting of the Representative Committee, and must be proposed by one member of that committee, seconded by another, and balloted for in the usual manner, when, unless there are five black balls against them, they shall be admitted and initiated according to the usual form.

6. No new law, alteration, or repeal of an existing law can be carried up to the General Meeting of the Club unless approved of by two-thirds of the representatives present at July Meeting. All notices of business to be brought before the Annual Representative Committee Meeting shall be sent to the secretary on or before the 1st of July, who shall, on or before July 15, send to the secretary of each club a note of the business to be taken up at the said Annual Meeting, and also the terms of any proposed new law, or alteration or repeal of an existing law.

7. All arrangements regarding prizes shall be made by the Representative Committee, and shall come into operation immediately after being made.

8. The Representative Committee, at their Annual Meeting, shall proceed to business in the following order:—1. Admission of clubs.

2. Reports on medal competitions. 3. Decisions on complaints or appeals. 4. Reports of committees. 5. Alterations on the constitution, rules, &c. 6. Appointment of committees. 7. General business. 8. Election of office-bearers. 9. Distribution of prizes.

9. The Representative Committee shall, every year, cause an *Annual* to be published, under the title of *The Annual of the Royal Caledonian Curling Club*. It shall contain a list of the office-bearers of the Royal Club; its rules and regulations; the local clubs associated with it, with the names of their office-bearers and members; proceedings of the club during the past year; reports of the prize competitions, and any other matter connected with curling which may appear of general interest to members. They shall also appoint a select committee from among the members of the Royal Club to superintend the publication of the *Annual*.

10. The Representative Committee shall annually appoint a Finance Committee, who shall audit the treasurer's accounts, as hereinafter provided, and whose docquet shall be published along with them in the next *Annual*. (*Vide* Section 16.)

11. The vice-presidents, finance committee, and committee on the *Annual* shall form a committee, to be called the Committee of Management, to assist the secretary in all matters relating to the business of the Royal Club. This committee to have power to admit new clubs after the July Meeting up to the 1st of November in each year. Three to be a quorum. The secretary to be convener of the committee.

12. The Representative Committee shall have power to elect, from amongst their number, sub-committees to manage the various parts of the club's business.

13. The Representative Committee shall, on the conclusion of business, adjourn to meet at such place and time during the winter as the meeting may deem most expedient. They may also appoint an assistant secretary in the locality determined on, in order to aid the general secretary in making arrangements for the adjourned meeting. The president or president-elect, or one of the vice-presidents, and six representatives to be a quorum. No part of the expenses of any adjourned meeting shall be defrayed from the general funds of the Royal Club, except such as are strictly necessary for convening the meeting, and carrying on the business of the same.

14. No business shall be transacted at adjourned meetings except the admission of new cubs, drawing for extra medals, and appointing umpires to superintend the extra competitions. The general secretary shall, if possible, attend these meetings, and receive £2, 2s. in full of his personal expenses.

15. The secretary shall be convener of the Representative Committee, and shall call special meetings thereof by circulars addressed to local secretaries, at any time he may deem it to be necessary, and also upon the requisition of twenty-one or more representative members.

16. The secretary shall, previous to 20th July in each year, prepare a note of what business he has ascertained is to be brought before the meeting.

17. The treasurer shall keep a classified account of his receipts and disbursements on account of the club. His books shall be balanced annually on 30th June, thereafter audited by the Finance Committee, and an abstract thereof published in the next *Annual*. The books shall be open for inspection to all members of the club for five days previous to the General Meeting in July, and to members of the Representative Committee at all times.

> NOTE.—At the Annual Meeting of the Representative Committee held on 25th July 1882, the Committee of Management were instructed to have the accounts audited by an accountant outside of the committee.

CHAPTER III.—ENTRANCE AND ANNUAL FEES.

1. All clubs, on admission, shall pay a fee according to the following scale, viz. :—If consisting of

100 ordinary members and upwards,	. . .	£1 10 0
50 and under 100,	. . . . .	1 5 0
8 ,, 50,	. . . . .	1 0 0

2. All clubs shall pay annually in advance, a fee according to the following scale, in respect of the number of ordinary members (regular and occasional), as printed in the last published *Annual*, the first year's subscription to be paid along with the entry-money :—If consisting of

8 ordinary members, and under 12,	£0 5 0	40 ordinary members, and under 50,	£0 16 0
12 ,, ,, 16,	0 7 0	50 ,, ,, 70,	1 0 0
16 ,, ,, 20,	0 9 0	70 ,, ,, 100,	1 5 0
20 ,, ,, 30,	0 12 0	100 and upwards, ...	1 10 0
30 ,, ,, 40,	0 14 0		

3. Every associated club, on publication of the *Annual*, shall receive and pay for them as under, viz.:— If consisting of

8 members (ordinary) & under 13,	2 *Annuals*.	33 members (ordinary) & under 38,	7 *Annuals*.
13 ,, ,, 18, 3 ,,		38 ,, ,, 43, 8 ,,
18 ,, ,, 23, 4 ,,		43 ,, ,, 48, 9 ,,
23 ,, ,, 28, 5 ,,		48 ,, ,, 53, 10 ,,
28 ,, ,, 33, 6 ,,			

and so on, adding one *Annual* for every five additional members. Each copy of the *Annual* is one shilling. The above rule does not apply to foreign clubs.

4. A common fund shall be formed from these and other sources, to be under the management of the Representative Committee, and from which shall be defrayed (1) the printing, advertising, and incidental expenses of the club ; (2) prizes given to be competed for by the associated clubs.

5. Clubs failing to pay the fees due at entry, or the subsequent annual fees, shall not be *entitled* to draw for medals, nor shall any associated club compete for a medal without producing to the umpire of the match satisfactory evidence of all fees due to the Royal Club having been paid.

6. If any club fall three years into arrear of its annual fees, it shall be struck off the list of the Royal Club, and not reponed except as a new club.

CHAPTER IV.—LOCAL CLUBS.

1. Printed forms shall be transmitted annually on 15th September, by the secretary of the Royal Club, to each of the local secretaries, in order that they may enter therein a list of the office-bearers and members of their respective clubs, for publication in the next *Annual*. And any local secretary failing to return this list to the secretary of the Royal Club by the first day of October following shall not only forfeit the right of his club to draw for medals, but the list will not, after that date, be receivable for publication in the *Annual* of that season.

> As great uniformity is desirable, the lists of office-bearers ought to include, so far as the club has them, the patron or patroness, president, vice-president, representative members, chaplain, treasurer, secretary, and committee or council, arranged in the order given in the printed form.

2. The list of members shall be classified under the titles of honorary, extraordinary, and ordinary. The ordinary members may be divided into regular and occasional.

> Each name to be arranged, as far as possible, chronologically, and the office-bearers to be inserted a second time in the list of members.

3. Clubs associated with the Royal Club shall, in all matches, adhere to the rules and regulations of the game in force in the Royal Club at the time, unless otherwise mutually agreed to in writing under the hands of the secretaries of the competing clubs.

4. All disputes arising between clubs or players associated with the Royal Club, except as hereinafter provided for, shall be referred to the award and decision of two neutral representative members resident in the district where the disputes arise. They shall act in the capacity of arbiters, and be chosen by the two disputants, each of whom shall name one; and said arbiters shall immediately on their appointment name an oversman, being also a representative member, to act and decide in the matter in the event of their differing in opinion; and whatever the award of said arbiters or oversman may be, even though informal, if in writing, it shall be final, and binding on all parties, provided that the Representative Committee of the Royal Club shall not find the procedure (not that regarding the merits) irregular. The umpire to have the right of appeal. Any complaint as to irregularity, in order to be received, must be lodged with the secretary of the Royal Club within ten days of the date of the award. In case the procedure be found irregular, the Representative Committee shall set aside the award, and order the disputants to begin the reference anew. Should either of the disputants allow three days to elapse without naming an arbiter, after being required in writing by the other so to do, both arbiters may be appointed by the other disputant; and failing the arbiters, when appointed, being able to agree upon an oversman, the secretary of the Royal Club, acting under advice of a committee, shall be bound to name one, on application being made to him by either of the disputants.

5. *Provincial Competitions.*—All rules and regulations relating thereto must be made by the province itself; and in no case will the Royal Club interfere, by appeal made to it or otherwise.

6. No curler, though belonging to two or more associated clubs, can be or appear on a list published in the *Annual* as an ordinary member (regular) of more than one of them at the same time; and unless otherwise previously agreed to in writing by the secretaries, or the acting skips present at a match, each club shall select its players from the list of ordinary members (regular) appearing in the last published *Annual*, or from those players whose names had been returned as regular members to be published in the next forthcoming *Annual*, as supplied to the secretary of the Royal Club for publication, and for that purpose a list of such players shall be furnished previous to the match by the secretary of each club to the other; and any club having a player thus disqualified engaged in the game shall forfeit all right to the Royal medal, even if awarded to it.

7. In all matches, other than those for district medals, all members whose names appear in the *Annual* may play.

8. In case the match be played on the ice of either of the parties, the strangers may select the rinks, subject always to the approval of the acting umpire.

9. Every challenge given by one club to another, and its acceptance, must be conveyed in writing by the respective secretaries.

CHAPTER V.—RULES OF THE GAME. *Vide* pp. 391-394.

CHAPTER VI.—MEDAL COMPETITIONS.

1. Only one class of medals shall hereafter be distributed by this club (except as after provided). They shall be called district medals, and be competed for according to the "Rules of the Game," by two clubs. The number of district medals to be issued in the first year of a rotation to be, as nearly as possible, a fourth of the whole associated clubs. The number awarded in the second year to be whatever is required, in conjunction with local medals, to complete the rotation.

2. Local medals will only be awarded during the second year of a rotation, in lieu of district medals, to such clubs as are, in the opinion of the Representative Committee, too far distant from other clubs to compete for district medals. Local medals shall be contested for by the members of the club, according to the rules for local competitions.

3. The drawing for medals shall take place at the July meeting; but if several clubs be admitted at the adjourned meeting in the first year of a rotation, a district medal may be given for each two newly-admitted clubs, to be balloted for between them, and such clubs as were unsuccessful in obtaining medals in July. No club shall receive two medals during the same rotation; and after a rotation has been completed, the whole clubs shall be arranged anew into pairs, and medals balloted for; it being understood that, before the very same clubs be again brought into competition, three years at least must elapse.

4. The Representative Committee shall have the sole power of disposing the clubs into pairs, balloting for medals, and appointing representatives to superintend competitions; but in any case where one of the competing clubs has become defunct, or has ceased to be a member of the Royal Club, the Committee of Management, along with the umpire, shall have authority to decide what club shall play with the other club for the medal. In arranging all competitions for district medals, distance shall be taken into account, and all specialties, including the relative number of the regular ordinary members. Clubs so situated that others cannot be found sufficiently near to compete with them shall not be included in the ballot of the first year of a rotation, in the hope of other clubs joining, which can be classed with them the following year; but they may receive local medals.

5. The representative appointed to be present at a district medal competition shall, at the request of the secretary of either club, fix the day, the hour, and the ice for the match, most suitable and mutually convenient, giving at least twenty-four hours' notice in writing to the secretaries of both clubs; and if either club fails to appear at the place and time appointed, without an excuse which is satisfactory to the representative or his deputy, and which had also been forthwith, after notice received, intimated to the opposing club, the medal shall be awarded offhand to the club which appears on the ice, and the club failing to appear on the ice shall be liable for the expenses of the club against whom they were to play (or appearing), unless they can give to the umpire a satisfactory reason for their non-appearance, provided the umpire be satisfied of its having complied with all the regulations. Should a district medal be awarded between two clubs for competition, and no umpire appointed by the Royal Club, the two clubs shall appoint an umpire, who shall have the same power as if appointed by the Royal Club, and should they fail to do so, the medal shall be awarded to the club willing to appoint an umpire, by arbiters chosen in accordance with Chapter IV., Section 4, of the Club Laws.

6. The representative appointed to act as umpire shall, in the event of his being unable, from any cause, to give notice of the match, or to attend thereat, depute a curler associated with the Royal Club, believed to

be well acquainted with the rules of the game, and not connected with either of the competing clubs, to act in his stead; but the report of the match to be transmitted to the secretary of the Royal Club shall be countersigned by the representative.

7. Should, however, the two clubs agree on the day, the hour, and the ice, notice shall be given thereof in writing by either secretary to the representative; and they may, in the event of his not being forward personally, or by deputy, at the hour intimated, appoint any associated curler, properly qualified, to act and report in his stead; and along with the report shall be transmitted the party's authority to act, which must be in writing.

8. When no ice can be had during the season within which the clubs have received medals, they must be competed for the first following opportunity.

9. All district medals shall be contested by at least eight players a side. If no arrangement in writing, fixing the number of players, takes place between the clubs, that number shall not be less than one-half of the (regular) ordinary members of the smaller club, as appearing in the last published *Annual*.

NOTE.—Clubs having 16 regular players produce and play 2 rinks.
  Above 16 and not more than   24   ,,   ,,   3   ,,
  ,,   24   ,,   ,,   32   ,,   ,,   4   ,,
  ,,   32   ,,   ,,   40   ,,   ,,   5   ,,
  ,,   40   ,,   ,,   48   ,,   ,,   6   ,,

10. The representative superintending a district medal competition, and the umpire of a local one, or their deputies, must, under the penalty of having their names struck off the lists of the Royal Club, prepare a short statement, and forward it forthwith to the secretary of the Royal Club, giving the information required by schedule sent for said purpose.

11. Umpires in all cases are enjoined to hear objections from the losing party before awarding medals; and if they shall find that neither club has complied, nor appears willing to comply, with the regulations, they shall return the medal to the secretary of the Royal Club, and report the circumstances, provided always that nothing contained in this rule shall affect the regulations contained in Chapter IV., Section 4.

CHAPTER VII.—RULES FOR GRAND MATCH. *Vide* pp. 276-277.

LOCAL MEDAL COMPETITION (POINT GAME). *Vide* pp. 414-416.

B.—PROVINCES (AS IN 1889).

I. STIRLINGSHIRE PROVINCE—
Airth Bruce Castle and Dunmore
Airthrey Castle
Alloa Prince of Wales
Alva
Bonnybridge
Borestone
Bridge of Allan
Camelon
Castlecary Castle
Denny
Denny Greens
Falkirk
Falkirk Callendar
Grangemouth
Lauriston & Zetland
Larbert
Redding Colliery
Sauchie & Bannockburn
Stenhouse and Carron
Stirling
Stirling Castle
West Quarter and Polmont

II. SCOTTISH CENTRAL PROVINCE—
Airthrey Castle
Ardoch
Ardoch Junior
Auchterarder
Blackford
Blair Drummond
Bridge of Allan
Callander
Doune
Dunblane
Dunblane Thistle
Kinbuck

III. TENTH PROVINCE—
Allander
Baldernock
Carbeth
Cardross
Duntocher
East Kilpatrick
Helensburgh
Kelvindock
Kilmaronock
Luss and Arrochar
Partick
Vale of Leven
Yoker

IV. NORTH-EASTERN PROVINCE—
Aberdeen
Aboyne
Alford
Ballater
Banchory
Braemar
Dyce
Ellon
Fyvie
Haddo House
Huntly
Inverurie
Pitfour
Strichen
Torphins
Turriff

V. TWELFTH PROVINCE—
Arthgowan
Auchenames
Barrhead
Barrhead Fereneze
Beith
  „ Fulwoodhead
  „ St Inans
Blythswood
Boreas
Dalry Iceland
  „ Union
Erskine
Garnock of Kilbirnie
Gourock
Greenock
Houston
Hurlet and Nitshill
Ladyland
Largs Thistle
Lochwinnoch
  „ Auchenbothie
  „ Castle Semple
  „ Garthland
Neilston
Paisley Iceland
  „ Union
Renfrewshire
  „ King's
Inch
St Mirren

VI. UPPER STRATHEARN PROVINCE—
Abercairny
Crieff
Drummond Castle
Lawers and Comrie
Logiealmond
Methven
Monzie
Monzievaird and Strowan
Muthill
Strathallan Meath Moss

VII. GLASGOW PROVINCE—
Airdrie Howlet
Bothwell
Bridgeton
Cadder
Cambuslang
Cambusnethan
Chryston
Coatbridge
Croy
Cumbernauld
Forrestfield
Glasgow Lilybank
Glasgow Northern
Govan
Kingston
Kirkintilloch
New Monkland
North Woodside
Rabbie Burns
Ruchazie
Rutherglen
Shettleston
Sir Colin Campbell
Willowbank

VIII. BORDER PROVINCE—
Branxholm and Borthwickbrae
Chirnside
Earlston
Galashiels
Hawick
Jedburgh
Kelso
Lauder
Liddesdale
Melrose
Selkirk
St Boswell's

IX. FORTH AND ENDRICK PROVINCE—
Aberfoyle
Ballikinrain
Balfron
Buchlyvie
Cardross and Kepp
Drymen
Fintry
Gargunnock
Gartmore
Kippen
Port of Menteith
Strathendrick
Thornhill

X. MIDLOTHIAN PROVINCE—
Coates
Corstorphine
Currie
Dalkeith
Drum
Edinburgh Northern
Glencorse
Holyrood
Kirknewton
Lasswade
Merchiston Castle (now Craiglockhart)
Merchiston
Midcalder
Oxenford
Penicuik
Ratho
Redhall
Rosslyn
Stow
Temple
Waverley
  „ Kierhill
West Calder

XI. WEST OF FIFE PROVINCE—
Aberdour
Broomhall
Crossgates
Dunibristle
Dunfermline
Lochgelly
Oakley
Saline
St Margaret's
Torry

XII. EAST OF FIFE PROVINCE—
Boarhills
Cambo
Elie
Hercules
Largo
Leven
Lundin and Montrave
Kilconquhar Junior
St Andrew's
Wemyss

APPENDICES. 433

XIII. DUNDEE AND PERTH PROVINCE—
Broughty Ferry   Fingask   Lundie   Perth
Camperdown   Friarton   Megginch   Rossie
Dundee   Inchmartine   Panmure   St Martin's
Errol and Murie

XIV. STRATHKELVIN PROVINCE—
Banton Junior   Kilsyth   Milton of Campsie   Townhead
Cadder   Kirkintilloch   Rob Roy   Waterside
Croy

XV. CUPAR DISTRICT PROVINCE—
Alulie   Balyarrow   Ladybank   Pitlessie
Auchit   Cupar   Markinch   Rothes
Balmerino   Falkland   Melville   Stratheden

FIG. 91. THE SPIRIT OF CURLING.

2 E

REV. JOHN KERR.

INDEX.

Abdie Club, 212, 363.
Aberdour Club, 39.
Adamson, Henry, 79, 83.
Ailsa Craig, 367.
Airthrey Loch, 208, 210, 269.
Aitchison, T. S., verses by, 112, 306.
Alloa Prince of Wales Club, 39; at Southport, 315.
Altrive Lake, 204.
Alyth Club, 40, 221.
Amateur Curling Club of Scotland, 231.
Anecdotes—Psammitichus, 5; Whirlie's eccentricities, 38; William Gourlay, 49; Aleck Cook, 50; 'the irate Clapperton,' 50; Lochmaben president and Lawrie Young, 50; Garthland, 59; masons at play, 60, n.; Laird of Barr, 150; Deacon Jardine, 152, n.; 'verra opposite,' 153; Hamilton v. M'Dowall, 180, n.; Terregles Club, 186; Mouswald v. Lochmaben, 188; the Ettrick Shepherd, 204; Meg Weir, 209; M'George, 240; Captain Ogilvy Dalgleish, 241; 'greatest duffer wins,' 258; Bailie Falshaw's bond, 287; ladies' bonspiel, 292, n.; club des barbiers, 308; collier seeing the deil curling, 368, n.; 'tak' what ye see o't,' 373; new way of clearing the rink, 377; Dumfriesian herd and artist, 387; fools, 388; 'soup,' 388; lunatics, 389; Doupar Robertson, 417; the 'Tutor,' 417; 'lie doun and dee,' 418.
Anderston Club, 182.
Annual, The, 281.
Ardgowan Club, stone from, 63.
Ardoch Club, 40, 216.
Arnott, Dr G. A. Walker, 89, n.; portrait, 214; 232, 283, 356, n., 362.
Artificial ponds—Cairnie's, 178, 187, 237; rules for formation of, 374.

Art of curling, 387.
Athole, Duke of, 220, 247, 252, 268.
Auchinleck Club, 177.
Auchterarder Club, 217, 233.
Ayr Club, 177.

Baillie, Sir William, 201.
Baird, Principal, 29, 219, 231, 256.
Balfour, Lord, of Burleigh, 213, 305.
Banknock Club, 209.
Barr, Andrew, 'the bannet,' 347.
Bathgate Club, 201.
Beef and greens, 195, 218, 378.
Begg, R. Burns, 35, 213, 232, 305.
Beith v. Lochwinnoch, 1783, 59; remarkable frost, 98.
Belfast Club, 317, 363.
Benevolence of curlers, 153.
Ben o' Tudor and Gordon of Kenmure, verses, 104.
Betting, 180, 201, 207, 240.
Blackie, Professor, 11.
Blairgowrie Club, 40, 132, 220, 263, n., 352.
Blast, The, 119.
Board, the, or rink, 394.
Bonspiel, 162-164; the parish, 262; provincial, 264.
Boomer, James, 317.
Borestone Club, 208.
Boswell, Sir Alex., poem by, 146; fatal duel, 177, 210.
Bothwell, 107.
Breadalbane, Marquis of, 31, 253, 289, 376.
Brechin Castle, stones at, 42.
Bridge of Allan Club, 208.
Bridie, J., verses by, 41, 133.
Broom, the, 158, 372, 407.
Broun, Sir Richard, 29, 58, 61, 70, 75, 119, 159, 173, 187, 220, 230, 359, 397, 404.
Brown's History of Sanquhar Curling Society, 125, 408.
Buccleuch, Duke of, 208.
Buchanan's History of Scotland, 17.
Burns, Robert, verses by, 101.

Caberfeidh Club, 302.
Cairnie, Dr J., 59, 65, 98, 140, 162; portrait, 178; elegy, 179; 180, 182, 220, 230, 233, 236, 249, 317, 359, 397, 410.
Callender, Thomas, 317, 321.
Cambusnethan, stones found at, 42, 182, 399; the twist at, 410.
Camden, *Brittannia*, 75, 89.
'Cammell,' Jamie, 135, 352.
Camshron, Pol (Paul Cameron), verses by, 228.
Canada, curling in, 322-342.
Canonmills Club—stones, 44; *Curler's March*, 26; songs, 107, 118; loch, 118; account of, 117-122.
Carlingwark Loch, 104, 193.
Carsebreck, 269, 274, 279, 286.
Carswell, J., 283, 377.
Carse of Gowrie's silver curling-stone, 74.
Cassels, Alexander, 254; portrait, 255; 286, 311.
Channel-stane, The, song, with music, 170; the chorus, 292.
Chirnside Club, 42.
Christie, J., verses by, 276.
Christopher North, 165, 195, 226.
Circular stone, third type, 52.
Clandeboye Club, 318.
Clergymen as curlers, 83, 257.
Clerk, Sir George, 196, 269.
Clerk, Sir James, 63.
Clerk, Sir John, 95.
Closeburn Club, 185.
Clubs in the eighteenth century, 114, 115; of transition period, 1800-1838, 172-175; furth of Scotland, 308; list of English, 312.
Clunie, stones found at, 42.
Clunie Club, 219.
Coates Club, 149, n., 375.
Cockburnspath Club, 204.
Copinsha stones, 89, 220.
Constitution of the Royal Club, 238, 425.
Coupar-Angus Club, 42; minutes of, 122, 220.
Cowan, Charles, 232, 239, 273, 283; portrait, 291.
Crampits, ancient, 56, 158.
Craufurd of Craufurdland, 176.
Crawford, Captain, on origin of curling, 16, n.
Crawford, Dr, *Crune of the Warlock of the Peil*, 180, n.
Crawfordjohn, 107.
Crieff Club, 219.

Crieff, stones found at Lochlane, 42.
Crossmichael Club, 190.
Crystal Palace Exhibition, 1851, stones in, 310.
Cunningham, James, verses by, 206.
Curler's Magazine, 90, n., 187.
Curler's March, 26; words with music, 92.
Curling court, 153, 359-364.
Curling-house, 375.
Currie Club, 198, 280, n.
Currie crampits, 158, 159.

Dalgleish, James Ogilvy, 212, 232, 239; portrait, 240; 264, 267, 283.
Dalton, St Bridgets Club, stone, 43.
Darnley as a curler, 77.
Davidson's verses, 51.
Davidson's *Thoughts on the Seasons*, 103.
Delvine Club, 40.
Distribution of clubs in Scotland, lists, 115, 172, 297; furth of Scotland, 308.
Dollar v. Devonvale Club, 213.
Douglas Bonspiel, a poem, 138.
Douglas St Bride's Club, minutes of, 136, 230, 353.
Doune Club's kuting-stone, 34, 43; minutes, 215.
Drummond, Jas., R.S.A., sketches by, 156, 157.
Dryfesdale, 107.
Duddingston Club — motto, 2; minutes of, 140; members, 144; rules, 145.
Duddingston Loch, 109, 149, 352.
Dufferin, Lord—portrait, 319; president of the Clandeboye Club, 318; in Russia, 320; in Canada, 327.
Dumbarton Club, 184.
Dumfries Club, 185.
Dunblane, old stones at, 29, 43; club, 209, 215.
Duncan, Rev. Henry, 186.
Dundas, Major Hamilton, 201.
Dundee Club, 224.
Dunfermline, stones at, 43; minutes of club, 114, 138.
Dunkeld, 219.
Duns, stones at, 43; club, 205.
Dyde, Colonel, 324, 331.

East Kilbride, stone from, 62.
Edinburgh, curling at, 44; the North Loch, 90, 194.
Edinburgh Castle, Origin of, song, 119.
Eglinton cup, 268.

INDEX.

Eglinton, Earl of, 177, 249; his rink, 396.
England, clubs in, 312.
Equipments, 367.
Ettrick Curling Club, 203.
Ettrick Shepherd, 189, n., 203, 204.
Etymological argument, 7.

Falkirk, 208.
Falshaw, Mr, 286.
Fenwick twist, 57, 330, 409.
Fergusson, Robert, verse by, 112.
Ferguson, Professor, 13, 283.
Fisher's *Winter Season*, 60, 108.
Fixed word of initiation, 356.
Flemish immigration, 20.
Foot-iron, Cairnie's, 159; improved form, 376.
Foreign clubs, distribution of, 308.
Forest Club, old stones, 45.
Forfar Club, 223.
Forrest, J. Clark, 305, 315, n.
Forrester, Mr, 266, 283.
Foulis, D., 343, 347.
Fountainhall's *Decisions*, 87.

'Gabions,' 80, 305.
Gall, James, 80.
Galloway, 189.
Gamgee, Professor, 314.
Gargunnock, stones at, 45.
Gibb, Alexander, 317.
Gibson-Craig, William, M.P., 248.
Gibson-Craig, Sir James, 283, 306, 310.
Giffen, Rev. C., 256; portrait, 257.
Gilbert, Mr, 239.
Gillespie, Professor, *Horæ Scoticæ*, No. I., 187, 406; *The Jolly Curlers*, 211.
Glaciarium, the, 313.
Gladsmuir, stone at, 45; club at, 204.
Glasgow Exhibition, stones in, 31.
Golf and curling, 4, 238, 402.
Golspie Club, 302.
Gordon, William, 201, 259.
Gourlay, William, 61, 404.
Graeme, James, *Poems*, 100; quoted, 387.
Grahame, George, 84.
Grahame, James, *British Georgics*, 109.
Grand match, 275; trophy, 277; gold badges, 277; results, 278; its future, 280.
Gray, David, *The Luggie*, 183.
Greenock Club, 180.

Greenshields, J. B., *The Annals of the Parish of Lesmahagow*, 10; 53, n.
Grierson, Rev. Thomas, 189.
Guthrie, William—kuting-stone, 35, 85, 176, 249.

Hack, the, 161.
Haddington, stones at, 45.
Hally, Rev. Mr William, 40, 116.
Hamilton, Bailie, 138, 417.
Hamilton, Duke of, *v.* M·Dowall of Garthland, 1784, 56, 180, 181.
Hamilton of Barr, 150.
Hamilton Club, minutes of, 128, 354; old crisp, 130; highest majority, 279.
Harvey, Sir George, 158, 162, 408.
Hawick, stones at, 45.
Heddle, Prof., on curling-stones, 380.
Heigh Linn, curlers, 181; word, 351.
Henderson, W. H., 33, 42.
'Hen-poo,' the, 206.
High Jinks, 153, 359, 363.
Highlands and curling, 33, 225, 303.
Historical and poetical references, 69.
Hogg, James, *see* Ettrick Shepherd.
Holden Challenge Shield, winners of, 1879-1889, 314.
Hollow-bottomed stones, 181, 334, 371, 399.
Holyrood Club, stones from, 64.

'Ice-sticks,' Bavarian game of, 13.
Icelanders' game of 'knattleikr,' 13.
Initiation, 351; 356.
Instructions as to choice of stones, 385, 395; use of flask, 373; curling ponds, 374; curling-house, 375; *rinks*, 377; playing from crampit, 400; the swing, 402; soling and delivering, 405; sweeping, 407; the twist, 409; skipping a rink, 412.
Inverness Club, 300, 363, 374.
Ireland, curling in, 316; 'stew' and 'black strap,' 378.
Iron 'stones,' 182, 334, 399.
Irvine Miscellany, quoted, 2.

Jamieson's Dictionary, 5, 7.
Jardine, Deacon, 152, 417.
Jedburgh, stones at, 45; club, 206.
Johnson, Dr Samuel, 54.
Johnston's *Edinburgh Magazine*, 195.
Jubilee dinner, 289.
Jubilee stone, 48.

Keats' sonnet to Ailsa Craig, 367.
Kellock, Willie, 347.
Kelso Club, 206.
Kelton Club, minutes of, 192.
Kelvin, curling on the, 182.
Kilian's Dictionary, *kluyten*, 9.
Kilmarnock, meeting at, in 1841, 249; clubs, &c., 176; the twist, 410.
Kilwinning, curling at. 85, 177.
Kinross Club, 114, 213, 233, 237, 357, 360.
Kirkbean Club, 189.
Kirkcudbright museum, stones at, 34, 'Kirkcudbrie' curlers, 191.
Kirkintilloch Club, 183.
Kirriemuir Club, 224.
Kirtlebridge, bonspiel at, in 1795, 309.
Kowe, the, 158, 372.
Kuting-stone, 27.

Ladies' bonspiels, 292, n.
Lasswade Club, 355.
Leeds Club, 312.
Lees, C., key to picture of match at Linlithgow 1848, 270.
Length of rink, 391.
Linlithgow, 33, 114; clubs, 201; grand match in 1848, 270.
Literary committee, 288.
Liverpool—club, 312; annual meeting at, in 1863, 313.
Livingston, Josiah, 285, 287, 306, 316.
Local medals, 258.
Loch Awe, curling on, 298.
Lochleven kuting-stone, 34; 114, 214, 237, 305.
Loch Lomond, bonspiel on, 1837, 184.
Lochmaben, 38, 45, 50, 188, 417.
Loch o' the Lowes, 204, 226.
Loch Scavaig, stones from, 189, n.
Lochwinnoch, 98, 180; meeting in 1850, 247, 269, 272; safety of, 279.
London, curling in, 309; its fog, 279.
Loquitur Rector, 65.
Lorne, Marquis of, portrait, 323; in Canada, 328, 349, 417.
Loyalty of curlers, 77, 165, 197.
Luggie, the, 183.

M'Diarmid's *Sketches from Nature*, 187, 263, 311.
M'Dougall, M., 348.
M'Dowall, Colonel, 271.
M'George, John, 143, 239, 240.

M'Inroy, W., 306, 316.
M'Kie, Nathan, letter from, 190.
Mackinnon, Professor, 11.
Maclagan, Alexander, verse by, 68.
Macnair, Captain, 31; 89, n.; *The Channel-stane*, 420, n.
Mactaggart's *Gallovidian Encyclopædia*, 28, 171, 191.
Maitland, Admiral, 212.
Maitland-Dougall, Admiral W. H., 261, 283.
Manitoba, curling in, 339.
Mansfield, Earl of, 242, 269.
Map, provincial, 286.
Markinch, stones at, 46.
Masson, Professor, 11.
Maule, Hon. Fox, 247, 310.
Menzies, Colonel, 182, 306.
Methven Club, 219.
Millar, James, advocate, 147; poem by, 148; queer position, 406.
Millar, James, the stone-blocker, 369.
Milwaukee, curling at, 343.
Mitchell, Hon. Alex., portrait, 343.
Montreal clubs, 324, 325, 353.
Mount Benger pond, 204.
Muir, Rev. Mr, verses by, 51, 71, n., 177, 289.
Muirkirk, 107; club minutes, 135.
Munich, game played in 1848, 13.
Murray, Rev. G., 34; verses by, 68, 191.
Muses Threnodie, 79.
Muthill, 40; stones at, 46; club minutes, 115, 219.
'Mysteries,' the, 351.

New Brunswick, curling in, 342.
Newfoundland, curling in, 339.
New Monkland Club, 280.
Newton Loch, stones from, 32.
Newtyle, stones at, 46.
New Zealand, curling in, 321.
Noddle Club dinner, 179.
North British Advertiser, 232, 313.
Northern Club, Edinburgh, 256, 375.
North Woodside Club, 182, 419.
Norway, curling in, 320.
Nova Scotia, curling in, 341.

Ogilvy, Sir John, portrait, 224; 273, 274.
Ontario, curling in, 331.
Orchard Lake Club, U.S.A., 343.
Origin of curling, 3.
Orwell Club, 214, 362.
Ossian's Poems, 71.

Otterston Club, 210.
Oxenfoord Castle, stones at, 67.

Paisley, game in, 181.
Palmer, Robert, 44, 199; portrait, 200; 265, 283, 286.
Paris International Exhibition, stones at, 307.
Parish bonspiel, 163, 185, 263.
Pate, Tam, 56, 65, 132, 180, n., 213, 250, 390, 410, 417.
Paterson, Captain, poem by, 138; elegy by, 179; 230, 410, n.
Peebles, 77; club, 201.
'Peebles, William,' first chaplain,139.
Penicuick Club, minutes of, 196.
Penicuick House, stones at, 63.
Pennant's *Tour in Scotland*, 55, 60, 99, 309.
Pennecuik, Dr Alex., prescription, 94.
Penninghame Club, 193.
Perth, meeting in 1843, 248.
Peterkin, W. A., 267, 283; *My Bonny Broomy Kowe*, 366.
Pitfour, stones at, 47; club, 299.
Playing out of turn, 393.
Poets, curling, 283.
Point game, 200; highest scores, old system, 260, 390; Quebec system, 329; rules for, 414; porting shot, 417.
Pond, the formation of, 373.
Position of curlers, 400-406.
Price of old stones, 124, 134, 222; of modern stones, 311, 370, 372.
Purdie, Thomas, 13.

Quebec, curling at, in 1854, 326.
Queen, Her Majesty the, and curling, 242.
Quoiting and curling, 9, 28, 36, n., 345.

Rain, Rev. T., verse by, 112, 167.
Ramsay, Rev. John, 6, 90, 118, 141, 149, 194, 215.
Ramsay, Allan, 95.
Rattray, 122, 419.
Renton, Dr, 237, 239, 248, 254, 286.
Rink, the size of, in 1772, 56; 155; Royal Club's plan of, 392; correct drawing of, 394.
Ritchie, Mr, 285.
Robertson, C., 76, 238.
Roslin tee-marker, 155; kutingstone from, 35.
Rosslyn Club, 198, 355.

Rothes Club, 262.
Rough block, second type, 36.
Royal patronage of curling, tradition as to, 73-78, 172, 242.
Royal Caledonian Curling Club—history, 229; first advertisement of, 232; inquiry as to sender, 233; first meeting of, 236; list of clubs attending second meeting, 236; president and secretary chosen, 237; framing of the constitution, 238; committee, 239; presentation of stones to Prince Albert, 242; changing name to Royal, 243; Prince of Wales as patron, 243; representative government, 244; headquarters, 246; meeting places, 247; presidents, 251; work done by Bailie Cassels, 255; office-bearers, list of, 1838-1890, 251; the clergy, 256; local medals, the old point game, 258; highest scores, 260; the parish bonspiel, 263; provincial spiels, 264; the grand match, 268; pond for grand match, 273; the *Annual*, 282; finance, 285; our patronesses, 292; progress, 296; the outlook, 304.
Rules—Muthill, 116; Douglas, 137; Dunfermline, 138; Duddingston, 145; Dumfries, 185; Lochmaben, 192; Kelton, 193; Peebles, 201; Orwell, 214; Ardoch, 216; Alyth, 223; grand match, 276; Royal Club, 391; local medal competition point game, 414.
Rusholme ice rink, 314.
Russel's, J. S., account of curling in Ontario, 332.
Russia, curling in, 320.
Ruthven, Dr George, 80; first of the brotherhood, 83; 179.

Samson, Tam, 63, 102, 176, 250.
Sanquhar Club, minutes of, 125; word and grip, 352.
Science of curling, 379.
Scot, Sir William of Harden, 87.
Scott, Sir W., *Guy Mannering*, 99.
Sefton, Earl of, 244, 313.
Shairp, Principal, verses by, 2, 272.
Shaw, Peter, record of, 377, n.
Sibbald, Sir Robt., *Scotia Illustrata*, 88.
Sidey, Dr, 35, 283; portrait, 284, 286; *The Curler's Grip*, 350.
Simpson, Rev. Dr, 256.

Skelton, James, W.S., 237, 285.
Skinner, Edward, 318.
Skipping a rink, 412.
Smith, A. Davidson, 287; portrait, 304, 305.
Snow-cleaner, 376.
Social gatherings, 52, 179, 186, 193, 210, 216, 218, 221, 223, 313, 325.
Societies, ancient curling, 113; their influence, 151.
Soling and delivering the stone, 405.
Somerville, Dr, of Currie, 151, 159, 178, 199, 258, 397.
Southport, the glaciarium at, 314; annual meeting at, in 1885, 315.
Spott Curling Club, 375.
Statistical Account of Scotland, 107.
Steel-bottomed stones, 181.
Stirling stones, 15n, 30, 69; club, 209.
Stones, ancient—three types of, 27, 70; curious mode of polishing, 60.
Stones, modern — loss of individuality, 65; manufacture of, 370-372; Ailsas, 384; Burnock Water, 384; Carsphairn, 384; Crawfordjohn, 384; Crieff, 385; Tinkernhill, 385; the choice of, 395; sole of, 396; as used in Canada, 333, 334.
Strathallan Meath Moss, club stones, 47; club, 217.
Strathmartine Club, 224.
Strathmore Club, 223.
Subscriptions to Dunfermline Club, 139; Duddingston Club, 143; Doune Club, 215; Dunblane Club, 215.
Sussex Express quoted, 311.
Sweeping, 393, 407.
Switzerland, curling in, 307.

Taylor, Rev. Dr, 7, n., 275, n., 410, n.
Tee, the, 155, 376.
Tee-ringer, 200.

Terregles Club, 185.
Thames, the, in 1684, 310, n.
The Choise, song, 121.
Thorburn, T., 31, 369.
Thornton Hall quarry, 62.
Three Open Winters, song, 120.
Thriepland, Sir Patrick Murray, 76.
Toddy, verses, 211.
Torphichen, kuting-stone from, 35.
Trickers, old, 160.
Tullibody Club, 213.
Turnbull, James, 201.
'Tutor,' the, 188, 418.
Tweeddale, 203; Marquis of, 407.
Tweedsmuir Club stone, 47.
Twist, the, 409.
Tynron, stone, 47; curlers, 204.

Uniform for the Abdie Club, 212; for the Royal Club, 358.
United States, curling in, 342.
Usher, J., verse by, 68.
Usher, T., 283, 287.

Wallace's *Isles of Orkney*, 88.
Wamphray, 107.
Wanlockhead curlers, 408.
Wannop, Rev. Canon, 45, 309.
Waterside Club, 183.
Watson, Walter, 181.
Weight of stones, ancient—28, 37, 40, 42, 43, 46, 47, 48, 61, 62, 63, 223; modern—311, 392, 395, 396.
Weir, T. Durham, 201, 239.
Welcome Hame, song, 121.
'Whirlie,' 38, 95.
Whitburn Club, 201.
Wigan Club, 312.
Williamson, John Wright, 213, 239; portrait, 357.
Willowbank Club's pond, 182.
Wilson, John, Cockburnspath, 48, 52, 60.
Windyedge Loch, 248.
Word, the, and the grip, 351; the long word, 356.

BOOKS

ON

SPORT & NATURAL HISTORY

PUBLISHED BY

DAVID DOUGLAS

MAY 1890.

One Volume, Royal 8vo. 50s.

WITH 40 FULL-PAGE ILLUSTRATIONS OF SCENERY AND ANIMAL LIFE, DRAWN BY
GEORGE REID, R.S.A., AND J. WYCLIFFE TAYLOR, AND ENGRAVED BY AMAND DURAND.

NATURAL HISTORY & SPORT

IN MORAY

By CHARLES ST. JOHN

AUTHOR OF "WILD SPORTS IN THE HIGHLANDS."

EDINBURGH: DAVID DOUGLAS
1882

Small Folio, price £21, with Sketches of Scenery and Animal Life by some of the best British and American Artists and Etchers.

THE
RISTIGOUCHE
AND ITS
SALMON FISHING

WITH A CHAPTER ON ANGLING LITERATURE

By DEAN SAGE

EDINBURGH: DAVID DOUGLAS

[Only 105 Copies printed.]

One Volume, Small 4to. 24s.

ALSO A CHEAPER EDITION, WITH LITHOGRAPHIC ILLUSTRATIONS,
DEMY 8VO. 12s.

WILD MEN & WILD BEASTS
Scenes in Camp & Jungle
By
Lt. Col. Gordon Cumming
Illustrated by
Col. R. Baigrie
and others.

EDINBURGH. DAVID DOUGLAS. MDCCCLXXI.

*In the Press: New and Revised Edition, with Illustrations from Nature
by various Artists. Royal 8vo.*

WILD SPORTS IN THE SOUTH

OR

THE CAMP-FIRES

OF THE

EVERGLADES

BY CHARLES E. WHITEHEAD

EDINBURGH: DAVID DOUGLAS

Two Volumes, Crown 8vo, Illustrated. 21s.

A TOUR IN
SUTHERLANDSHIRE

WITH EXTRACTS FROM THE FIELD BOOKS OF A SPORTSMAN AND NATURALIST

By CHARLES ST. JOHN

AUTHOR OF "NATURAL HISTORY AND SPORT IN MORAY"

SECOND EDITION

WITH AN APPENDIX ON THE FAUNA OF SUTHERLAND
BY J. A. HARVIE-BROWN AND T. E. BUCKLEY

EDINBURGH: DAVID DOUGLAS
1884

One Volume, Demy 8vo, with Maps and Illustrations. 12s.

NOTES AND SKETCHES

FROM THE

WILD COASTS OF NIPON

WITH CHAPTERS ON CRUISING AFTER PIRATES
IN CHINESE WATERS

BY CAPTAIN H. C. ST. JOHN, R.N.

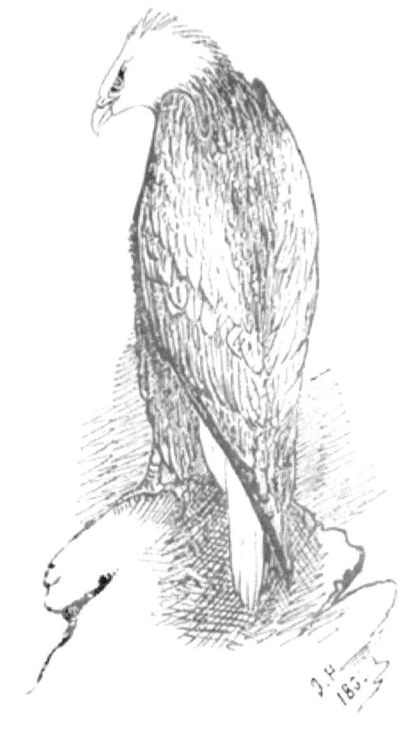

EDINBURGH: DAVID DOUGLAS

One Volume, Demy 8vo. 18s.

SASKATCHEWAN
AND
THE ROCKY MOUNTAINS

A DIARY AND NARRATIVE OF TRAVEL, SPORT, AND ADVENTURE DURING
A JOURNEY THROUGH THE HUDSON BAY COMPANY'S TERRITORIES

By THE EARL OF SOUTHESK, K.T.

WITH MAPS AND ILLUSTRATIONS

EDINBURGH: DAVID DOUGLAS

One Volume, Demy 8vo, with Etchings and Map. 8s. 6d.

THE
CAPERCAILLIE IN SCOTLAND

WITH SOME ACCOUNT OF THE EXTENSION OF ITS RANGE SINCE ITS
RESTORATION AT TAYMOUTH IN 1837 AND 1838

By J. A. HARVIE-BROWN, F.Z.S.
MEMBER OF THE BRITISH ORNITHOLOGISTS' UNION, ETC.

EDINBURGH: DAVID DOUGLAS. MDCCCLXXIX

One Volume, Demy 8vo, 21s. New Edition, Rewritten and Enlarged, with 40 full-page Plates from Instantaneous Photographs.

Modern Horsemanship

THREE SCHOOLS OF RIDING

An Original Method of Teaching the Art

BY MEANS OF

Pictures from the Life

BY EDWARD L. ANDERSON

EDINBURGH: DAVID DOUGLAS

MDCCCLXXXIX

In the Press. In One Volume, Small 4to, with Illustrations from the Author's Sketch Book.

THE BIRDS OF IONA & MULL

BY THE LATE H. D. GRAHAM

EDINBURGH: DAVID DOUGLAS: MDCCCXC.

One Volume, Demy 8vo. 15s.

THE ART OF GOLF

By SIR WALTER SIMPSON, BART.

With 20 Illustrations from Instantaneous Photographs of Professional Players, chiefly by A. F. Macfie, Esq.

EDINBURGH: DAVID DOUGLAS

One Volume, Royal 8vo. 31s. 6d.

A HISTORY OF CURLING

SCOTLAND'S AIN GAME

AND OF FIFTY YEARS OF
THE ROYAL CALEDONIAN CURLING CLUB

By JOHN KERR, M.A.

MINISTER OF THE PARISH OF DIRLETON

With 15 *full-page Plates from Original Sketches by Sir W. Fettes Douglas, P.R.S.A., George Reid, R.S.A., John Smart, R.S.A., R. Alexander, R.S.A., and others; and over one hundred illustrations in the text.* (*Also in Demy 8vo, without the Photogravure Plates,* 10s. 6d.)

EDINBURGH: DAVID DOUGLAS

Vol. I., Demy 8vo, Price 15s.
Profusely Illustrated with Etchings and Lithographs.
Vol. II., completing the work, in the Press.

THE
BIRDS OF BERWICKSHIRE

WITH REMARKS ON THEIR LOCAL DISTRIBUTION
MIGRATION, AND HABITS, AND ALSO ON THE
FOLK-LORE, PROVERBS, POPULAR RHYMES
AND SAYINGS CONNECTED WITH THEM

BY

GEORGE MUIRHEAD, F.R.S.E., F.Z.S.

MEMBER OF THE BRITISH ORNITHOLOGISTS' UNION, MEMBER OF THE
BERWICKSHIRE NATURALISTS' CLUB, ETC.

EDINBURGH: DAVID DOUGLAS
1889

In One Volume, Small 4to, with Maps, and Illustrated by Etchings, Cuts, Lithographs and Photogravure plates. 42s.

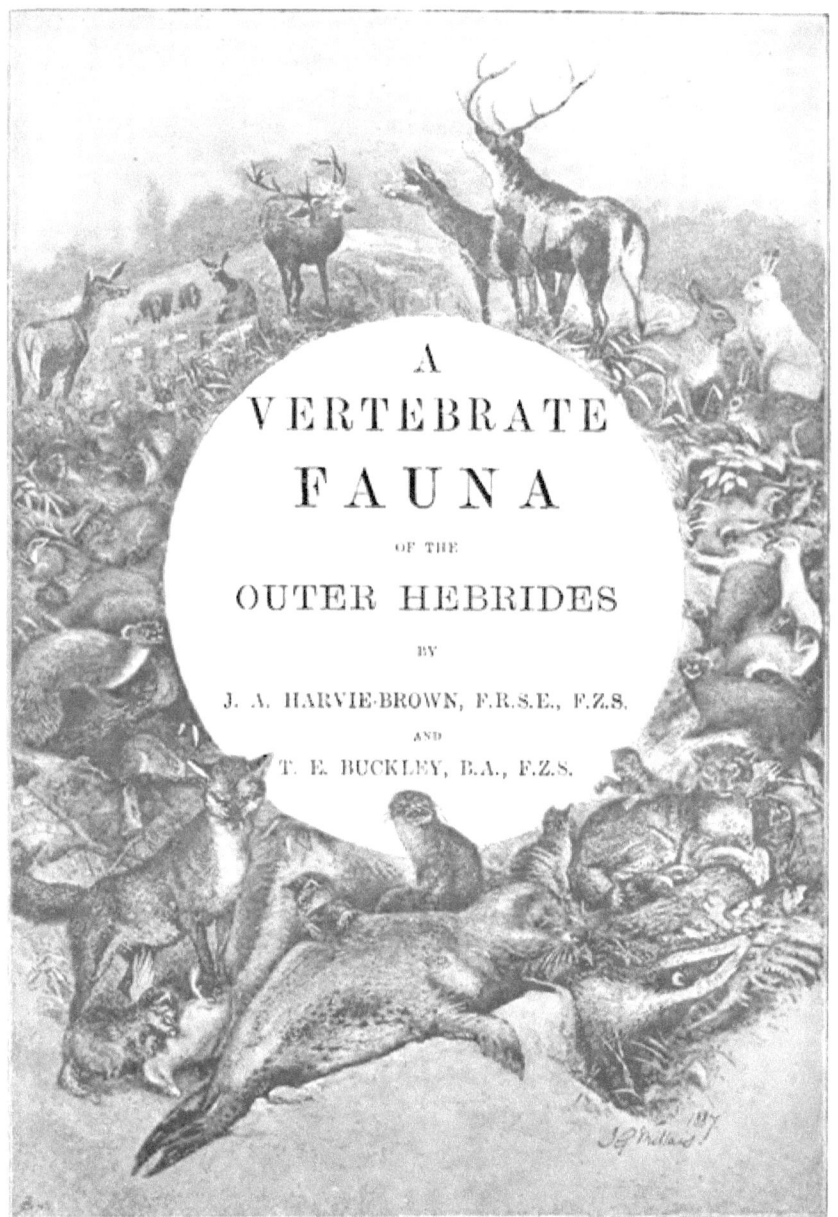

A VERTEBRATE FAUNA
OF THE
OUTER HEBRIDES

BY

J. A. HARVIE-BROWN, F.R.S.E., F.Z.S.

AND

T. E. BUCKLEY, B.A., F.Z.S.

EDINBURGH: DAVID DOUGLAS, CASTLE STREET

A TREATISE ON ANGLING.

HOW TO CATCH TROUT
By THREE ANGLERS.
Illustrated. Price 1s., by Post, 1s. 2d.

The aim of this book is to give within the smallest space possible such practical information and advice as will enable the beginner without further instruction to attain moderate proficiency in the use of every legitimate lure.

"A delightful little book, and one of great value to anglers."—*Scotsman.*
"The advice given . . . is always sound."—*Field.*
"As perfect a compendium of the subject as can be compressed within eighty-three pages of easily read matter."—*Scotch Waters.*
"A well written and thoroughly practical little work."—*Land and Water.*
"The most practical and instructive work of its kind in the literature of angling."—*Dundee Advertiser.*

ALEX. PORTER.
THE GAMEKEEPER'S MANUAL
BEING AN EPITOME OF THE GAME LAWS OF ENGLAND AND SCOTLAND, AND OF THE GUN LICENCES AND WILD BIRDS ACTS

FOR THE USE OF GAMEKEEPERS AND OTHERS INTERESTED
IN THE PRESERVATION OF GAME

By ALEXANDER PORTER, CHIEF CONSTABLE OF ROXBURGHSHIRE

Second Edition. Crown 8vo, Price 3s., Post free.

"A concise and valuable epitome to the Game Laws specially addressed to those who are engaged in protecting game."—*Scotsman.*
"Quite a store-house of useful information. . . . Although not pretending to be a 'law book,' this work will certainly serve the purpose of one; no subject being omitted that comes within the province of the game laws."—*Glasgow Herald.*

ROBERT MORETON.
ON HORSE-BREAKING
By ROBERT MORETON.
Second Edition. One Volume, Crown 8vo. Price 1s.

COLONEL CAMPBELL.
MY INDIAN JOURNAL
CONTAINING DESCRIPTIONS OF THE PRINCIPAL FIELD SPORTS OF INDIA, WITH NOTES ON THE NATURAL HISTORY AND HABITS OF THE WILD ANIMALS OF THE COUNTRY

By COLONEL WALTER CAMPBELL, AUTHOR OF "The Old Forest Ranger."

Small Demy 8vo, with Drawings on Stone by Wolf. Price 16s.

GENERAL GORDON.
THE ROOF OF THE WORLD
BEING THE NARRATIVE OF A JOURNEY OVER THE HIGH PLATEAU OF TIBET
TO THE RUSSIAN FRONTIER, AND THE OXUS SOURCES ON PAMIR.

By MAJOR-GENERAL T. E. GORDON, C.S.I.

With Numerous Illustrations. Royal 8vo. Price 31s. 6d.

EDINBURGH: DAVID DOUGLAS.